The Samurai

The Samurai
A military history

S. R. TURNBULL

Osprey Publishing London

First published in 1977 by
Osprey Publishing Limited
12–14 Long Acre, London WC2E 9LP
Member company of the George Philip Group

Reprinted 1979
Second reprint 1983

British Library Cataloguing in Publication Data

Turnbull, S. R.
    The Samurai.
    1. Samurai—History
    i. Title
    305.5'2   DS827.S3
ISBN 0-85045-097-7

Filmset and printed by
BAS Printers Limited, Over Wallop, Hampshire

for Jo

Foreword

Japan entered the modern world in 1868 in the name of a restoration of the Emperor, a shadowy figure who for centuries had been totally removed from real power by successive hegemons of a samurai class of warrior rulers. Yet there was little that was radical or revolutionary about the Meiji Restoration of 1868, at least in its early stages; for it was engineered by members of the samurai class itself and the Emperor remained what he had been since ancient times, a legitimizer of government by others. Within a decade the new samurai rulers had set Japan firmly on the course of modernization, and though they were obliged in the process to dissolve the feudal privileges of their own class, former samurai in fact became leaders in all areas of modern Japanese society. More importantly, they brought into the modern age a samurai spirit of military honor and conduct that was to remain one of the principal guidelines for behaviour in Japan until at least World War II, when Japanese soldiers lugged antique samurai swords into battle and went down before enemy fire in suicidal *banzai* charges.

To a great extent the story of the samurai has been the story of Japan during most of the past millennium and it is surely premature to relegate the samurai tradition entirely to the past. For one thing, it is impossible to understand contemporary Japanese society and behavior without knowledge of the values of premodern Japan and these values were evolved primarily by the samurai. More than most other modern people, the Japanese remain bound by ties of personal commitment and responsibility that have often been labelled as 'feudal'. Whether or not 'feudal' is a proper term in the modern context, there is clearly much in Japanese behavior even today that is a direct legacy of the samurai past.

In addition to its importance in informing us about Japanese behavior in general, the history of the samurai is enormously colorful and exciting. No one knows exactly when samurai first appeared in the provinces of Japan. The oldest written accounts that provide meaningful information about them date from the tenth century. But it seems certain that a provincial fighting *élite* had existed from much earlier times, perhaps as far back as the protohistorical tomb period of the fourth and fifth centuries. From the tenth century on the samurai increasingly consolidated their territorial bases and, by the late twelfth century, also appeared on the stage of central rule in Japan.

One of the most striking things about the samurai rise to dominance at this time in Japanese history was that it was achieved not by overthrowing or destroying the courtier class in Kyōto that had until then ruled the country as ministers to the throne but by gradually displacing it. Despite their largely rustic origins, the samurai much admired the social brilliance and classical culture of the courtiers and sought eagerly to emulate their ways. After the seat of military power was established in Kyōto in the fourteenth century, samurai mingled freely with courtiers and themselves became exemplary patrons of the arts. Indeed, the Ashikaga shōguns of this age were far more successful in the latter role than as keepers of the peace, since there was almost constant civil war during their time of rule (1336–1573).

Thus, when the wars were finally brought to an end in the late sixteenth century and lasting peace established by the Tokugawa house of shōguns, the samurai had a long and rich tradition not only of military conduct but also of encouragement of the arts and culture. The Tokugawa period (1600–1867), moreover, provided the samurai with their first real opportunity to direct their attention to the art of governing the country by civil rather than coercive means. The longevity and almost unbroken tranquility of the age attest to the adaptability and success of the samurai in making the transformation from warriors to bureaucrats. At the same time they never lost the conception of themselves as fighting men, even though generations passed with no wars; and indeed it was during the Tokugawa period of peace that the samurai evolved the code of *bushidō* or the 'way of the warrior'. Romanticizing the fighting prowess of their forbears of earlier times and reflecting upon their new moral and intellectual responsibilities as civil rulers, the samurai created in *bushidō* a guide for conduct that served the Japanese people as a whole well even when they were forced, in response to Western intrusion at mid-nineteenth century, to make the transition to the modern era.

After a period, following World War II, during which their own guilt over wartime militarism made them wish to forget their samurai past, the Japanese in recent years have come to see things once again in clearer perspective and have enthusiastically responded to television serials, movies, and the like that recount the swashbuckling exploits of the samurai of bygone eras.

S. R. Turnbull has written a lively—often rousing—account of the samurai. Delving first for the earliest traces of a warrior tradition in the mythology and prehistory of Japan, he examines the evolution of the samurai class from its provincial beginnings through its centuries of glory and ascendancy and, finally, to its dissolution in the early Meiji period. Turnbull is especially to be commended for providing a sound background for his narrative. His primary interest is in military history, and he is at his best in describing battles and campaigns; but he always deals with military developments with careful attention to the larger scheme of events from which they emerged. There is a tendency, it seems, for most contemporary writers in English on Japan to slight purely military history. *The Samurai* is an excellent corrective to this tendency.

H. Paul Varley
Columbia University

viii

Author's Preface

'Samurai' has become a familiar word, conjuring up a picture of a proud, individual warrior making and accepting challenges to combat. Behind this popular image lies the richer picture of the samurai as a member of a complex web of organization and tradition geared to warfare for centuries of a nation's history.

This book is concerned with the origin and development of the samurai as a military man, from the semi-legendary figures of Japanese mythology to the ruling class of Japan during her years of isolation. The period of Restoration in the mid-nineteenth century is treated only briefly here, but it is interesting to note that it is but a hundred years since the wearing of swords was forbidden to all but the armed forces, an act both real and symbolic in marking the passing of the samurai.

The actual definition of a samurai changed considerably throughout his history, so the reader is recommended to see the samurai initially as a high-ranking warrior in service to a master. To think of a samurai as a Japanese knight is a helpful analogy.

As this book is about people I make no apology for the inclusion of a large number of Japanese names. To ease the task of the reader, I ignore the infuriating samurai habit of changing one's name every few years, and have referred to each individual by the name by which he is best known – family name first, given name second – in the old Japanese style. For example Tokugawa Ieyasu (i.e. Ieyasu of the house of Tokugawa) began life as Takechiyo and became Matsudaira Motonobu at the age of fifteen. A year later he became Matsudaira Motoyasu. When he was twenty he changed his given name to Ieyasu, and at twenty-seven discarded his family name in favour of Tokugawa. After his death he was deified as Tō-shō-gū. We shall call him Tokugawa Ieyasu throughout.

I have also made the reading of dates simpler by converting all the lunar dates in the old chronicles, epics, and legends, to the Western calendar using Bramsen's *Japanese Chronological Tables*. The romanization used is the Hepburn System. All pronunciation is phonetic, the syllables beginning with a consonant. A line above 'o' or 'u' lengthens the vowel. To avoid tautologies, and ugly combinations of Japanese and English words, I have retained certain suffixes in names and titles, namely '-gawa' (river); '-ji' (Buddhist temple or monastery); '-yama' (mountain or hill); and '-shima' (island).

In addition to the acknowledgements given under particular illustrations, I would like to mention the following individuals and institutions, whose contributions towards this work have been a great help to me:

Roger Cleeve, of Osprey Publishing Ltd., for his prompt and efficient advice during the preparation of this book; Gilbert Smith, for translations from the Japanese; K. B. Gardner, Deputy Keeper in the Department of Oriental Manuscripts and Printed Books at the British Library, for guiding me through his Department's resources, and for supplying the Japanese originals on which I based my maps; John Anderson, for allowing me to use his collection to illustrate the development of armour, and all my colleagues in the Northern Branch of the To-ken Society of Great Britain, the organization which has done so much to foster serious study of Japanese arms and armour. In particular I would like to thank my friend Ian Bottomley, whose collection has supplied several illustrations, and who put at my disposal the unpublished manuscript of his study of Japanese armour, produced in collaboration with Mr J. Hopson.

B. W. Robinson, of the Victoria and Albert Museum; H. R. Robinson of the Armouries, H.M. Tower of London; Dr Naoyoshi Ii, Mayor of Hikone; Yoshinobu Tokugawa, Director of the Tokugawa Reimeikai Foundation; Yoshimi Hayashi, Director of the Akizuki Museum, Fukuoka; Laurie Allen, of Ryde, N.S.W., Australia and Louis Allen of Durham University, have made useful contributions and offered helpful advice during the book's preparation. I. G. Clark and E. G. Heath have advised on the practical side of book publication, and Signora S. Rossi has kindly supplied me with translations from the Italian. Dr M. Tonge, my former colleague at Downing College, Cambridge, supplied me with some valuable Korean material. I would like to thank the Japan Society of London for permission to quote from their *Transactions*.

Above all I wish to thank my wife Jo, without whose constant support and encouragement none of what follows would have been possible.

Stockport.   S. R. Turnbull, M.A.
November 1975

Contents

Illustrations

Colour plates between pages 144–5 and 208–9

Illustrations in the text

Conventional Periods of Japanese History

Japanese history is conveniently divided into the following periods, the names referring to the seat of government at the time.

Nara	646–793
Heian	794–1184
Kamakura	1185–1367
Muromachi	1368–1575
Azuchi-Momoyama	1576–1614
Edo (Tokugawa)	1615–1867

In feudal times the wealth of a samurai was assessed in terms of *koku*. One *koku* of rice was supposed to be the amount required to feed one man for one year. It was equivalent to almost 5 bushels, or 180·4 litres.

1. Gods and heroes

When Heaven and Earth were one, and male and female were as yet unseparated, all that existed was a chaotic mass containing within it the germs of life.

Then appeared the shape of a reed shoot, which arose out of the chaos as the lighter, purer essence rose to form Heaven, while the heavier element settled down and became Earth. This mysterious form became transformed, as suddenly as it had appeared, into the first of the gods, Kuni-toko-tachi, 'The Deity Master of the August Centre of Heaven'.

Other deities appeared, all of whom were born alone until the coming of a pair of deities, Izanagi and Izanami, 'The Male who invites', and 'The Female who invites'. Together they stood on the floating bridge of Heaven and gazed down with curiosity upon the Earth as it floated beneath them. At the command of the elder deities they were given a coral spear ornamented with jewels, which they thrust into the Ocean and stirred its waters. Withdrawing the tip of the spear they allowed water to drip from its point. The drops coagulated and formed islands, upon one of which the heavenly pair descended, and raised the coral spear as the centre pole and foundation of their house. Japan was created.

This account of the beginnings of Japanese history is given in the oldest written records of Japan, the *Koji-ki* and the *Nihongi*, both of which were written in the early part of the eighth century A.D. In this creation myth we find the first statement of certain aspects of Japanese tradition, the most noteworthy being the divine ancestry of the Japanese rulers, and the appearance, right from the beginning of time, of the symbol of a weapon. Had our anonymous chronicler wished to be a prophet as well as a recorder, he could not have chosen more apt a metaphor for the following ten centuries, for until modern times the weapon of war, realized by the Japanese sword, was indeed to be the foundation of the house, and a pattern of struggle and armed conflict was to characterize its growth.

To some extent the seeds of conflict were sown right from the start, for the drops of water that fell from the spear coagulated in a most haphazard and untidy fashion. Instead of coagulating into one large piece of land they split into a myriad of tiny pieces, which appear to have joined rather grudgingly into four main islands. The largest of the four, which is called Honshū, arranged itself into the shape of an

1

1 The ideal. A figure of Honda Tadakatsu (1548–1610) made for the Boys' Festival. (Victoria and Albert Museum.)

elongated crescent. At its southern tip appeared the tidier form of Kyūshū, which assumed a ragged western edge out of sheer spite. The simple little island of Shikoku tucked itself in between the other two, to leave between itself and Honshū the long and beautiful waterway called the Inland Sea. The fourth island, Hokkaidō, coalesced at the cold northern tip of Honshū. So far north did this fall that it remained neglected until comparatively recent times, and plays no part in our history. Thus the reader need trouble himself with only three main islands, and a handful of minor ones that will be introduced as they enter the story. (Map, Fig. 2.)

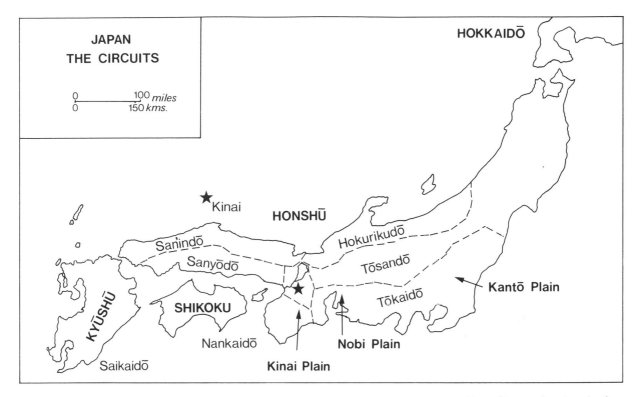

In the map:

JAPAN
THE CIRCUITS

0   100 *miles*
0   150 *kms.*

HOKKAIDŌ

★ Kinai

HONSHŪ

Sanindō
Sanyōdō

Hokurikudō
Tōsandō

★

Tōkaidō

Kantō Plain

KYŪSHŪ

SHIKOKU

Nankaidō

Nobi Plain

Saikaidō

Kinai Plain

2 Map of Japan, showing the four main islands, the medieval geographical circuits, and the three great alluvial plains.

In addition to a complicated shape, Japan was also given a curious position. It is placed one hundred miles across the sea from the southern tip of Korea, with two of the little Japanese islands *en route*, narrowing the gap between the Japanese mainland and Korea to fifty miles. Now this is close enough to make a journey practicable, but not close enough to make it convenient. Thus the Japanese have been able to assimilate from Asia what they wanted, and to keep out what they did not. In the whole of the history of the samurai we will meet with only one case of foreign invasion. Incidentally we shall meet with only one case of Japanese aggression overseas, for wide moats work both ways.

In spite of these advantages the creators of Japan had indeed made a land fit only for heroes. The islands, by their very shape, ensured that communications would remain a problem. So it was with a particularly sly turn of mind that the deities ensured that 80 per cent of the land surface should be mountainous, of which nearly six hundred mountains should top 6,000 feet, and one, the legendary Mount Fuji, should rise to 12,000. Place upon these mountains a rich vegetation, with many a swift flowing river and clear lake, and add a climate that gives sharply defined seasons of warm humid summers and snowy winters, dramatic springs and melancholy autumns. Collect the remaining 20 per cent of fertile land into but three main areas, and arrange for the occasional typhoon and earthquake just to remind the natives of the Creators' unseen hand, and you have a country that from today's aircraft gives the impression of wrinkled brilliant green

3

velvet. Yet, in the period of time we are discussing, merely to keep alive must have been an adventure.

The three great areas of fertile land lie along the eastern edge of Honshū. The largest is the Kantō plain, covering about 5,000 square miles. The others are the Nobi and the Kinai plains. The struggle for possession of these lands is the key to Japanese history. Throughout the ages these flatlands have attracted the bulk of the Japanese population, and they now carry the great metropolises of Tōkyō, Nagoya and Ōsaka respectively.

The Kinai plain, by its position in the centre of Honshū, has tended to become the 'hub' of Japan, as Lake Biwa, whose northern shores lie among mountains and which empties into the sea, neatly divides Japan in two. Furthermore, until modern times the capital has always been situated in the Kinai, so that it has become known as the area of the 'Home Provinces'. Throughout this book the terms 'Western' and 'Eastern' Japan refer to these directions from the Kinai. For many years the main lines of communication in Japan have been along the coasts, either westwards along the Inland Sea to Western Honshū, Kyūshū and Shikoku, or east and north along the famous Tōkaidō, the ancient highway made famous by the artist Hiroshige and his series of woodblock prints. Having thus set the scene, let us return to the gods.

We do not have to read far into the ancient chronicles before we find mention of the first actual sword in mythology. This weapon belonged to Izanagi. He used it to kill his son the Fire God, whose birth had caused Izanami extremes of pain. Izanami was so distraught that she abandoned Izanagi and crept away into the Underworld. Filled with remorse at the accomplishment of the first murder, and grieving for his wife, Izanagi, like Orpheus, followed her, to rescue her from the clutches of the Gods of Hell. His attempt proved unsuccessful, and he was pursued on his return journey by the Eight Thunder Deities and other assorted unpleasant spirits, against whom he wielded the sword with deft skill. After his return he performed numerous ablutions to rid himself of the pollution of Hades.

The Fire God had not been their sole offspring, for two deities had preceded him. The eldest was Amaterasu, the Goddess of the Sun, who was followed by Susano-o, 'the Impetuous Male'. Susano-o appears to have been an unsettling companion, given to fits of temper which he enlivened by tossing thunderbolts across the sky. During one of his tantrums his gentle sister became so alarmed by his violent behaviour, which included flinging a dead horse at her, that she fled from his sight and locked herself in a cave. At this all the people of the world were much distressed, for with the Sun Goddess hiding away the world had been plunged into darkness. So they conferred together as to the best way of enticing her out again and hit on the idea of making for her the most beautiful gifts imaginable.

A certain 'One-Eyed Deity' as he was called, forged an iron mirror. This heavenly craftsman is traditionally regarded as the father of the art of sword-making, and it is interesting to note that the one-eyed

4

Cyclopes of Greek legend were also famous for their metal-working.

The other gift was a necklace of precious jewels which, together with the mirror, was hung on a tree at the mouth of the cave. By the sounds of dancing and laughter Amaterasu was induced to peep round the edge of the stone at the cave's entrance, where she caught sight of her features reflected in the mirror. Her own beauty made her stop and stare, and before she had a chance to return to the cave its mouth was blocked completely. So was light restored to the world.

On at least one occasion, however, Susano-o's violent ways were put to good use. In the province of Izumo lived a great serpent, with eight heads and tails, and its tails filled eight valleys. Its eyes were like the sun and the moon, and on its back grew forests. This serpent, who swallowed people, had a particular taste for young maidens. Susano-o undertook to kill the serpent. Choosing an attractive young maiden as bait, he lay in wait for the serpent, his father's sword in hand, and with a prodigious quantity of *sake* (Japanese rice wine) as an added enticement for the monster. Eventually the serpent came, ignored the maiden, and stuck its eight heads into the *sake*, which it drank with relish. Before long the beast was intoxicated, and an easy prey for Susano-o, who furiously began to hew it to pieces. When he reached the serpent's tail, however, his blade was turned, and he discovered another sword in its tail. As it was a very fine blade he took it and presented it to his sister, and because that portion of the serpent's anatomy had been covered with black clouds he called the sword 'Ame no murakomo no tsurugi' or 'Cloud Cluster Sword'.

As the first born, Amaterasu had inherited the Earth, and some time afterward sent her grandson Ninigi to rule over the islands of Japan which her parents had created. When Ninigi was about to leave Heaven she gave him three items that would ease his passage through the world – the mirror, the jewels, and the sword. Thus armed with the objects that were to become the Japanese Crown Jewels, Prince Ninigi descended from Heaven to the top of Mount Takachiko in Kyūshū. He married, and eventually passed the regalia on to his grandson Jimmu, the first earthly Emperor of Japan.

In Gilbert and Sullivan's *The Mikado*, Pooh Bah claims to be able to trace his ancestry back to a 'protoplasmal primordial atomic globule'. Perhaps Gilbert knew of the Japanese creation myths, describing the emergence of life from a shapeless chaotic form; but, satire notwithstanding, the present Emperor of Japan can look back on 123 Imperial ancestors, the oldest established ruling house in the world. Admittedly the existence of Jimmu, the first Emperor, is very doubtful. According to legend Jimmu took sword in hand and left Kyūshū for Honshū, fighting many fierce battles on the way against all manner of foes, including eighty earth spiders, who were speedily vanquished, once again, with the help of liquor. He ascended the throne of Japan on the traditionally given date of 11 February, 660 B.C., which is still celebrated in Japan with a public holiday.

The more down-to-earth but no less violent testimony of archaeology tells of the existence of man in the Japanese archipelago for the past 100,000 years. For the first 90,000 years Japan was linked to the main land mass of Asia. Then the oceans were swelled by the melting of the glaciers of the last ice age, and Japan was cut off from Asia by the straits that were to have such an influence on her later history.

In the now isolated Japan lived the hairy Ainu, the Japanese aborigines who still exist in Hokkaidō. From about 500 B.C. the Ainu began to be supplanted by the Mongolian type of people associated with modern Japan. They arrived gradually over the next few hundred years, bringing with them the potter's wheel, bronze, iron and the cultivation of rice. Their sharp iron swords, which within a few generations were to become the most deadly examples of their art, helped the invaders push back the indigenous tribesmen. Although the Ainu contributed little to Japanese culture, some interbreeding certainly took place, and they are probably responsible for the relative hairiness of the Japanese compared with other Mongoloid peoples.

By the time of the tenth Emperor, Sujin (c. A.D. 200), the mythological accounts were beginning to combine with a primitive animism to form Japan's indigenous religion of 'Shintō' – 'The Way of the Gods'. One essential of Shintō is that certain places, perhaps waterfalls, mountain tops or rock formations possessing unusual beauty or grandeur, are the abodes of the gods. Such places became a focus for Shintō worship, and it was more than likely that a Shintō shrine would be built there, instantly recognizable by the characteristic gateway, the 'torii', shaped like the Greek letter π. Under Shintō all the universe was united, and the holy places were a corner of creation where man might identify with nature and adore the makers of it. Shintō offered no great interpretation of the world, but invited man to partake in it by associating himself with the natural phenomena of trees, earth, water, birth, life and death.

This attitude of harmony with nature is nowhere shown better than at Sujin's foundation of the Grand Shrines of Ise, built to serve as a centre of worship of Amaterasu the Sun Goddess. The remarkable complex of buildings is of the utmost simplicity of construction, and to emphasize the fact that they are not a permanent monument but a living part of their environment, the Shrines have been demolished and rebuilt every twenty years since their foundation.

Not unnaturally the Shintō tradition is closely associated with the enduring institution of the Emperor, who claims descent from the deity of Ise. Thus the foundations of Ise have been especially revered by the Japanese people, and as we shall see in later chapters, in times of national crisis it is to Ise that they have turned.

Emperor Sujin is also noteworthy for two other innovations. Faced with the threat of rebellion, he appointed four generals to lead armies to the four quarters of the country. The generals were each given the title 'Shōgun' (roughly translatable as 'Commander in Chief'), the first time in Japanese history that this word, which was to achieve such importance in the years to come, was used. Sujin's other innovation was simpler but no less dramatic. He invented income tax!

Sujin was followed by Emperor Keikō, whose son now demands our attention. This character, Prince Yamato, represents a transitional stage between gods and heroes. He is, in a way, a forerunner of the samurai heroes of later times. He still fights monsters, but possesses entirely human characteristics, and it is worth examining the Yamato legend because of the pattern he set for the samurai tradition. 'He' is a misnomer, for Yamato is certainly a composite character, whose exploits, suitably embellished and exaggerated, are those of the many warriors sent out on expeditions in the early centuries of the Christian era.

In bravery Yamato equalled any knight of the Round Table, but the chivalric spirit is conspicuous by its absence. Yamato's career as a swordsman begins by the murder of his elder brother as a punishment for being late for dinner. This so shocked his father, the Emperor Keikō, that Yamato was despatched to Kyūshū where he might put his warlike energies to some use by opposing the enemies of the throne. Before setting out, the youth visited his aunt, the high-priestess of the Great Shrine of Ise, who presented him with the sacred sword 'Cloud Cluster'. However, it was a trick, and not swordsmanship, that encompassed Yamato's first victory of the campaign. He arrived at the house of his enemy and observed that it was heavily guarded, while there was much activity within in preparation for a banquet. The Prince thereupon disguised himself as a girl and joined in the merry-making, sitting between the two chieftains who were gradually becoming intoxicated. When they least suspected it, Yamato drew the sword from his robe and slew them both.

His mission accomplished, Yamato set off for home, stopping on the way to subdue another local chieftain in the province of Izumo. Once more he resorted to trickery to attain his ends. He first cultivated the friendship of the chieftain, to the extent of establishing a strong bond between them. Then he secretly manufactured a dummy sword of wood, which he wore in his belt. One day he invited the chieftain to bathe with him in a river. They left their swords on the river bank, and on emerging from the water Yamato suggested that they exchange swords as a further pledge of friendship. This his comrade readily agreed to do, and also responded to Yamato's challenge to a friendly duel with their new swords. Of course the luckless chieftain soon discovered that the sword he now held was of wood, and Prince Yamato cut him down with ease.

So far Prince Yamato seems a most unattractive hero, and quite unlike the ideal of the samurai warrior. But after his return home his character appears to change, and he becomes the archetype of the wandering hero who dies an early and tragic death, a theme to be repeated time and again in the history of the samurai.

As Yamato set out on his travels once more, the great serpent slain by Susano-o, miraculously restored, appeared in front of him on the road, and demanded the return of the sword Cloud Cluster. Yamato merrily jumped over the serpent and continued on his way. The only further interruption to Yamato's progress was a beautiful maiden named Iwato-hime, with whom he fell intensely in love. He finally managed to drag himself away from her, and proceeded on his way in the direction of Mount Fuji. Here some enemies invited Yamato to join them in a stag hunt, and when he was engrossed in the chase they set fire to the long grass in order to burn him to death. So the prince drew Cloud Cluster from its scabbard and, swinging it furiously about him, cut his way through the burning grass to safety. Thus Cloud Cluster came to be known as 'Kusanagi no tsurugi' ('the Grass-mowing Sword').

After this narrow escape he returned to Iwato-hime. But realizing that he could not stay for ever, Yamato left as a memento his most treasured possession, Cloud Cluster or Grass-mower, which Iwato-hime tearfully took and hung from the branches of a mulberry tree. Now the great serpent, resentful that Yamato had escaped him, was lying in wait for the hero on his return journey. Yamato paid no more heed to the monster than on the former occasion, but sprang clear over him and passed on. This time, however, the tip of his foot touched the serpent as he leapt. Before long he was seized with a fever that spread through his whole body. He managed to obtain some relief by bathing his foot in a cool stream, but though the fever subsided the sickness was still with him and he collapsed.

As the prince lay on his sick bed he longed to see Iwato-hime once again. Then his eyes fell upon her, for she had followed him on his journey. Thus were his spirits temporarily raised, but his condition was rapidly deteriorating, until eventually he died, and was changed into a white bird which flew away to the south. This tragic ending to Yamato's career contains features which we will meet again, in particular the solitary nature of the hero, hunted down by his enemies until he meets a tragic death. The idea of the samurai as an individual heroic warrior is one that has persisted to our times, and Yamato is the first of the line.

Leaving aside the fabulous aspects of the Yamato story we can see within it the tremendous conflict that was going on in Japan at the time. The nation was composed of a number of clans, of which the strongest was the Imperial family. They strove to exert their right – claimed through their alleged descent from the Sun Goddess – to command the Empire. When occasion arose, the Emperor himself led the army, or some high-ranking officer was appointed Shōgun. A Shōgunal commission to go forth and make war was a short-term one. Similarly, weapons of war were the property of the state, stored away in times of peace, and served out periodically when required for fighting or training purposes. There was no such thing as a samurai or knightly class among these early warriors, for the duty of service fell upon all subjects alike, though certain clans received special privileges. In particular the Ōtomo clan were honoured as the hereditary palace guards.

Such a life, where death was commonplace, bred a strong spirit among the people, and the spartan life practised by the kinsmen of the early warrior-emperors was later adopted by the samurai. To the early emperors cleanliness was next to godliness, and with the memory of Izanagi's return from Hell, they performed countless ceremonies of ritual purification, especially after battle. There was no fear of dying, but of the pollution and decay that death brings. Thus it was regarded as necessary to vacate any house in which a death had taken place. This rule applied equally to the Imperial Palace, so that for the first few centuries there was no permanent capital of Japan.

So emperors and capitals came and went, and the shrine of the Sun Goddess continued to be torn down and rebuilt every twenty years, while the institution of the Emperor, maintained by the mirror of knowledge, the sword of power and the jewels of kingship, flourished and grew.

On one occasion an emperor's consort played her part in the extension of empire. The Empress Jingō led a divinely assisted expedition to Korea, foreshadowing a further invasion in this direction a thousand years later. She was pregnant at the time, and on her return to Japan gave birth to a son who was to become Emperor Ōjin. On his death he was deified and worshipped as Hachiman the War God, a deity later attracting enormous respect from the samurai.

Hachiman, along with the rest of the Shintō pantheon, did not long enjoy the undisputed adoration of the Japanese, for in the early sixth century A.D. there came alien gods to Japan. A missionary from a kingdom in Southern Korea brought an image of Buddha.

The religion of Buddhism was already ten centuries old when it reached Japan, and had lost much of its purity and asceticism. The first the Japanese were to see of the new religion was a glittering gold image of Buddha. The appeal of the new teaching, and the richness of the Chinese culture associated with it, represented a threat to the omnipotence of the Emperor, and at first there was great opposition to it. But strangely enough, the most enthusiastic advocate of Buddhism turned out to be a member of the Imperial family, a crown prince called Shotoku. He was a great scholar, and worked towards the integration of Buddhism with his native Shintō, whereby the gods of Shintō could be looked upon as manifestations of Buddha himself. In A.D. 607 Shotoku sent the first of many official embassies to China, and was working on a system of reform for Japan based on Chinese teachings when he died at the age of forty-nine in 621. His plans, however, did not die with him, but were put into effect by a high-ranking courtier called Fujiwara Kamatari. He was the first of a very long line of Fujiwaras who were to make their mark upon Japanese life.

The Great Reforms were complicated, and far-reaching in their effects. Essentially they involved the emasculation of the patriarchal clan system in Japan, which threatened the stability of the Imperial rule, and its replacement by a bureaucracy under the Emperor based

3 Statue of Shaka Nyorai, the healing Buddha. (Courtesy of Christie's.)

on the Chinese model. The Fujiwara therefore began to reconstruct Japan as a miniature version of T'ang China. All the statutes, traditions and mores of the T'ang empire were to be copied and adapted for Japanese use, as the Chinese had, to their eyes, the perfect system of government. With that peculiar Japanese talent for absorption and imitation that can still be seen today, the people of the rising sun set out enthusiastically to parallel the people of the setting sun.

The most concrete of Fujiwara's endeavours was the founding in 710 of Japan's first permanent capital city, Nara. Nara was laid out after the style of T'ang China's capital, Chang-an. Chang-an's rectangular shape with its straight, broad streets running at right angles to one another, was scaled down to a size of about two-and-a-half by three miles, though in fact it proved too big for the population and the western half of the city was never built.

Thirty years later Nara suffered an epidemic of smallpox which began to decimate the population. Prayers for relief were offered by the Buddhist priesthood and so effective did they appear to be that Emperor Shomu decided to construct a huge bronze statue of Buddha, to be housed in a great wooden temple, as an offering and propitiation. The site of Nara had been chosen partly because near by stood two Buddhist temples, the Hōryū-ji (founded in 607) and the Yakushu-ji (founded in 680). Now there was to be another temple for Nara, so grand in its scope as to surpass anything that had been seen before. The new temple was to be called the 'Tōdai-ji', the 'Great Eastern Temple'. Monasteries were also to be endowed in all provinces of the country to ensure Buddha's protection for the Japanese people.

It may be thought that the Sun Goddess had been conveniently forgotten, but this was not so. With due respect for his ancestors, Emperor Shomu despatched a messenger to the priests of Ise to enquire of Amaterasu's opinion of the project. Her views were evidently favourable, for as soon as the messenger returned with the deity's approval, work began on the casting of the gigantic image.

The statue, representing Buddha seated with his hand raised in blessing, may be seen today inside the great temple built to house it. It is fifty-three feet high and is cast in an alloy of bronze. Thousands of workers were engaged upon it day and night, and so much copper went into it (the present image weighs 551 tons) that it is said to have caused a shortage of the metal. In 749 gold was discovered in Northern Honshū, and soon sufficient was mined to cover the entire statue with the precious metal. The Daibutsuden, the building which actually houses the image within the Tōdai-ji compound, is still the largest wooden building in the world under one roof, although subsequent rebuilding has somewhat reduced its original dimensions.

Even more remarkable than the building itself was the ceremony of dedication which followed its completion in 749. Emperor Shomu, attended by the highest dignitaries in the land, proceeded to the Tōdai-ji and stood before the great image. He faced it from the south in the attitude of a subject paying homage to a ruler, and there professed

4 The Daibutsuden, or Great Buddha Hall, of the Tōdai-ji. (Kyodo News Service.)

himself to be the humble servant of the three precious things, Buddha, the Law, and the priesthood. Capitulation to the alien god could go no further, for by those words and actions Emperor Shomu virtually proclaimed Buddhism to be the established church of Japan, and set in motion a chain of events that were to give the Buddhist priesthood powers that would shake the very throne of the Emperor himself.

It is the failures of the programme of the Great Reforms rather than its successes that are most important to the history of the samurai. The most glorious failure was the reform of land tenure, by which land was to become the property of the state, which would then re-distribute it at two *tan* (about half an acre) for every male over five years old, and two-thirds of this for every female. The new owners paid various taxes which included a period of compulsory military service.

There were obvious dangers here, dangers that multiplied when the landowners wrung concessions out of the government in the form of rank land, awarded in accordance with the rank held; gift land, which speaks for itself; and merit land, which was awarded for especially meritorious service. Salary land and rank land were liable for rice tax only, as was merit land, but gift land somehow became completely tax free, for it was regarded as being a direct gift from the Emperor. As only an Imperial edict was required to bestow gift land the powers behind the throne saw the tax-free gift land as a means of recovering their former property. Gift land also had the advantage of becoming a permanent family possession, a quality it began to share with salary land when adroit manipulation of the bureaucratic system tended to ensure that certain offices became hereditary.

One category of land that escaped the land reform was the possessions of the great religious foundations. Even before the consecration of the

5 Five storey pagoda of the Kōfuku‐ji. (Kyodo News Service.)

Tōdai‐ji the Buddhist priesthood were aware which way the economic wind was blowing, and saw to it that their pious acts led not only to the elimination of plague and pestilence, but also the elimination of tax.

With such a concession, and the bureaucratic patronage to which we have already referred, the temples' wealth and power grew enormously, while the government became increasingly desperate in the search for new lands to donate. As an example of the power of the temples we may examine the record of the Tōdai‐ji. Being especially blessed from the time of its foundation, the Tōdai‐ji had in 747, two years before the dedication of the Great Buddha, 1,000 houses under its ownership, spread around the central provinces. In 758 Emperor Shomu gave the Tōdai‐ji 5,000 houses covering thirty‐eight provinces of Japan. Under these circumstances the temples became economic centres to which the whole people looked. The Imperial Court paid little attention to the common people, while the priests took them under their wing and taught them how to build bridges, construct dams and various other practical skills. This benevolence was rooted in good experience, for the priests were among the best educated people in Japan. Many had studied in China, and the combination of a training in Chinese economics and great wealth made land speculation an attractive pastime. An edict of 746 had forbidden the temples to trade in land, but there was no prohibition against developing virgin land, and indeed this was seen by the Court as being of long-term benefit to the community.

By the end of the eighth century the great monasteries of Nara were beginning to exert political as well as economic pressure. The neighbouring foundation of Kōfuku-ji had also grown rapidly since its foundation in A.D. 669.

Disaffection between temple and court, culminating in a scandal concerning a Buddhist High Priest and an Empress, led to the decision to move the capital. In 784 the Court left Nara for Nagaoka, some miles farther north, but this new site proved unsatisfactory and in 794 the capital was established in Kyōto. There it remained until supplanted by modern Tōkyō in 1868.

Once again Chang-an was taken as the model, and the new master-piece of town planning, surrounded by cherry trees and weeping willows, presented the eye with such a picture of grace and beauty that it was named 'Heian-kyō', 'The Capital of Peace and Tranquility'. But if the Courtiers expected peace and tranquility in the streets of Kyōto they were to be disappointed, particularly in the matter of interference from the Buddhist Church.

In 767 there was born a monk called Saichō, now posthumously referred to as 'Dengyō Daishi'. Disgusted by the wordliness of his colleagues at Nara, Saichō had left to seek spiritual peace on a mountain. His wanderings eventually led him to the hills west of Lake Biwa, and here in 788 he founded a temple, the Enryaku-ji, near the summit of Mount Hiei. This was six years before the founding of Kyōto, so that when the new capital was built there was Saichō's temple, five miles north-east among the densely wooded hills. To the superstitious courtiers Enryaku-ji assumed great importance, for – according to the rules of Chinese geomancy – evil could attack a city from the north-east, the direction known as the 'demon gate'. As the new capital had to have as auspicious a beginning as possible, the presence of the Enryaku-ji was regarded as being a very good omen, and the new foundation attained the status of guardian of Kyōto. Further proof of the gods' pleasure lay in the additional presence on Mount Hiei of the shrine of an important Shintō deity, the King of the Mountain. Blessings were heaped upon Enryaku-ji such as even the Tōdai-ji had not known! As it grew, its buildings spread over Mount Hiei, and an abbot of Enryaku-ji founded a daughter-temple called Mii-dera (or Onjō-ji) at the foot of the mountain near Lake Biwa. Within a few years, the monasteries of Kyōto grew to rival in wealth and power those left behind in Nara. Great resentment was felt in the Southern Capital as Nara was now called, as the citizens saw their privilege and patronage being wrested from them.

As we have already seen, the nobles and the monasteries had found it comparatively easy to avoid paying taxes. The smaller landowners, or those with no great aristocratic connections, found it less easy to opt out. To people in this position a convenient device suggested itself. They nominally handed over their land to a landowner who paid little or no tax – a monastery for example. The new owner registered these commended lands in his own name, thus removing them from the tax roll, then returned the lands intact to their owner. All the protector required from the 'donor' was an annual tribute, considerably less than the standard rate, and a tacit understanding to keep his mouth shut. As this system, known as 'kishin', developed, the means of donation became more sophisticated. A landowner might find it advantageous literally to donate his land to a temple, and become 'sōji' or manorial governor of it. As the farmers working on these free lands escaped the tyranny of the local (official) tax collectors, the people flocked to the manors or the temple lands. The benefits to the noble who accepted lands were considerable, for he thereby increased his land yield without the business of opening up virgin territory. Such a convenient and profitable arrangement was not easily checked, for the corruption of *kishin* extended high up into the bureaucracy. Prohibitions were issued against it, but so many were growing fat on the proceeds that the traffic went on.

The Fujiwara family did particularly well out of the system of *kishin*. It will be recalled that it was the founder of this illustrious house who had begun Shotoku's reforms. Ever since Kamatari's rise to power the Fujiwara had prospered, dominating the counsels of the Emperor, and had begun a process of infiltration into the Imperial line. The principle of the Fujiwara takeover was quite simple. They bred and reared beautiful daughters who were married to succeeding crown princes. So successful were they that between A.D. 724 and 1900 (the birth of the present Emperor) no less than fifty-four out of the line of seventy-six emperors were born to girls from this family.

During the eighth and ninth centuries the Imperial Court became a Fujiwara club, and the Emperor himself, the descendant of warriors, gradually became dehumanized and god-like. Even his name was discarded and replaced by euphemistic titles, the best known of which is 'The Mikado' which literally means 'Worshipful Gateway'. A custom developed by which the Emperor would abdicate, while still a young man, in favour of an infant relative who could more easily be manipulated, and whose power would be purely nominal. But breeding such a fertile cohort of princesses inevitably leads to complications, for in every generation there appeared disaffected persons who were passed over as heirs, not to mention non-Fujiwara Imperial relatives who stood little chance of promotion. These aristocrats tactfully left the capital to seek their fortunes elsewhere. This simple departure of discarded royalty seemed convenient at the time, for they settled far from Kyōto, and many married into the ancient clans. Yet the Court's policy was sowing dragon's teeth, from which armed men would shortly grow.

14

2. Buddha and Bushi

In the preceding chapter we saw how the land reforms were the first casualties in the failure of the Great Reforms. With their failure, the obligation of national military service in return for land was eroded by the practice of *kishin*. The concept of a national conscript army had collapsed. In Kyōto, where noble families vied with one another for the sinecure of mounting guard at the Palace, there was no shortage of volunteers for 'military service', but in the eastern and northern provinces, where the aboriginal Ainu were still to be found, there was a continuing security problem. Besides the Ainu there were other sporadic rebellions to be put down, and persistent forays by bandits and highwaymen. The conscript system having failed, security in these outlying areas passed more and more into local hands. The Court nobles, enjoying the languid life that has come down to us in such novels as *The Tale of Genji*, were most unwilling to undertake a Shōgunal commission to subdue enemies, and were indeed so preoccupied with life in the capital that garrisons in outlying areas were actually reduced and the soldiers brought back to guard the city.

The men upon whom fell the task of maintaining law and order were landowners who had grown rich, more than likely on *kishin*. A number were also dispossessed aristocrats who had left the Fujiwara-dominated Court to seek their fortunes. Under the landowners were a large number of smaller farmers and land-holders whom *kishin* had made dependent. It involved no great shift of emphasis for this economic dependence to become a military one in the face of danger. Also there had been a tendency for the bonds formed by *kishin* to be strengthened by marriage between interested parties, so that over the years a master/servant relationship grew, whose bonds were strong and whose loyalties were local and personal. When trouble threatened the servant would follow his master's lead.

Supporters of the powerful landowners called themselves 'samurai', which is roughly translatable as 'those who serve'. ('Samurai' comes from the verb 'samurau' or 'saburau' which means 'to serve'.) The original meaning of 'samurai' may seem to have no military connotation, but the definition of a samurai changes considerably through Japanese history. Another word, 'bushi', is also familiar from such combinations as 'bushi-dō', the 'Way of the Warrior'. 'Bushi', however, does not imply the master-servant relationship, and may be regarded as a general term for a fighting man or warrior.

It would be misleading to see the rise of the samurai as a democratic movement, which the picture of brave farmers uniting behind a champion to defend their interests, may suggest. With few exceptions, the powerful landowner who was the nucleus round whom the military force gathered, was of noble, and often royal blood. It is interesting to note that, in the provinces, although actual military prowess was the test of leadership, an aristocratic pedigree was a definite asset in attracting support. As this support grew, so did the sense of identity based on a newly established idea of the clan. The clans of the pre-Reform era, which the land reforms had set out to abolish, reappeared as the samurai clans. The effect of *kishin* had been to make the social unit much wider than hitherto, as it encompassed many unrelated families and persons round the core of a family unit. The tendency was for the leadership to come from the immediate family, while the bulk of the samurai were not direct relations.

As we have seen, Eastern and Northern Japan were the centres of rebellious activity, and it was there, or more specifically in the Kantō plain, that the samurai had their beginning. The Kantō was an ideal situation for such trends to develop. It was three hundred miles from Kyōto and its influence. There were hundreds of square miles of virgin territory to be cultivated, and there were sporadic attacks by Ainu to keep the warriors on their mettle. Quite early in the Heian period the fighting qualities of the 'Kantō-bushi' were recognized, and some were even recruited for the defence of Kyūshū.

The arrangement was convenient for the Kyōto Court, but they must have been completely engrossed in Court intrigue not to have realized the danger of allowing this growth of samurai clans. In effect, the government had transferred its entire military and policing duties to a handful of dispossessed aristocrats whose loyalties were local and personal. In the last chapter the settling of non–Fujiwara nobles in the east was likened to sowing dragon's teeth. These seeds had now sprouted, and like Jason's crops, were bringing forth armed men.

Two names stand out above all the new clans in the east. These are the clans of Taira and Minamoto. The Taira grew out of the policy of farming out excess nobles, and the name 'Taira' was first adopted by one Takami, the grandson of Emperor Kammu, the founder of Kyōto, who reigned 781–806. Seeing his progress blocked at Court this young man moved east and settled in the Kantō plain. His son rose to be a provincial governor, and his six grandsons achieved positions of power and respectability. Thus the name of Taira became a popular one for *kishin*, marriage or alliance.

In time the Minamoto grew to rival the Taira. They too were of royal descent, and were forced to move east because the large number of princes being born was putting a strain on the Court's budget. The first Minamoto was Tsunemoto, son of one of these princes and a grandson of Emperor Seiwa. Other branches developed, such as the 'Murakami-Genji', and the ''Uda-Genji'. 'Genji' is the Chinese pronunciation of the written character which in Japanese is read 'Minamoto'.

Similarly the Taira are often referred to as the 'Heike' of 'Heiji'. The Taira and the Minamoto made their names by rendering military service to the government. Before describing examples of such service, let us take a look at the samurai themselves.

We are fortunate in the artists of old Japan having left us a rich pictorial record of early samurai warriors. These illustrations, most of which are painted on long narrative scrolls, together with extant specimens of arms and armour, give us a vivid picture of military life in those days. It was about this time that the Japanese suit of armour acquired the characteristic shape which makes it instantly recognizable. The very early forms of armour, which we only know from excavations of tombs dating from the fourth or fifth centuries A.D., were of plate construction, replaced about the fifth century by styles imported from continental Asia. The Asiatic style of 'lamellar' armour, whereby the armour is made up of numerous scales fastened together, rather than plates, can trace its ancestry back to Ancient Egypt and Assyria. Once adopted by the Japanese it became a style they were to make uniquely their own. During the seventh and eighth centuries the lamellar armour was worn as a large, clumsy coat, which gradually evolved into the armour worn by the samurai. This is the first real 'samurai' armour, and is known as 'yoroi'.

The principle behind the construction of yoroi is very simple. Several pieces of metal or leather are bound tightly together to make a flexible, resilient plate. The strip thus formed of 'kozane', as the scales were called, would be about a foot long, varying in length according to which part of the armour it would form. The strip was covered in leather and carefully lacquered to make it waterproof. A series of these strips were then bound together with thick silk or leather thong. These cords, known as the armour's 'odoshi' or 'lacing' were brightly coloured, and it is the pattern they made which provided the decorative effect on the armour.

The whole of the armour was made in this way, and it can be seen from the samurai in the scroll paintings that this construction gave the armour its box-like appearance. Three sides of the 'box' – the front, left and rear – were made as one. The right side, or 'waidate' was put on first and tied securely under the armpit and over the left shoulder. The large, heavy shoulder plates, 'sode', fastened to each shoulder strap by thongs or cords, and to prevent them from flying loose or rising to leave the arms unprotected, were fastened at the rear to a large ornamental bow called an 'agemaki'. The agemaki, which was usually red, hung from a ring at the top of the back and had the shape of a cross.

Further details of the armour can be seen in Plate II, which shows the 'kon ito odoshi yoroi' or 'blue thread laced armour' preserved at Ōyamazumi Shrine on Ōmishima Island in the Inland Sea. This armour, one of the oldest suits still in existence, has been carefully restored to its former glory. What appears to be a breastplate is the 'tsurubashiri' designed to present a smooth passage to the bowstring when the bow is discharged. Like all plain surfaces on the armour it was covered with a sheet of dyed leather, usually patterned in an intricate and attractive design. Hanging down in front of the tsurubashiri are two appendages designed to protect the supporting cords of the armour. These were fastened by toggles. Over the right breast is the 'sendan no ita', which is like a miniature shoulder plate. On the left is the 'kyūbi no ita', a rigid iron plate covered in leather.

At this period the samurai wore an armoured sleeve, or 'kote', on the left arm only, so as to leave the right free for drawing the bow. The armoured sleeve was simply a cloth bag reinforced with iron plates along its outer edge, and fastened under the opposite armpit. Under the armour the samurai wore a 'yoroi-hitatare' or 'armour robe' which was ornately embroidered and ornamented with pom-poms. The large baggy trousers tucked into shinguards, and the full sleeves were gathered at the wrists by tying cords. For convenience the left sleeve was not forced into the armour sleeve but pulled out and tucked into the belt. The shinguards were simply three iron plates that folded and fastened round the leg. Bearskin fur boots and leather archery gloves completed the warrior's equipment below the neck.

The helmets shown on the scrolls are typical of the heavy headgear worn with yoroi. The bowl of the helmet consisted of a series of iron plates riveted together with large conical rivets, whose heads were left projecting from the surface of the helmet. In the crown of the helmet was a large hole, called the 'tehen'. It is perhaps surprising to hear of a helmet with a hole in it, but its most likely function was to allow the pigtail of hair to pass through. When, in later years, an inner lining for the helmet was introduced, the tehen was discarded. The large curving neckpiece of the helmet (the shikoro) is made of kozane in the same way as the rest of the armour. Note how the ends of the shikoro are made to curve upwards and outwards as a protection for the face. These projections, called 'fukigayeshi' were covered with patterned leather, as was the peak. A final decoration was the small agemaki bow tied at the rear of the helmet.

A number of the warriors illustrated in this book are wearing face protectors in the form of iron plates hung round the forehead and down the cheeks. The details can be seen most clearly in the fierce looking bushi (without a helmet) in the *Heiji Monogatari* scroll, who is carrying a head. (Fig. 6.)

The samurai's dress just described was by no means a strictly followed uniform, as the accompanying illustrations show. Minor variations in costume can probably be attributed to rank. The essential division is between the mounted warrior and the foot soldier. The suit of armour of the latter was not the box-like yoroi but a much simpler wrap-round style called the 'haramaki' (often erroneously called the 'dō-maru').

As to weapons, we may note the almost universal possession of a sword, and also the dagger, bow, and the curious heavy glaive known as a naginata. At this time the mystique that was to grow around the

Japanese sword had not developed. By the eleventh century, however, the sword had become the almost perfect weapon, and in its shape, construction and mode of use, had already attained its final, deadly form. Yet it was but one weapon among many, and the legends of the Japanese sword, like those of the samurai themselves, had yet to be made. The swords of these early warriors resembled most closely the sword shown in Fig. 19. This form is known as a 'tachi', the sword being suspended from a belt, the cutting edge downwards. This was the invariable means of carrying the sword, as can be seen from the scroll paintings. It was the only really practical way of wearing a sword with the bulky yoroi armour. Fastened to the scabbard is a wooden or basketwork disc which holds the spare bowstring. At this time the bow was the most important weapon and the mark of the samurai. Bows were of composite construction like most Asiatic styles, being made of strips of bamboo and other woods bound round with rattan. A curious and unique feature of the Japanese bow is that the hand-grip is not central on the shaft but one third of the way up. This was to enable the bow to be discharged more easily from the saddle of a galloping horse. The samurai was essentially a mounted archer, and hours of practice were given to shooting from horseback with the long bamboo arrows. A selection of arrowheads is shown in Fig. 18. Different heads were designed for different purposes. The open 'V'-shaped heads, like a pair of scissors, were intended for cutting the cords of an armour. An interesting arrowhead, not illustrated here, had a large perforated wooden bulb which whistled as it flew through the air. This was used for signalling and for intimidating the enemy. The arrows were carried in a quiver fastened on the right side of the body from which arrows were drawn by pulling out and down, rather than over the shoulder in the Western fashion.

The weapons and armour described here clearly indicate that the peaceful bureaucracy which had held sway since the Great Reforms was giving way to new military pressure. Although fighting the Ainu on the government's behalf gave the frontier samurai good experience of warfare, the real lessons in military science came from action against their own kind. These rebellions are insignificant when viewed against the overall trend of Japanese history, but were of great importance in the development of the samurai tradition. In later years the samurai were to be spurred on by exhortations to emulate the deeds of their ancestors. When challenging an opponent to individual combat it became the custom to proclaim one's pedigree and the history of one's house. These ancestors were the samurai who fought with Minamoto Yoshiie in the campaigns known as the 'Early Nine Years' War' and the 'Later Three Years' War', and it was their deeds that were being proclaimed two or three centuries later.

Yoshiie represents the beginning of the military tradition in the Minamoto family, and his descendants were proud to have his name to shout above the din of battle. He first came to prominence during the Early Nine Years' War (1051–63) waged by his father.

6 Warriors armed with bows, swords and naginata. From the *Heiji Monogatari Emaki*. ('Picture Scroll of the Heiji War'.) (Courtesy, Museum of Fine Arts, Boston.)

The extreme north of Honshū, consisting of the twin provinces of Dewa and Mutsu, was the last outpost of the Kyōto hegemony. In addition to the official Governor there was also an officer responsible for the 'welfare' [sic] of the aborigines. By long tradition this office had been held within the Abe family and by 1050 the then incumbent, Abe Yoritoki, had so profited from the position that the government thought it wise to restrain his activities. They appointed Minamoto Yoriyoshi to the post of Governor and Commander-in-Chief. Yoriyoshi had served under his father against various local rebels, but it was the presence on this campaign of Yoriyoshi's eldest son Yoshiie, then a boy of fifteen, that was to make the name of Minamoto known and feared throughout the land.

In 1057, after some desultory fighting, the corrupt Abe Yoritoki was killed by a stray arrow, but his son Sadato continued the struggle. At the end of 1057 Sadato entrenched himself with 4,000 men in a position at Kawasaki where he was attacked by the Minamoto, father and son, at the head of a mere 1,800 troops. The attack failed, and as the Minamoto pulled back to regroup a terrific blizzard began. Under cover of driving snow Abe Sadato launched a furious attack against the discomfited Minamoto. In a fierce rearguard action the Minamoto began a retreat from which Yoriyoshi, Yoshiie and five other commanders survived. For his bravery during the retreat Yoshiie earned the sobriquet of 'Hachiman-taro' the 'First Born of Hachiman – God of War'.

In 1062 the Minamoto, reinforced by allies from the Kiyowara family, returned to the fray with 10,000 men. Abe Sadato put up a fierce resistance from his stockade at Kuriyagawa. This was a deadly affair. Boys of thirteen fought beside old men, and even women joined in the fray, which continued without remission for two days and nights. At last the weight of numbers told, and Sadato capitulated. A few months later Yoshiie rode into Kyōto carrying Sadato's head. This was the form of trophy which, throughout samurai history, was to furnish the best proof of a task successfully accomplished. Legend has it that during the fighting in front of the stockade at Kuriyagawa, Yoshiie, in his direst need, had uttered a prayer to his patron Hachiman. He promised the deity that if victory were granted him he would establish a shrine to Hachiman. Thus, in 1063, while on the way to Kyōto with his grisly spoils of war, Yoshiie broke his journey at Tsurugaoka, now part of the town of Kamakura near Tōkyō, and there founded the Tsurugaoka Hachiman Shrine, which was to become the glory and honour of the Minamoto.

The elder Minamoto, Yoriyoshi, died in 1082, and a year later Minamoto Yoshiie set out on the campaign known as the Later Three Years' War. Kiyowara, who had allied himself with the Minamoto during the Early Nine Years' War, had been rewarded by a position of rank in Northern Honshū. Like Abe before him he allowed power to corrupt him, and his son and grandson had profited from his excesses. Yoshiie took the field against them.

The bulk of the fighting of the Later Three Years' War consisted of a protracted siege of the fortress stockade of Kanezawa, which gave Yoshiie much opportunity to put into practice the military arts he had learned at his father's knee. On the way to invest the Kanezawa fortress, Yoshiie observed a flock of wild geese rising in disordered flight from a distant forest. He at once concluded, correctly, that an ambush had been laid. What is significant in this incident is that the rule that the rising of birds indicated an ambush was one that Yoshiie had learnt from an Ancient Chinese manual on the art of war. Here was proof that a rising military class took its profession seriously enough to study a work that a few generations before would have been regarded as unspeakably vulgar.

As the siege went on the samurai virtues of bravery and loyalty crystallized in the actual danger and comradeship of the warriors' life. Assault after assault was beaten off, and Yoshiie exhorted his men again and again to bravery. In his camp he set aside seats for the brave and for the cowards. At the close of each day's campaigning each samurai was assigned to the position he had earned. In time that samurai fatalism, which was soon to be regarded as the warrior's special character-

7 Samurai in camp, preparing and eating food. A detail from *Gosannen Kassen Emaki*. ('Picture scroll of the Later Three Years' War'.) (Tōkyō National Museum.)

23

istic, asserted itself. One samurai, of sixteen years of age, named Kamakura Gongoro Kagemasa received an arrow in his eye during an attack. He calmly snapped off the shaft and shot the man who had delivered it. During a lull in the fighting a fellow samurai attempted to extract the arrow head, but it was so firmly implanted that he could only get a grip on it by planting his foot firmly on Gongoro's face and pulling with all his might. At this Gongoro greatly protested that it was an insult to tread on the face of a samurai, and that his comrade would pay for it with his life!

An interesting sequel to this story is that the actual incident recounted above was recalled and quoted by a descendent of Gongoro one hundred years later. When Kajiwara Kagetoki, an illustrious samurai in his own right, entered the fighting at the Battle of Ichi-no-tani in 1184 he proclaimed himself loudly to the enemy in these terms, recorded in the epic *Heike Monogatari*:

'Ho! I am Kajiwara Heizō Kagetoki, descended in the fifth generation from Gongoro Kagemasa of Kamakura, renowned warrior of the East country and match for any thousand men! At the age of sixteen I rode in the van of Hachiman-taro Yoshiie at the siege of Sembuku Kanezawa in Dewa and, receiving an arrow in my left eye through the helmet, I plucked it forth and with it shot down the marksman who sent it, thereby gaining honours and leaving a name to posterity!'

Two points can be noted here. First, that the story has been embellished so that the arrow is plucked from his eye and used to kill the enemy, and secondly that Kajiwara Kagetoki claims that he performed the feat and not his ancestor. Perhaps in the heat of the battle he hoped his enemy would be incapable of mental arithmetic, for if the situation was as he described Kagetoki would by then be at least 117 years old!

As the siege of Kanezawa dragged on, even the samurai of the Minamoto begged Yoshiie to withdraw. He refused, telling them to burn their wooden shelters for warmth, for Kanezawa would be theirs on the morrow. In a final desperate attack the Minamoto were indeed victorious, and a large number of heads were added to Yoshiie's collection.

But were the government grateful for the privations endured on their behalf? Indeed they were not, for they had earlier turned down a request from Yoshiie for an official Shōgunal commission, and now that he had undertaken the campaign on his own, and at his own expense, no reward was forthcoming. Disgusted at the government's attitude, Yoshiie flung the heads of the rebels into a ditch, and rewarded his samurai out of his own resources. This was necessary, for in those early days loyalty to the point of death had a strong mercenary aspect.

By their refusal to reward Yoshiie the Court set a very dangerous precedent. If Yoshiie was to be regarded as a suppressor of rebels then it was essential that he should be seen to be acting on the government's behalf. If the Later Three Years' War was to be regarded as a private war between the Minamoto and the Kiyowara then the government were in fact sanctioning a *droit de guerre*, as no steps were taken to punish them. In such ways the government revealed their utter lack of understanding of the changed conditions of life in Japan.

There were many rebellions like the Later Three Years' War and the other emerging samurai family, the Taira, played their part. Oddly enough, the Taira tended to be employed in the south and west of Japan, whereas the Minamoto confined their activities to the north and east. The Taira made their name largely as quellers of the pirates along the Inland Sea and the coasts of Kyūshū. It was this service that made the sea routes safe for trade with China. As the Minamoto identified their clan with the Hachiman Shrine of Tsurugaoka, so the Taira patronized the Shrine of Itsukushima, or Miyajima, a lovely island on the Inland Sea about twelve miles from Hiroshima. The Taira made Itsukushima their own, and lavished much wealth and attention on it.

Thus by the beginning of the twelfth century there were three very powerful families in Japan, the Fujiwara, who controlled the reins of government and the genetics of the Royal Family, the rebel-quelling Minamoto, and the pirate-quelling Taira. There was, in addition, another growing military power to which we now turn.

Ever since the time of the moving of the capital from Nara to Kyōto there had existed a rivalry between the older temples of Nara and the new foundations of Enryaku-ji and Mii-dera on Mount Hiei. In August 963 a religious conclave had been held at the Palace by Imperial command, to which twenty priests from Nara and Mount Hiei had been summoned to discuss some principles of religion. The ensuing debate proved endless, and added further to the discord. Nor was there perfect peace within the two centres. In 968 the priests of the Tōdai-ji actually fought with their neighbours of the Kōfuku-ji for the possession of land whose ownership was disputed. In 981 an unpopular choice for Abbot of the Enryaku-ji led to the priests of that temple dividing into two factions, and even attempting to kill one of the nominees.

In a time of political uncertainty the growing riches of the temples were an inviting lure to any samurai leader willing, for a while, to put religion on one side. There was also a threat from the government tax-collectors, who were much bolder in their dealings with the taxable monastic lands than they were with 'donated' samurai holdings. Consequently the monasteries of Mount Hiei began to regard it as essential to maintain a private army for the maintenance of their rights and privileges, and to withstand the deprivation of others. The Kōfuku-ji was forced to follow suit when the Enryaku-ji attacked the Gion shrine in Kyōto, which was subject to the Kōfuku-ji. Soon most of the great monasteries of Kyōto and Nara could number thousands of men under arms, and for the next two hundred years their invasions were to alarm

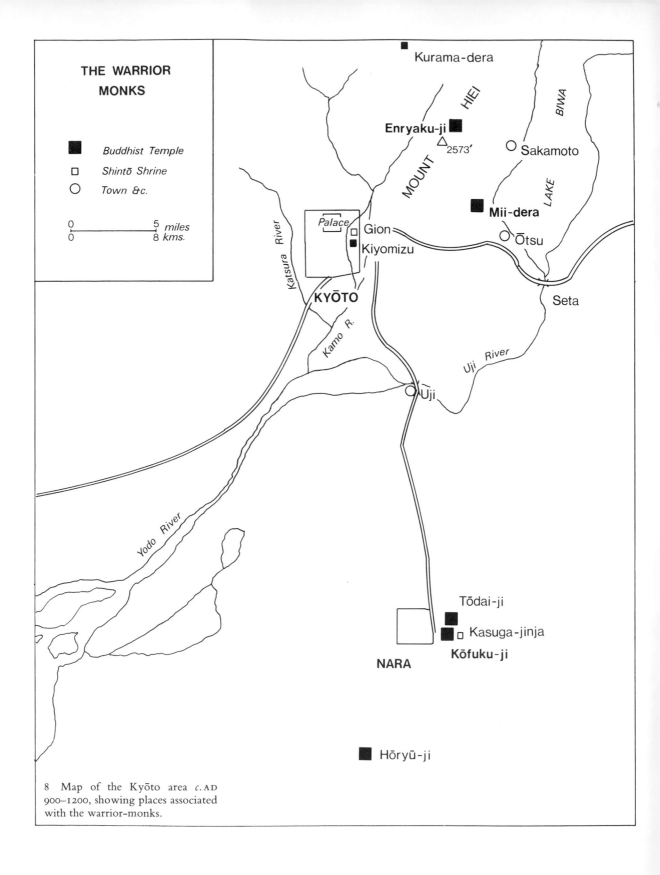

THE WARRIOR
MONKS

■   Buddhist Temple

□   Shintō Shrine

○   Town &c.

0   5   miles
0   8   kms.

Kurama-dera

MOUNT HIEI

Enryaku-ji

2573'

BIWA

○ Sakamoto

LAKE

Mii-dera

Katsura River

Palace

Gion

Kiyomizu

○ Ōtsu

KYŌTO

Kamo R.

Seta

Uji River

○ Uji

Yodo River

Tōdai-ji

Kasuga-jinja

Kōfuku-ji

NARA

■ Hōryū-ji

8   Map of the Kyōto area *c.*AD
900–1200, showing places associated
with the warrior-monks.

the superstitious Courtiers and terrify the ordinary citizens of Kyōto.

The warrior-monks, or soldier priests, as they are variously called, were formidable. Their military skills approached those of the emergent samurai. To swell the numbers of their armies, monasteries deliberately recruited men to the priesthood for no reason other than their being trained in warfare. These recruits, known as 'sōhei', were often absconded peasants or petty criminals, and did most of the fighting on the temples' behalf. The priesthood had traditionally been a gentleman's profession, although many upper class 'gakushō' (scholar priests), would readily join in battle if the need arose. In Kyōto, most of the trouble caused by the monks came from the direction of Mount Hiei, and the term loosely used to describe them was 'yama-bushi' (mountain warriors). The choice of phrase was unfortunate, for there was (and still is) a sect of Buddhist friars called 'yamabushi', meaning mountain sleepers (the written characters are different), who toured the country preaching and doing good. This has led to much confusion.

Two particular painted scrolls depict warrior-monks in detail. The first is *Tengu Zōshi* from which Figs 9 and 10 are taken. Here the monks are shown in their full heavy robes with the large cowl wrapped round the face. The outer robes were sometimes dyed with oil of cloves, producing a light brown colour, or were left a plain off-white. On their feet the monks wear sandals or 'geta' (wooden clogs). Figure 11

9 Warrior-monks in full robes. From the scroll *Tengu Zōshi*. (Tōkyō National Museum. Photograph: Kokusai Bunka Shinkokai.)

10 Warrior-monks armed with naginata. From the scroll *Tengu Zōshi*. (Tōkyō National Museum. Photograph: Kokusai Bunka Shinkokai.)

shows the monks in more warlike mood. Most have donned their robes over a suit of armour, which, judging by the shape of the 'kusazuri', the skirt of the armour, is not a yoroi but a simple footsoldier's haramaki. Some are wearing yoroi, with a 'hachimaki' or head towel, in place of the cowl. Figure 12, from the scroll *Kasuga Gongen Reikenki* depicts sōhei of the Kōfuku-ji defending their temple from attack. Most of the defenders, whom we may assume are all monks, have abandoned their monkish habit in favour of the more practical suit of armour. An unusual feature of the group shown here is the warrior behind the tree in the centre who is wearing a veil with eye-slits, no doubt to conceal his identity. The monk's traditional weapon was the 'naginata' previously referred to. The version used at this time was called a 'shōbuzukuri-naginata', with a blade up to four feet long. Its slashing strokes, usual in fighting, could produce some nasty wounds.

The monks' other weapon was the fear of the gods they represented. Every monk possessed a rosary, and would readily 'tell his beads' to bring down a curse upon an offender. The Courtiers, whose lives were so strictly geared to the demands of religion and augury, were particularly vulnerable to such treatment. Mount Hiei was their sacred guardian, even though the house of the gods had been turned into a den of thieves. It is probable that four out of every five warrior-monks had not properly entered the priesthood, beyond accepting a purely nominal shaving of the head.

Often the monks would emphasize their presence by carrying into battle, a huge portable 'mikoshi' (shrine) wherein the god was supposed to dwell. The mikoshi, illustrated in Fig. 11, was carried on long poles by about twenty monks. An offence against the mikoshi was regarded as an assault on the deity itself. During one upheaval, following the murder of a Mount Hiei monk by a Courtier, the great mikoshi of Mount Hiei, which was said to hold the spirit of the Mountain King, was carried at the head of a monk army into the streets of Kyōto. The monks stood around it and chanted the six hundred volumes of the *Dai Hannya Kyō* – a Buddhist Sutra, as a curse. Sometimes the mikoshi would be left in the streets while the monks returned to the mountain. Here it would remain, to the dread of the townspeople, until the monks' demands were satisfied.

However, the monks' greatest fury was reserved for inter-temple disputes. These were not religious wars as we know them, for doctrinal

11 Warrior-monks carrying the 'mikoshi' or portable shrine, in which the spirit of the god was supposed to dwell.

12   Sōhei (warrior monks) of the Kōfuku-ji fighting samurai. From the scroll *Kasuga Gongen Reikenki* ('Miracles of the Kasuga Gongen'). (Imperial Household collection. Photograph: Kokusai Bunka Shinkokai.)

differences mattered little, and the arguments were usually over land or prestige. The issue was frequently settled by burning down the opposing temple. Alliances were frequently formed, and as easily broken. In 989 and 1006 the Enryaku-ji took arms against the Kōfuku-ji. In 1036 Enryaku-ji fought Mii-dera. In 1081 Enryaku-ji united with Mii-dera against the Kōfuku-ji, and during the dispute Kōfuku-ji burned Mii-dera and carried off much loot. Later in the same year Enryaku-ji burned Mii-dera over a succession dispute. In 1113 Enryaku-ji burned the Kiyomizu temple during a dispute over the election of an abbot. In 1140 Enryaku-ji attacked Mii-dera once again, and in 1142 Mii-dera attacked the Enryaku-ji. So the long catalogue goes on, until the monks' warlike activities were swallowed up in the great war that swept the country.

An incident that occurred in 1081 was significant. In January the people of Ōmi, who were subject to the Enryaku-ji, attacked the inhabitants of Otsu, who were under Mii-dera. Though the men of Otsu complained to the Enryaku-ji, nothing was done, so they reported the incident to Mii-dera, who suggested that the men refuse ever to work again for the Enryaku-ji. This angered the Enryaku-ji, who in June sent forces to attack Mii-dera. Mii-dera was ready for them. The attack was beaten off, only to be renewed with increased vigour. The Abbot of Enryaku-ji personally led the attack and spurred his followers on to such exertions that when the flames subsided they had destroyed 294 halls, 15 sutra store houses, 6 bell towers, 4 tabernacles, 624 monastic residences and more than 1,500 dwelling houses – in fact the whole place was destroyed except for a handful of buildings. Hereupon the monks of Mii-dera assaulted Enryaku-ji with a large army. The Court, greatly alarmed, sent soldiers to check them, but in September the attack went ahead, and rumours began circulating in the Capital that the two temples were about to unite and descend upon Kyōto. The Imperial Court, in an excess of fear, turned to the only force who could possibly withstand such an attack. They granted a Shōgunal commission for defending the capital to Minamoto Yoshiie! This stalwart, covered with the reflected glory of the Early Nine Years' War and who two years later was to set out on the Later Three Years' War, accepted the commission with alacrity. The capital was fortified by the samurai, but the expected attack never materialized. Yoshiie returned to his normal duties.

Ten years later, in 1092, the Court again found the Minamoto useful against the monks. On behalf of the government Minamoto Yoshichika, Yoshiie's second son, confiscated a manor in Mino province which had recently been established by the Enryaku-ji. Yoshichika claimed, quite rightly, that he was acting only in accordance with the law which forbade trading in land by the temples. Nevertheless the monks insisted they were in the right and sent a large force into Kyōto. Faced with the power of the Minamoto they grudgingly withdrew.

In spite of the turbulence of the priests the Imperial Family continued to shower gifts of land, gold and silver upon the temples. Perhaps they hoped thereby to buy their favour, but it seemed not to work, for whenever the Court tried meddling in the appointment of clergy there was a furious outcry and the usual flare-up of monastic anger through the city streets. Although they knew that they possessed sufficient force to overpower the temples, the Court, and the Fujiwara family as a whole, were too devout Buddhists to treat the monks as they deserved, and in spite of the presence of the samurai the priests grew even more haughty and self indulgent.

In 1146 a young samurai called Taira Kiyomori had his first dramatic clash with the monks. Kiyomori was a talented young man of doubtful parentage. His official father was Taira Tadamori, a great queller of the pirates, who had been given, as a reward for services, the Emperor's favourite concubine. Nine months later she gave birth to Kiyomori, so the young man had some pretensions to Imperial blood. On the day of the Gion Festival in 1146 one of Kiyomori's attendants quarrelled with a priest of the Gion Shrine. Vowing revenge for the implied insult to his name Kiyomori led a band of samurai to attack the priest-army of Gion. They were carrying the mikoshi at the time. According to some accounts Kiyomori showed an admirable samurai disregard for religious scruples and fired an arrow at the mikoshi, which struck the gong on the front, proclaiming far and near the act of sacrilege. Enraged at the offence to a mikoshi the Enryaku-ji sent 7,000 warrior-monks into Kyōto, who uttered all manner of curses and demanded Kiyomori's immediate banishment. Certain members of the Fujiwara family, jealous of the growing popularity of the samurai and of Kiyomori in particular, urged the Emperor to pass sentence, but the Court knowing they now depended entirely upon the samurai for protection, exonerated Kiyomori on his payment of a small fine.

During the two centuries under discussion the Enryaku-ji alone appealed no less than seventy times to the Emperor with armed force, not to mention numerous incidents between and within the temples themselves. Thus the temples which had helped in the collapse of the land reforms and the growth of private manors, were to make the Court reliant upon the power of the samurai near at home, as well as in the far distant provinces. It is not too much to say that the warrior-monks ushered in the military age of Japan, for by their incursions the Taira and the Minamoto were able to see that the Emperor had no clothes.

The best comment on the monks was made by the ex-Emperor Shirakawa, who looked out of his palace during one of their demonstrations and muttered sadly, 'Though I am ruler of Japan, there are three things which are beyond my control; the rapids on the Kamo River, the fall of the dice at gambling, and the monks of the mountain!'

It was now only a matter of time before the samurai would be called upon to settle internal matters at Court, instead of merely providing its external defence. Such an occasion presented itself in the year 1156, in the 'Hōgen Incident', so called after the era name of the year in which it happened. The background to the Hōgen Incident is complicated, but may be summarized as follows.

During the Heian period the curious practice developed among the Emperors of Japan of abdicating while still comparatively young in favour of an infant son or nephew. Those who took such a course of action were known as 'Cloistered Emperors', owing to the fact that it was convenient, upon resigning the post, to have one's head shaved and enter the priesthood.

By the year 1150 there was a child Emperor, Emperor Konoe, and no fewer than two ex-Emperors, father and son, Toba and Sutoku. As the health of the Emperor Konoe was not good, it was decided to appoint a Crown Prince ready for the sovereign's expected demise. With so much royal blood among the Court a number of different suggestions were made, but when Emperor Konoe died of poison, all was confusion. Ex-Emperor Sutoku wished to become Emperor once again, for his abdication had been rather forced, to put it mildly, while ex-Emperor Toba described the throne for another of his sons. His will prevailed so that on 22 November 1155, Toba's fourth son became Emperor Go-Shirakawa. Ex-Emperor Sutoku, egged on by partisan Fujiwara followers, determined to regain his throne by force. There were plenty of troops around to call upon, including the upstart families from the provinces who had recently been making a name for themselves, not to mention the various cohorts of warrior-monks. Just at this juncture, on 20 July 1156, ex-Emperor Toba died. With correct filial piety Sutoku went to attend the solemn funeral. He was met at the entrance and informed that according to the dying wishes of his father no place was to be found for him at the service. Sutoku was mortally offended, and sent out orders for all the samurai in the near-by provinces who had declared their support, to move troops up to the capital with the greatest of speed. A similar message was also sent to the warrior-monks of Nara.

By and large the samurai who responded to Sutoku's call, and to the similar one sent by the incumbent Emperor Go-Shirakawa, did not divide along clan lines, but along more personal lines of court rank and commitment. So it came to pass that the forces that gathered on both sides for the Hōgen fight consisted of mixtures of Taira and Minamoto clansmen. For Sutoku the Taira contingent was in the hands of Tadamasa, uncle of Kiyomori. The Minamoto were led by the then head of the clan, Tameyoshi, grandson of Hachiman-taro Yoshiie, and certain of his sons, notably Tametomo, a giant of a man and a superb archer.

A notable absentee from Tameyoshi's contingent was his son and heir Yoshitomo, who had joined the other side. When Emperor Go-Shirakawa's summons went out he was the first to respond, and put 400 picked samurai at his sovereign's command. On 29 July he was joined by Taira Kiyomori, who had so infuriated the warrior-monks twelve years before. Troops were sent out to seize strategic positions on the approach roads to the capital, and block the expected advance of the warrior-monks. Within ten days of the death of ex-

Emperor Toba the mourners at his funeral had divided themselves into two camps, the supporters of Emperor Go-Shirakawa in the Imperial Palace, and Sutoku's forces two miles away in an old Imperial residence called the Shirakawa-den. Here Sutoku held a council of war, presided over by Minamoto Tameyoshi and his giant son Tametomo. The latter was only seventeen years old, but is said to have been seven feet tall and possessed extreme muscular strength. His bow was eight and a half feet long, and took three ordinary men to bend it. By some accident of birth, or excess of practice, he had acquired a left arm that was four inches longer than his right, enabling him to draw the bow-string to a considerable length, and fire arrows with terrific force. He also possessed enormous self confidence, and made the suggestion, based on sound military experience, that they should launch a night attack on the Palace. He continued: 'There are probably no brave men in the Emperor's party except my brother Yoshitomo, and if he comes forward for single combat with me, I shall shoot him in the throat. How much more insignificant are the weak arrows of such a man as Kiyomori! I would turn them off with the sleeves of my armour or kick them aside with my feet!'

But Tametomo's wise counsel was of no avail, for Sutoku's chief military adviser, Fujiwara Yorinaga, favoured caution. They should wait, he urged, until morning when they would be joined by the warrior-monks. Unfortunately Tametomo had to yield to the opinion of higher authority, and in so doing realized that they were doomed. Neither the morning nor the monks were likely to come, for the monks would as readily join their opponents, and Tametomo suspected that the night attack he had proposed was shortly to be launched against themselves.

So began the first battle between Taira and Minamoto samurai. The chronicle of the events of the night of 29 July 1156, recorded as the *Hōgen Monogatari* or the 'Tale of Hōgen', gives the impression of an almost leisurely courtesy between the two armies. All the classic forms of samurai warfare were obeyed to the letter, in a gentlemanly fashion that was never to be repeated. Certain curious incidents happened. For example, Taira Kiyomori was advancing to the attack when it occurred to him that the day, the eleventh on the lunar calendar, was one on which the east is an unlucky direction. Consequently he veered round to the north to avoid having to shoot his arrows in an easterly direction. Also, before the attack began, giant Tametomo had an argument with one of his brothers about who should be first into the attack. This was one of the earliest examples of what was to become a samurai obsession. In this case it was settled by a compromise; the brother led the attack and Tametomo went to defend the most dangerous place, which his brother was to specify.

According to the *Hōgen Monogatari* the action began with the shouting of war cries, pedigrees and personal achievements. There followed an archery duel in the dark, during which Tametomo caused great alarm by sending an arrow clean through one samurai to wound another. Tametomo was holding the Western Gate, and it was against this position that his elder brother Yoshitomo made his advance. Tametomo hoped to frighten him into retreating, so he loosed an arrow at Yoshitomo's helmet. The arrow tore off one of the projecting rivets and buried itself into the gatepost. Tametomo was about to loose another shaft when he was challenged by two samurai who addressed him as follows:

'We are Ōba Kageyoshi and Saburo Kagechika, descendants of Kamakura Gongoro Kagemasa, who when he was sixteen years old in the Three Years' War of Hachiman Taro, at the attack made on Kanezawa castle in Dewa province, went out in the van of battle and was hit in the left eye by an arrow. . . . The arrow tore his eye out and left it hanging on the first plate of his helmet, but he sent an arrow in reply and killed his enemy.'

The same story again, but no doubt any descendant of Kamakura Gongoro was a worthy opponent for Tametomo. He fixed a 'humming bulb' arrow to his bow and let fly. The arrow made a loud scream as it flew through the air, and cut off at the knee the left leg of Ōba Kageyoshi, who was standing about twenty yards away. The arrow passed on and hit his horse, whereupon the wooden arrowhead shattered into pieces. Saburo Kagechika leapt from his horse to prevent the taking of Kageyoshi's head, and lifting his wounded comrade on to his shoulder, carried him away.

Minamoto Yoshitomo realized that his father and brother were prepared to put up a long and spirited defence, so orders were given to set fire to the Shirakawa-den. There had been no rain for some time, and a strong wind was blowing. The buildings ignited like tinder, and soon the glow of the burning palace illuminated the sky for miles around. There was no course open to the defenders but flight, for the peculiar Japanese tradition of suicide had yet to be established. As the Sutoku supporters fled the blazing building they were picked off by archers. Fujiwara Yorinaga, who had advised Sutoku against the proposed night attack, fell in this way, but the remaining leaders were all captured, including Kiyomori's uncle Tadamasa, and the redoubtable Minamoto pair Tameyoshi and Tametomo. So ended the brief but bloody Hōgen Incident. Although short and limited in its political effects, the Hōgen Incident marks the emergence of the samurai as an integral part of the politics of the central government.

The most pressing question was what to do with the defeated supporters of Sutoku. The only major Taira clan member to have supported him was Kiyomori's unpopular uncle Tadamasa, whose execution Kiyomori gleefully ordered. This set a precedent for Yoshitomo to follow, but dare he order the execution of his own father and brother? If he did not, said the now secure Emperor Go-Shirakawa, the execution would have to be entrusted to Kiyomori. Such a disgrace would have been an eternal slur on the Minamoto family, so it was with the greatest regret that Yoshitomo ordered one of his own samurai to behead his father. A compromise was reached concerning Tametomo, who was banished, the precaution having been taken of cutting the sinews of his arm so that he could never wield a bow again. In fact, during his years of exile his arms healed, and he fired his last arrow at a boatload of Taira samurai. The arrow smashed through the hull just below the water level, sinking the vessel with the loss of all hands. Tametomo then retired and committed suicide by cutting open his abdomen with a dagger, the first recorded instance of 'hara-kiri', that was to become such a feature of the samurai way of death.

Ex-Emperor Sutoku was also banished, and died in misery in 1164.

The horror of these events was increased considerably by the knowledge that for three and a half centuries no high officer of the Emperor had been executed, furthermore the Court was still in mourning for ex-Emperor Toba, and it was against all precedent to execute any offenders during such a time. Nevertheless seventy of Sutoku's supporters came to kneel in the blood pit of Rokujō-ga-hara.

So the new Emperor Go-Shirakawa was safe. It was his triumph, but the real winner in the affair was Taira Kiyomori, whose rise in Court rank now became dramatic. Kiyomori had more political skills than military, and began to play the Fujiwara at their own game of matchmaking. In future, Kiyomori hoped, the wives and concubines of Emperors would be Taira instead of Fujiwara. Of course there were still Minamoto at Court, those of the clan who had managed to choose the right side in 1156. Notably, of course, Minamoto Yoshitomo, whose sorrowful countenance soon attracted the attention of one of the Fujiwara hangers-on, Fujiwara Nobuyori. Nobuyori's aspirations were directed against a fellow Fujiwara, Shinzei by name, so he devised a little plot, and somewhere along the line whispered to Yoshitomo the fateful word 'revenge!'.

Meanwhile, Emperor Go-Shirakawa, on whose behalf the war had been fought, soon decided that he had had enough of being a real Emperor and abdicated in favour of his fifteen-year old son, who became Emperor Nijō. Thus, so soon after the trouble caused by the Cloistered-Emperor system, Japan once again had a Cloistered Emperor.

This time rebellion was bound to turn into a direct Taira/Minamoto clash. Taira Kiyomori was a loyal subject of both Emperor and ex-Emperor, so to avoid being branded as rebels the Minamoto would have to kidnap both sovereigns while Kiyomori was out of town, and then make the Emperor declare Kiyomori a rebel. The plot was hatched in apparently complete secrecy, and on 14 January 1160 came the moment to strike. Suspecting nothing, Taira Kiyomori and his eldest son Shigemori left Kyōto for a private pilgrimage to Kumano, eighty miles due south. The conspirators allowed five days for Kiyomori to get well clear of the capital, and on the night of the fifth launched an attack on the palace of the ex-Emperor, which stood on San-jō (third avenue). Five hundred Minamoto samurai flung themselves at the gates, and soon the whole Sanjō Palace was ablaze. Ex-Emperor Go-Shirakawa was taken, and the young Emperor Nijō was surrounded at the Imperial Palace and confined there.

Figures 6 and 13 are taken from the scroll known as *Heiji Monogatari* which deals with the events of these turbulent few days known as the 'Heiji Incident' after the era name once again. Surely no more vivid picture of samurai activity has ever been painted than that portion of the scroll illustrated in Fig. 13, entitled 'The Burning of the Sanjō Palace'. Smoke and flames rise above the palace roofs, while tough country 'bushi' search under the floorboards for more victims to decapitate. The overall impression is one of a surging mass of horses and men, fleeing Court ladies, and crashing timbers. After the attack Minamoto Yoshitomo honoured his deal with Fujiwara Nobuyori and attacked the mansion of Nobuyori's enemy, Shinzei. Shinzei escaped, but not for long, as attested by Plate III, from another section of the *Heiji Monogatari*, which depicts a group of samurai returning to Nobuyori, who is seated in an oxcart, with the trophy he so desired.

13 The burning of the Sanjō Palace during the 'Heiji Incident', 1160. From the scroll *Heiji Monogatari Emaki* ('Picture scroll of the Heiji War'). (Courtesy, Museum of Fine Arts, Boston.)

Among the incidents of the attack on the Sanjō Palace one deserves mention for its wry humour. The retreating Taira forces were fighting a rearguard action, when Taira Yorimori, one of Kiyomori's younger brothers, was assailed by a Minamoto samurai armed with a 'kumade'. This weapon resembled an animal paw of iron mounted on a long wooden shaft. The attacker swung his kumade against Yorimori, and its claw bit into the bowl of his helmet and stuck fast. Before the samurai could pull Yorimori off his horse the latter turned in the saddle and sliced through the shaft of the kumade with his sword. He then made off with this unusual battle trophy still projecting from his helmet, to the amusement of all.

So far the conspirators had had it all their own way, but Kiyomori had learned of the rebellion while still on his way to Kumano, and was now returning to Kyōto with a handful of men. Urged on by his gallant son Shigemori, the Taira leader boldly entered the capital, and made straight for his mansion, called Rokuhara, as yet unassailed by the Minamoto. From this moment on the tide began to turn in favour of the Taira. On the night of 4 February the Taira pulled off a dramatic

coup, and snatched Emperor Nijō from under the very noses of the Minamoto. The Emperor was but a youth, and was disguised as a girl by a band of Taira partisans, who escorted his Majesty through the labyrinthine complexities of the Palace and past the Minamoto guards. About the same time ex-Emperor Go-Shirakawa made good his escape from the Minamoto headquarters.

The news of the twin disaster was brought to Nobuyori, who was drunk when the message arrived. The following morning the seriousness of the situation became apparent, and two hours later a thousand Taira samurai under Shigemori and Yorimori attacked the Minamoto head-quarters. The Minamoto managed to hold their ground until a feigned retreat by the Taira led them into reckless pursuit. As the Minamoto streamed out, the Taira forced their way in, until the positions of attackers and defenders were completely reversed. Yoshitomo then resolved to make an attack in force on the Taira headquarters of Rokuhara. The attempt was a disastrous failure, as one of the Minamoto leaders refused to move. This was Yorimasa, a warrior who had seen long service under the Emperor, and who was loath to betray years of loyalty for a clan feud. So Yoshitomo was compelled to flee from Kyōto to the east. As they left the capital his party ran headlong into the monks of the Enryaku-ji. After many casualties the Minamoto fought their way as far as the bridge of Seta, at the southern tip of Lake Biwa, and here Yoshitomo ordered his men to break up and scatter.

Yoshitomo headed up in to the mountains with three of his sons, Yoshihira, Tomonaga and Yoritomo, the latter a boy of fourteen who had performed his 'gembuku' (manhood ceremony), only shortly before the Heiji battle. In their flight they were hindered by storms and blizzards, and by the wounded Tomonaga, who begged his father to kill him. At last Yoshitomo agreed to the horrid request, but Tomonaga's sacrifice was to prove of little use, for the trio had gone but a short distance before the Taira caught up with them in their hiding place. Yoshitomo was finally murdered in his bath.

There followed such a savage series of executions as to make the beheading of Tameyoshi after Hōgen seem a trifling incident. By orders of Kiyomori the executioner decapitated Minamoto Yoshihira and Fujiwara Nobuyori. The body of Tomonaga was exhumed, the head cut off and sent to join that of his father on public display, along with numerous lesser warriors. There remained four young Minamoto sons. Yoritomo, who had fought by his father's side, was banished to Izu, to be brought up in a Taira household. The others were still in the care of their mother, Tokiwa, who on hearing of the death of her husband fled from Kyōto, her youngest baby clasped to her bosom, another strapped to her back, and the eldest clutching her hand. The flight of Tokiwa has been a source of inspiration to Japanese artists ever since, the blood from her footprints on the snow symbolizing the red of the Taira flag staining the white of the Minamoto. And Tokiwa would have escaped, had it not been for the ruthless Kiyomori, who tortured Tokiwa's mother until the old lady disclosed her daughter's whereabouts. At last, however, a measure of humanity touched Kiyomori, aided greatly by Tokiwa's radiant beauty, and he agreed to spare the lives of her children if she became his concubine. So the three boys were neither executed nor exiled, but sent to various monasteries for training as priests. (See Appendix I for the Minamoto family tree.)

With the death of the exiled Tametomo in 1164 there was but one adult Minamoto left alive, the venerable old Yorimasa, who had refused to attack during the Heiji Incident. He represented no threat to the Taira, and was tolerated in Court. By 1180 Taira Kiyomori was virtually ruler of Japan, with ex-Emperor Go-Shirakawa firmly under his thumb. In that year his dream came true for with the accession of Emperor Antoku he became Imperial Grandfather. He had beaten the Fujiwara at their own game.

So it must have come as something of a surprise to Kiyomori to hear in 1180 that there was a Minamoto plot against the Taira.

41

3. The Gempei War

The Gempei War, which lasted from 1180 until 1185, is the most celebrated of all the encounters fought between samurai. It was the consummation of the samurai ideal, a fight to the death between two entire clans. In its time the Gempei War produced a handful of the greatest samurai heroes Japan has ever seen, whose exploits were to be recounted and sung for years to come, until they acquired almost mythological status.

The Gempei War was fought between the Taira and the Minamoto clans, with many other allied families joining in. The name 'Gempei' is formed by the union of the Chinese pronunciation of their names, 'Genji' and 'Heike', into the compound 'Gempei'. The war has often been compared with the Wars of the Roses, an analogy suggested by the Minamoto use of white as an insignia and the Taira red.

The reader may be forgiven for asking whether, after the incidents of 1156 and 1160, there were any Minamoto left to challenge the Taira. In 1180 there certainly appeared to be none, not even to the eyes of Taira Kiyomori, but it will be recalled that the sentence passed on the Minamoto children had been banishment, not execution. Twenty years had now passed. One of the four had died young, but the remaining three sons of Yoshitomo had now grown to manhood.

The first action of the Gempei War, however, came not from the sons of Yoshitomo but from the one Minamoto left in the Taira-dominated Court. This was the veteran warrior Minamoto Yorimasa, who was now seventy-four years old. Because of his advanced age and loyal service he was a most unlikely rebel, yet because of his unique position at Court he and his sons had become the butt for numerous Taira insults, and his progress in Court rank had been slow. Minamoto Yorimasa did not have to look far to find an excuse for turning his growing personal dislike of the Taira into open rebellion. There was in the Court a disgruntled Crown Prince, Mochihito, the second son of ex-Emperor Go-Shirakawa, who had twice been passed over in succession to the throne, the second time in 1180 when the accession of Emperor Antoku had made Kiyomori Imperial Grandfather. The accession of Antoku, who was only three years old, was such a bare-faced Taira plot as to make Prince Mochihito receptive to revolutionary suggestions from anywhere. Minamoto Yorimasa provided the stimulus, and promised to provide the support.

As in the Minamoto rising of 1160, the plotters chose a time when

Taira Kiyomori and his grandson Emperor were absent from Kyōto. It was the custom for a newly enthroned sovereign to make a royal progress to the most hallowed religious foundations in the land. Normally these would have included the Nara and Mount Hiei temples, but as Emperor Antoku was the Taira's puppet the Imperial visit was made to the Taira family favourite of Itsukushima. This provided the plotters with an excellent excuse for enlisting the support of the warrior-monks. When the coast was clear Prince Mochihito issued a proclamation:

'The pronouncement of His Excellency the Prince declares that Kiyomori, Munemori and others, using the prestige of their office and their influence, have invited rebellion and have overthrown the nation. They have caused the officials and the people to suffer, seizing and plundering the five inner provinces and the seven circuits. They have confined the Ex-sovereign, exiled public officials, and inflicted death and banishment, drowning and imprisonment. They have robbed property and seized lands, usurped and bestowed offices. . . . They have despoiled the graves of Princes and cut off the head of one, defied the Emperor and destroyed Buddhist law in a manner unprecedented in history.

'This being so, let those of the Minamoto, the Fujiwara and the brave now living in the provinces of the three circuits now add their efforts to the cause. If there be those who are not of like mind they shall be regarded as partisans of Kiyomori and they shall suffer pain of death, exile or imprisonment. If there be those who perform meritoriously, despatch missions to me and inform me of their names and deeds, I shall, without fail, following my enthronement, bestow rewards upon them according to their wishes. Proclaim this message in all the provinces and carry out the terms of this pronouncement.

5 May 1180.'

A copy of the proclamation was taken by Minamoto Yukiie to Minamoto Yoritomo, the eldest of the three surviving sons of Yoshitomo, now living in exile in Izu. Careless talk on his journey brought the plot to the ears of Taira spies, and soon Taira samurai were searching Prince Mochihito's Kyōto residence in an effort to find him, but he had fled to the monks of Mii-dera.

How little Kiyomori knew of the plot may be judged from the fact that he sent Minamoto Yorimasa to attack Mii-dera and bring back the Prince. It was time for Yorimasa to show his true colours, so he set fire to his Kyōto home and joined the Prince, accompanied by fifty trusty retainers. It was now important that the insurgents, whose plot had been so prematurely sprung, should hold on until there was a general Minamoto rising in the east. However, Yorimasa's small contingent, even though augmented by the monks of Mii-dera,

14 The Phoenix Hall of the Byōdō-in at Uji. Minamoto Yorimasa committed suicide here after the Battle of Uji, 1180. (Photograph by the Author.)

was likely to prove insufficient against the Taira, who were whipping up 20,000 men to attack the temple. The sole hope for the Minamoto was the support of the monasteries but, as we have seen in a previous insurrection, they were doubtful allies. Urgent messages were sent to the Enryaku-ji, whom Kiyomori had recently bribed lavishly, and to the Kōfuku-ji of Nara, who promised support.

Yorimasa suggested a night attack on the Taira headquarters of Rokuhara. There was a strong wind blowing, making it easy to set fire to the building and perhaps kidnap Taira Kiyomori amid the resulting confusion. But for the second time in a generation the bold advice of the Minamoto was turned down. It was decided to evacuate Mii-dera and join the monks of Nara at the Kōfuku-ji. In the small hours of the morning the Prince, Yorimasa, and their pitifully small force of loyal monks and Minamoto samurai – perhaps as few as 300 men in all – set out from Mount Hiei in a desperate race for Nara.

The reader will notice from Fig. 8 that their route would take them almost directly south. The main road from Kyōto to Nara crossed the Uji river at the town of the same name. The bridge over the River Uji was of extreme strategic importance, as the Uji, which farther on becomes the Yodo, makes a convenient outer moat for Kyōto between Lake Biwa and the sea. By the time the small Minamoto force had reached Uji the Prince was extremely tired, so it was decided to rest with the river between them and the pursuing Taira.

On the southern (Nara) side of the Ujigawa stands the Byōdō-in, which includes among its buildings the exceptionally beautiful Phoenix Hall. It was originally the country villa of a Fujiwara nobleman who later converted it into a temple. The Byōdō-in was chosen as a resting place for the Prince, while Yorimasa sent out scouts to watch the river and the road to the north in case of a Taira attack. As an added precaution the Minamoto samurai tore up about twenty yards of the planking of the long wooden bridge. There they waited for whichever group would arrive first, their monk allies from Nara or the Taira.

As dawn broke the Taira samurai arrived on the northern bank. Little could be seen of them by the Minamoto, for they were shrouded in the thick early morning mist, but the Taira made their presence known by raising their warcry. The Minamoto replied, and the Taira vanguard galloped straight on to the bridge, and straight through the hole in the middle of it! As the mist cleared a fierce duel of arrows began across the swift flowing river. The monks proved to be good archers, firing their shafts clean through the large wooden shields the Taira had erected. Minamoto Yorimasa removed his helmet to facilitate drawing his bow. In his heart he knew that this fight was likely to prove his last.

At this point the more intrepid elements in the monk army began to clamber across the beams of the bridge to engage the Taira in individual combat. The first across was Tajima, who threw the sheath of his naginata into the river and strode out alone on to the bridge. This made him an instant target for all the arrows the Taira could fire

15 Tajima the arrow-cutter. Tajima was a monk of Mii-dera, who used his naginata to deflect arrows fired at him during the Battle of Uji, 1180. Ivory statuette. (Lloyd collection, Manchester Museum.)

at him, which he took on his armour, ducked to avoid, or knocked to one side with his whirling naginata. This earned him the nickname of 'Tajima the arrow cutter'. Soon another monk followed him on to the bridge. This was Jomyō, who despatched at least twenty-six Taira with bow, naginata, sword and dagger in succession. Behind Jomyō was Ichirai Hochi, who was exceedingly frustrated by Jomyō's completely blocking the narrow beam. Thirsting for action, Ichirai seized Jomyō by the neck-guard of his helmet, placed his foot on the beam of the bridge, and vaulted over Jomyō to the front, where he fought bravely until he fell. Jomyō retired and counted sixty-three arrows sticking out of his armour like the spines of a hedgehog.

The fighting across the broken bridge continued for much of the day until the beams were littered with the bodies of the slain. Some fought across to their opponents' side and returned with heads. Others, severely wounded, jumped into the river. There was still no sign of the Nara monks, and the Taira commanders, Tomomori and Shigehira (two sons of Kiyomori) and their uncle Tadanori, began to consider the possibility of making the fifty-mile detour via the bridge of Seta. The idea was scorned by an eighteen-year old samurai called Ashikaga Tadatsuna, who advocated fording the fast flowing river there and then. His three hundred samurai of the Ashikaga made ready to follow him, so he gave them some useful advice, recorded in the *Heike Monogatari*: 'Join hands and go across in line. If your horse's head gets pulled down, lift it up . . . if the enemy shoots do not draw bow in return; keep your head down and your neck-piece well sloped upwards, but not too far or you will be shot in the crown of your helmet.'

The latter remark obviously refers to the tehen, the hole in the crown of the Japanese helmet.

So, giving the Ashikaga warcry, the whole force crossed safely. Gallant Tadatsuna had the distinction of being the first to emerge, dripping wet, on the southern bank. Not even in the excitement of the moment, did he forget the formalities of combat, but stood up in his stirrups and proclaimed loudly: 'I am Ashikaga no Tara Tadatsuna of Shimotsuke, descended in the tenth generation from Tawara Toda Hidesato, the renowned warrior.'

Finishing his speech, he spurred his horse and fought his way as far as the gateway of the Byōdō-in. The *Azuma Kagami*, a contemporary chronicle, records of him that:

'There will be no warrior in future ages like this Tadatsuna. He excelled all others in three things: namely, his physical strength, which equalled that of a hundred men; his voice, which reverberated for a distance of ten ri [about 25 miles!] and his teeth, which were one inch in length.'

The Taira main body were a little shamefaced at the gallantry of their allies, so Taira Tomomori led the rest of the army down the bank in a mass attempt at crossing. For a brief moment the weight of men and horses almost dammed the river, until the pressure of water behind them became so intense that the mass heaved and broke, and the Taira samurai were carried hither and thither by the force of the current. Most of them emerged eventually, for the attentions of the Minamoto had been absorbed by the attack from the Ashikaga. Soon the Taira forced their foes back within the gate of the Byōdō-in. In the confusion Prince Mochihito attempted to escape towards Nara while Yorimasa and his sons held back the overwhelming Taira assault. Yorimasa was struck in the right elbow by an arrow and withdrew, while his younger son Kanetsuna held off a band of Taira samurai eager for the old man's head. An arrow struck Kanetsuna under the helmet, and Nakatsuna, the elder son, fell mortally wounded, but not until they had held off the Taira long enough for their father to commit what has come to be regarded as the classic example of hara-kiri.

Yorimasa's suicide, though not the first in Japanese history, for he was preceded by 'giant' Tametomo and a score or so of anonymous samurai during that day's battle, was performed with such finesse that it served as a model of the noblest way by which a defeated samurai could take his leave of the world. While his sons held the gate the septuagenarian samurai calmly wrote a farewell poem on the back of his war-fan, which read:

> Like a fossil tree from which we gather no flowers
> Sad has been my life, fated no fruit to produce.

He then thrust the point of his dagger into his abdomen, and cut himself open. He was soon dead. A faithful retainer took his head, fastened stones to it and sunk it in the river where no Taira trophy hunter might find it. Yorimasa's elder son Nakatsuna joined his father in a ritual death.

Self-inflicted death has never been confined to the Japanese race, but the Japanese tradition of hara-kiri of which in Yorimasa we see the first example, is surely the only form of suicide that was deliberately intended to be extremely painful. So horrible was the idea of hara-kiri that even the samurai modified it in later years to a purely nominal stabbing, while a friendly second cut off the victim's head.

With the Minamoto heroes out of the way the Taira swept through the Byōdō-in and out along the Nara road in pursuit of the Prince, whom they overtook in front of a Shintō shrine, where the instigator of the plot died in a hail of arrows. A few hours later 7,000 warrior-monks set out from Nara, but being informed of the rebellion's speedy end they hastily returned to their temples, while the Taira rode in triumph to Kyōto, the heads of the Prince and the sons of Yorimasa borne triumphantly before them.

The Battle of Uji, fought on 20 June, 1180, marked the sudden and dramatic end of the first insurrection of the Gempei War. Scarcely before the call to arms had reached the Minamoto in the east Prince Mochihito was dead, and the rebellion which he had proclaimed was over. This premature revolt nearly spelled the end of the warrior-monks as an institution, for when the dust had settled after the Battle of Uji, Taira Kiyomori was bent on revenge. On 19 December, 1180, Taira Tomomori was sent to punish Mii-dera. Ten thousand Taira

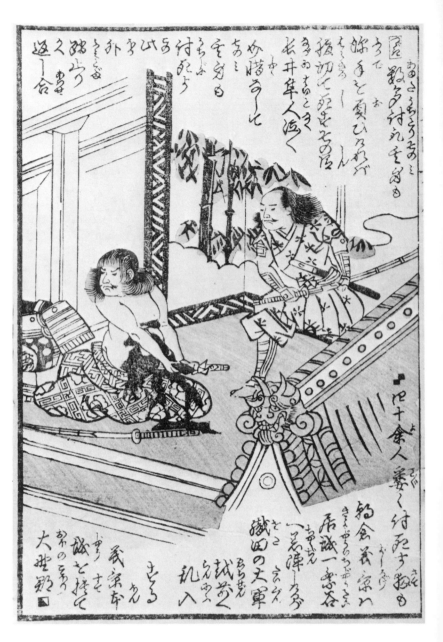

16 Hara-kiri. A warrior commits suicide in the way that the ritual later developed, whereby a trusted friend stands by to decapitate the victim. (E. G. Heath collection.)

samurai attacked at dawn. The monks had made a barrier of wooden shields and fallen trees, and the fighting continued all day until the monastery was set alight. The damage was no greater than any inflicted by the monks themselves in their heyday, but much worse was in store for Nara, as the Kōfuku-ji and the Tōdai-ji had sent a force to aid Mochihito, even though they arrived too late. Kiyomori first tried to make a political alliance with the 'gakushō', the scholar priests of the temples, hoping that they would be able to subdue their turbulent sōhei. But it was too late for negotiations. The monks replied to

Kiyomori's message by beating the messenger and forcibly shaving his head, so that he fled back to the capital pale and terrified. To add insult to injury the Nara sōhei made a great wooden head which they called the head of Kiyomori, and kicked it about in the courtyard.

Kiyomori still behaved with caution, and sent a force of five hundred samurai with orders, even though provoked, to use no violence. The monks promptly attacked the deputation, seized sixty or so of the samurai and cut off their heads, which were displayed around the Pool of Sarusawa, opposite the southern gate of the Kōfuku-ji. Finally a full scale attack on Nara was launched. Command was given to Taira Shigehira, a veteran of Uji and not one of Kiyomori's most attractive offspring. Shigehira was subject to fits of rage, an affliction that was beginning to affect his father to a pronounced degree. The monks saw the danger they faced, and made preparations to withstand the assault. Seven thousand monks, young and old, sōhei and gakushō alike, made ready to defend their temples. Ditches were dug across the roads and palisades erected, while the monk-archers waited behind large wooden shields. Most of the monks fought on foot. The mounted samurai launched repeated charges at them, but were held off until nightfall by the stubborn defenders, who were inspired by a valiant priest called Yogaku, a man of immense strength who wore two suits of armour, one over the other.

As it grew dark Taira Shigehira decided to use that most deadly of weapons in the samurai armoury – fire. We have seen incendiarism used before, but it was always a risky business, as Shigehira no doubt knew when he ordered some of his men to chop up wooden shields for torches and set fire to some buildings outside the gate. It was 5 pm, and as the wind was changing in all directions the flames spread rapidly through the temple compound, leaping from storehouse to pagoda, from pagoda to bell tower. As the *Heike Monogatari* recounts:

> 'Those who were too old to flee, and the unattached laymen, children and girls, thinking to save themselves went up into the upper storey of the Daibutsuden (The Hall of the Great Buddha of Tōdai-ji) and pulled up the ladders behind them so that the enemy could not follow, but the flames reached them first, and such a great crying arose that could not be surpassed even by the sinners amid the flames of Tapana, Pratapana and Avitchi, fiercest of the Eight Hot Hells.'

The Kōfuku-ji was burned to the ground, and so was the Tōdai-ji, the 'Great Eastern Temple', pride of Emperor Shomu four centuries before. With it fell the idol before which the Emperor had knelt.

> '. . . the colossal statue of Vairochana Buddha of copper and gold, whose domed head towered up into the clouds, from which gleamed the sacred jewel of his lofty forehead, fused with the heat,

so that its fullmoon features fell to the pavement below, while its body melted into a shapeless mass . . . surely never before had there been such a destruction. . . . Even the dew of Mount Kasuga changed its hue, and the wind howled mournfully on Mount Mikasa.'

In all, 3,500 died in the fire, and only the Shōsō-in, the Imperial Storehouse of Emperor Shomu, escaped the blaze to remain to this day. The heads of 1,000 monks who died in the attack were displayed on the gate or carried back to Kyōto. Months later, when important services were due to be conducted, not a single priest could be found in the whole of Nara.

Taira Kiyomori died on 20 March 1181, leaving this sad legacy behind him. He was feverish at the last, and babbled, not of green fields, but of revenge. 'When I am dead,' he said, 'do not perform any Buddhist rites for me, only slay Yoritomo and cut off his head and lay it before my tomb. That will be the best offering you can make for me either in this world or the next.' To understand the significance of these dying words we will have to go back a few months in the Gempei War.

Yoritomo

The man whose head Kiyomori so desired was the eldest of the three surviving Minamoto children whom Kiyomori had banished in 1160. Yoritomo was then fourteen, and had been sent to Izu, the mountainous peninsula on the Tōkaidō. Izu was Taira territory, and the young man was put under the care of Itō Sukechika, a Fujiwara ally of the Taira, whose guardianship was monitored by Hōjō Tokimasa, a local land-owner of Taira descent. Itō Sukechika proved to be a lenient guardian, and the young Minamoto flourished in his practice of the arts of war, and also had much time to consider how disastrous the premature and over-enthusiastic use of military skill had proved for his family. It is also recorded that Yoritomo enlivened his study of warfare and politics by the more pleasant pastime popularly called sowing wild oats. The result was that his guardian discovered that he had become the grand-father of a Minamoto baby. This enraged the loyal Taira so much that he killed the child, and would have done away with Yoritomo as well had the latter not fled for safety to Hōjō Tokimasa, where he promptly fell in love with Hōjō's daughter, and eventually married her.

Legend has it that during his banishment Yoritomo was visited by a wandering priest called Mongaku, who presented him with the skull of his father Yoshitomo, thereby goading him into rebellion against the Taira. But it was not the head of his father that first made Yoritomo consider an insurgence against the Taira, but the receipt, on 23 May 1180, of the proclamation of Prince Mochihito. It was not long after this that he received the news of the Battle of Uji, which confirmed his earlier thoughts that premature action meant the ruin of the Minamoto. On 13 July Yoritomo received further bad news. Taira Kiyomori had ordered his capture and execution. To whom this task had been assigned his informant did not know, but it was likely to have been Taira Kanetaka, the Deputy Governor of the area. Yoritomo's precarious situation was aggravated when, towards the end of August, Ōba Kagechika, one of the fiercest Taira partisans in the Izu region, returned home after helping to win the Battle of Uji. This brought another enemy close to hand, and one with a considerable fighting force.

For twenty years Yoritomo had contemplated the folly of making hasty rebellions, so it must have been with some trepidation that he decided to break out of the stranglehold being placed upon him by attacking Yamagi, the headquarters of the Deputy, Taira Kanetaka. The raid was launched on 8 September, and resulted in Kanetaka's death. Strange to relate, Yoritomo took no part in the actual raid, but stayed back at the mansion of his father-in-law, Hōjō Tokimasa, praying for victory. Yoritomo was a statesman, not a general, and we will see him in this guise throughout the Gempei War, leaving the fighting to other members of his family.

Now that his nearest enemy was dead, Yoritomo could break out of Izu (Fig. 17). The peninsula is only about ten miles wide at the northern neck, its narrowest point, so Yoritomo headed out of Izu into Sagami on 11 September. Two days later he was joined by the first Minamoto supporters to rally round his flag, the Miura.

17 Map showing the campaigns of Yoritomo at the start of the Gempei War.

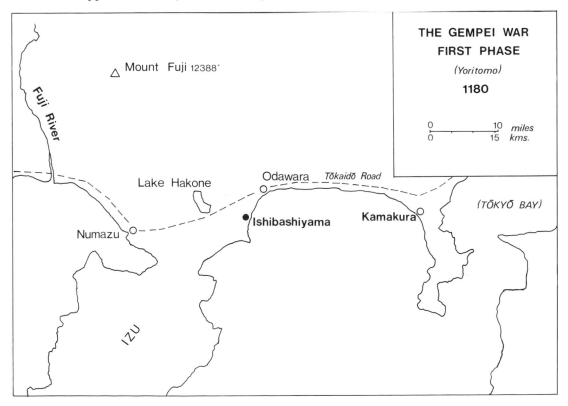

51

The chief Taira partisan was Ōba Kagechika. With the speed of action that characterized the Taira dash at the Battle of Uji, Ōba rallied the Taira and pursued his prey. Yoritomo was outnumbered by about ten to one when the Taira caught up with him at Ishibashiyama on 14 September. The resulting Battle of Ishibashiyama was almost as great a disaster for the Minamoto as the Battle of Uji had been. Fearful lest Yoritomo should be reinforced, Ōba Kagechika led the Taira forces in a fierce night attack on Yoritomo's position. Ishibashiyama was a narrow valley near the sea coast, giving little room for manoeuvre and certainly no opportunity whatsoever for the formalities of combat. Pitch darkness, a gale, and torrential rain added to the confusion of the mêlée. One can imagine the determination with which the rough country samurai went about their deadly business. There was no time for the shouting of pedigrees or the challenge of a worthy opponent, just the muddy and bloody scuffle of a bitter fight.

When the battle was over the tiny Minamoto force had been almost annihilated, but Ōba Kagechika paid dearly for his advantageous night attack, for in the height of the battle Minamoto Yoritomo slipped away into the mountains. Many thrilling tales have been told of the following five days as Yoritomo was hunted through the Hakone mountains. The best known concerns Kajiwara Kagetoki, then in the service of the Taira, but later to become one of Yoritomo's staunchest supporters. Yoritomo was hiding in the hollow trunk of a tree, which Kajiwara was sent to investigate. The latter was even then secretly in sympathy with the Minamoto cause. Seeing Yoritomo in the tree he stuck his bow into the trunk and dislodged two doves, which was sufficient to convince the other pursuers that the birds were the sole occupants. The story has added significance in that the dove is regarded as the messenger of Hachiman the War God, the patron of the Minamoto.

Eventually Yoritomo succeeded in reaching the sea coast at Cape Manazuru, where he took a boat and, accompanied by a handful of followers, crossed to Awa province, which was Minamoto territory. He travelled through Awa and round the coast of what is now Tōkyō Bay, gathering adherents as he went. Within a month his small following had grown to a vast army, with which he entered the little fishing village of Kamakura. Here he resolved to make his headquarters, and Kamakura, which was to give its name to a period of Japanese history lasting a century and a half, became the focus for the Minamoto rebellion. However, Yoritomo did not have long to relax and enjoy his new found popularity, for intelligence was brought to him that a large Taira army had left Kyōto for the east. This was at the beginning of November 1180, a month before the Taira punitive army was to set off to burn Mii-dera. Up to that moment the Taira had not suffered a single reverse, but Taira Kiyomori did not appreciate that the situation had changed considerably in the past few months. In dealing with the uprisings of Hōgen, Heiji and Prince Mochihito's late attempt, the Taira had been fighting on their own ground. Now they were faced with a Minamoto uprising 300 miles to the east, in traditional Minamoto territory.

Kiyomori assigned the task of quelling the Minamoto to the least able member of his family, Taira Koremori, his grandson by his late son Shigemori. Koremori was twenty years old, with little experience of fighting. The *Heike Monogatari* tells us that 'his costume and bearing were beautiful beyond the power of brush to depict'. Serving under him was to be Tadanori, Kiyomori's brother and a veteran of Uji. The sole comfort that the Taira could expect in the Kantō was the support of the allies who had so thoroughly thrashed Yoritomo at Ishibashiyama. Before proceeding against the Taira advance, Yoritomo took steps to neutralize this threat by sending his father-in-law Hōjō Tokimasa to rouse the Takeda family in Suruga. This he did with great speed, and the combined efforts of Minamoto and Takeda ensured that Yoritomo was able to proceed unmolested along the Tōkaidō. His army crossed the Ashigara Pass in the Hakone mountains and descended into Suruga, beneath the lofty slopes of Mount Fuji. They came to a halt on the eastern bank of the Fujigawa, or River Fuji, for across the wide expanse of shallow water and reeds fluttered the red pennons of the Taira. For the first time since the Gempei War had started two great armies of the Taira and Minamoto faced each other in battle array. It was 9 November 1180.

Accounts of what happened next are confused and contradictory. Some authorities speak of the Battle of the Fujigawa which, as we shall see, is very wide of the mark. What is certain, however, is that the Taira were feeling very uncomfortable and not a little homesick, which did nothing to increase their confidence as they gazed across the wide, flat river bed. Some accounts say that the Takeda launched an attack on the Taira flank during the night. The *Heike Monogatari* has a more poetic account:

'Also about the middle of the same night the water-fowl of the marshes of Mount Fuji were startled by something or other, and suddenly rose all together with a whirring of wings like the sound of thunder or a mighty wind, and the Taira soldiers hearing it shouted out: "It is the army of the Minamoto coming to attack us! There are hundreds of thousands of them." So, panic-stricken, they abandoned their positions and fled precipitately without even taking their belongings with them, for so great was their haste that some snatched up their bows without arrows, or arrows without any bow, springing on to each other's horses, and even mounting tethered animals and whipping them up so that they galloped round and round the post to which they were tied.'

In all probability the Taira retreat was by no means as desperate or as panic-stricken as these accounts would have us believe. To withdraw from the Fujigawa was a sensible step in view of their extended

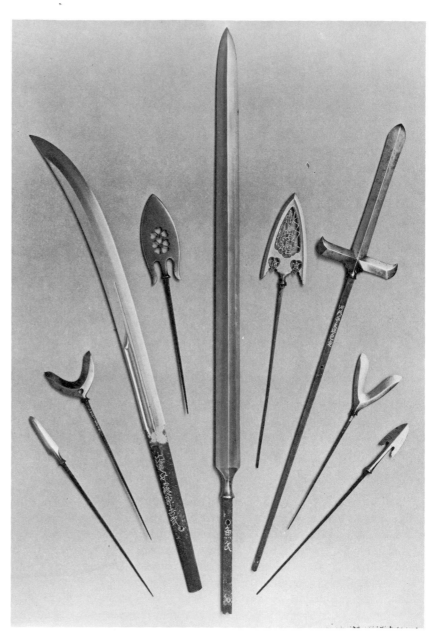

18 Various spear and arrow heads.
(Victoria and Albert Museum.)

lines of communication and the fact that ahead lay the Ashigara Pass
and the Hakone mountains. But stories grow in the telling, and the
Taira's strategic withdrawal was conducted at some speed, for they
were back in Kyōto twelve days later. As for the Minamoto, they
advanced to the attack the following morning and found 'not so much
as a fly stirring in the Taira camp'. Yoritomo wisely attributed his
'victory' to the divine intervention of Hachiman, and made obeisance
to his household god. The good sense of the Taira in retreating was
followed by the equally wise decision of the Minamoto not to pursue.

Consolidate the east, suggested Yoritomo's advisers. This course of action was adopted for some time to come, the Minamoto fighting various small campaigns, gaining allies and liquidating enemies.

Yoshinaka

We now turn another page in the story of the Gempei War to consider the career of Minamoto Yoshinaka. His name has not yet been mentioned in the complicated genealogy of the Minamoto family, so he will require some introduction.

Yoshinaka was Yoritomo's cousin. He was the son of Yoshikata, a younger brother of Yoshitomo. Yoshikata is therefore the fourth son of Tameyoshi to be mentioned in this book, the others being Yoshitomo, Tametomo 'the giant', and Yoritomo's uncle Yukiie, who took the Prince's proclamation east to the Minamoto. The Author here confesses to a certain regard for Yoshinaka. He was a rough country samurai with an impetuous nature and no manners, in short the perfect example of how the samurai really were! His meteoric career encompasses some of the most exciting episodes of the Gempei War. Compared with Yoshinaka, Yoritomo is dull and solid.

Yoshinaka's life was hazardous from his birth. His father, Yoshikata, was killed in 1155. He had taken the precaution of concealing his pregnant wife, and the white banner of the clan, in the home of a friendly peasant. The enemy tried to capture his wife and the peasant woman. To facilitate escape they split up, the peasant woman heading towards Lake Biwa. To escape the pursuing samurai she jumped into the lake and swam towards some barges. As she drew near them she realized to her horror that the boats were full of enemy samurai, who struck at her with their swords, cutting off her right arm which held the Minamoto flag. The arm sank to the bottom of the lake, followed soon by her dead body. Four days later the peasant woman's son fished his mother's arm out of the lake and took it, still clutching the flag, to the hut where Yoshikata's wife was about to give birth to the infant Yoshinaka.

The legend continues that a samurai called Saitō Sanemori was sent to arrest Yoshikata's widow and kill the child if it were a boy, but that Sanemori was so moved by compassion that he could not carry out the order. He accordingly returned to his master with the hand of the peasant woman as proof that he had killed the baby. With the active connivance of Sanemori the baby Yoshinaka was spirited away into the mountainous district of Kiso in Shinano, where he was brought up. He adopted the surname of 'Kiso' in preference to Minamoto, and it is as Kiso Yoshinaka that he is generally known. Yoshinaka grew to be a mighty man of war, and was twenty-eight years old when he received his copy of Prince Mochihito's proclamation. Like his cousin, Yoshinaka responded readily, but the snows of winter cut short any campaigns among the mountains, so the year 1180 ended with little action on his part. Early 1181 was marked by the burning of Nara and the death of Kiyomori. After the Fujigawa incident the Taira policy became one

19 A sword of 'tachi' form, carried with the cutting edge downwards. (Courtesy of Sotheby & Co.)

55

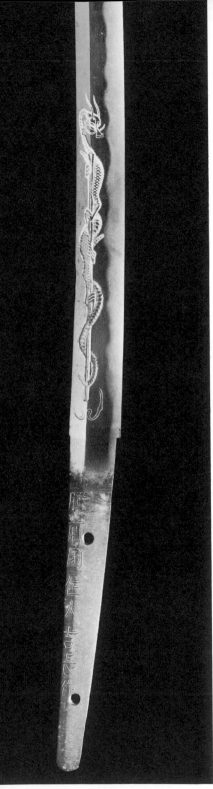

20 Sword blade with 'horimono', chiselled decoration. (Courtesy of Sotheby & Co.)

of consolidation. In April a Taira force advanced into Owari province where they inflicted a crushing defeat on Minamoto Yukiie. Yukiie seems to have had little military skill and even less luck. He led the Minamoto in an attack across the river Sunomata with the object of taking the Taira by surprise, but they calmly let him advance right into the middle of their throng and then counterattacked furiously, aiming their swords and arrows at any samurai whose armour was wet. The result of the battle, on 25 April 1181, was the complete rout of Yukiie, who ran off to join the nearest Minamoto army, which happened to be that of Yoshinaka.

As spring gave way to summer there were three great power blocs in Japan; the Taira, based on Kyōto; Minamoto Yoritomo in Kamakura; and Kiso Yoshinaka in Shinano. But for fourteen months a different enemy was to take its toll of the population. A succession of droughts and floods ruined the harvests of 1180 and 1181, and there followed a pestilence and plague so violent that it decimated the population of the Home Provinces. There were many who saw in these dire events the wrath of the Gods against the clan whose troops had burned Nara. Their conclusions were reinforced considerably by the observation that the Kantō, seat of Yoritomo, escaped lightly.

When hostilities recommenced in July 1182 they began at a furious pace. The Taira, under the leadership of Munemori since his father's death, appointed Jō Sukenaga to the unenviable post of chastiser of Yoshinaka, for the sole reason that, being lord of Echigo, he was the next Taira ally that Yoshinaka would probably attack. Jō took up the challenge, was defeated, and promptly died. Yoshinaka meanwhile had over-run Kōzuke, but as this was dangerously close to his cousin's sphere of influence he veered off to the north and made a wide sweep through Echigo, Etchū, Kaga, Echizen and Wakasa, knocking Taira allies right, left and centre. (These provinces are illustrated in Fig. 54.) Yoshinaka was now master of the Hokurikudō (see Fig. 2). So fast and so dramatic was Yoshinaka's advance that by the end of the summer of 1182 his territory extended to within forty miles of Kyōto. He may have considered a direct attack on Kyōto from the north, but in fact this did not happen, as Yoshinaka had good reasons to wait while famine and pestilence did his work for him.

Meanwhile Yoritomo was watching his cousin's progress very closely. To quote an old Chinese saying, 'There cannot be two suns in heaven.' Yoritomo now referred to himself as Lord Kamakura, and saw in Yoshinaka one who was unlikely to be satisfied with a position inferior to his own. Accordingly, in early spring, 1183, Yoritomo sent an army into the mountains to attack Yoshinaka. Fortunately common sense prevailed, and after some careful parleying both sides withdrew, Yoritomo to ponder his next move, Yoshinaka to face a new threat from the Taira.

By the end of April the Taira felt strong enough to launch a full-scale attack against Yoshinaka, who posed a greater threat to them than Yoritomo. It was a fatal decision, and one that is unlikely to have

56

been taken had Kiyomori still been alive. The Taira chief, Munemori, showed that he had profited not at all from the lesson of the Fujigawa incident, by proceeding to raise a large army to march just as far in a different direction. Since the time of the Fujigawa retreat the spirit and health of the Taira followers had greatly deteriorated. Nevertheless an attempt was made to raise, levy, recruit or coerce a nominal force of 100,000 men for the expedition against Yoshinaka. The methods used to obtain this impossibly large figure, which exceeds most of the great armies of the sixteenth century, remind one of the pressgang. Even men who had previously been exempt from military service were 'called up', including the woodcutters of the Wazuka forest in Yamato. 'We carry neither bows nor swords,' they protested. 'When in the forest thirty-seven men do their work and twenty-seven of them are levied as soldiers, this is outrageous and should be stopped.'

The makeshift army was put under the command of Taira Koremori, the beautiful samurai who had retreated from the Fujigawa. Under him were Taira Michimori, Taira Tadanori, Taira Tsunemasa, Taira Kiyofusa and Taira Tomonori. They set out on 10 May, and were so badly organized that their supplies ran out when they were only nine miles from Kyōto. For the rest of the expedition the army would have to feed off the land already ravaged by famine and plague. The foraging that took place was nothing short of pillaging, as the Taira locusts appropriated everything they could lay their hands on along the narrow strip of land between Lake Biwa and the mountains. Ironically Ōmi province was traditional Taira territory and had supplied many men for the army. The sack of these fields, which had so recently recovered from the effects of the 1181 disasters, caused many of the inhabitants to flee in terror or disgust. No doubt many of the army followed their example.

One group who were unconcerned about the soldiers' behaviour was the subordinate group of generals, who had practically no military experience behind them. Koremori and Michimori pressed on, but the others stopped off at Lake Biwa for a little sightseeing, even sparing the time to take a boat out on the lake so that Tsunemasa could indulge his poetic muse: 'The scene filled Tsunemasa with ecstasy, and he quickly alighted from the boat and climbed up on to the island, gazing at the beauty of the landscape with a heart too full for words.'

Such emotions, which somewhat soften the usual image of the samurai, were rather out of place when the poet was in command of an army that was probably deserting faster than it was marching.

Meanwhile the head of the Taira column was nearing its Rubicon. The ancient border between Ōmi and the most southerly of the Hokurikudō provinces, Wakasa and Echizen, lay at the top of a ridge 2,500 feet high at its peak (see map, Fig. 54). Many a samurai must have paused as he reached the crest, and turned back to gaze at Lake Biwa glittering in the sunshine, with Kyōto somewhere fifty miles to the south, and felt a genuine emotion above that of Tsunemasa's poetry. It is not for nothing that the flat lands around Kyōto are called the Home Provinces. Descending the ridge the view of home vanished forever and, as the samurai saw spread out before him the long sweep of the Japan Sea coastline with the mountains of the north forming a menacing backdrop, he surely realized that not only was he entering Echizen province, he was entering enemy territory.

If the Taira had any curiosity about where the enemy actually were, it was shortly to be dispelled. On about 17 May, a week after leaving the capital, the vanguard of the Taira made contact with some of Yoshinaka's troops, a garrison he had posted in Echizen at a place called Hiuchi-yama. Their position, called Hiuchi-jō, or Hiuchi Castle, was not an inspiring feudal fortress but a stockade reinforced with earthworks and rocks. The designers of 'Fort Hiuchi' obviously had an eye for terrain. It was built on a strong position with mountains and crags all round it. In front of it the Minamoto had built a dam, so that the waters of the river had risen to form a moat. According to the *Heike Monogatari*, a traitor in the garrison fired an arrow into the Taira camp telling them to breach the dam and run the water off. It would be odd if none of the besiegers had realized this already, but they followed the suggestion and succeeded in taking the fort.

So the Taira army continued on its way. Hiuchi had been taken on or about 20 May. Five days later they entered Kaga province, where they met a further light Minamoto force at a place called Ataka. Like Hiuchi, this skirmish provided Kiso Yoshinaka with the information he desired. He now knew the strength and direction of advance of the Taira, and could hazard a fair guess at their morale. As to their route, they were obviously by-passing the mountainous interior (now the Haku-san National Park), to turn east across the narrow neck of the Noto peninsula into Etchū province and on into Echigo. To reach Etchū they would now have to cross the central mountain chain at its northern end where the elevation is more that of large hills. So much could be deduced, and it was also more than likely that they would cross by one pass and one pass alone, the Pass of Kurikara.

It is very difficult when working from the old chronicles and epics, to work out exactly what happened during the next few days. The Taira apparently divided their army into two parts, the larger of which was under the command of Koremori and Michimori. This army crossed the central ridge by the Pass of Kurikara and decided to rest on Tonami-yama, which was probably on the eastern side. The *Heike Monogatari* gives Yoshinaka the credit for persuading them to rest. He realized that the Taira were thirsting for a decisive battle as they had the larger force. Yoshinaka had a plan, and for its successful operation the whole Taira army had to be held stationary near the top of the pass. Yoshinaka therefore ordered thirty white flags to be carried to the top of a hill called Kurosaka which overlooked Tonami-yama. This fooled the Taira into thinking that ahead of them lay a superior host, so they dismounted and rested, keeping the overall advantage of height.

Below Tonami-yama, where the pass crossed the ridge, was a valley also called Kurikara. It would appear that this valley was open at its eastern, or Etchū, end, but deteriorated to a narrow path on its western, Kaga, side. To a traveller heading east the Kurikara valley would not be seen until he had crossed the pass and had descended some way down the eastern slopes, from where it would appear to be a valley that cut right through the mountain. This was the conclusion that Yoshinaka hoped would be drawn by a panic-stricken army. He had no doubt heard the story about the water birds of the Fujigawa. He was now going to try the same trick, but with stronger meat!

The Taira spent the night of 1 June, 1183, encamped upon Tonami-yama, while Yoshinaka grouped his forces, and sent picked bands round behind Kurosaka Hill to station themselves at the rear of the Taira positions. During the day of 2 June they engaged the Taira in a leisurely and gentlemanly battle, designed to keep their enemies occupied until nightfall. The Minamoto indulged themselves to the full in the extravagant formalities of battle. There was an archery duel with humming-bulb arrows; then a duel with sharp-pointed arrows; then individual combats between small groups; and finally a pitched battle between one hundred men from each side. The Minamoto sent no more to join in so that the contest was prolonged. As it grew dark the water-birds arose, only this time the water-birds had been replaced by a herd of oxen. The herd, enraged by flaming pine torches fastened to their horns, stampeded on to the Taira flank. Immediately the rest of the Minamoto, who had concealed themselves until that moment, flung themselves into the fray. The shock caused the Taira to withdraw rapidly, and as Yoshinaka had planned, they saw their sole means of escape to be the Kurikara valley, into which they had been unerringly funnelled. Once inside the gorge, 'those behind cried "Forward!"', and those before cried, "Back!"', as the Minamoto samurai followed after them. The *Heike Monogatari* notes:

> 'Thus did some seventy thousand horsemen of the Taira perish, buried in this one deep valley; the mountain streams ran with their blood and the mound of their corpses was like a small hill; and in this valley, it is said, there can be seen the marks of arrows and swords even to this day.'

So concluded the first defeat the Taira had suffered since the war began. The Battle of Kurikara, or Tonami-yama, marks a turning point in the Gempei War.

After joining up with his uncle, Minamoto Yukiie, who, true to form, had been defeated by the smaller Taira army in Noto, Yoshinaka began a vigorous pursuit of the Taira, who were now re-tracing their steps to the capital with all speed. The Minamoto caught up with them on 12 June at Shinowara in Kaga, and on the following day a fierce battle took place. The Battle of Shinowara, although a comparatively minor affair, is interesting for an incident that happened after it was over. Yoshinaka was seated on his camp stool inspecting the heads of the slain, when a samurai approached him bearing a head. The samurai was puzzled by the trophy, for his victim had refused to declare his name. Also he had been wearing a red brocade under-robe which was reserved for generals, yet he had no personal retainers fighting with him. Yoshinaka examined the head, and fancied he saw the features of Saitō Sanemori, the samurai who had saved his life when a baby. But the hair on the head was jet-black, and Sanemori would by then have been an old man. An officer was summoned who had known Sanemori well, and he recalled that Sanemori had once told him that should he be called upon to fight after the age of sixty he would dye his hair black so as not to feel inferior to the younger samurai. Yoshinaka took the head to a stream and washed it, and immediately black dye began to flow from the hair. It was indeed Sanemori, who had obtained permission from the Taira generals to wear a red brocade armour robe in what he had expected would be his last fight.

Meanwhile the news of the Taira defeat had spread to Kyōto, throwing the capital into a state of panic. Preparations were made for the defence of the city against Yoshinaka. Taira Munemori approached the Enryaku-ji for help. The haughty monks, as unpredictable as ever, scorned their plea, and on 11 August received Yoshinaka's army into the Enryaku-ji. Three days later the Taira evacuated the capital, taking with them the child Emperor Antoku, the Crown Jewels, and most of the Royal Family. A notable exception was the wily old ex-Emperor Go-Shirakawa, who hurried off to join Yoshinaka.

On 17 August, 1183, ex-Emperor Go-Shirakawa re-entered Kyōto, escorted by Minamoto Yoshinaka and Minamoto Yukiie. For the first time since 1160 a Minamoto army had entered the capital in triumph.

4. The fall of the house of Taira

Minamoto Yoshitsune, brother of Yoritomo, cousin of Yoshinaka, and the youngest of the surviving sons of Yoshitomo, now demands our attention. For his military prowess alone, Yoshitsune would still be remembered. Yet legend has woven round his name a web of mystery and romance unequalled by any other who bore the name of samurai. Most of this chapter will therefore be concerned with this outstanding samurai round whom whole books, plays and poems have been written for the past eight hundred years.

Yoshitsune is the perfect samurai. He is skilled in the arts of war; he is attended by the archetypal faithful companion; his relations with the fair sex add a strange note of chivalry; and he meets his end in the most tragic circumstances. All the ingredients of the Japanese hero are present in Yoshitsune.

He was born in 1159, the year before the ill-fated Heiji Incident which resulted in the death of his father. Yoshitsune was then confined in the monastery of Kurama-dera for instruction in the peaceful ways of the priesthood, as Kurama-dera was singularly deficient of warrior-monks. Not surprisingly, the young Minamoto, with much military tradition in his blood, did not take kindly to the monastic discipline, and tutored himself secretly in the martial arts. Legend tells us that Yoshitsune's instructors in the ways of sword-fighting were the 'tengu', small goblins – half men and half bird – who inhabited the mountains. Yoshitsune used to slip out of the monastery at night and fence with these talented creatures. The tengu found him to be a promising pupil, and taught him numerous cuts and guards with the sword, as well as the use of a war-fan for defence, and, stranger still, how to fight with a tea-kettle!

About 1174 Yoshitsune left Kurama-dera to perform his manhood ceremony under the auspices of Fujiwara Hidehira, whose territory was the far north of Honshū. On his way north Yoshitsune showed his promise in vanquishing a number of brigands. He also showed his first attraction to the opposite sex, but for rather unusual motives. Yoshitsune was eager to read a certain book, a Chinese treatise on warfare, which was owned by a Taira lord. The lord had a beautiful daughter, whom Yoshitsune proceeded to seduce. He first serenaded her by flute outside her window, and having gained her attentions, and shortly her affections, visited her for sixteen nights, during which he pursued his conquest of the maiden and the study of the book.

It was about this time that Yoshitsune had his first meeting with the giant monk Benkei, one of the most popular figures in Japanese mythology. Benkei is as well known as Yoshitsune himself, and there are interesting parallels between their adventures and our own Robin Hood and Friar Tuck. Benkei had been born after a gestation period of three years as a big boy with a mouth full of teeth and long hair. As he was rather a handful he was entrusted to the care of the Enryaku-ji. In time, however, Benkei proved too lively and quarrelsome for even the warrior-monks to handle, and he was politely asked to leave.

After leaving Enryaku-ji Benkei found an abandoned shrine, where he established himself as a one-man monastery. One night his sense of humour got the better of him, and he tried to play a joke on Mii-dera, which was but a short distance away. Mii-dera had a prize bell, whose clear tones were known throughout Japan. That night Benkei entered Mii-dera, cut the bell from its supports, and lifted the half ton of bronze on to his broad shoulders. The story continues that Benkei had not gone far up the mountain when he became anxious to hear the sound that his newly acquired bell would make. So he put it down, and struck it a terrific blow with an uprooted sapling. Alas! The bell gave out no lovely tone, but merely complained that it wanted to go home. In disgust Benkei kicked the bell, which started to roll back down the hill, gathering speed as it went. It eventually came to rest back in Mii-dera, where the indignant monks insisted that Benkei replace their bell forthwith. This Benkei agreed to do, in return for a cauldron of bean soup. The cauldron and the bell are preserved at Mii-dera as 'proof' to this day.

Benkei's meeting with Yoshitsune took place on the Gojō bridge in Kyōto. Benkei's latest hobby was collecting swords – other people's! He had acquired 999 fine specimens of the swordmakers' art by the time he saw, walking towards the bridge, a young lad carrying at his belt a magnificent sword. It was to prove no easy conquest, for the young Yoshitsune engaged Benkei in such a dazzling display of swordsmanship that the latter abjectly surrendered, swearing eternal friendship and service to Yoshitsune. From that time on the names of Yoshitsune and Benkei were firmly linked.

In 1180 Yoshitsune became a historical figure. After the Fujigawa incident he was re-united with his brother Yoritomo, and entered his service at Kamakura. One of his first commissions turned out to be directed against a member of his own family – his cousin Yoshinaka.

The entry of Yoshinaka's troops into Kyōto had been as much of a shock to Yoritomo as it had to the Taira and Yoshinaka was now making himself very unpopular. If any of the frightened city dwellers had been ready to greet the triumphant soldiery as liberators from a Taira yoke they soon saw the error of their judgements. During and after their entry the samurai of Yoshinaka and Yukiie behaved like a mob to whom a conquered city had been given for pillage. The rough mountain-men from Shinano were wild, dangerous and hungry, robbing Minamoto and Taira supporters alike. Yoshinaka made no

attempt to stop them, and ex-Emperor Go-Shirakawa realized that Yoshinaka was no political animal. He had noticed with satisfaction that relations between Yoshinaka and Yukiie were by no means cordial. The Court had in fact roared with laughter at the antics of these two country-bred boors. When Go-Shirakawa had received them in audience they had argued about precedence, and compromised by walking in side by side, to the amusement of all. To a man brought up in the rarified atmosphere of the Heian Court such behaviour was unfitting.

Towards the end of 1183 Yoshinaka and Yukiie left Kyōto for the daunting task of finding, and vanquishing, the Taira who had retreated to their own territory, the Inland Sea (Fig. 25). It was thus with ease that Yoshinaka was trounced at Mizushima on 17 November, and Yukiie at Muroyama a week or so later. These were serious reverses that sent a ragged and weary Minamoto army back to the capital.

Yoshinaka's position grew daily worse. Yoritomo was making threatening noises from Kamakura, so Yukiie, seeing which way things were going, abandoned Yoshinaka to his fate. Yoshinaka thrashed about wildly. He put Go-Shirakawa under house arrest, fortified his mansion, and even proposed an alliance with the Taira against Yoritomo! Eventually in February 1184 all his plans came to nothing, as news was brought to him of a large army under Yoshitsune heading for Kyōto.

21 Lacquer tray depicting Yoshitsune, assisted by tengu, fighting Benkei on the Gojō Bridge in Kyōto. (Lloyd collection, Manchester Museum.)

63

Yoshinaka stayed in the capital, and sent two of his best captains to hold the Uji river. He was planning to use the river as his predecessor Minamoto Yorimasa had four years before, only this time the natural moat of the Uji was to be used in reverse. Following Yorimasa's example they tore up the planking of the Uji bridge, and as an added precaution hammered stakes with a hawser attached into the river bed. It would take a hardy soul to ford the river anyway, for the river, swollen by the melted snow, was in spate.

However, when the Kamakura army arrived it was all Yoshitsune could do to prevent his entire army galloping straight into the flood in a mass attempt to emulate the deeds of heroes. Hatakeyama Shigetada was about to force his horse down the river bank when his attention was caught by two warriors farther upstream, who were apparently having a private race across the river. Their names were Kajiwara Kagesue and Sasaki Takatsuna, and their rivalry at Uji has probably inspired more artists than any other incident in the history of the samurai. There are numerous sword guards, prints and screens depicting the incident, and Sasaki's rather dirty trick to win:

'Kajiwara was about three yards in front of Sasaki. "Kajiwara Dono! Your saddle girth seems to be loose; this is the greatest river in the Western Provinces, so you had better tighten it up." Thus warned, Kajiwara dropped the reins on to his horse's mane, kicked his feet from the stirrups, and, leaning forward in the saddle, loosened the girth and tightened it afresh. While he was thus engaged, however, Sasaki rode on past him and leapt his horse into the river.'

Realizing that he had been tricked, Kajiwara dashed in after him, but his lead could not be gained, even though Sasaki found the hawser in mid-stream and had to cut it with his sword. So Sasaki Takatsuna became the first across the Ujigawa.

A little-known incident occurred directly afterwards. Hatakeyama Shigetada's horse had been shot under him, so that he was forced to swim for his life. As he was clambering out on the opposite side he felt a tug at his leg. It was a young samurai called Oguchi Shigechika, at whose manhood ceremony Hatakeyama had officiated. Oguchi had also lost his horse and was too weak to climb out, so Hatakeyama gripped him by the scruff of the neck and hauled him on to the bank. The young man recovered himself, stood erect, and, drawing his sword, proclaimed, 'Oguchi Shigechika of Musashi is the first to cross the Ujigawa on foot!'

Once the crossing had been made the defeat of Yoshinaka followed as swiftly as that of Yorimasa in 1180. Minamoto Noriyori, Yoshitsune's other brother, had also crossed the Uji at Seta, and now both armies were heading for Kyōto. The end was near. 'Last year he rode forth from Shinano with fifty thousand horsemen, now he flees along the

22 Two forms of Japanese dagger, a 'tanto' and an 'aikuchi', the latter having no guard. The aikuchi is traditionally the knife used to perform hara-kiri. (Courtesy of Sotheby & Co.)

23 Painted screen depicting Sasaki Takatsuna (on left) racing Kajiwara Kagesue for the honour of being the first across the Ujigawa into battle in 1184. (Victoria and Albert Museum.)

river-bed with but six retainers, already lost in the melancholy twilight where lies the nether world.'

With him rode his wife, Tomoe Gozen. Tomoe was a warrior woman noted for her bravery. Together with her brother Imai Kanehira she joined Yoshinaka in a last desperate charge against Yoshitsune's samurai. After cutting off one samurai's head Tomoe withdrew, and Imai suggested that Yoshinaka should retire to the safety of some near-by woods to commit hara-kiri while he held the enemy off. The *Heike Monogatari* describes what happened next:

'Yoshinaka rode off alone toward Awazu, and it was the twenty-third day of the first month. It was now nearly dark and all the land was covered in thin ice, so that none could distinguish the deep rice fields, and he had not gone far before his horse plunged heavily into the muddy ooze beneath. Right up to the neck it floundered, and though Kiso plied whip and spur with might and main, it was all to no purpose, for he could not stir it.'

As Yoshinaka turned in his saddle an arrow hit him in the face. Two samurai ran to him and struck off his head. Yoshinaka's retainer, Imai Kanehira, was still fighting when this occurred, and 'When he saw that his master was indeed slain he cried out: "Alas, for whom now have I to fight? See, you fellows of the East Country, I will show you how the mightiest champion in Japan can end his life!" And he thrust the point of the sword in his mouth and flung himself headlong from his horse, so that he was pierced through and died.'

With the death of Yoshinaka the Gempei War enters its last phase, and the name of Yoshitsune dominates the narrative. On 13 March 1184 Yoshitsune and Noriyori set out to succeed where their cousin had failed, finally to make an end of the Taira.

The Taira had one outstanding advantage, they were fighting on their own ground. The seafaring tradition the Taira had built up while they were quelling pirates now came into its own. After leaving the capital they had strengthened their bases along the Inland Sea. One was on an island called Hikoshima in the narrow strait between Honshū and Kyūshū. A second was at Yashima, off the coast of Shikoku, and the third was near the site of the present-day city of Kobe in Settsu. As the Taira had access to a large number of boats, and the skill to manage them, they were in a very strong position indeed.

Yoshitsune decided to concentrate his first attack against the base near Kobe called Fukuhara, which consisted largely of a fortress called Ichi-no-tani. This was no castle, but a stockade, albeit a strong and extensive one. It was built in a very clever position for a sea-faring family, for at Ichi-no-tani high cliffs surrounded a narrow strip of land and beach. These cliffs formed the fort's northern wall, while the southern side opened on to the sea, where the Taira fleet lay at anchor. The plan of the Minamoto attack was to send Noriyori along the coast from the

24 The spectacular suicide of Imai Kanehira after the death of Kiso Yoshinaka in 1184. From a seventeenth-century wood-block printed edition of *Heike Monogatari*. (Author's collection.)

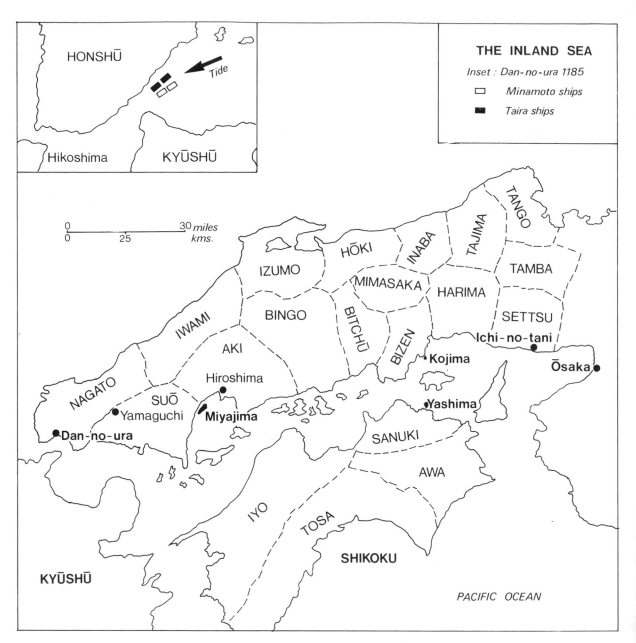

THE INLAND SEA

Inset : Dan-no-ura 1185

☐   *Minamoto ships*

■   *Taira ships*

HONSHŪ

Tide

Hikoshima   KYŪSHŪ

0   30 *miles*
0   25   *kms.*

TANGO

TAJIMA

HŌKI   INABA

IZUMO   MIMASAKA   TAMBA

HARIMA

BINGO   BITCHŪ   SETTSU

IWAMI   BIZEN   Ichi-no-tani

AKI   •Kojima   Ōsaka•

Hiroshima

NAGATO   SUŌ   •Yashima

Yamaguchi   **Miyajima**

•**Dan-no-ura**   SANUKI

AWA

IYO

TOSA

SHIKOKU

KYŪSHŪ

PACIFIC OCEAN

25   Map of the Inland Sea, showing the campaigns of Yoshitsune and Noriyori, 1184–5.

east, while Yoshitsune circled round through Settsu to deliver a simultaneous attack from the west. If the attacks were delivered quickly and successfully it should be possible to break the Taira lines before they had a chance of escaping to sea with the Emperor.

On the night of 18 March Yoshitsune's army over-ran a Taira outpost called Mikusayama, about twenty miles due north of Ichi-no-tani. He then turned south, and sent Doi Sanehira on with the main body of troops while he led a small band of samurai towards the cliffs at the rear of the fortress. When he and his men reached the top of the cliffs they saw that the battle had started. The fighting was fierce, but neither side appeared to be gaining the upper hand. Yoshitsune had about two hundred samurai with him, including Benkei, who knew a guide acquainted with a practicable descent to the rear of the fort. The descent was said to be so steep that not even monkeys would go down. To test this proposition Yoshitsune sent two riderless horses down the path. When they made the descent safely Yoshitsune concluded that his men could do better than the monkeys and followed. 'So steep was the descent that the stirrups of the hinder man struck against the helmet or armour of the one in front of him, and so dangerous did it look that they averted their eyes as they went down.'

So they reached the bottom, and charged into the undefended rear of the fort of Ichi-no-tani. As they galloped through they set fire to anything that would burn, and the Taira made a rush for the boats. The Emperor had already been placed on board, so one prize at least would be denied to the Minamoto. It also looked as if the roll of heads that day would be insignificant as high ranking samurai fought for places in the remaining boats, and flung common soldiers into the sea.

For those left behind a series of desperate struggles lay ahead which are recorded in detail in the *Heike Monogatari*. The first is the death of Taira Tadanori, the victor of Uji and a survivor of Kurikara. He was escaping towards the beach when Okabe Tadazumi, an ambitious Minamoto samurai, espied him and followed at full gallop, eager to bring down so noble a prize. When challenged Tadanori turned and cried out, 'We are friends! We are friends!', and continued on his way. As he turned, however, Okabe noticed that he had adopted the effeminate custom of blackening his teeth. This confirmed that he must be a Taira courtier, so Tadanori was engaged in combat and the first noble Taira head was struck from off its shoulders.

Meanwhile his nephew Shigehira, the destroyer of Nara, was also making for the boats. His fast steed had outdistanced all pursuers until an arrow struck it in the rump. Shigehira leapt from his horse's back into the shallow water, hoping to commit suicide by drowning, but the water was too shallow and he drew his dagger to perform hara-kiri. At that moment up rode a Minamoto samurai, who seized Shigehira and carried him off as a prisoner, an unusual action to take.

On another part of the beach the most celebrated individual combat in samurai history was taking place. Kumagai Naozane was riding along a narrow path in the hope of intercepting some high-ranking Taira. Just then he spotted a single horseman, whose armour was richly decorated, in the act of swimming his horse out to the boats. Kumagai Naozane challenged him to return, so the man rode back and gave battle. Kumagai proved the stronger. He hauled the stranger off his horse, then sprang on him to cut off his head. As he tore the helmet from the samurai's head he saw the face of a sixteen-year-old youth with a powdered face and blackened teeth. Kumagai's own son had been wounded during the attack on the stockade, and he was moved

to pity at the sight of the boy now at his mercy. Kumagai was about to let him go, but saw that all around swarmed the Minamoto samurai.

'"If you must die, let it be by my hand, and I will see that prayers are said for your re-birth in bliss." "Indeed it must be so," said the young warrior, "so take off my head at once." Then Kumagai weeping bitterly, and so overcome by his compassion for the fair youth that his eyes swam and his hand trembled until he could scarcely wield his blade, hardly knowing what he did, at last cut off his head.'

As Kumagai was wrapping up the head he discovered a flute in the young man's belt. The previous night Kumagai had heard a flute being played, and had reflected that none of the tough Minamoto warriors could play the flute. From this time on Kumagai turned towards the religious life, and the death of the young man, called Taira Atsumori, entered samurai mythology.

Ichi-no-tani was a great defeat for the Taira. Ten of the late Kiyomori's relatives were killed and one captured. The one bright ray of hope was the escape of the child Emperor to the Taira base of Yashima.

There followed a quiet spell of six months while Yoritomo sent reinforcements from Kamakura to Yoshitsune. Yoshitsune was to pursue the Taira by sea, while his brother Noriyori marched along the coast of the Inland Sea towards the Taira base at Hikoshima. On 8 October 1184 Noriyori set out for the west. He is a shadowy figure compared with his illustrious brothers, but he had been given no mean task. His journey would take him through solidly pro-Taira territory, and to further his discomfort the Taira had complete control of the sea. Noriyori's supply lines therefore became hopelessly extended, and once again we see the unedifying spectacle of an army living off a land which had already been stripped. The Taira had an outpost on the Inland Sea coast at Kojima, where Taira Tomomori, who had escaped from Ichi-no-tani, gave Noriyori the only real fight of the campaign. The action is interesting because a samurai called Sasaki Moritsuna performed an unusual feat of arms. He was the elder brother of Sasaki Takatsuna, who had won the famous race across the Ujigawa. Moritsuna now excelled his brother by racing his horse across the narrow strip of sea dividing Kojima from the mainland, thus leading the Minamoto into battle. Apart from this excitement Noriyori's army merely plodded on. By February 1185 Noriyori was sending messages to Kamakura describing the low morale and listlessness of his army. He warned Yoritomo that many would desert if given the chance. He also begged for horses and boats, for they were stalled in western Honshū, and could not cross to Kyūshū. Eventually some were commandeered, and the weary army 'invaded' Kyūshū. One of the samurai, weak from lack of food, sold his armour to buy a boat to help his comrades on their way.

26 Minamoto Yoshitsune leads his men in the celebrated rear attack on Ichi-no-tani, 1184. From a seventeenth-century wood-block printed edition of *Heike Monogatari*. (Author's collection.)

27 (*above and on following five pages*)
Tsuba (sword guards). The centre
pair depict samurai during the
Gempei War. (Courtesy of Sotheby
& Co.)

While Noriyori was marching westwards his younger brother was
stealing all the glory. A fleet, of sorts, had been assembled at Watanabe
for a sea-borne raid upon Yashima, the Taira base on Shikoku. For the
first time the Minamoto were really taking to the water, a prospect
which daunted many of the mountain samurai. Kajiwara Kagetoki,
who had saved Yoritomo's life in the 'wood-doves' incident, was
particularly critical of Yoshitsune's maritime preparations. He pointed
out to Yoshitsune that the way the oars had been arranged on the boats
would make it difficult for them to reverse. Yoshitsune was very
caustic in his reply. 'We have no intention of retreating', he said, words

which stung Kajiwara to the quick. The overall aim of the strategy embodied in the Yashima raid was at all costs to avoid a sea battle with the Taira, at which the Minamoto would almost certainly come off worse. The planned course avoided the direct sea route to Yashima, and was aimed south of the island of Awaji, to land on Shikoku about thirty miles along the coast from Yashima, from where an attack could be launched overland.

Yashima is a volcanic plateau that is today connected with the mainland of Shikoku by a land bridge, but at the time of the Gempei it was isolated, although the channel was shallow and easily fordable

by man and horse. No doubt the Taira would have posted sentries on the plateau's sides, but in spite of its obvious natural fortifications the Taira base was not on top of the plateau but on the beach between the island and the mainland, with their life-saving fleet stationed in the shallows.

By the middle of March Yoshitsune's preparations were complete, and the army set sail about 22 March. The weather was bad, with a fierce storm raging, which Yoshitsune hoped would add an element of surprise to their attack. His samurai did not share his enthusiasm, and many had to be forced on to the boats at sword point. They sailed

overnight, in the teeth of the furious gale, landing on Shikoku the
next morning. Once they had recovered their wits the samurai saddled
up and set off at full speed for Yashima.

Yoshitsune's 'visiting card' at Yashima was the same that had
proved effective at Ichi-no-tani. Anything that would burn was burned,
and under cover of the pall of smoke the small Minamoto force swept
down to the sea. Once again the Emperor was bustled into a boat,
but instead of heading for the open sea the boats drew up in the narrow
channel between Yashima and the mainland, no doubt with the intention of inflicting as much damage as possible on the Minamoto

before slipping away. As the water was so shallow the Minamoto were able to wade out on their horses and give battle to the Taira samurai in the boats. Yoshitsune himself took a brave part in this unusual combat. In the struggle he dropped his bow and was fishing for it in the sea when his retainers shouted to him not to risk his life for a bow. Yoshitsune replied that as his bow was an ordinary one, and not like that borne by his uncle 'giant' Tametomo, the Taira would be likely to make fun of him if they found it. So Yoshitsune persisted until the bow was found, and his image remained intact. The most celebrated incident of the Battle of Yashima occurred when someone in the Taira

boats conceived the idea of suspending a fan from the mast and inviting the Minamoto to shoot it down, thereby wasting their ammunition. The fan, which bore the design of a bright red sun's disc, fluttered in the breeze and presented a very difficult target on a moving boat. A volunteer was found called Nasu Munetaka, an eighteen-year-old samurai. He was wary of displaying his skill in front of such an audience, but he agreed to try, and fitted a humming-bulb arrow to his bow. The arrow found its mark, hitting the fan on the rivet and shattering it, flinging the pieces into the sea. In later years the descendants of Munetaka took a fan with a sun's disc as their family badge or 'mon'.

As the sun began to set the Taira withdrew to the shelter of Shido Bay, directly east of Yashima. The Minamoto crossed to Yashima and washed the blood and salt water out of their armour in a pool that remains to this day. This was a sensible precaution against rust, which would soon eat into a part where the lacquer had cracked. The Taira lingered at Shido for another day, then set out on the long voyage to their sole remaining refuge at Hikoshima. The Taira had lost few casualties at Yashima, but their voyage to Hikoshima, where Noriyori held the coasts, was likely to prove a decisive move.

Yoshitsune's greatest asset was now his success. The samurai leaders had seen him defeat the Taira on two occasions and hurried to associate themselves with the white flag of the Minamoto. In particular Yoshitsune was pleased to receive the allegiance of several sea-going samurai commanders, who helped to transport the eager Minamoto army by sea towards the most decisive battle in Japanese history – Dan-no-ura.

To follow this, the final struggle of the Gempei War, the reader is referred to the inset diagram in Fig. 25. The situation on the eve of battle, 24 April 1185, was as follows: The Taira fleet, commanded by Taira Tomomori, were based on Hikoshima where they could command the western approaches to the Shimonoseki Strait. As the Minamoto fleet advanced swiftly from the direction of Shikoku the Taira fleet left its base and took to the sea, as had been their practice since Ichino-tani. They sailed eastwards through the strait until they were level with Ta-no-ura on Kyūshū, a few miles east of the modern city of Kita-Kyūshū. Simultaneously the Minamoto gradually advanced to Manjushima Island. The two fleets were then about two miles apart.

The mood among the Taira was one of forced self-confidence. They were by far the most experienced side at sea-warfare, but owing to the allegiances recently made to Yoshitsune the Minamoto fleet outnumbered them by about 850 to 400, and these new additions were as well versed in sea fighting as the Taira. Taira Tomomori made a stirring speech to his clansmen, reminding them that this time there would be no retreat. They should pay no heed to the risk to their lives, but fight as bravely as they could. Taira Kagekiyo added a peroration, calling on his fellow samurai to make Yoshitsune the main object of their attack. They could not mistake him, said Kagekiyo, for he was 'a little fellow with a fair complexion and his front teeth stick out a bit'. The only samurai of whom Tomomori had doubts was one Taguchi Shigeyoshi. Suspecting a possible defection, Tomomori asked Munemori for permission to deprive Shigeyoshi of his head. The request was turned down, and as the battle was about to begin Shigeyoshi was allowed to take his place in the Taira battle line. As a precaution the Emperor had been placed on an ordinary ship, while the large 'flagship' hung with streamers acted as a decoy. The boats used were very simple affairs. They had no armaments of their own, and merely served as floating platforms for samurai.

The Minamoto went into battle with bows and sterns abreast,

while the Taira formed three squadrons. Fighting began between six and eight in the morning of 25 April 1185, opposite a beach on the Honshū shore called Dan-no-ura. The Taira took advantage of the tide, at that time flowing in an easterly direction, to bear down upon the Minamoto. When the leading boats were about 350 yards apart a spirited archery duel began, and as the current was slow the Taira marksmen made grim execution. The battle seemed to be going their way, and Tomomori continued to press the advantage while conditions allowed.

At about 11 o'clock the fleets closed, and the fight for Yoshitsune became fast and furious. Taira Noritsune came close to capturing him when he fought his way on to Yoshitsune's boat. Yoshitsune leapt for his life to another boat, and while he made his escape three samurai tackled Noritsune, who kicked one overboard, and, seizing the others under each arm, jumped into the sea to commit suicide. By now two factors had changed the situation considerably. The tide had turned, giving the Minamoto the weather position, so they were now forcing the Taira towards Dan-no-ura while the tide ran at eight knots. The second development was the expected defection of Taguchi Shigeyoshi, who suddenly hauled down the red flag of the Taira and pulled away to join Yoshitsune. Once on board Yoshitsune's boat he divulged the exact location of the Emperor, so the full force of the Minamoto was directed against this one ship.

More confusion was caused among the Taira by an order from Yoshitsune for the archers to concentrate on the rowers and steerers. Soon several Taira boats were spinning helplessly in the current, and as the Minamoto bore down upon them Tomomori knew that all was lost. He went on board the vessel containing the child Emperor to announce that as the battle was lost suicide was the only answer. Accordingly the Emperor's grandmother, Kiyomori's widow, took the eight-year-old sovereign in her arms and walked slowly to the side of the ship. There she and the child prayed to their Imperial Ancestress of Ise, and the Buddha who protected their land, and with the words, 'In the depths of the ocean we have a capital', sank with him beneath the waves.

Thus began the most tragic mass suicide in the history of the samurai. The Emperor's mother was next to jump into the sea, but was hauled out by a Minamoto samurai who caught her hair in a rake. The wife of Shigehira was also about to jump when an arrow pinned her skirt to the side of the ship, forcing her to drop the casket she was carrying. It turned out to contain the Sacred Mirror, one of the items of the Regalia. The Sacred Sword had already been flung into the sea. Meanwhile Taira Norimori and Tsunemori placed heavy anchors on their armour and, hand in hand, leapt into the sea. Three other members of the family, Sukemori, Arimori and Yukimori did likewise, but Munemori, the head of the clan and a weak character, stood around waiting to see what would happen, until a samurai, disgusted at his leader's example, pushed him over the side. Munemori was a good swimmer, if nothing else, and managed to keep afloat until the Minamoto took him prisoner. The supposed cowardice of Munemori was remarked upon by his mother shortly before she jumped into the sea with the child Emperor. She is said to have confided in her family that Munemori was not the son of his illustrious father Kiyomori but had been exchanged at birth with an umbrella merchant for a daughter.

The final suicide that day was committed by Taira Tomomori. He put on two suits of armour to weigh his body down, and jumped into the sea.

'And now the whole sea was red with the banners and insignia they had torn off and thrown away, so that it looked like the waters of the Tatsuta-gawa when it is flecked with the maple leaves that the wind brings down in autumn, while the white breakers that rolled up on the beach were dyed a scarlet colour. The deserted empty ships rocked mournfully on the waves, driven aimlessly hither and thither by the wind and tide.'

The Battle of Dan-no-ura marked the utter destruction of the Taira. Hardly one of the names recorded here survived this conflict, and with Dan-no-ura the name of Taira disappeared from Japanese history. No other victory in the story of the samurai was so complete and so decisive as the eclipse of the Taira at Dan-no-ura. The sheer scale of the family's destruction has earned the battle an immortal place in the rich world of Japanese ghost stories. Such an awful engulfing of human life made a profound impression upon the psyche of a superstitious people. For centuries sailors avoided the area of Dan-no-ura lest they catch sight of the restless ghosts of the Taira condemned to wander the waves. Peasants in their fancy saw ghostly armies bailing out the sea with bottomless dippers, attempting to cleanse the sea of the stain of years ago. A better known legend concerns the Heike crabs, which are said to contain within their shells the spirits of the dead samurai. (Their shells do indeed bear the shape of a human face, when perused with some imagination.)

The Gempei War had now come to an end, making Minamoto Yoritomo, 'Lord of Kamakura', the effective ruler of Japan. The steps he took to establish his position differed widely from those of the Taira and Fujiwara. Yoritomo elected to rule from Kamakura, and in 1192 was proclaimed 'Seii-tai shōgun'. The title of 'Shōgun' or 'Barbarian-subduing Commander-in-Chief' was the temporary commission granted by the Emperor for the suppression of rebels. Yoritomo made the temporary commission into a permanent one, for the Shōgunal commission that the new Emperor gave Yoritomo was not handed back until 4 January 1868! Yoritomo had therefore established a hereditary military dictatorship to remain forever within the Minamoto family, called the 'Shōgunate' or the 'Bakufu', the latter word deriving from the maku, the large curtains that surrounded a commander's camp

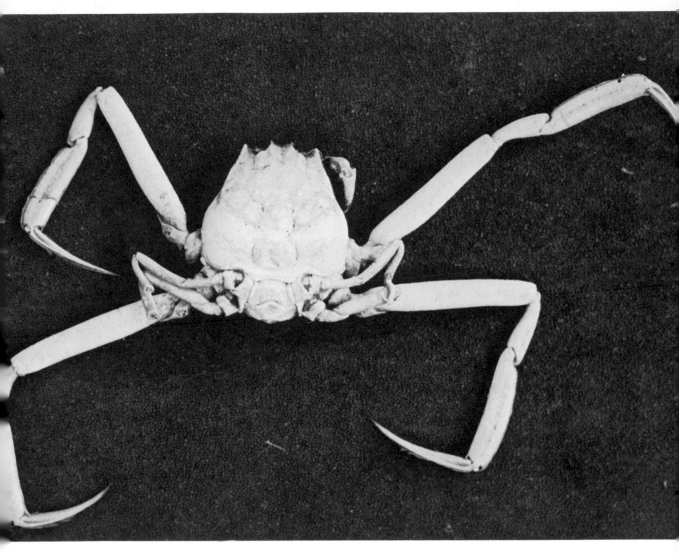

on the field of battle. The Shōgunate was a government of the samurai, by the samurai and for the samurai. It retained the Emperor, but shifted the whole emphasis of political power to the only real power that remained in the land – the samurai. The samurai were the real victors of the Gempei War.

As for the greatest of the samurai, their rewards were slight. Intense jealousy and suspicion of Yoshitsune led Yoritomo to outlaw the brother who had done so much to help him gain his position. For four years after Dan-no-ura Yoshitsune was hunted through Japan like a wild animal. With a handful of faithful companions, including the trusty Benkei, Yoshitsune managed to elude his brother's spies and the armies searching for him. These adventures have raised Yoshitsune from the status of a samurai general to a mythological figure, supplying artists and playwrights with endless inspiration. He encounters ghosts

28 Heike Crab. These crabs are supposed to contain the spirits of the samurai slain at Dan-no-ura, 1185. A human face may be discerned on the shell, when it is scrutinized with some imagination! (Author's collection.)

29 Minamoto Yoritomo (1147–99), the founder of the Shōgunate, the hereditary military dictatorship that lasted seven hundred years. (Studio M.)

of the Taira while travelling by sea, and one particular narrow escape is worth mentioning, as it neatly illustrates the master-servant relationship of lord and samurai.

Yoritomo set up a series of roadblocks in an effort to find Yoshitsune, who was reported to be travelling in the guise of a yamabushi (itinerant Buddhist friar). When Yoshitsune and his men arrived at one such barrier Benkei managed to convince the guard that they were genuine yamabushi, and even managed to extort a subscription for the re-building of the Tōdai-ji. They were about to pass through the barrier when a vigilant sentry recognized Yoshitsune and challenged the party to halt. With admirable presence of mind Benkei turned and struck Yoshitsune with his staff, calling upon him to hurry and not delay their journey. The guard therefore let them pass, perfectly satisfied at their genuineness, for no servant would dare strike his master.

Yoshitsune's flight ended at the bank of the Koromogawa in Northern Honshū, where he and his band of followers prepared to fight the Shōgun's armies. They were soon overwhelmed, so Benkei held the foe off while Yoshitsune retired to commit suicide. Benkei stood there defiantly, naginata in hand, and so terrible did he look that none dared approach him, until a mounted samurai, galloping by, caught Benkei in his slipstream and he fell over. It was only then that the Shōgunal samurai realized that he had been dead for some time.

Meanwhile Yoshitsune committed hara-kiri, or, as some say, escaped, for there is an old Japanese tradition that Yoshitsune escaped to the mainland of Asia and there joined the Mongols, taking the name of Genghis Khan. At this point the legend takes off into pure fantasy, but there is no doubt that Yoshitsune remains the archetypal Japanese hero, the lonely, wandering figure who dies a tragic death, in whose encounters with ghosts and heroes we see the last flickering of heroic myth. From now on the samurai, for all their bravery, remain with their feet firmly planted on the earth.

Leaving aside the legendary aspects of the Gempei War, we can see it as a period of immense change in Japanese life. By 1180 the Taira had mastered the techniques of court intrigue and the accepted ways to power, but were toppled because these methods were already obsolete when they began to use them. In 1185 the Minamoto seized power by the sword, and confirmed it by extending to the whole of Japan what Yoritomo had been building up in the Kantō – a military based feudal dictatorship.

Yoritomo's supremacy was completed by the extermination in 1186 of Minamoto Yukiie, and of Noriyori in 1193. Yet his supreme power was not to place him in the hall of fame, for while every Japanese schoolboy can relate the tales of Yoshitsune and Benkei, Yoritomo belongs to the dry world of political history, and not to the stirring epic of the samurai. In 1199 Yoritomo was thrown from his horse, sustaining severe injuries from which he later died. A popular version of the accident makes his horse rear at the appearance of the ghost of Yoshitsune, which neatly expresses the popular opinion of Yoritomo.

5. Their finest hour

With the death of Minamoto Yoritomo the fortunes of the house of Minamoto, which had risen so rapidly in the Gempei War, went as speedily into a decline. Within thirty years of the founding of the Kamakura Shōgunate the third and last Minamoto Shōgun had been assassinated, and his place taken by the Hōjō. For a century and a half the power of the Shōgunate fell under the control of this family, although they respected the tradition that required the title of Shōgun to be kept within the Minamoto family, and took the title of 'Shikken', or Regent, instead. Thus the Shōgun, who had manipulated a puppet Emperor, became himself a puppet of the Hōjō Regency, and it was under a Hōjō, not a Minamoto, that the military government of Japan faced its most serious crisis – the Mongol invasions of 1274 and 1281.

The Mongol attempts at conquest are particularly interesting as providing the only time in the history of the samurai when Japan suffered foreign invasion. It forced a radical reappraisal on the samurai, who for two centuries had fought only each other, to face up to an alien foe whose ways of warfare differed from their own. Furthermore, it marks the one time in their history when the samurai were Japanese first and foremost, and the nation stood united as never before.

Before describing the Mongol invasions it will be necessary to discuss certain points concerning what had been happening in Japan during the century following the Gempei War. In one way the country had undergone a great change, for the late twelfth and early thirteenth centuries witnessed a religious revival in Japan. The reader will recall that the activities of the warrior-monks had led to the virtual destruction of the old established monastic centres of Nara and Mount Hiei. After the Gempei War Yoritomo supervised the reconstruction of the Nara temples, and was generous in his attitude to the expansion of Buddhism at both centres. But by far the greatest contribution to the development of Buddhism in Japan at the time came not from the old monasteries but from a handful of new sects, some of which had sprung up before the Gempei War, and had grown in the early thirteenth century. The first of these sects sprung from a monk called Hōnen-Shōnin, who was born in 1133. Seen in the context of a world torn by civil war, famine, treachery and death it is not surprising that Japan was receptive to a creed of despair. His sect of 'Jōdo' (the 'Pure Land') called upon the faithful to admit that the world was vile and evil, and that it would be impossible to attain Buddhahood within it. They should therefore cease chasing such a shadow and put their faith in what was to come after death, where by faith in Amida Buddha they would be received into bliss. Entrance into the 'Pure Land', said Hōnen, could be expected only if prayer was maintained, and he set an example to his followers by repeating the name of Amida as many as 60,000 times a day.

Hōnen's doctrine of despair did not endear itself to the samurai, who had little to despair about. They inclined far more to an off-shoot Jōdo sect called 'Shinshū' or 'Ikkō'. Its founder, Shinran Shōnin, began preaching about 1224, after the jealous monks of Mount Hiei had contrived for him to be exiled to the Kantō. He taught that the salvation that the Jōdo sect promised was not put off until the hour of one's death, but was available here and now. 'Call on the name of Amida and you will be saved – now!' was Shinran's message. He rejected all acts of religiosity such as spells, incantations and exorcisms, and insisted on prayer alone. He further enraged the monks of Mount Hiei by rejecting the notion of celibacy of the clergy and the Buddhist prohibition against eating meat. With such restrictions lifted the sect grew in strength, and the full extent of its power became apparent in the unrest of the fifteenth century.

But neither Jōdo nor Ikkō captured the hearts of the samurai. This honour was to be conferred upon that sect of Buddhism best known in the West, namely Zen. Indeed so familiar is 'Zen Buddhism' that to many Zen is synonymous with Buddhism itself. It had been introduced into Japan during the seventh century, but had no success until it was re-introduced by the monk Eisai in 1192. To explain the tenets of Zen in a few lines is a problem itself worthy of Zen, but suffice it to say that Zen was the sect of contemplation, that saw salvation as coming from within rather than from without. To this end Zen stressed the need for the practice of meditation. The believer must put from his mind all worldly thoughts and desires. By so doing he will arrive at the knowledge of the law and nature of Buddha without being influenced by other dissenting doctrines. How, then, could a mystical religion of contemplation appeal so strongly to the samurai, when they were men of action? The answer lies partly in what Zen offered, for it provided essentially a way of salvation which the believer worked out for himself, and this would find great sympathy among the wielders of bow and sword. Also its practices were austere and its demands spartan, making it but a short distance from the halls of Kamakura to the corridors of contemplation. Finally the abstraction of Zen took a man out of himself, on to a plane superior to his surroundings, where he might examine his own fate and defy it. In short, Zen provided a philosophical framework ideally suited to the samurai ideals that had developed in the eleventh century and come to fruition in the Gempei War.

There is one final aspect of the religious revival to consider, one which is curiously relevant to the study of the Mongol Invasions. In 1222 there was born in the Kantō area a certain Nichiren, who studied as a monk in the Enryaku-ji, whence he returned in 1253 and began a vigorous campaign of preaching. In 1253 he preached a sermon which began 'Namu myōhō renge kyō' or 'Hail to the Lotus of the Divine Law', a phrase which later became the motto and battlecry of his sect. Nichiren called upon the nation to reject the teachings of all other sects, new and old, and to seek truth by searching the scriptures, for enlightenment and salvation would only come from the words of Buddha himself, enshrined within the *Lotus Sutra*. Nichiren was a wandering preacher, and attracted his audiences by gongs, drums and chants. In time, because of the resentment his views aroused, his followers became known for being defiant and fanatical to the point of pugnacity, and in fact the Nichiren developed into the only really bigoted Buddhist sect. Nichiren was the one true faith, and all others were false and damnable. Legend has lavishly embellished his last years. According to tradition, when Nichiren was delivered to be executed the sword blade shattered on his neck.

Yet this strange, tub-thumping preacher rendered his nation a service greater than the rest of the religious coterie put together, for he helped to restore to the Japanese their sense of nationhood. Ever since Buddhism had forced the indigenous cult of Shintō into second place the flower of Japanese nationalism had faded. Nichiren determined to make his sect a national Church, and aimed his enthusiastic preaching to the national as well as the individual conscience. His appeal to the Japanese as a nation took its most dramatic turn when he warned them that unless they repented of their sins the wrath of Heaven would shortly descend upon them in the shape of foreign invasion! In this Nichiren proved an astute observer of the political situation, and a skilled awakener of conscience. When the threat came the resistance of Japan had been given a firm moral and ideological framework.

The background to the invasions that Nichiren preached about is, briefly, as follows. While Japan, in the fullness of time, grew towards a centralized government with real power, finally realized by Yoritomo's Shōgunate, the fortunes of China, from whom Japan had received so much inspiration, declined under the pressure of Barbarian attacks from the north. From 960 until 1120 the Sung dynasty ruled China, and throughout this period China was swept by hordes of invaders, first the Tartars, who managed to blackmail the Emperor into paying them to stay away, then a second, the 'Golden' horde of Tartars, whom the Emperor had originally recruited to get rid of the first horde; and finally the Mongols, those fierce horsemen whose depredations extended as far as Europe.

By 1259 Kublai Khan, the Great Khan of the Mongols, and the grandson of the famous Genghis Khan, had made himself Emperor of China, and in 1264 moved his capital to the city now known as Peking. By the time of Kublai's accession China's neighbour Korea had also acknowledged the supremacy of the Mongols, so that the Mongol power stretched to within fifty miles of Japanese territory. In 1266 Kublai Khan despatched two ambassadors to Japan, but the mission was prevented by fierce storms in the Korea Straits, to the relief of the Koreans who had been ordered to accompany them.

The position of Korea in the subsequent developments is an un-enviable one. Korea had only submitted to Mongol domination after fierce assault had beaten her to her knees. The history of that unhappy country has always been one of a buffer between great powers, and in 1266 Korea was at its lowest ebb. Korea desired nothing but peace with Japan, yet was faced with the terrible prospect that, should Kublai proceed with his conquests, Korea would be unavoidably involved. The simple fact was that the Mongols were no sailors and had no fleet, their reputation having been won from the horse's back. The Koreans were sailors and possessed a large fleet. They were also now the slaves of the Mongols. Should the invasion go ahead it would sail in Korean vessels, with probably a Korean contingent on board. For their part the Japanese sought nothing but the most cordial relations with Korea. The extent of their goodwill was shown by the severity with which the Japanese invariably put down their own pirates who raided Korean soil.

In 1268 Kublai's envoys at last made the crossing of the Strait and presented a letter to the local Bakufu representative in Kyūshū. Japanese spies in Korea had given the Shōgunate, or rather the Hōjō Regency, a good idea of what to expect:

'[We] by the Grace and decree of Heaven, Emperor of Great Mongolia, present a letter to the King of Japan.

'We have pondered that from ancient times even the princes of small states have striven to cultivate friendly intercourse with those of adjoining territories.

'To how much greater extent have Our ancestors, who have received the Middle Empire by the inscrutable decrees, become known in numerous far off foreign lands, all of whom have reverenced their power and majesty!

'When we first ascended the throne, many innocent people in Korea were suffering from continuous war. Thereupon we put an end to the fighting, restored their territories, and liberated the captives both old and young. . . .

'. . . We beg that hereafter you, O King, will establish friendly relations with us so that the sages may make the four seas their home.

'Is it reasonable to refuse intercourse with each other? It will lead to war, and who is there who likes such a state of things!

'Think of this, O King!'

The letter immediately threw the Imperial Court into a panic, though their fear of the Mongol was mitigated somewhat by anger at the reference to the Emperor of Japan, the descendant of the Sun-Goddess, as a mere King, while pointedly retaining the Imperial title for Kublai Khan. The letter had arrived during preparations for the fiftieth anniversary of the accession of ex-Emperor Go-Saga, and plans for this were hurriedly put aside while a reply to the threatening letter was framed.

Had the Imperial Court still been the effective rulers of Japan then the ensuing few years might have had a disastrous effect on the country's history. But the power now lay with Kamakura, and Kublai was threatening fighting men, not courtiers. The Bakufu contemptuously dismissed the Court's reply, and their answer to the Great Khan remained a polite 'no comment'. While the Mongol ambassadors returned empty handed, the samurai prepared to defend their country.

On 18 April 1268 the Regent Hōjō Masamura retired from office to occupy the position of chief of staff of the Bakufu. He was succeeded as Regent by Hōjō Tokimune, a samurai of eighteen, and the perfect symbol of the nation's resolve. He appealed to the samurai to put aside all clan differences and feuds, and unite as one for the defence of hearth and home. That his appeal was a success was in no small way attributable to the foundations which Yoritomo had laid. Had the Mongols chosen to invade Japan a century earlier the results might have proved very different.

As soon as his first embassy had failed in 1268 Kublai Khan began preparations for war. There were several diplomatic exchanges between 1268 and 1274, but all were treated with contempt by the Japanese. It is clear from the invasion preparations that Kublai greatly underestimated the fighting capacities of the Japanese, for his army was to consist of no more than 25,000 Mongols, in addition to the Koreans impressed into transport and fighting roles. As expected, Korea bore much of the brunt of assembling the throng, for in 1268 Kublai sent word to the King of Korea to furnish troops and ships for the invasion. As Korea was in such straitened circumstances the King protested that he could not comply with the order, nor could he arrange to supply the oxen and ploughs demanded to increase the supply of rice for the invasions. In 1273, 5,000 Mongol troops arrived in Korea as an advance guard, and found the country so impoverished that foodstuffs had to be ferried down to them from China.

The Mongol fleet set sail in November 1274 for the island of Tsushima. Here the defences were in the hands of Sō Sukekuni, who was the grandson of Taira Tomomori, the last to commit suicide at Dan-no-ura. It is worth noting that the Japanese made no attempt to harass the fleet as it crossed the Straits, for the Japanese had no capability to do so. There was so little of a naval tradition in Japan, apart from the pirates, that all legitimate commerce in the days of peace had been carried in Chinese ships. In spite of the heroic efforts of Sukekuni, Tsushima was overrun by sheer weight of numbers, and the same fate befell Iki Island a few days later. The inhabitants of both islands were subjected to the shocking cruelty of the Mongols, which horrified the Japanese samurai, to whom fighting was a business conducted between fighting men, and which did not include the murder of innocent women and children. This was the first indication the Japanese had that the Mongols fought to a tradition entirely alien from their own.

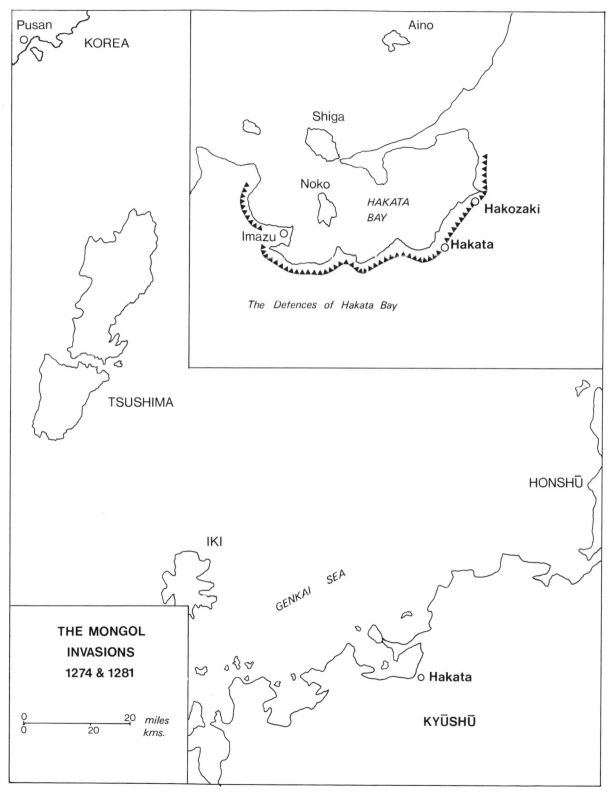

Pusan

KOREA

Aino

Shiga

Noko

HAKATA BAY

Imazu

Hakozaki

Hakata

The Defences of Hakata Bay

TSUSHIMA

HONSHŪ

IKI

GENKAI SEA

THE MONGOL

INVASIONS

1274 & 1281

0 — 20 *miles*

0 — 20 *kms.*

○ **Hakata**

KYŪSHŪ

30 Map showing the Mongol attempts at invasion, 1274 and 1281.

How strange and terrible the Mongols were was brought home forcibly on 19 November when the Mongol fleet entered Hakata Bay and landed at Imazu. At dawn the next day the Mongol army, supported by the ships lying off shore, launched an attack on Hakata, during which the samurai learnt several lessons about their enemies.

The first lesson concerned tactics. The samurai's bravery, which was in some ways his greatest strength, proved now to be a weakness. The tradition of being first into battle, collecting heads and particularly of challenging a worthy opponent to individual combat, proved to be completely irrelevant against a foreign enemy. As we saw during the Gempei War, the actual practice of formal combat played a relatively small part in the overall conduct of battles, but it was an enduring myth in which every samurai believed. When it is remembered that it was nearly a century since the Gempei War, and that in that time there had been only one relatively minor clash of arms (in 1221), then there is no doubt that the majority of samurai desired above all else to engage a single Mongol in a duel and cut off his head, thus emulating the deeds of his ancestors whose exploits had grown in glamour with every year that had passed.

In contrast, the Mongols who had fought their way through China and Korea, had been fighting, as distinct from merely training, for the best part of their lives. They fought in close formation like a Macedonian phalanx, and against this Mongol phalanx the samurai horsemen flung themselves with incredible bravery, for bravery was the greatest asset they possessed.

With one exception the Mongol weapons were inferior to the Japanese. They fought with straight spears, and swords that were no comparison to the keen blades of the samurai. But, according to the *Taihei ki*, a fourteenth-century military history, they had one 'secret weapon':

'When the fighting began, mighty iron balls known as teppō were [flung?]. They rolled down the hills like cartwheels, sounded like thunder and looked like bolts of lightning. Two or three thousand of them were [thrown?] at a time, and many soldiers were burned to death.'

Figure 31, which is taken from *Mōko Shūrai Ekotoba* (the Scroll of the Mongol Invasions), painted shortly after the war, depicts one of these 'iron balls' exploding slightly in front of, and above, a Japanese warrior. It is highly unlikely that these bombs were discharged by explosive. More probably they were fired by a sort of catapult, for the Mongols also possessed powerful crossbows and siege-engines.

Finally, on the subject of military differences, it is sad to record that Japanese archery was not what it had been. Admittedly the defence of the country had fallen entirely on the shoulders of the Kyūshū samurai, whose bows were lighter and weaker than those of the Kantō,

but there is evidence that even in the Kantō the martial arts had been neglected in the 'piping time of peace'.

In spite of all their bravery the Japanese were forced to retreat to the safety of some ancient fortifications built six centuries before. Behind this defence-line of moats and embankments the samurai waited. 'We lamented all through the night,' wrote one, 'thinking that we were doomed and would be destroyed to the last man and that no seeds would be left to fill the nine provinces.' Their hope lay with the reinforcements expected from Shikoku and Honshū, for whom word had been sent as the first news from Tsushima had arrived. The Bakufu had acted as swiftly as its immense line of communication allowed, and commands to levy troops had gone out to all areas, including Kyūshū. But before any such orders or reinforcements reached Kyūshū there was not a single Mongol left on Japanese soil.

It would appear that the resistance put up by the Japanese had greatly surprised the Mongol leaders, who knew that reinforcements might reach the Japanese at any moment. They were also suffering from a shortage of arrows, for they had prepared only for a 'blitzkrieg' and shot arrows in thick random clouds. They also feared a possible night attack by the Japanese over ground they knew well, during which the primitive techniques of the Japanese would come to the fore. So the Mongols ordered a tactical withdrawal, and to cover the re-embarkation the great shrine of Hakozaki was fired, together with several villages along the shore. As the Japanese crouched in their trenches they saw the sky red with fire, and witnessed the destruction of 'the temples of their gods'.

The fire was short lived, for that night a great wind blew, and with it came a deluge of rain. The storm caught the Mongol fleet as it was leaving harbour, and flung the ships hither and thither. Those that had reached the open sea were tossed on the fierce waves, and one ran aground on Shiga spit as it left Hakata Bay. Korean records tell us that 13,000 men lost their lives in this expedition, many by drowning. The first invasion was over.

31 A Mongol firebomb exploding in front of a mounted samurai. From *Mōko Shūrai Ekotaba* ('The scroll of the Mongol Invasion'). (Imperial Household collection.)

Between 1274 and 1281 the Mongols were too preoccupied with the conquest of Southern China to worry about completing their designs on Japan. As the Japanese kept themselves well informed as to Mongol activities a further attack was anticipated, so the Shōgunate used the time to organize proper defences. In particular, a stone wall was erected along the coast of Hakata Bay (see inset diagram, Fig. 30). It may have been as long as twenty-five miles, was about fifteen feet high, and was cleverly constructed so that horses could be ridden up the sloping defensive side while the side facing the sea was vertical. It is arguable that the energy that went into constructing the wall might have been put to better use in building an ocean-going fleet of war vessels, capable of taking the fight to the enemy. This was in fact suggested, and a raid on the Mongol homeland was planned by certain Kyūshū samurai, but the proposal was finally turned down on the grounds of expense, and all extra naval preparations were confined to building small and easily handled ships for use in coastal waters.

Plans were also made for the speedy and large-scale supply of manpower that would be needed when the second invasion arrived. The four extreme western provinces of Honshū were given responsibility for defence of the seas immediately in their area. Kyūshū was organized with a rota for garrisoning the coast, and in case of a surprise attack on the Hokurikudō, forces were mobilized there. Steps were also taken to ensure that everyone called by the summons complied with the order.

By 1279 Kublai's conquest of China was virtually complete, putting the vast maritime resources of South China into his hands. Again Korea was expected to furnish additional men and ships, and in fact supplied 900 ships, 10,000 Korean soldiers, and 17,000 Korean sailors. This force assembled at Aiura in Korea, and was joined by 15,000 Chinese and Mongols. They were to spearhead the attack, and would be followed by a vast Chinese army of 100,000 men plus 60,000 sailors in 3,500 ships. This second squadron, known as the 'South of the Yangtze' force, was to meet the eastern force by 2 July at Iki, and combine for the attack on Kyūshū.

The eastern (Korea) army set sail on 22 May 1281 and invaded Tsushima on 9 June. The resistance was far fiercer than during the first invasion both on Tsushima and Iki, which was attacked on 14 June. The Chinese fleet had not yet set sail, for its commanders were having difficulty in manning and provisioning such a vast host, so the Eastern army tried to steal a march on its allies by advancing ahead of schedule. On 21 June lookouts on the Kyūshū coast made out the 'tasselled prows and fluted sails' of the invader's fleet. This, however, proved to be but part of the Mongol force, designed to act as a diversion from the main attack on Kyūshū by launching an attack on western Honshū. As this detachment sailed along, the main body headed for Hakata Bay, and attempted to land troops on Shiga spit, at the extreme end of the wall and an excellent place for turning the Japanese flank. So fierce did the resistance prove that only one unit was able to land even after several days of continuous fighting. As the wall was held from end to end, the

Japanese were able to change defence into offence, and put out from Hakata in small, swift and highly manoeuvrable boats (ten to fifteen men per boat) to harass the Mongol ships in night-time hit-and-run raids. The fanatical samurai would close with a Mongol ship, knock down their own mast for a bridge whereby to board the enemy vessel, attack the Mongols at close quarters, and then return. On one occasion thirty samurai swam out to a ship, cut off the heads of the crew, and swam back. Another celebrated incident concerns a certain Kusano Jiro, who raided a Mongol ship in broad daylight. In spite of a hail of darts, one of which took off Kusano's left arm, the ship was fired and twenty-one heads taken.

The most famous of these 'little ship' raids was led by Kono Michiari, who also set out in broad daylight with two boatloads of men, apparently unarmed. The Mongols thought they were coming to surrender, so held their fire. The Japanese boats came alongside, the masts were let down, and the samurai boarded. Kono Michiari killed the captain of the ship, and escaped under cover of the burning vessel taking a high ranking officer with him as captive.

Eventually the Mongols withdrew to regroup at Takashima Island on 30 June, and tried to land farther along the coast. Again they were repulsed. Forced to remain on board their cramped ships, with scarcely enough breathing space in the scorching heat, three thousand men were carried off by an epidemic, and the ships themselves began to rot. As the Yangtze force had still not arrived the Mongols were forced to wait and suffer the Japanese raids.

On 16 July the advance vessels of the Yangtze arrived at Iki, and on 12 August the great armada combined for the final, decisive assault on Japan. The noise made by the drums and cheers when the two navies met could be heard on land, and stiffened the defenders' resolve still further. As the climax of the campaign approached the Japanese realized that individual valour would not be sufficient to save them from the hand of the invader, and the whole nation bent the knee in prayer to the gods for the overthrow of the Mongols. The ex-Emperor Kameyama turned in the hour of crisis to the founder of his house, and sent a proxy to Ise to petition his Imperial Ancestress the Sun Goddess for divine help. The prayer was answered.

On the same evening as the prayer was offered, 15 August 1281, there appeared in the sky a cloud, no bigger, perhaps, than a man's hand. The cloud grew and spread, until an early and lurid darkness blotted out the setting sun over the Genkai Sea where the Mongol armada lay. Then the wind began to rise, its wild moan being heard for some time before its force began to be seen on the surface of the sea. The waves grew, and the Mongol boats began to rock fiercely as the wind developed into a terrific tornado, which whipped up the water and flung it against the ships, carrying them towards the rocks, tossing them against one another, or simply blowing them completely over. The force of wind and wave smashed the armada to matchwood, so that the sea looked 'as if divining rods had been scattered'.

93

When the 'kami-kaze' or 'divine wind', as it was immediately dubbed, subsided, the samurai gleefully went about the task of mopping up survivors. The total loss of life was truly enormous, the Chinese fleet alone losing over half its 100,000 men. So ended the final attempt at invasion. Kublai Khan planned a third, but it was never attempted. The effect on Japanese pride was colossal, for the kami-kaze was literally regarded as a weapon from heaven, and from that time onwards the kami-kaze came to be seen as a symbol of Japan's divine protection, and the shrine of Ise earned more honour and respect than ever before. It may interest the reader to note that in adopting the name 'kami-kaze' the suicide pilots of the Second World War were deliberately identifying themselves with the divine tempest.

There is a slightly unsavoury rider to this heroic tale. The defeat of the Mongol armada had been a campaign in which no territory had been captured, so that when claims for reward started coming in there was no new land to bestow. Also, as the Shōgunate believed most strongly in the divine nature of the kami-kaze the religious foundations claimed pride of place in the distribution of any lands that should be made available. For example, a certain temple in Kyūshū proclaimed:

'. . . earnest prayers were offered; when the wicked invaders again arrived in 1281 and all persons, believing that the expulsion of the enemy could be effected only by divine will and never by human power . . . reverently looked up to heaven, [and] a divine storm rose in mighty force and scattered the enemy ships, and the enemy perished all at once. This was the victory achieved by the Heavenly-complete, greatly free, heavenly deity.'

Some temples went so far as to make up stories to obtain a better reward. In 1309 the Chief Priest of a Shintō shrine in Kyūshū complained that he had not yet received a reward, even though in 1274 the God of the shrine had shot arrows from its sanctuary, and that just before the kami-kaze blew three purple banners on top of the shrine had pointed towards the Mongol fleet!

With such competition the samurai had to be very insistent on their demands for reward. In fact none was granted until 1286. To this pressure we owe the *Mōko Shūrai Ekotoba*, from which Plates VI–VIII are taken. Takezaki Suenaga had it painted to illustrate his exploits in support of a claim for reward.

The Hōjō Regency was soon financially embarrassed by rewards, payment for religious services, and the maintenance of coastal defence for the next thirty years. The strain it put on the Shōgunate contributed not a little to the eventual collapse of the Hōjō domination, which is discussed in the next chapter. The temples alone did well out of it. The kami-kaze would have been an ill wind had it blown nobody any good.

6. Acts of loyalty

The fourteenth century in Japan is a period of contradictions. To some extent it was the golden age of disloyalty, where allegiances changed readily and frequently against a background of sporadic and increasingly irrelevant warfare. Yet it produced the most outstanding example of fidelity in the history of the samurai.

The long war of the fourteenth century arose out of the juxtaposition of two unlikely characters, a military dictator who was idle and dissipated, and an Emperor who was vigorous and active. The dictator was the Shōgunal Regent Hōjō Takatoki, whose greatest delights in life were dog-fighting, dancing and sex. The Emperor was Go-Daigo, who, on his succession to the throne in 1318 saw in the decline of the Hōjō Regency an opportunity to restore the Imperial power to the position it had formerly occupied, where he, as Emperor, would rule and not merely reign.

When the Bakufu forces failed to subdue a minor revolt in the north of Japan, Go-Daigo's challenge could be brought out into the open, and setting up one of his sons as Abbot of Mount Hiei, he began to court the old standby of the rebel, the warrior-monks. Among the samurai who rallied to his cause came one whose name has come to represent the ideal of the samurai warrior, Kusunoki Massashige. So in 1331 Japan found itself with the phenomenon of a samurai who was loyal to the Emperor. If that should strike the reader as odd, let him consider how the Emperors of Japan had been treated since the days of the Fujiwara. We have seen Emperors kept behind screens; we have seen them deposed, manipulated, kidnapped, and in one case drowned. They have been treated as pawns rather than as kings, reduced to rubber stamps for declarations of rebellion, or relegated to perpetual childhood under the system of 'Cloister Government'. Now we have a samurai who declares himself for the Emperor, as a living, human, adult Monarch, inspiring in his followers that same loyalty for which the feudal lords of two centuries ago had become proverbial.

Kusunoki Masashige was born in 1294 of Minamoto stock. Legend has it that Emperor Go-Daigo had a dream in which he was sheltering under a camphor tree ('Kusunoki'), and that this dream led him to the surname of the warrior who would support him.

In 1331 Go-Daigo left Kyōto with the Imperial Regalia and took refuge in the temple on the summit of Mount Kasagi. The Bakufu troops fancied that he might be hiding in the Enryaku-ji, and attacked

32　The Emperor Go-Daigo (1319–38). Wooden statuette in the Nyoirin-ji, Yoshino, traditionally supposed to have been carved by Go-Daigo himself during his years of exile.

95

33 Kusunoki Masashige (1294–1336), the outstanding example of samurai loyalty. Ivory statuette. (Lloyd collection, Manchester Museum.)

Mount Hiei in great force. The 'Prince Abbot' of Enryaku-ji escaped to join Kusunoki Masashige at Akasaka fortress in Kawachi, whose defences Kusunoki had hurriedly strengthened. The fortress consisted of a rectangular palisade 650 yards square, with simple wooden towers around the walls. Two hundred samurai manned Akasaka, while the remaining three hundred of Kusunoki's army positioned themselves on a neighbouring wooded hill.

The Bakufu samurai, seeing that the fortress was of such light construction and without moats or ditches, attempted to rush the walls, but were repulsed by the accurate archery of the defenders. The generals withdrew their men, and were resting in preparation for a renewed assault when the Loyalist force on the near-by hill fell on them, and Kusunoki led a sally out of the fortress driving the enemy back several miles. As the assaults of the Bakufu grew in intensity so did Kusunoki's ingenuity. Huge logs were suspended on the steep slopes of the hill by ropes, which the defenders cut when the attackers climbed on to them. Rocks, boiling water and pitch kept them off the walls.

The siege then developed into a blockade, which soon left Kusunoki with scarcely five days' provisions. He resolved to evacuate the fort, and planned an ingenious ruse to cover his tracks. A vast funeral pyre was prepared and covered with the bodies of the slain, and when all was ready the garrison stole away in twos and threes under cover of darkness, escaping by their superior knowledge of the forests and hills around. When all had disappeared, one samurai, who had volunteered to stay behind, set fire to the mound of corpses. At the sight of flames the Bakufu hastily advanced to find the solitary samurai who told them tearfully of the mass suicide of the great Kusunoki clan. The scene was too realistic to raise doubts, and the weeper was allowed to escape. Soon afterwards Kusunoki attacked and regained possession of Akasaka. Unfortunately this second occupation only lasted thirty days, for the Bakufu at last reduced it by cutting a trench which drained off its water supply. Once again Kusunoki escaped.

Emperor Go-Daigo had been less fortunate than his loyal followers, and had been captured after an attack on Kasagi. In 1332 he was exiled to Oki Island, but exile proved to be ineffective, and a year later he returned, hidden under seaweed in a fishing boat. By this time the whole of Western Japan was in turmoil, largely owing to the inspiring example of Kusunoki Masashige, who had now entrenched himself in the fortress of Chihaya, and was successfully tying down a large proportion of the Bakufu force in their endeavours to dislodge him, while daily gaining adherents for the Loyalist cause.

The attack on Chihaya cost the Bakufu dear, and after the first assault eight scribes were occupied for three days in listing the dead. It was a naturally strong position, being built on a hill separated by a deep valley from the hills around it. The ground was so difficult that the position was thought impregnable upon two sides, and nearly so upon the others.

The Bakufu had employed the trick that had worked at Akasaka, cutting off the water supply. But the defenders had their own well, and continued to reply to every attempt at forcing the siege with the usual shower of rocks and missiles. The besiegers tried to match cunning with cunning, and constructed a large wooden bridge which they dropped over the steepest and narrowest part of the ravine. On the day of the assault, when the bridge was packed with samurai, the defenders set fire to it.

In desperation the Bakufu tried bribery, and sent a message by arrow to one of Kusunoki's army whose loyalty was questionable. However the samurai took it straight to Kusunoki, who saw an opportunity for a trap. The Loyalists cut a deep trench behind the tower that was to be 'betrayed', and on a dark moonless night the enemy were admitted. As the leaders stumbled into the pit they were showered with missiles, and retreated so fast that the main body of the army took it to be a sortie by the garrison, and attacked their own men.

Kusunoki's defence of Chihaya, which contributed greatly to the Imperial cause, is regarded as one of the finest achievements in Japanese military history. Campaigns such as this led to the first change in samurai warfare since the Mongol invasions. The act of defending a fortress, or attacking one for a long period of time, made the use of horses unnecessary except as transport. The box-like 'yoroi' armour proved clumsy when dismounted, so with the increase in fighting on foot the design of Japanese armour was gradually modified. As the two-part construction of the yoroi made it slow to put on, it was replaced by a one-piece suit of armour that was basically the design worn previously only by the footsoldiers. In the hand-to-hand fighting of siegework the bow and arrow were an inconvenience, so gradually the features of yoroi that had been designed for mounted archers were discarded. The leather 'breastplate' disappeared, and the heavy skirts of the yoroi were replaced by several separate skirt pieces called 'kusazuri'. For close fighting many samurai chose a short bladed naginata, or a particularly vicious looking long sword called a 'no-dachi', similar to an old style naginata with a blade length of up to four feet. As a defence against sweeping strokes a form of thigh guard was introduced, and the helmet neckguard was made to sweep outwards rather than curve down so that the weapons might be more easily wielded. Two armoured sleeves were now worn, protection for the face was increased, and light sandals replaced fur riding boots.

It must be emphasized that these changes occurred gradually between about 1350 and 1500. Yoroi were still made and worn up to the end of the sixteenth century.

When Go-Daigo returned from exile the Bakufu decided to by-pass Kusunoki's outpost and launch a direct and speedy attack against the Emperor. They ordered one of their best generals, Ashikaga Takauji to march from Kamakura against Go-Daigo. Takauji, who was born in 1305, was a veteran of the assaults on Akasaka and Chihaya. He emerges as a sly, cunning character, who realized that his family, who were of Minamoto stock, might have much to gain from the present

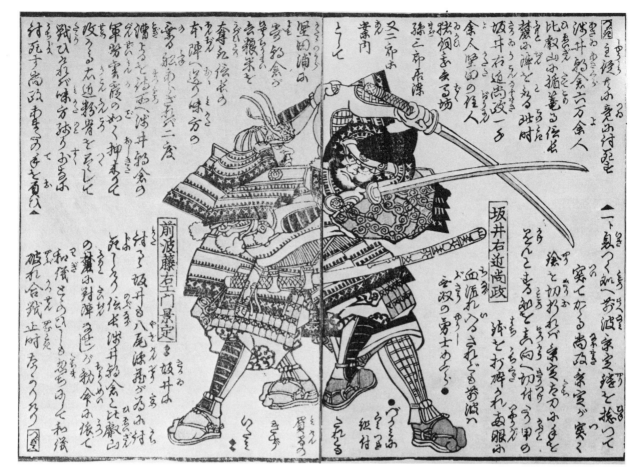

confusion. Consequently, as soon as his army was clear of Kamakura he declared his support for the Imperialist cause. On 10 June 1333 Ashikaga Takauji attacked Kyōto and killed the Bakufu representative there. This was a terrific blow to the Hōjō, but worse was to come. As many of the Bakufu samurai were still sitting in front of Chihaya Castle, the defences of Kamakura had been greatly weakened, and this weakness was exploited by another Minamoto descendant, Nitta Yoshisada. On or about 20 June Nitta Yoshisada raised the flag of revolt in his home province of Kōzuke, and his personal following soon grew to a vast army. Fighting all the way, the new Loyalist army under Nitta advanced on Kamakura.

Nitta's samurai marched to Kamakura in three columns. As the city was built among heavily wooded mountains the only approaches to it from the east or west lay along narrow valleys and tunnels. Thus the Bakufu were able to maintain a stubborn defence, and the leading Loyalist column was wiped out. Nitta eventually arrived at the sea coast at Inamuragasaki, where according to legend, he mounted the rocks and prayed to the Sun Goddess for help in destroying the usurpers of her descendants' power. As earnest of his intentions he flung his sword into

34 Close combat. As the mounted archer was rendered less effective by improvements in armour and the increase in fighting on foot, the Japanese sword at last came into its own. (E. G. Heath collection.)

the sea, and the waters parted like the Red Sea before Moses. In simpler language he waited for low tide and crossed the sands to attack the city from the south! Kamakura fell on 5 July, and the despised Hōjō Regent performed one last brave act when he committed suicide.

So Go-Daigo regained his throne, a more absolute monarch than any of his line for centuries. But if he thought that the clock could be turned back four hundred years, and the samurai, whose swords had secured his throne, would revert to being the military police and pirate quellers of an idle Court, he was much mistaken. It is unlikely that the wise Go-Daigo ever thought along these lines, but now the Hōjō Bakufu had fallen the Imperial power was the only government in existence.

Dissension began to arise when Go-Daigo commenced the necessary business of rewarding his loyal followers. Kusunoki and Nitta were well satisfied, but Ashikaga Takauji made his indignant dissatisfaction widely known. Events soon allowed him to pursue the course of action that he had been contemplating for some time. Hōjō Tokiyuki, a son of the late Takatoki, made a sudden attack on Kamakura and recaptured it in the name of the Hōjō family. Ashikaga Takauji was appointed to chastise the 'rebel', which he did without delay, proving his great military ability and his capacity for attracting men to his standard. Once established in Kamakura his behaviour became extremely suspicious. He soon declared hostilities against Nitta Yoshisada and seized his lands in Kōzuke. The result was that Go-Daigo's erstwhile supporter had abolished one Shōgunate to found another, and the war started again, with Nitta and Kusunoki supporting the Emperor against the Ashikaga house.

Ashikaga Takauji entered Kyōto on 25 February 1336, but was speedily displaced by Loyalists under Kitabatake Akiie, who joined forces with the monks of the Enryaku-ji. The Ashikaga troops allied themselves with Mii-dera, and here Kitabatake launched his attack. It was the old story of monk against monk, and once again in its chequered history Mii-dera was burnt to the ground. Takauji and his brother Tadayoshi were pursued by the victorious Loyalists until they were literally chased off the end of Honshū, and forced to cross to Kyūshū to attempt to raise support. Here Ashikaga Takauji hoped that support would be forthcoming, for when he had begun his revolt the previous November he had sent out identical calls to arms to several great warriors, chiefly in western Japan. That set in motion a chain of events that was to affect all samurai, forcing them to declare for one side or the other. One of these actual documents is preserved in the records of the Shibuya family of Iriki in Southern Kyūshū:

'[To Shibuya Shigemoto]
   Nitta Yoshisada shall be vanquished. It is hereby ordered that you gather the men of your family and immediately hasten to present yourselves.

17 November 1335   ASHIKAGA TAKAUJI'

Nitta Yoshisada, the leader of the Loyalist forces, was named as the enemy in order to avoid a direct reference to the person of the Emperor. The call was brief but effective, and when in March 1336 Takauji beat his precipitate retreat into Kyūshū the support waiting for him must have been most reassuring. As well as the Shibuya and other small families, the three powerful clans of Kyūshū, the Shimazu, the Shōni and the Ōtomo declared for the Ashikaga. Chief among their opponents in Kyūshū was the Kikuchi family, and the rivals soon met in battle at Tadara beach, near Hakata, on 14 April. This spot, three miles of white sand against a backcloth of green pinetrees, was surely the most picturesque battlefield in Japanese history. The resulting clash was a great victory for the Ashikaga, and within a month Ashikaga Takauji, with a greatly increased following, was on his way back to Kyōto.

The Shibuya lent their weight to the Ashikaga triumph in Kyūshū, and received prompt reward, as shown by a letter signed by Takauji the day before he left Hakata for Kyōto in May. In it he made a grant of land to Shibuya Shigemune, of the Taki branch of the family, 'as reward for his merit'. The Shibuya may well have accompanied Takauji on his advance to Kyōto. If they did so, then they would have been present at the decisive Battle of the Minatogawa.

The battle took place as Takauji was moving along the Inland Sea coast. At Tomo, about half way on the road to Kyōto, a council of war was held, at which it was decided to advance in two bodies, one by sea under Takauji, and the other by land under Ashikaga Tadayoshi, with a vanguard supplied by Shōni Yorihisa, who had come up from Kyūshū. As the two armies moved eastwards they were joined by a large sea borne reinforcement from Shikoku under the Hosokawa. On 24 June Takauji had reached Kojima in Bizen, and on 4 July dropped anchor off Akashi. Meanwhile the land forces had reached Ichi-no-tani, the scene of Yoshitsune's celebrated victory over the Taira in 1184. It was an auspicious place to spend the night before a battle.

There was some alarm at the news among the Loyalist supporters in Kyōto, as Nitta Yoshisada had been forced to withdraw in the face of the strong Ashikaga advance. Emperor Go-Daigo sent for Kusunoki Masashige and ordered him to reinforce Nitta. In an echo of the Hōgen Incident the military mind gave its opinion, and had it rejected. To Kusunoki the risk of a pitched battle was too dangerous to contemplate, and he advised Go-Daigo to take refuge on Mount Hiei, whereupon Takauji would be tempted to enter the capital. He could then be attacked by the combined force of monks and samurai, and Nitta would cut off his retreat. But the wise counsels of samurai were of no avail, and Kusunoki reluctantly accepted the Emperor's decision. In this most perfect example of samurai loyalty he made up his mind to die in battle, and set off with the conviction that he would never return. As he left, he told his son Masatsura that although he was prepared to forfeit his life for the Emperor he did it willingly, because he knew that some day Masatsura, then only ten years old, would take up the cause.

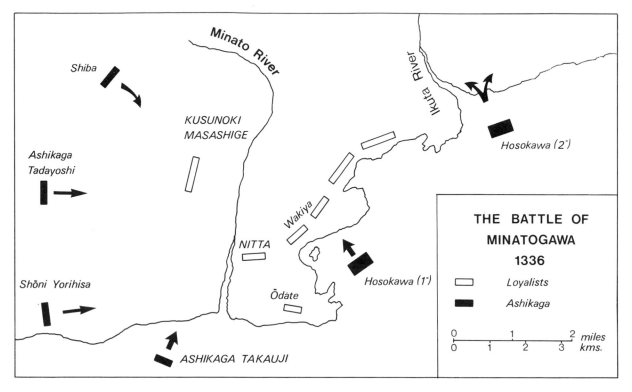

Shiba

Minato River

KUSUNOKI
MASASHIGE

Ashikaga
Tadayoshi

Ikuta River

Hosokawa (2°)

Wakiya

NITTA

Shōni Yorihisa

Ōdàte

Hosokawa (1°)

THE BATTLE OF
MINATOGAWA
1336

☐ Loyalists

■ Ashikaga

0   1   2 miles
0   1   2   3 kms.

ASHIKAGA TAKAUJI

35 Map showing the Battle of
Minatogawa, 1336.

Faced with the prospect of attack by sea as well as by land the
Loyalists took up their positions as shown in Fig. 35. Nitta Yoshisada,
who was in overall command, covered the sea coast from the Minato
River to the Ikuta River, while Kusunoki faced the land force of
Ashikaga Tadayoshi with his back to the Minato River. Tadayoshi
divided his army into three parts. He took the centre, leaving Shōni
to proceed along the coast and keep in touch with the fleet, while
Shiba mounted some high ground to threaten Kusunoki's flank.

The first fighting took place as Hosokawa's troops tried to land.
The Loyalist resistance was spirited, and Hosokawa's samurai were
driven back to their boats, and forced to move along the coast towards
the east. Meanwhile Nitta received an assault from Shōni, and as
Hosokawa soon managed to land at the mouth of the Ikuta River,
Nitta began to withdraw to face the new threat. This left Kusunoki
isolated on the other side of the Minato River. He managed to hold
off Tadayoshi and Shiba, but was put under severe pressure by the
landing of Takauji. Nitta was driven from the field by Hosokawa, and
by late afternoon, 5 July 1336, Kusunoki was being attacked from all
sides in the blazing heat. Eventually, covered with wounds, Kusunoki
Masashige committed hara-kiri, and the Loyalist cause was lost.

Thus Kusunoki Masashige entered the pantheon of Japanese heroes,
to join Prince Yamato and Yoshitsune as a paragon of samurai virtue.
In his life, as in his death, he was a solitary figure, perfect for the role
in which he was cast. His loyalty to the Emperor was unquestionable,

and of all Go-Daigo's supporters Kusunoki made the greatest sacrifices. At the time of the Meiji Restoration, five centuries later, it was Kusunoki Masashige who inspired the samurai who were inculcating the new devotion to the Emperor. In the fourteenth century Kusunoki stands supreme, as an example of loyalty that revered the person and not merely the institution of sovereignty.

Decisive though Minatogawa was, it did not end the fighting. The Ashikaga force entered Kyōto in triumph on 8 July, and Go-Daigo fled to Mount Hiei. Takauji set up another prince as Emperor Kōmyō, and to this new sovereign Go-Daigo surrendered the Crown Jewels on 12 November. But it afterwards turned out that these were not the genuine items of Regalia, but merely duplicates fabricated for the occasion. Go-Daigo thereupon left Mount Hiei for Yoshino, in the mountains south of Nara, and reigned from there as the legitimate sovereign. From 1337 until 1392 Japan had to deal with the odd problem of having two Emperors, the legitimate line in Yoshino known as the Southern Court, and the Ashikaga nominee in Kyōto known as the Northern Court.

Hostilities between the Courts continued throughout the period of schism. In 1338 Ashikaga Takauji was proclaimed officially as the first Ashikaga Shōgun. In the same year Nitta Yoshisada was killed, to be followed in 1339 by Emperor Go-Daigo, who is said to have died with a sword in his right hand and the *Lotus Sutra* in his left. Honouring the request of his father, Kusunoki Masatsura kept the flame of Loyalist resistance alive, and in 1347 took the leadership of the Southern Court army under Go-Daigo's successor, the twelve-year-old Go-Murakami. In 1348 he was attacked by Ashikaga troops under Kō Moronao and Kō Moroyasu. He promptly withdrew to Yoshino, where the young Emperor received him, and told him that he trusted the Kusunoki clan as he trusted his own elbows and thighs. At this Masatsura was greatly moved, and with his men worshipped at the tomb of Go-Daigo, upon which they cut their names with their swords. As he was leaving, Masatsura wrote a farewell poem on the temple door with an arrowhead. It read:

> 'I could not return, I presume,
> So I will keep my name
> Among those who are dead with bows.'

36 Door from the Nyoirin-ji, Yoshino, bearing the last poem of Kusunoki Masatsura (1326–48).

The door, still bearing the poem, is preserved at the Nyoirin-ji temple to this day. Masatsura set out from Yoshino with the small force, and was overtaken by the enemy at Shijo Nawate, and here, on 4 February 1348, took place the last stand of the Kusunoki clan. Masatsura was killed along with his brother Masatoki and his cousin Wada Takahide.

With the passing of the Kusunoki family the struggle between the Courts degenerated into a scramble for land, where the claims of the

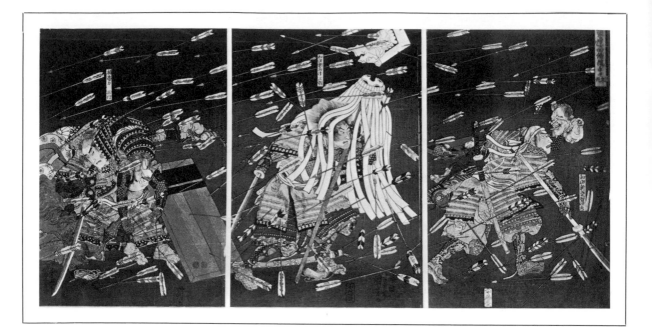

37 The last stand of the Kusunoki at the Battle of Shijō Nawate, 1348. Print by Utagawa Kuniyoshi (1798–1861). (Victoria and Albert Museum.)

rival dynasties were conveniently put aside in favour of personal jealousies and political ambitions. There is an element of farce about certain families' activities during the war, for they changed sides with bewildering rapidity. The most ridiculous situations arose when families who desired nothing but peaceful neutrality found themselves forced to declare for one side or the other. To choose the losing side meant financial ruin for the family. To safeguard against any such eventuality some families actually arranged for different branches to support different sides, so that any confiscated lands would remain in the family. This could result in mock warfare, as Sir James Murdoch says in his *History of Japan*: 'One party would erect a fort or stockade in a strategic position and provision themselves to maintain it; the other would raise a similar structure in the immediate neighbourhood. In the encounters between the two garrisons sword wounds were exceedingly rare, although there were occasional accidents in the exchange of arrows. The party whose provisions first gave out would retire. Thus when the recruiting agents appeared, the opposing chiefs could urge that they were too closely pressed at home to be able to spare any men for distant expeditions.'

The Iriki documents show how little the nominal 'causes' of the two Courts affected the Shibuya family, who had supported Takauji when he fled to Kyūshū. On 22 September Ashikaga Takauji recorded 'that the loyal acts of Shibuya Shigekatsu (the adopted son of Shigemoto, to whom the call to arms had been addressed) are excellent and will be rewarded.' Several months later Ashikaga Takauji was again recruiting, and wrote to 'the entire family of Shibuya' (see Appendix I for the Shibuya genealogy):

'Regarding the uprising of the insurgents of Satsuma province. We hear that you have rendered loyal service at arms in the province, which is excellent. In brief, we are despatching forces, you shall again start, and evermore distinguish yourselves by acts of loyalty.

27 May 1337   ASHIKAGA TAKAUJI'

Within a year the Shibuya had rendered 'acts of loyalty' by dividing into two factions, Southern and Northern, and fighting one another. The Tōgō and Taki branches of the family followed Takauji's call to arms and joined the Northern Court supporters. The Southern Court was followed by the Ketō and Iriki branches, including Shibuya Shigekatsu, who had been rewarded for his loyalty to the Northern Court the year before! That personal gain lay at the root of the fighting is clear from the extant documentation, which includes several reports known as 'gun–chū shō' (letters reporting loyal acts in war). After a battle in which he had rendered service, the samurai drew up a careful account of his exploits, describing his feats, his encounters with the enemy, and citing trustworthy eyewitnesses. The commander would certify the report, and it would then be forwarded to the appropriate authority for consideration of reward. Occasionally a commander would submit his own report on a samurai's conduct.

In July 1339 Shibuya Shigekatsu led the Iriki samurai in an attack on Ikari-yama, a fortress on the Sendai River being held for the Northern Court by the Tōgō branch of the family. In the vanguard was a samurai of the Izumi clan, who 'led the van at peril of death, and was the first to fall into the moat together with his horse, being wounded on the right hand.' Whether or not this worthy fellow submitted a report is not known, but a *gun–chū shō* was certainly forthcoming from one of the defenders, Saburo Toshimasa, who wrote his report in the third person, and had the advantage of naming his own commanding officer as witness to his feats:

'. . . [On 29 July] Toshimasa fought [at the turret] by the river; but hearing on the same day, at the hour of the cock, that the enemy had broken down the main entrance of the fortress, [Toshimasa] hastened to the main entrance and did service, and repulsed the enemy. These acts were witnessed at the same place by Sakawa Hisakage. . . .

'. . . At the night battle of 1 August, when the enemy tried to break down the entrance [facing] the river, and our forces issued from the little gate [facing] the river with a view to dispersing the enemy, Toshimasa as [leader of] these forces went out of the fortress and repulsed the enemy, as was witnessed by the present commander.

'. . . Therefore in order that at once, in accordance with the facts of his service at arms, [his merits] be reported, and also that he be granted a certifying seal, he presents a brief statement thus.

August 1339.'

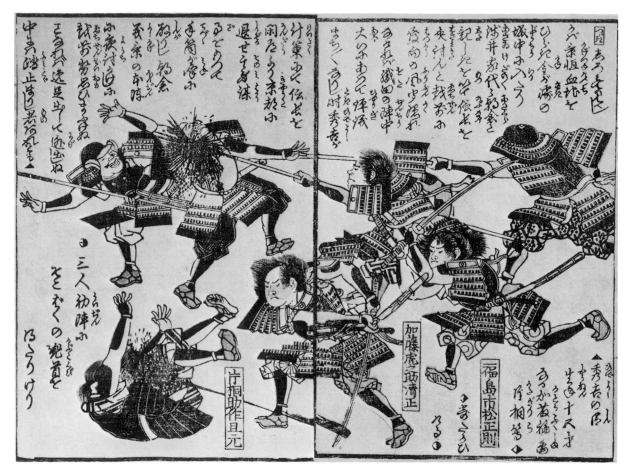

38 Samurai in action in classic style, where warfare was conducted at a run. (E. G. Heath collection.)

The document was countersigned by the commanding officer, Sakawa Hisakage, and sent to Ashikaga Takauji in Kyōto. As Hisakage had personally witnessed Toshimasa's exploits he felt sufficiently confident of the latter's eventual reward to grant Toshimasa some vacated land there and then, promising to increase the reward when more land became available and the necessary authority had been obtained.

The failure to take Ikari-yama was a small setback to the Southern cause. The following year Prince Kanenaga, who had been invested by his late father, Emperor Go-Daigo, with the control of affairs in Kyūshū, arrived in Satsuma. His coming put new heart into the Southern Court followers, and those branches of the Shibuya who had supported the Southern Court hastened to pledge their allegiance. They were joined by the Tōgō branch, who thought it wise to change sides when royalty was present, while the Terao branch, who had hitherto been lukewarm in their loyalty towards the Southern Court, received overtures from the other side. Soon the Shibuya samurai who had chosen the Northern faction were drawn into hostilities on behalf of their powerful neighbours the Shimazu, who were the strongest supporters of the Ashikaga's puppet in Southern Kyūshū. One of their kinsmen, Shimazu Tadakuni, had risen in revolt, and had come near to attacking the Satsuma capital of Kagoshima. In 1346 the Shibuya lent their aid, which led to Nikaidō Yukinaka, the Shimazu general at the fortress of Ikebe, writing the following report on the disgraceful conduct of the Shibuya family:

'. . . Next, as men of the Shibuya family had built defences at No-zaki village, in Yukinaka's domain, and guarded them as an aid to the present fortress, the rebels came in large force on 21 July, and in order to take No-zaki by assault, established a counter fortress . . . near by. On 19 September, at the hour of the hare, all the men of Shibuya, without leaving a single soul, deserted the fortress and withdrew.'

The letter ended in dramatic style, as Nikaidō Yukinaka reported on their present plight in Ikebe fortress:

'. . . the means of procuring supplies has been exhausted; it has therefore been resolved that shortly the crops should be cut and a last battle given, to certain death. Therefore it is prayed that, not only for the pacification of the province, but also for the succour of this fortress, orders be speedily issued, inspiring the [defenders'] courage to achieve loyal services. Since the roads are difficult, [the signatories] beg leave to write on half sheets. It is desired that the import of this letter be presented [to the lord]. With reverence,

NIKAIDŌ YUKINAKA
ISAKU MUNEHISA'

The plea must have been heard, for Ikebe was still in the hands of the Shimazu two years later. As regards the desertion by the Shibuya, the above report was forwarded by Shimazu Sadahisa to Ashikaga Tadayoshi, which was the most that the Shimazu could effectively do, as the Shibuya were not their vassals, but merely happened to live in the same province. Ashikaga Tadayoshi wrote back:

'Your frequent reports on the war in Satsuma have been read. . . . [you report that] men of the Shibuya family and others deserted the camp and returned home. If this is true, it is exceedingly wrong. They should again be called forth by strict order. If they are still obdurate, we shall, on receiving a renewed report, confiscate their domains. . . . Ordered thus.

3 January 1347   ASHIKAGA TADAYOSHI'

39 A white and red silk-laced suit of armour of 'haramaki' style, opening at the back. (Ōyamazumi Shrine Museum, Ōmishima.)

One branch of the Shibuya however, the Okamoto, remained loyal to the Shimazu, and therefore to the Northern Court. Shibuya (Okamoto) Shigeoki, Shigekatsu's brother, took part in a heroic defence of the fortress of Tōfuku-ji, and presented the following *gun-chū shō*, countersigned by his commander, Hatakeyama Naoaki:

'Shibuya Shigeoki reports his loyal service in war. [Shigeoki] was the first to hasten to [the fortress] Tōfuku-ji on the 11 July. While he was awaiting the arrival of the forces on our side, at the hour of the hare, on 14 July, thousands of Kumano pirates and other men rushed in from both land and sea. Though deficient in numbers, [Shigeoki] defended [the fortress] at the peril of his life, killed several rebels, and repulsed the enemy. The retainer Tō-shirō was wounded [a sword cut on the forehead]. These circumstances were witnessed by Nomoto Magoshichi, the attendant [of the commander] who fought at the same time.'

Such heroics led to Shigeoki being summoned to war again, this time by the Shōgun's Deputy in Kyūshū, Isshiki Noriuji. In Honshū the fortunes of the Northern Court were looking a little brighter owing to the death in February 1348 of the valiant Kusunoki Masatsura, but in Kyūshū the Shimazu, as the chief supporters, were by no means having it all their own way. The fortress of Ikebe was again in trouble:

'It is reported that the rebels of Satsuma province have [of late] been particularly turbulent. You shall render loyal service in war in strict obedience, and succour the fortress of Ikebe. Therefore the order is conveyed thus.

19 March 1348   ISSHIKI NORIUJI.'

Discretion, however, is said to be the better part of valour, and six months later Shibuya Shigeoki received a further letter from the Deputy:

'Since it was rumoured that the rebels of Satsuma province would attack the fortress of Ikebe. It has previously been ordered that you should give it your aid. It is reported that this has not been done. What is the reason? You shall speedily hasten thither and subdue [the enemy]. Therefore the order is conveyed thus.

10 September 1348   ISSHIKI NORIUJI.'

The reason for Shigeoki's failure to act may be guessed from the fact that in 1351 he changed sides on receipt of a call to arms issued by Prince Kanenaga of the Southern Court. A similar summons was sent to his brother Shibuya Shigekatsu of the Iriki branch, of whom we last

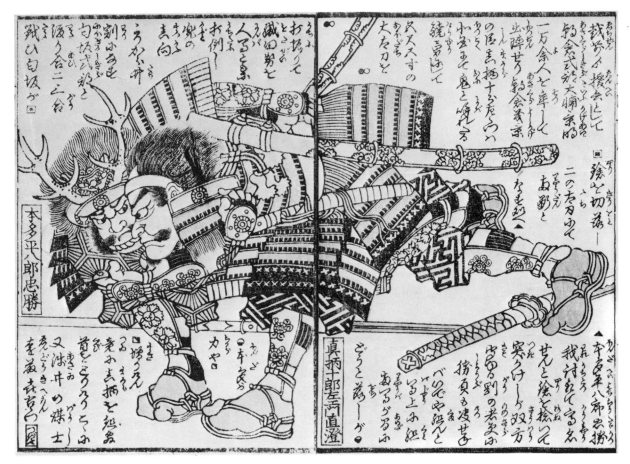

heard in 1339 when he attacked Ikari-yama on the Southern Court's behalf. The tone of the letter implies that at some time between 1339 and 1348 Shigekatsu had changed sides for the second time, back to the Northern Court!

    '[To] The residence of Shibuya Shigekatsu.
    '[His Majesty] has heard that you would come to his side. You shall at once attach yourself to the Prince and do loyal military service. Any distinguished service which you may render will be rewarded. The Imperial pleasure is hereby conveyed.

25 August 1351'

    Both Shigekatsu and Shigeoki responded to the call, and did good service. This put the Shibuya family in an equivocal position, for the complex web of Japanese politics at this time forced a temporary and unholy alliance between the Prince and the Shimazu clan, who until then had been his deadliest enemies in the whole of Kyūshū. The alliance implied that Shibuya Shigeoki had effectively not changed sides at all,

40 Grappling. Considering the number of weapons about the samurai's person it is unlikely that bare hands decided the outcome of an individual combat except on rare occasions. (E. G. Heath collection.)

for his former master was now allied with his present master. As Shigeoki's own operations were directed entirely against his own kinsmen, the Tōgō branch (who had already once changed sides themselves), the actual cause for which he was fighting probably never entered his head. All that mattered was that on 10 January 1352, Shigeoki submitted another *gun-chū shō*, citing his commander as witness. 'Distinguished service' was again recorded.

For the next six years no service for either side is recorded for the Shibuya family. As this period was a bad time for their powerful neighbours, the Shimazu, it is likely that the Shibuya sat back to await developments, in case the mighty Shimazu were vanquished, and with them the cause of the Northern Court in that area of Japan.

In 1358 the Prince wrote to Shibuya Shigeoki acknowledging a pledge of support that, presumably, he must have received a few months earlier. However, 1362 found Shigeoki returned to the Northern side when he supported the Shimazu in their campaigns against the Izumi. The following document is the last record we have of him on the battle-field. Note that it is signed by the second Ashikaga Shōgun, Takauji having died from cancer in 1358:

'It has recently been reported that since the second month of last year you have rendered loyal service in battles in Satsuma. That was excellent. It is hereby commanded that you shall continue evermore to achieve distinguished service in arms.

24 September 1362   ASHIKAGA YOSHIAKIRA.'

Shibuya Shigekatsu, meanwhile, had gone as a guest to the White Jade Pavilion, leaving the affairs of the Iriki branch of the family in the hands of his son and heir, Shigekado. In 1364 Shigekado was approached by the Southern Court and promised rewards for service, which Shigekado began to render, while his son, Shigeyori, joined the Northern Court. In 1365 Shigeyori received a letter of commendation from the Shōgunal Deputy rewarding his loyal service. A year later he changed sides, and received a letter in similar vein from the representative of the Prince.

By 1371 the popularity of the Southern Court in Kyūshū so alarmed the Shōgun that a new, more able Deputy was appointed to the island, Imagawa Ryō-shun. He was both a general and a diplomat, and on his arrival in Kyūshū began to canvass for support. The Iriki Shibuya received three calls to arms between December 1372 and March 1373, promising them that their domains would be undisturbed and would indeed be increased should special service be rendered. However the Iriki remained loyal (if the word can still be used) to the Southern Court, and had already fought gallantly on the side of Imagawa's enemies when the first of his calls reached them. On 24 July 1372 Shibuya Shigekado led the Iriki samurai with contingents from the

Ketō, Tōgō and Taki branches, against the fortress of Mine, held for the Shimazu by Yamada Tadafusa. The besiegers were at first repulsed, but Shigekado climbed down into the moat and, as he was clambering up the opposite bank to the fortress, his helmet was broken by a rock thrown from the ramparts. He fell into the moat and perished. Inspired by his example the Shibuya attacked with renewed vigour, taking the fort and the commander's head. They moved on and invested Ikari-yama, before which Shigekado's father had failed in 1339. Shimazu Ujihisa hurried to raise the siege, and at the approach of a fresh Shimazu army the Shibuya prudently withdrew, thus avoiding a showdown between the two clans.

Shibuya Shigekado's heroism did not go unrewarded, for Prince Kanenaga wrote to Shigeyori:

'His Imperial Highness has heard with praise that your father died at the battle of Mine fortress in Satsuma. You will be rewarded. By order, his word is transmitted thus.

11 January 1373'

In 1375 Shibuya Shigeyori, in spite of such generosity, changed sides again, but by now the notion of Southern Court or Northern Court had become utterly meaningless. The Shimazu were always loyal at heart to the Shōgun, but disliked his deputy, and this led to a series of defections by the Shimazu. As for the Shibuya, the main motive for their choice of side was their unwillingness to serve with the Shimazu. So, whichever side the Shimazu chose, the Shibuya would immediately shift to the other.

In December 1375 the Shōgunal Deputy acknowledged Shibuya Shigeyori's services, and two years later the Shibuya fought for the Shōgun against the Shimazu. As late as 1385 the Shibuya were still in arms against the Shimazu, ostensibly on behalf of the Shōgunate, but by now the original cause was forgotten. Prince Kanenaga died in 1383, and finally, on 16 December, 1392, the Southern Court capitulated unconditionally. The Emperor of the South, Go-Kameyama, abdicated, and transferred the Imperial Regalia to the Emperor Go-Komatsu of the North. It was the end of the schism that had divided the country for fifty-six years.

The decline in the samurai ideal during the war between the Courts is reflected in the virtual abandonment of the old formalities of combat, such as the calling of pedigrees and the challenge of a worthy opponent. In the 'Golden Age of the Turncoat' anyone was a worthy opponent, and the grandiose challenge was replaced by the anonymous missile. Looking at the fourteenth century in the light of the Shibuya's experiences, the loyalty of Kusunoki Masashige becomes almost unique in its steadfastness. One may question whether the majority of the samurai of the fourteenth century were capable of being loyal to anyone, let alone the Emperor.

7. The age of the Country at War

From the tribulations of Princes we now turn to the opposite end of the social spectrum. So far, the Japanese peasant has hardly been mentioned in our history, but as the fourteenth century gives way to the fifteenth it is this neglected and despised class of humanity that first demands our attention. The peasant farmer lived his life against a constant background of warfare in which he took little part. As warfare became a more professional business during the Wars between the Courts the idea of the 'samurai-farmer' began to disappear. The high-ranking samurai, at any rate, did nothing but fight, and the lowest ranking peasant did nothing but till the soil. In between the two extremes was a wide and shadowy borderline of small landowners who, when not campaigning, had to cultivate their lands for reasons of sheer economic necessity, and the more prosperous sort of peasant. These may well have been wealthier than a neighbouring 'ji-samurai', as the small landowners were called, and would not be averse to carrying arms. At this time the status of the samurai was by no means rigid, and the opportunities for upward social mobility and promotion in military rank were there for anyone who had the drive and ability to seize them.

To some extent the Japanese peasant was in a curious position. Unlike his counterpart in contemporary Europe the seemingly endless wars that cut swathes of destruction across his rice fields affected his person very little. Largely because the wars were civil wars the peasant had little to fear from armies. There was no rape or slaughter of civilians, and if his flimsy hut was burned down it could easily be rebuilt. The only real danger was the risk of starvation when crops were trampled or stolen. Apart from this the peasant was largely an irrelevance to the samurai as he rode proudly by to fight his next meaningless engagement. What the peasant dreaded was not the scourge of war, but disease, famine, and above all the tax-collector, who in Ashikaga times was known to have exacted a rate of up to seventy per cent of all that the peasant produced.

In the early years of the fifteenth century the worm began to turn. In the whole of Japanese history there had never been anything akin to a peasant rising, yet suddenly, the people who had been as docile as sheep for hundreds of years seemed completely changed. With the organizational skills of the ji-samurai, and the impetus of their warlike nature, a genuine popular mood of indignation found expression in the formation of leagues for mutual defence, or 'ikki'. Very soon the ikki were to take their grievances to the seats of power, as the warrior-monks had done centuries earlier, and a series of 'peasants' revolts' began.

The first ikki appeared during the later years of the War between the Courts, but it was not until 1428 that the inhabitants of Kyōto felt the fury of the mob. In that year there was a massive uprising against certain financial edicts aimed at the peasants. As if this were a signal to the discontented masses there were similar risings all over the country. In 1441 Kyōto suffered the fiercest rising of all, which unlike the 1428 demonstration was carefully planned months beforehand. The peasants chose their moment well, and marched on Kyōto while the samurai of the Ashikaga Bakufu were engaged far away in Harima province. On 15 September the ikki gathered in the approaches to the city, where there was a fierce clash between them and samurai of the Kyōgōku clan. There were ten casualties on the ikki side and fifty-three on the other. Four days later the mob began rioting and burning on the fringe of Kyōto, and on 21 September thousands of ikki members attacked the city, seized strategic buildings and blocked roads. To the citizens it must have seemed as if the world had gone mad. Within two days Kyōto was completely cut off from the outside world. Chronicles of the time, like the following from the Tōji district of Kyōto, sound like war reports:

'The ikki from east of the road that descends from Toba and Kisshōin occupied Tōji. There were about two or three thousand of them. On the same day the Tamba-guchi ikki entered Imanishinomiya with about one thousand men. . . . They have ringed the city with camps. . . . Every day they raid into the centre of the city'.

The main targets of the ikki attack were the pawnbrokers and moneylenders, with a view to forcing the cancellation of bad debts. But the mob's fury did not end there, and after a week of indiscriminate rioting and looting the Bakufu was forced to issue a debt-cancelling edict. The success of the 1441 riot having established a pattern, the ikki returned to Kyōto in 1447, 1451, 1457, and 1461. Although none reached the scale of the 1441 riot several were quite impressive in their scope. During the 1457 disturbances a full-scale battle took place between ikki members and mercenary samurai hired by the moneylenders. The ikki successfully vanquished the mercenaries, then took on a Bakufu army of 800 samurai and soundly beat them.

For a dissatisfied peasant there was an alternative to rioting. This was to abscond and join an army. Local lords often needed fighting men, and the loose organization of their armies made it easy for a peasant to join up. All he required were weapons and armour. These items could easily be obtained in view of the number of dead and wounded samurai to be found in most localities. The possibility of reward was slight, as reward was becoming increasingly dependent on the *gun-chū shō* report, but there was always loot to be had. A good commander could make successful use of these peasant soldiers, who were called 'ashigaru', a word which literally means 'light feet'. As they were also very light-fingered discipline was a major problem.

The rise of the ikki and the ashigaru is the first indication of the trend referred to by Japanese historians as 'gekokujō' (the low oppress the high), which reached its zenith fifty or so years later when old established warrior houses were overthrown by their own vassals, or even by ikki. However, in the 1460s the high were too busy digging their own graves to worry about the low. In 1467 there began the Civil War of Ōnin, surely the most wasteful and destructive war that the samurai ever conducted.

The most remarkable feature about the Ōnin War, which began during the first year of the year period of 'Ōnin', hence the name, was that practically all the fighting took place within Kyōto itself. At the time of the outbreak of hostilities in 1467 the capital was still a magnificent city. It had received a new lease of life with the fall of Kamakura, as Ashikaga Takauji had regarded Kamakura as too remote from the centre of political life, and had brought the Ashikaga Shōgunate to Kyōto. The Bakufu headquarters were in the district known as 'Muromachi', which gave its name to the Muromachi Period of Japanese history. In 1378 Ashikaga Yoshimitsu, the third Ashikaga Shōgun, built a magnificent palace named 'Hana-no-Gosho', or The Palace of Flowers, which was, significantly, twice the size of the Imperial Palace. Incidentally, Yoshimitsu's other contribution to Japanese architecture was the 'Kinkaku-ji', the world famous Gold Pavilion, built to the west of the city.

41   *Gekokujō* (the low oppress the high) in its most savage form. A group of ashigaru overpower a wounded samurai. (E. G. Heath collection.)

114

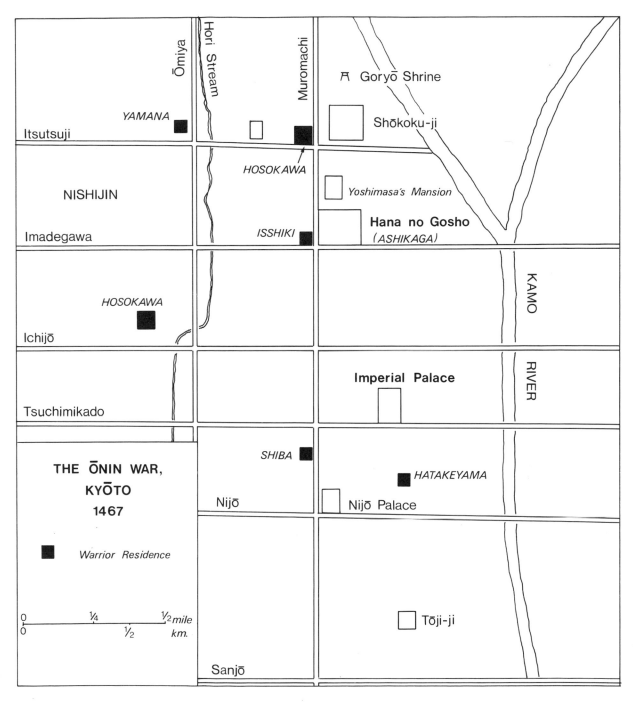

Itsutsuji

Ōmiya

Hori Stream

Muromachi

YAMANA

Goryō Shrine

Shōkoku-ji

HOSOKAWA

NISHIJIN

Imadegawa

Yoshimasa's Mansion

Hana no Gosho
(ASHIKAGA)

ISSHIKI

HOSOKAWA

Ichijō

KAMO

RIVER

Imperial Palace

Tsuchimikado

THE ŌNIN WAR,
KYŌTO
1467

SHIBA

Nijō

HATAKEYAMA

Nijō Palace

Warrior Residence

| 0 | ¼ | ½ mile |
| 0 | ½ | km. |

Tōji-ji

Sanjō

The establishment of the Bakufu headquarters in Muromachi led many of the major military houses to build their mansions near by. Thus by 1467 most of the important samurai maintained residences within a small area of Northern Kyōto, bounded on the south by Sanjō (third avenue) and on the east by the Kamo River. In 1467 this graceful

42 Map showing the part of Kyōto affected by the Ōnin War (1467–77).

115

district, within a matter of months, became a battlefield. To follow the subsequent activities the reader is referred to the map in Fig. 42, which shows clearly that Kyōto still retained its grid system of intersecting avenues and streets. As the city was almost completely destroyed during the Ōnin War the positions of the warrior residences are only approximate, and are taken from descriptions of their location.

The actual causes of the Ōnin War were complicated, and were in fact little more than excuses for conflict between the two most powerful warrior families in Kyōto at the time, the Yamana and the Hosokawa. The leader of the Yamana, Mochitoyo, was an excessively ambitious leader of men. He had been born in 1401, and inherited the domains of his father in 1435. In 1441 he had entered the priesthood, taking the name of Yamana Sōzen, by which he is usually known. His excessive rages and tantrums, which drove him near to fits, earned him the nickname of the 'Red Monk', for during such attacks his countenance became scarlet.

Strange to relate, his enemy, Hosokawa Katsumoto, was his son-in-law. Katsumoto, born in 1430, was of a character diametrically opposite to that of his tempestuous father-in-law. While the Red Monk raged Hosokawa kept calm. His administration was able and his followers were content. He remained above all intrigue, preferring to let others intrigue for him.

For a number of years previous to Ōnin the two rivals had been meddling in the affairs of other families. There was a succession dispute in the Hatakeyama family in 1450, and soon after one in the Shiba. Yamana made as much political capital as he could out of the situations, hoping thereby to gain allies for the eventual showdown with Hosokawa. Eventually there came an ideal excuse for a dispute. The Ashikaga Shōgun, Yoshimasa, expressed a desire to abdicate. This was not a political move to rule behind the scenes as a sort of 'Cloistered-Shōgun', but rather a gesture of complete and utter boredom. Yoshimasa was an aesthete, who spent his days in poetic fancy, indulging his passion for beauty and the arts. This left him no time for the affairs of state, except for the necessary business of tax-collection to pay for his pleasures. He spent vast sums on entertainments, and ran up such huge bills that he was once forced to pawn his suit of armour – perhaps the one thing he least desired to keep. Yoshimasa had no son to whom he could pass the Shōgunate, so he brought out his brother Yoshimi from a monastery and startled the young man by proclaiming him as his heir. Unfortunately, a year later Yoshimasa's wife gave birth to a son, and hastened to proclaim the rights of her offspring. Yamana Sōzen offered his support for the cause of the infant Yoshihisa, while Hosokawa Katsumoto pledged his loyalty to the brother Yoshimi. The two rivals had now arranged themselves on opposite sides in a dispute concerning the highest in the land.

Both Yamana and Hosokawa realized that their long-awaited conflict was nigh, so they summoned the forces at their disposal. Yamana could muster 80,000, including allies, while Hosokawa could raise 85,000, and his men were more dependable. It soon became clear that the battlefield was to be the city itself, as both sides looked around for suitable houses to use as headquarters and studied the strategic position of the northern streets.

At this point Ashikaga Yoshimasa began to appreciate the danger that threatened, and issued a warning to both commanders that whosoever struck the first blow would be declared a rebel, and would have to suffer the consequences. This was no idle threat, for to be declared a rebel would tend to alienate the clan from all support, and give an excuse to any adventurer to attack the 'rebel's' domains.

By the first year of Ōnin tension was rising in the city. Samurai began gathering at the rival mansions, but the citizens made a brave show of carrying on as usual. In February 1467 Hosokawa received reports that Ōuchi, a lord from the Western Provinces, was marching to Kyōto with 20,000 men in support of Yamana. At the end of the month the mansion of one of Hosokawa's generals mysteriously went up in flames. In April Hosokawa samurai attacked a group of Yamana's troops bringing rice into the city. The crisis was imminent, and all the citizens who could flee began evacuating the city. The younger members of the Royal Family were moved south for safety, and the guard on the Imperial Palace was doubled as rumours flew about of impending attacks. At the Hosokawa mansion the sliding doors and translucent screens were removed from the walls, and replaced by wooden shutters inlaid with clay as a protection against fire. Under the command of Katsumoto's foster son the Hosokawa samurai gathered in the garden, hidden from enemy view by the high walls.

The fighting began at the end of May, when the Hosokawa attacked the mansion of Isshiki, one of Yamana's generals, directly across Muromachi Street from the palace of Flowers. The fighting continued for a few days, and as it spread gave some indication of the ruin that was to come. In the wake of the fighting came the looting and burning, and soon the whole block containing the Isshiki mansion was burned out. For the next month similar raids and attacks continued, and the samurai virtues flourished amidst the ruin of a fine city. One warrior wrote a pathetic message to Hosokawa at the conclusion of a particularly fierce day's fighting. 'We are tired,' he wrote. 'Would you please send me a cask of sake? I will share it with Masanaga, then we will commit hara-kiri together.'

The anonymous samurai still thought of his comrades in spite of his own despair, and concluded with a plea for extra weapons to be forwarded, as a number of their arrow bearers had 'got lost' that morning.

By the beginning of July much of Northern Kyōto had been reduced to rubble and ashes. Barricades had been built across the streets, and as the houses disappeared the defences were augmented by trenches, particularly across the wide Ichijō (first avenue) where opposing lines of trenches were dug by both sides. The front lines of both armies were now becoming established. Yamana's defences were centred west of

Muromachi Street, roughly bounded by the streets Itsusuji and Ōmiya, with the main encampment between Itsusuji and Imadegawa, an area still known as 'Nishijin' (western camp). The Hosokawa had been forced into a smaller area east of Muromachi and north of Imadegawa, which contained the Ashikaga Palace of Flowers and a large Zen monastery called the Shōkoku-ji. It also contained one of Hosokawa's residences. The other, on Ichijō, had long since been abandoned to the Yamana.

The Hosokawa's sole success during this month was to persuade the Shōgun to have Yamana declared the rebel, even though Hosokawa had struck the first blow, but the declaration stopped short of granting Hosokawa a commission to subdue his rival. Meanwhile Yamana had received reinforcements. In September Ōuchi Masahiro arrived, and his 20,000 troops put new heart into the rebel Red Monk, so that he stepped up the offensive. Hosokawa's communications were already cut to the west, and on 29 September Yamana began to isolate him from the south by attacking and burning the Imperial Palace. The Emperor was not there, as Hosokawa had anticipated Yamana's action and removed him to the Palace of Flowers.

At the end of October Yamana attacked the Shōkoku-ji, having first bribed a monk to set fire to it. The great Zen establishment was very near Yoshimasa's mansion, and the conflagration alarmed the ladies inside. The Shōgun, however, was unperturbed, and in his usual high spirits continued with a drinking party. Fighting went on among the hot ashes until night fell, and both sides retired exhausted. The carnage had been fearful, and the narrow streets were choked with corpses. Ōuchi Masahiro filled eight carts with the heads of the slain. There were many more, which the tired samurai merely tossed into the nearest ditch. It is no wonder that at the end of 1467 a Shōgunal official could write:

'The flowery capital that we thought would last for ever has to our surprise become the lair of foxes and wolves. In the past there have been revolts and disasters, but in this first year of Ōnin the laws of gods and Emperors have been broken and all the sects are perishing.

'Now the city that you know
Has become an empty moor,
From which the skylark rises
While your tears fall.'

During the first few months of 1468 the fighting abated somewhat, yet, incredibly, the Ōnin War still had nine years to run. The pile of ashes that had been the Shōkoku-ji was recaptured, and Hosokawa's men made a raid on the Yamana supply line. But from April the fighting settled down into the tedium of what was virtually trench warfare, as the two sides glared at each other from barricades and prepared positions. No-man's-land was an expanse of blackened timbers being slowly buried under a growth of weeds, divided in two by a trench twenty feet wide and ten feet deep. The Yamana hoped to starve the Hosokawa into submission, and indeed looked likely to do so for they controlled seven out of the eight exits from the city. Yet no impression was made either way.

So the months passed, enlivened by the occasional raid on the opposing positions, and bombardment by catapults from the Hosokawa side. Behind the lines high-ranking samurai amused themselves by composing verse and acting Chinese drama. What real fighting took place during 1468 had moved out to the borders of the city, while the lines remained relatively tranquil. The Tenryū-ji, a monastery on the eastern outskirts of Kyōto, fell victim in this way.

As the months grew into years even the fire-breathing Red Monk began to long for peace. Hosokawa was greatly inclined the same way, but between them they had raised up a Frankenstein's monster. The Ōnin War began to assume a bizarre and terrible life of its own which even their efforts could not stop. The fighting had now spread to the provinces, and their allies and subordinates were so carried away with euphoria that a truce was impossible. So many ashigaru had been recruited that neither army knew exactly what fighting was going on. In desperation Hosokawa thought of becoming a monk, and Yamana contemplated hara-kiri. However, release from their worries was nearer than expected, for the Red Monk died on 16 May 1473, and on the following 6 June Hosokawa followed him. Ōuchi Masahiro was now left in command of the Western forces, upon whom the stigma of 'rebel' was at last having some effect. Finally, on the night of 17 December 1477, the sky of Kyōto glowed red as the Western army burned their positions and melted away into the night, leaving the capital city of Japan 'one with Nineveh and Tyre'.

As the samurai moved out, the mob moved in. Bands of rioters, many of whom were ashigaru, continuing the struggle, occupied those portions of the city that had been spared during the war. Monasteries were invaded, where the bells were rung day and night to announce the mob's presence to the citizenry. Pawnbrokers were looted. Sake brewers were broken into and their stocks distributed among the rioters, making the whole affair one vast drunken brawl.

It may occur to the reader to ask what Shōgun Yoshimasa, whose title, after all, means 'Barbarian-subduing Commander-in-Chief', was doing to alleviate the problem. It is hardly exaggerating to say that Yoshimasa fiddled while Kyōto burned. He had not managed to abdicate from the post of Shōgun until 1474, and as Yoshihisa was then only nine years old he continued to rule, and ruled very badly. His utter detachment from reality, which was noted at the beginning of the Ōnin War, continued unabated throughout, and at the end of the war he commenced the building of a 'stately pleasure dome' at Higashiyama, the hills to the east of Kyōto. Its buildings included the 'Ginkaku-ji' or silver pavilion, built in imitation of his grandfather's Golden Pavilion.

It was never actually covered with silver foil as the money ran out before the building was completed. Here Yoshimasa held flower-viewing parties and poetry readings, and developed the tea ceremony as the last vestiges of Ashikaga power fell about his ears.

An indication of the shape of things to come was given in 1485, the year the Tudor Dynasty was established in England. The fighting spawned by the Ōnin War was particularly fierce in Yamashiro province, where the main contenders were two branches of the Hatakeyama family. Their armies had reached stalemate, and sat glowering at each other while consuming the substance of the agricultural population. In 1485 the ji-samurai and local peasants deserted *en masse* from the rival armies. They formed a fortified camp of their own, from which they issued an ultimatum, consisting of three demands, to the commanders:

1. Both armies to withdraw immediately from Yamashiro.
2. All manors to be restored to their owners.
3. All toll barriers to be demolished.

Within two weeks all three demands had been met in full. From this victory Yamashiro ikki went from strength to strength. In 1486 they proclaimed a provisional government for Yamashiro after a meeting in the historic Byōdō-in at Uji.

By far the most important development in ikki took place at this time in Kaga province. It will be recalled that one of the most important religious revivals of the thirteenth century was the founding of the Ikkō sect, with its belief in salvation by faith in Amida. The head of the sect in the fifteenth century was Rennyō (1415–99) who achieved such fame as a preacher that in 1465 the monks of the Enryaku-ji had burned his house and forced him to flee. He then began touring the country, and in 1471 settled in Kaga, where he built a church which was constantly thronged with believers, most of whom came of peasant stock, for Rennyō's repudiation of the aristocratic side of Buddhism, and his scriptures written in a simple style, appealed directly to these people. The Ikkō sect had always allowed priests to marry, and Rennyō took advantage of this to leave twenty-nine children behind him when he died at the ripe old age of eighty-four.

Kaga province had become inextricably wound up in the Ōnin War, and Togashi Masachika, a prominent lord in Kaga, enlisted the aid of the fanatical Ikkō believers in his struggle. This was the beginning of the Ikkō-ikki, an army that resembled the warrior-monks of Hiei in its ecclesiastical basis, and excelled them in its warlike fury. The Ikkō-ikki received tremendous support, particularly from the lower classes. Ikkō taught that death in battle was a death rewarded by paradise, so nothing ever daunted them. The more they were attacked, the firmer they combined; the more they were put down the higher they rose. In 1488 they revolted against samurai control and expelled

Togashi, so that the government of Kaga passed into their hands. In 1496 they commenced the construction of the Ishiyama Hongan-ji, an immense fortified 'cathedral' at the mouth of the Yodo River. The military skill of these monks may be judged from the fact that on the site of Ishiyama Hongan-ji now stands Ōsaka Castle.

The rise of the Ikkō-ikki was but one example of the process of *gekokujō* (the low oppress the high), that swept Japan in the latter half of the fifteenth century. Soon the aggregate of private wars, of which the Ōnin is the best known but only one example, became combined into a single struggle for survival with rapidly changing alliances, triumphs and disasters, that was to last for over a century. Borrowing an expression from the Chinese, the years from 1490 to 1600 are called the 'Sengoku jidai', which is best translated as 'the Age of the Country at War'. It was war on a scale vaster and more terrible than Japan had yet experienced.

The remainder of this chapter is devoted to the clans who survived and prospered. To survive at all was no mean feat, and by the year 1500 certain names had disappeared altogether. Shiba, Yamana, Hatakeyama and Isshiki, whose mansions had graced the Kyōto skyline, had by the turn of the century fought each other into virtual extinction. Other clans were removed by far less distinguished opponents. For example, in Mino the old house of Toki was destined to succumb to one Saitō Toshimasa, who had begun his adult life as a priest, then became an oil merchant, and commenced his military career by murdering the samurai who had adopted him. In Kyūshū, the Shōni and the Kikuchi disappeared. In Shikoku the Chōsokabe rose to power because of the misfortunes of their overlords, and finally came to grief themselves. In Kaga province, as we noted above, the local lord went under to the Ikkō-ikki. In the Kantō, traditionally the fountainhead of the samurai, events moved so rapidly and with so little reference to Kyōto that Eastern Japan may as well have been a foreign country. The Kantō furnishes us with the first of the families that prospered in the midst of war, the Hōjō.

In about 1490 there occurred within the Ashikaga family an incident typical of the times. Ashikaga Masatomo, a brother of Yoshimasa, ordered his son Chacha to enter the priesthood. The son refused, and murdered his father. The crime was an excellent opportunity for any soldier of fortune to exact revenge, and practise a little *gekokujō* by the way. The challenge was taken up with righteous indignation by an obscure samurai called Ise Shinkuro. Shinkuro attacked Chacha in his fortress of Horigoye, at the northern end of the Izu peninsula. He forced Chacha to commit suicide, thereby ensuring for himself the Mastery of Izu. Having thus suddenly risen to power he changed his name, as the samurai were so prone to do, and chose to call himself Hōjō. He had, of course, no connection with the late line of Hōjō regents, who had disappeared without trace during the fourteenth century, but the name had a nice militaristic ring about it, and spuriously implied aristocratic connections. (He did attempt to legalize it later by marrying his son to a descendant of the original Hōjō.) At the same time he had his head shaved, and took the Buddhist name of Sōun. It is by the name of Hōjō Sōun that this remarkable character is known.

When he was safely established at Izu, Sōun looked eastwards to Sagami, where the strategic fortress town of Odawara dominated the province. Sōun made friends with the young man who had recently inherited the domain, and one day in 1494 Sōun was invited to attend a deer hunt. It was soon obvious that deer were not the prey, when Sōun's men murdered the young lord, leaving Sōun free to take possession of Odawara. He now turned his attention towards Musashi province and the immediate area of modern Tōkyō. By 1518 he had completed the conquest of Sagami, and established fortresses to guard his northern flanks. Hōjō Sōun died in 1519, leaving his son Ujitsuna to continue the conquest of the Kantō. He took advantage of an internal dispute in the powerful Uesugi family to seize their castle of Edo, which is now the site of the Imperial Palace in Tōkyō. Ujitsuna spread his defence along the Sumida River and held out against the Uesugi until his death in 1541. His son, Ujiyasu, brought his grandfather's plans to their consummation by utterly defeating the Uesugi forces at Kawagoe Castle in 1542.

Here we have three generations of a family (see Appendix I for genealogy) sprung from nowhere and owing allegiance to none but themselves, rising to power by a combination of naked aggression and underhand treachery. Had the Ashikaga Bakufu retained but a fraction of its original power then activities such as those of the Hōjō would have been utterly impossible to contemplate, but by the sixteenth century the Shōgunate had become a trifling irrelevance.

Such treachery as the murder during a hunt was regarded as above board by the samurai of the time, whose motto was 'survival of the fittest'. In fact Hōjō Sōun was regarded as the epitome of martial virtue, for he left his son a testament in twenty-one articles, dealing with the administrative aspects of the samurai life. Certain passages give a vivid picture of its rule:

'One ought always to believe in the Gods and Buddhas.

'Go to bed before 8 pm. Thieves generally break in between 12 and 2 am, so if you spend the evening in useless talk and go to bed late you are likely to lose your valuables and your reputation as well. Save the firing and the light that will be wasted by staying up late and get up at four in the morning. Have a cold bath and say your prayers, and after you have dressed give your orders for the day to your wife and children and retainers and so be ready to go on duty before six. . . .

'Before you wash go and inspect everything from the lavatory to the stable and outside the garden gate and give orders to clean anywhere that needs it.

'Do not think you need necessarily have as fine swords and clothing as your neighbour. As long as they are not disreputable they will do. And if you borrow and so lose your independence you will be despised.

'When on duty . . . see that your hair is done properly.

'Riding on horseback ought to be practised when off duty. If a man is well trained on foot he will only have to get used to handling the reins etc.

'The best friend a man can have is reading and writing, and the bad ones to avoid are Go and chess and flute and pipe.'

The testament ends in grand style with a very apposite remark:

'The literary and martial arts are, it is unnecessary to say, to be practised always. The ancient rule declares that letters are the left hand and militarism the right. Neither must be neglected.'

The family that suffered most from the Hōjō's calculated belligerence were the Uesugi, who had practically torn themselves to pieces by the time that Hōjō Sōun started on them. The last Uesugi to withstand the Hōjō was Norimasa, who fled from the Kantō in 1551 to Echigo, the wild, mountainous province in the Hokurikudō. Here he was forced to place himself under the protection of his erstwhile vassal, Nagao Kagetora. Like Hōjō Sōun, Kagetora knew the value of a famous name, so arranged to be adopted by Uesugi Norimasa. The following year, 1552, he had his head shaved and from then on was known as Uesugi Kenshin, one of the most distinguished names in the military annals of the sixteenth century. As heir by adoption to the waning fortunes of the Uesugi family, Kenshin conducted a series of raids against the Hōjō, but he is best known for his hostilities against another neighbour, Takeda Shingen, and it is to this other worthy, whose name is always linked with Kenshin, that we now turn.

Takeda Shingen, or Harunobu as he was called before shaving his head in 1551, is one of the most colourful characters in Japanese history. He was born in 1521, and his first aggressive acts were directed against his own father, who planned to disinherit him in favour of a younger brother. The young Harunobu revolted, and placed his father in the custody of a neighbour, whereupon he assumed full control of the province of Kai. The adventurous young lord then expanded, to use a polite term, into Shinano, which was under the control of Murakami Yoshikiyo. Murakami was defeated in 1547, and asked for help from his nearest neighbour, who happened to be Uesugi Kenshin.

Thus began a series of wars between Kenshin and Shingen celebrated

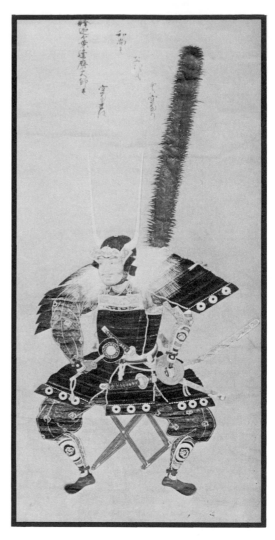

43 Uesugi Kenshin (1530–78). A good likeness of this famous samurai leader. (Koya-san Treasure House.)

in military romance. Their encounters, reminiscent of Percy and Douglas, had one remarkable and amusing feature. They were all fought in the same place, year after year! The battlefield was an area of flat land in Shinano called Kawanakajima where the rivers Saigawa and Chikuma-gawa meet. In 1553, 1554, 1555, 1556, 1557, and 1563 their forces gave battle on the plain of Kawanakajima. In some encounters, when one side had gained a tactical advantage over the other, both armies with-drew, like a gigantic game of chess with human pieces. Perhaps, in view of the later slaughter in which both armies would become involved, the gentle jousting of Kawanakajima was no bad idea for letting off steam. The Battles of Kawanakajima are a unique episode in Japanese history.

The respect in which Kenshin and Shingen held each other is best illustrated by the famous 'salt incident'. As Shingen's provinces lay in the mountains he was consequently dependent upon the good offices

of the Hōjō for the supply of salt. During one of the Kawanakajima campaigns the current Hōjō cut off Shingen's salt supply. Kenshin, hearing of Shingen's dilemma, commented that Hōjō had performed a very mean act, and sent Shingen some salt from his own province, which bordered on the Sea of Japan. He added, 'I do not fight with salt, but with the sword.'

When he was not fighting his annual battle with Kenshin, an event he must have anticipated with great pleasure, Takeda Shingen was administering his domains wisely and well. From a military point of view he was a skilled performer, as we shall see when he engages more powerful opponents later in life. He relied so much on his tactical prowess that in an age of fortress-building he never erected one, preferring to meet his enemy in the field. This necessitated strict discipline and good organization, and Shingen was among the first to introduce these virtues to the ashigaru, who were a troublesome command for the

44 Takeda Shingen (1521–73), a noted warrior and administrator. (Koya-san Treasure House.)

45 One of the many battles of Kawanakajima, between Uesugi Kenshin and Takeda Shingen. Although highly stylized, the degree of discipline possessed by these two rivals makes such an ordered arrangement of troops not improbable. (From a print in the Author's collection, Studio M.)

46 A face mask. (L. J. Anderson collection.)

best general. In this, and in other military developments, Shingen was in the forefront of innovation. He was ably supported by a team of faithful generals such as Baba Nobuharu and Yamamoto Kansuke.

There is a story told of one such old retainer who led a division of the Takeda Army into a certain battle accompanied by his youngest son. It was the lad's first experience of warfare and, full of pride, he turned to his father and proclaimed, 'Now I am going into battle, I forget my wife and family.' The response he received surprised him, for his father became very angry. He turned on the young man and retorted, 'A true samurai cannot possibly forget his wife and family when he goes into battle, because a true samurai never thinks of them at any time!'

Shingen's generals well understood the subtle psychological effect of a well-maintained army. Yamagata Masakage, one of his best generals, used to pick out the samurai who were wearing red-lacquered armour and put them into the front ranks to make a brave show. Shingen's ideals were emblazoned on his standard in gold ideographs, 'Steady as a mountain, attack like fire, still as a wood, swift as the wind. In heaven and earth I alone am to be revered.'

His military approach was partially dictated by necessity. Based on mountainous Kai and Shinano his campaigns had to be offensive, sweeping down from the mountains on to the plains. Difficulties of transport outside Kai made him keep his campaigns short, three days or four days perhaps, and forty or fifty days at the most. To do the work in so short a time required large resources in both men and materials, and he possessed both, as is shown by the following analysis of his army:

Takeda Shingen's personal bodyguard	6,373
Kai province, 788 villages yielding 3,740 horsemen plus four retainers each, under Oyamada, Baba *et al.*	14,960
Kai, ashigaru leaders (including samurai)	285
Kai, ashigaru	785
Shinano	2,020
Eastern Kōzuke	1,035
Suruga	430
Tōtōmi	320
Hida	150
Etchū	170
Musashi	180
Officials, cooks, couriers etc.	9,340
plus various pirates, mercenaries etc.	

This gives a grand total of about 45,000 men. Shingen was able to control and feed such a host because his administration was sound, even though a little patriarchal. In some ways his administration was ahead of its time, for he allowed the farmers to pay taxes in money as

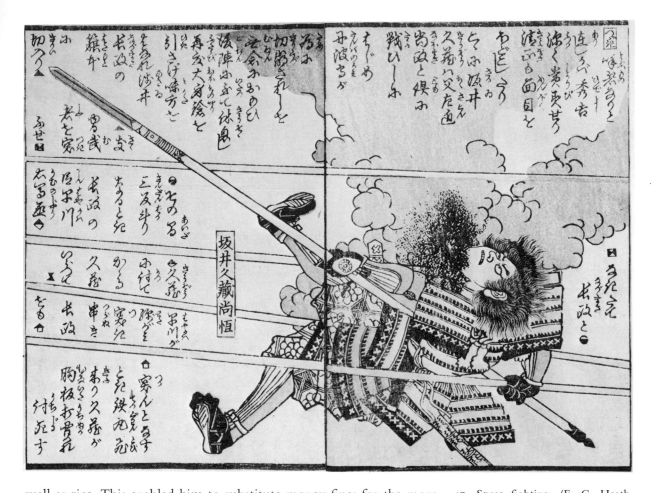

47 Spear fighting. (E. G. Heath collection.)

well as rice. This enabled him to substitute money fines for the more usual corporal punishment, leading to a better relationship with the peasants. The peasants were also fully appreciative of the fact that Shingen was one of the few daimyō (as these new feudal lords were called), who taxed the samurai and the temples along with the farmers. Shingen always kept wartime requirements in mind. He ensured that the roads were maintained in good repair, and organized an efficient courier service. He could afford to be lavish in his expenditure, for he was literally sitting on a gold mine. The precious metal had been mined in Kai for centuries, and the Takeda gold reserves were the backbone of his economic strength.

It is tempting to see Shingen's kingdom as a land of happy, hard-working peasants who laid down their tools and took up their swords in defence of their beloved lord, and where unpleasant movements like the ikki would never take root. Nor is this impression far from the truth, for the farmers did talk of 'Shingen-Kō', or 'Prince Shingen' as they called him, with affectionate respect and reverence. The system that Shingen devised was paid the highest of compliments long after his death, when Tokugawa Ieyasu based his great administration on the Takeda model. Essentially, where Takeda Shingen was more successful than other warlords was in his ability to strike a happy balance between having a large army of ashigaru, who had received a modicum of military training, and not thereby denuding the fields of agricultural workers. The most notorious for raising soldiers from his peasants was Hōjō Ujiyasu (Sōun's grandson 1515–70). If the following regulations, issued at some time when he was fighting Uesugi Kenshin, were obeyed, it is hard to see how agriculture in his provinces could possibly be kept going:

'1.   All men, including those of the samurai class, in this country district are ordered to come and be registered on the twentieth day of this month. They are to bring with them a gun, a spear, or any kind of weapon, if they happen to possess one, without fearing to get into trouble.

'2.   If it is known afterwards that even one man in this district concealed himself and did not respond to the call, such man, no matter whether he is a district commissioner or a peasant, shall be beheaded.

'3.   All the men, from fifteen to seventy years of age, are ordered to come; not even a monkey-tamer will be let off.'

There follow several sections urging recruits to polish their spears and make paper flags, and giving alternative arrangements should the weather prove inclement on the day of muster. Those without arms are ordered to bring hoes or sickles, and even Buddhist priests are invited to 'do their duty'. It finishes with dire warnings and promises of reward. To such a lord all men were soldiers.

The rise of 'new men' such as Hōjō Sōun and Takeda Shingen was often dramatic, but no process of *gekokujō* was so theatrical as the downfall of the Ōuchi clan, who were ousted by one vassal and avenged by another. We last heard of Ōuchi in the person of Ōuchi Masahiro, who had taken Yamana's part in the Ōnin War. His son Yoshioki was a warlike character, and brought the family fortunes to a high point before his death in 1528. At first it was thought that his son Yoshitaka was of similar mettle, but success made Yoshitaka careless, and after soundly beating some enemies in Kyūshū, he returned to his mansion at Yamaguchi and devoted himself to the pleasures of art and literature. Like the Hōjō stronghold of Odawara, Yamaguchi was a flourishing commercial centre, and its position on the Inland Sea made it ideal for trade with China. A defeat which he suffered in 1543 convinced Yoshitaka that warfare was too dangerous an occupation for civilized man, so he wallowed more than ever in amusements, his pleasure increased by the company of refugee courtiers from Kyōto, who had left the capital for the relative tranquility of Yoshitaka's domains.

Meanwhile his two principal retainers, Mōri Motonari and Sue Harukata, who were much closer to reality than was their master, begged him in vain to put aside his effeminate pursuits lest some ambitious

48   Holder and staff for a 'sashi-mono', the little banner worn at the back of the armour to facilitate identification in battle. (L. J. Anderson collection.)

samurai should take advantage of the situation and try some *gekokujō*. As Mōri and Sue had warned, a coup was arranged, and as if to further the accuracy of his predictions, Sue arranged it! In spite of Yoshitaka's pleas for aid, few of his erstwhile cronies would help him, and after an unsuccessful attempt at flight he was besieged by the rebel and committed suicide.

So far Mōri Motonari had taken no part in the affair, but felt in-honour-bound to avenge his late master. So for the next few years Mōri plotted in secret, all the while putting on a show of respect for Sue and an appreciation of his evident power. Apart from a certain native cunning Mōri had a powerful advantage in the persons of three fine sons. His heir was Mōri Takamoto, born in 1523, who eventually predeceased his father. The second son was called Motoharu. He was born in 1530, and had been adopted into the Kikkawa clan. Takakage, who was two years younger, had also been adopted, in this case into the Kobayakawa. The two younger brothers, whose military reputation was second to none, were nicknamed 'The Two Rivers' (Ryō-gawa) from the common ideograph in their adoptive names.

In 1554 Mōri began hostilities but, faced with an enemy who could muster 30,000 men, decided that a strategem was necessary. Now it happened that certain of Mōri's generals had suggested fortifying the island of Miyajima. This island, also known as Itsukushima, contained the shrine so beloved of the Taira clan. It lies about twelve miles south west of Hiroshima. There is an old tradition connected with Miyajima. It was once a strictly enforced religious rule that Miyajima should not be polluted by the occurrence on it of either a birth or a death. There is still no cemetery on Miyajima; the dead are buried on the mainland and the mourners undergo purification rituals before returning. Mōri Motonari was fully aware of this rule, but was enough of an opportunist to put religion on one side and treat the holy island as a potential Trojan Horse.

So Mōri constructed a fortress on Miyajima, set ostentatiously near the Great Shrine. The castle was manned in May 1555, and Mōri began publicly to bewail his 'folly' in building a castle that could so easily be captured by Sue, who soon obligingly commandeered a fleet of junks and captured Miyajima in an almost bloodless struggle. Mōri, in the meantime, was busy capturing Kusatsu, directly across the strait, thus cutting off Sue's means of retreat. The latter fortified the castle with a garrison of 500 men, and encamped the rest of the army on the island. An impressive show of strength, no doubt, but the fact that Sue had his entire army on the island with him made the situation look uncomfortably like a siege!

For Mōri it was a question of how and when to launch a surprise attack. The odds were five to one, but surprise would be easy to achieve, as Sue in his watery fastness felt sufficiently secure to dispense with sentries. The Mōri army eventually set sail on a dark October night during a blinding rainstorm. They were transported across the strait by pirates, whom Mōri ordered to return after landing his army, so

49 'Jinbaori', the surcoat worn over armour by high ranking samurai in camp. (Richards collection, Manchester Museum.)

that no boats would be available for a retreating enemy. The army was divided in two. One contingent, under the Mōri, father and son, and the other son Kikkawa, sailed round the northern tip of the island to land on a beach a mile or so behind Sue's camp. The other force, slightly less at 1,500 men under Kobayakawa, sailed directly down the strait for a few miles, then doubled back when out of sight of the castle to make a frontal assault at dawn, the same time that the others attacked the rear. The surprise was total, and to the accompaniment of shell trumpets the Mōri samurai carried all before them. Finding that there were no boats in which to escape the Sue troops committed suicide by the hundred, either by drowning, or by the time-honoured method. (See map, Fig. 51.)

As for the pollution of death, Mōri Motonari saw to it that the island was wiped clean of blood. The Gods evidently approved, for the victory of Miyajima raised his family to a position of pre-eminence in Western Japan. Once again the utter irrelevance of the Ashikaga Shōgunate had been demonstrated.

The reader may have sensed that, with the breakdown of a central authority, the nature of warfare itself was again changing, or if not exactly changing, then widening in scope. War now involved much more than ordering campaigns and leading men into battle. There had always been underhand tricks throughout samurai history, but whereas in the Gempei War those who employed them stand out as the villains that they were, in the 'Age of War' the knife in the dark was both legitimate and necessary. War had left the battlefield and entered the bedchamber. The textbooks of the 'new men' were the Chinese treatises on warfare, that contained principles and directions for spying, assas-

50 The renowned samurai Honda Tadakatsu (1548–1610) as a young man. (Tokugawa Art Museum, Nagoya.)

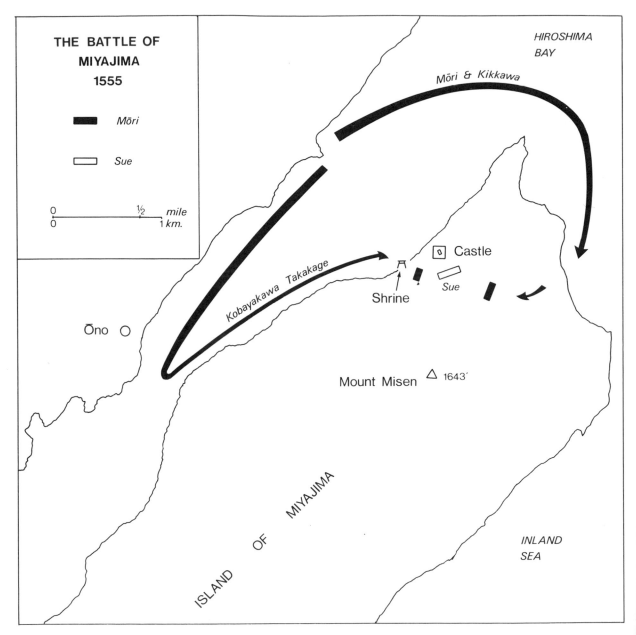

THE BATTLE OF
MIYAJIMA
1555

Mōri

Sue

0   ½   mile
0   1 km.

Mōri & Kikkawa

Castle

Kobayakawa Takakage

Sue

Shrine

Ōno ○

Mount Misen   △ 1643ʹ

ISLAND   OF   MIYAJIMA

INLAND
SEA

51 Map showing the Battle of
Miyajima (Itsukushima), 1555.

sination, and all forms of underhand espionage. Even if a samurai did
not employ such tactics, he had to be aware of them if he wished his
head to remain securely on his shoulders. Mōri Motonari once remarked that it was wise not to trust anyone, not even close relatives.
Matsuura, the daimyō of Hirado Island, off Kyūshū, used to keep a
club in his bathroom. Takeda Shingen had two doors on his lavatory.
It is believed that certain feudal lords used to hire assassins to remove
enemies. These 'ninja', as they were called, are a problem to historians,
owing to the lack of contemporary reference to them. Their trade was

one of stealth and darkness, and many seemingly natural deaths may be attributable to them.

Interesting evidence of the changing times is seen in the styles of armour. Campaigns were now of much longer duration, and certain problems were discovered with the close-lacing of the cords of the armour. According to the seventeenth-century authority, Sakakibara Kōzan:

'. . . when soaked with water they are very heavy and cannot be quickly dried, so that in summer the weight is oppressive and in winter the whole may freeze. Moreover no amount of washing will completely free the lacing from any mud which may have penetrated it, so that on a long and distant campaign it becomes evil-smelling and overrun by ants and lice, with consequent ill effects upon the health of the wearer.'

Also the close lacing would retain a spear point instead of letting it glide off harmlessly. So the close-lacing (kebiki odoshi) was replaced by a lacing spaced in pairs of cords (sugake odoshi). This had the added advantage of a considerable saving of the armour maker's time, whose order books were probably always full! Two other innovations in armour date from this period. The first was the development of armour for the face from a simple set of plates to a metal face mask, which soon acquired features and often a bristly horsehair moustache. As simpler styles of armour were of largely uniform appearance, the *sashimono*, a small flag worn on the back and bearing a badge or other identifying design, was introduced to facilitate recognition on the battlefield.

The theme of this chapter has been *gekokujō*, the low oppressing the high, and in fact throughout the Age of the Country at War the social group that achieved most was the peasantry. Their well-being had suddenly become of vital concern to the daimyō, as they needed their produce and person for the armies. If a group of peasants were harshly treated they had only to cross the provincial border and they could till the fields of an enemy. In military affairs also it was the great age of opportunity for the lowerclass warrior. An ashigaru with military skill could rise to be a high-ranking samurai, for there was no closed clique to keep him out. Like land, loot and surnames, rank was there for the taking. Every ashigaru in a feudal army carried a general's war fan in his knapsack.

At the opposite extreme of the social spectrum the misery of the age was utterly degrading. As an institution the Emperor had ceased to be of any practical importance. As wars raged, no money came in from the Imperial estates, and the throne became bankrupt. When Emperor Go-Tsuchi-Mikado died in 1501 the Court could not even afford to bury him, and the Coronation of his successor was delayed for twenty years owing to lack of funds, when a gift from, of all people, the Ikkō monks, made it possible. Emperor Go-Nara (1527–32) lived in a wooden hut for a palace and children made mud pies outside his

52 This armour and the following illustrate the change in styles of armour produced by the long campaigns of the Sengoku Period. A haramaki laced with 'kebiki odoshi', close-spaced lacing. (I. D. Bottomley collection.)

53 Suit of armour, 'nuinobe-dō' style, laced in 'sugake odoshi', lacing spaced in pairs. (I. D. Bottomley collection.)

front door. To raise cash he sold his autograph to passers-by, and it is recorded that an Imperial banquet consisted of rice cakes and dog soup. The finances of the Shōgunate were little better, and even though this discredited organization had long since ceased to wield any power, ambition still ruled, and to obtain the paltry position of Shōgun men were prepared to murder their own father.

In conclusion, by the middle of the sixteenth century Japan was in a worse state of confusion than had ever existed in the country's history. There was no longer any central government, while warlords fought for their own little kingdoms, allying with and betraying each other at frequent intervals. Sandwiched in between them were hundreds of smaller families, all engaged in the highly respectable business of stealing each other's land. Yet for ten years or so the seeds that would restore peace to the country had been growing, and this will be the theme of the following chapters.

8. Saints and samurai

Our theme now becomes the re-unification of Japan, a largely military undertaking which entailed radical changes in the status, organization and weaponry of the samurai. The adoption of a new weapon into the samurai arsenal played a large part in the developments leading to this re-unification.

In 1543 or 1542, a Chinese junk containing three Portuguese traders was blown off course by a typhoon, and driven on to the shores of Tanegashima Island off the coast of southern Kyūshū. The three travellers were the first Europeans to set foot in Japan. Although their appearance and strange dress aroused curiosity, what really excited the Japanese were the firearms they carried. An eyewitness recalled:

'In their hands they carried something two or three feet long, straight on the outside with a passage inside, and made of a heavy substance. The inner passage runs through it although it is closed at the end. At its side there is an aperture which is the passageway for fire. Its shape defies comparison with anything I know. To use it, fill it with powder and small lead pellets. Set up a small white target on a bank. Grip the object in your hand, compose your body, and closing one eye apply fire to the aperture. Then the pellet hits the target squarely. The explosion is like lightning and the report like thunder.'

It is more than likely that the Japanese were acquainted with the primitive Chinese 'hand-guns' of the time, and it will be remembered that the Mongols had pelted their forefathers with exploding bombs in 1274, but the weapons brought by the Portuguese were undoubtedly the first real 'firearms' that had ever reached their country. The weapons were of the type known as an 'arquebus', or 'matchlock', which were light enough to be held without the aid of the rest used for the heavier 'musket'. The potential of the new weapon for warfare was immediately realized. As we saw in the last chapter these were exceedingly warlike times, and the needs of the moment had lifted Japanese technology to the level where it could cope with the innovation. Both psychologically and technologically the arquebuses arrived at exactly the right time. After a month of lessons the Lord of Tanegashima purchased the two specimens for a colossal sum of money, and gave the guns to his master

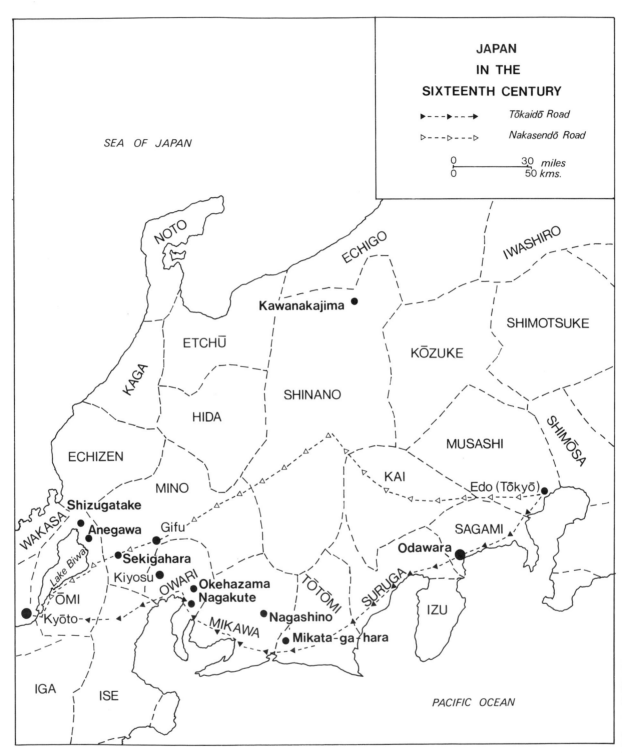

54 Map of Central Japan in the
sixteenth century, showing major
battles, lines of communication, and
provinces.

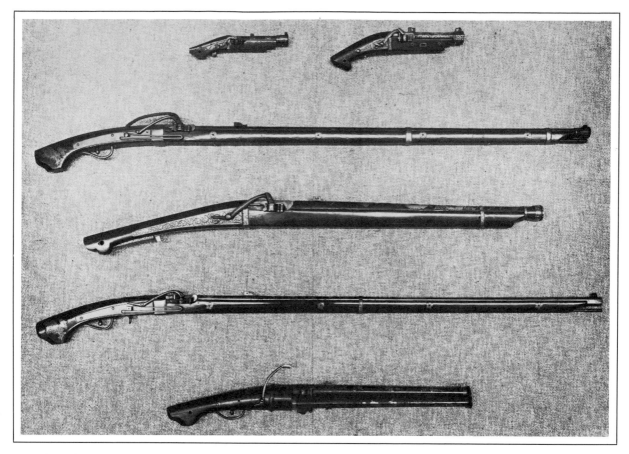

swordsmith to copy. The latter was puzzled by certain technical problems, such as how to close the end of the barrel, but when a Portuguese
vessel called in a few months later he exchanged his daughter for a
series of lessons in gunmaking, and soon his workshop was turning out
home-produced imitations as good as the originals. The technique
soon spread, and within a few years blacksmiths were journeying to
Kyūshū from Honshū to learn the gunmaker's art.

The Japanese arquebus is illustrated in Figs 55–7. The three weapons
in the centre of Fig. 55 show clearly what they looked like, and 56 and
57 show how they were used. The match, an impregnated cord, was
held in the serpentine, the 'S'-shaped lever. By pulling the trigger the
ignited and spluttering match was dropped on to the touch hole,
protected by a tight fitting brass cover to guard against accidents. The
process of ramming bullet and powder down the barrel may not have
posed many problems of safety, but the introduction of the finer priming
powder into the pan must have necessitated the complete removal of
the match from the immediate vicinity. It is not clear how this was
done. Some illustrations show the arquebusier with a length of match
wound round his arm, but this may be spare, as it would have required
about six feet of match to keep a gun alight all day. Some muskets

55 Japanese arquebuses (matchlock
guns), including pistols and a three-
barrelled 'revolver'. (Victoria and
Albert Museum.)

139

56 The process of firing an arque-bus, from ramming to actual firing. From *Nakajima-ryū kō jutsu densho*. (Kyōto University Library.)

have holes in the stock through which the match was passed. Figure 56 shows the processes of firing from ramming to actual ignition. The second and third men from the right are priming the pan, while the fourth is cocking the serpentine.

With that traditional Japanese talent for imitation and improvement a number of innovations were introduced. Lacquered cases were made for keeping the guns dry when not in use. One of the oddest improvements, which probably dates from the seventeenth century or later, is shown in Fig. 115.

The arquebus did have certain major disadvantages. The process of loading took time, and it was by no means as accurate as the bow. Yet in 1555 Takeda Shingen purchased 300 muskets, and in 1571 addressed the following order to his commanders:

'Hereafter guns will be the most important weapons. Therefore decrease the number of spears [in your armies] and have the most capable men carry guns. Furthermore, when you assemble your soldiers, test their marksmanship and order that the selection of [gunners] be in accordance with the results [of your test].'

One additional reason for the popularity of the arquebus lies with the changing social composition of armies. We have noted a decline in the use and potential of the Japanese bow from before the Mongol invasions, and that with the increase in the size and scope of armies the lower classes were beginning to play a greater part. Now whereas it took years of practice and the development of strong muscles to shoot

57 Firing arquebuses. From *Budo Geijutsu hiden zue* painted by Ichi-yusai Kuniyoshi, 1855. (National Diet Library, Tōkyō.)

well with the bow, a peasant could be taught within a few days to shoot an arquebus with all the accuracy of which the weapon was capable. In short, the arquebus was the ideal weapon for the ashigaru. However this is not to say that they were given them to use, as these expensive weapons were probably kept initially as samurai prestige objects.

To Shimazu Takahisa goes the honour of being the first warlord to fire an arquebus in anger. This was in 1549. Takeda Shingen and Uesugi Kenshin used them during their periodic battles at Kawana-kajima, and Mōri's troops fired on Sue at Miyajima, but while they

58 The unifiers of Japan. Oda Nobunaga piles the rice; Toyotomi Hideyoshi kneads the dough; Tokugawa Ieyasu eats the cake. The fourth figure introduced to help Nobunaga is Akechi Mitsuhide.

were a useful addition to the samurai armoury, none of these very able warlords really appreciated the true potential of firearms. It was thirty years from their introduction to Japan before a warlord was to see the most effective way of using a large number of inaccurate weapons, a discovery which considerably assisted the re-unification programme, as we shall see.

The unification of Japan is essentially the story of three men, all of whom were born within eight years of one another. They all began their careers as bold samurai, and ended them as statesmen. By the end of the sixteenth century all three had fought side by side, and against one another.

The three men are Oda Nobunaga, born in 1534, Toyotomi Hideyoshi (1538), and Tokugawa Ieyasu (1542). In the last chapter we saw how the decline of the Ashikaga Shōgunate enabled several powerful warlords to set up practically independent kingdoms throughout Japan. Now it is more than likely that such men, particularly Hōjō and Takeda, had an underlying ambition to copy Ashikaga Takauji's activities of 1335–6 and march on Kyōto, setting up either another Shōgunate or using a puppet Shōgun. But because the situation had changed so much in the intervening two centuries such a move was no longer practical, for absence from one's home province inevitably left the way open for an attack by a neighbour. If Hōjō, for example, had descended upon Kyōto with the strength that would have been needed, then Takeda Shingen would have marched into Sagami. While Shingen was in Sagami Uesugi Kenshin could march on Kai! In fact the warlords were too busy watching and fighting one another to consider an assault on the capital. Had things been different, Takeda Shingen would certainly have proved more than capable of ruling Japan as well as he ruled Kai. As it was, the mantle of conquering hero fell on the shoulders of a young, minor warlord called Oda Nobunaga.

The Oda family were small landowners in Owari province, who rose to the mastery of the whole province between the years 1530 and 1539 by the now familiar process of *gekokujō*. In 1551 young Nobunaga inherited his father's growing domains. As he was only seventeen years old he faced great opposition from other members of the family, whom he opposed with the ruthlessness that was to prove his main characteristic. In the same year that Nobunaga was inheriting a fortune, another young man was busy making his. Toyotomi Hideyoshi was also born in Owari, but of peasant stock. While still young he ran away from the temple where his peasant parents had hoped he would become a priest, and joined a local army as an ashigaru. One day his master entrusted him with a sum of money. He absconded with it, purchased a suit of armour and weapons, and joined Nobunaga's army, again as an ashigaru. This was in 1558. Nobunaga had an eye for talent, and Hideyoshi's subsequent progress up the ranks developed at a rate unequalled by any other samurai in the history of Japan.

The year 1558 also saw the first battle in which the third member of our trio fought. Tokugawa Ieyasu was a seventeen-year-old samurai

in the service of Imagawa Yoshimoto, who ruled Mikawa, Tōtōmi
and Suruga, the next three provinces along the Tōkaidō from Oda's
Owari. Possession of these provinces put Imagawa into the same
league as Hōjō, Uesugi and Takeda, but he lacked their military and
administrative skills. Tokugawa Ieyasu's first battle for Imagawa was
conducted against Oda Nobunaga. Ieyasu attacked one of Nobunaga's
fortresses, set fire to it and gave Nobunaga a rough time when he tried
to re-take it. In 1559 Ieyasu again embarrassed Nobunaga by provisioning Imagawa's frontier fortress of Ōtaka while creating a diversion
which Nobunaga fell for. Ieyasu's tremendous self-confidence endeared
him to Imagawa, who was planning greater things, for Imagawa was
destined to be the first of the warlords to attempt a march on Kyōto.
His rear was fairly secure, because Suruga was divided from Hōjō's

Sagami by the Hakone mountains, and at the time when the operation was planned Hōjō Ujiyasu was busy fighting Uesugi Kenshin. So Imagawa set out in June 1560 with 25,000 samurai drawn from all three of his provinces. Lying between him and Kyōto were but three provinces, and the first was Oda Nobunaga's Owari.

Oda Nobunaga's headquarters were at the fortress of Kiyosu, near the present-day city of Nagoya. On 22 June 1560 he was informed that one of his frontier fortresses, Marune, had fallen to a dawn attack by Tokugawa Ieyasu. Ieyasu's assault had been swift and powerful, making good use of concentrated arquebus fire. A few hours later another frontier fort fell, leaving nothing between Imagawa's 25,000 men and Oda's small army in Kiyosu. To the surprise of his advisers Nobunaga decided to take the offensive. His force cannot have been much in excess of 2,000 men, yet with odds of twelve to one he still set off from Kiyosu humming a tune and appearing to be without a care in the world.

Nobunaga's scouts reported that Imagawa was resting his troops at a place called Dengaku-hazama, near a little village named Okehazama. It was countryside that Nobunaga knew well. Dengaku-hazama was a narrow gorge, an ideal place for a surprise attack if the conditions were right. The scouts added that the Imagawa army were celebrating their victories with food and drink while Yoshimoto viewed the heads. So Nobunaga moved up towards Imagawa's camp, and set up a position some distance away. An array of flags and dummy troops made of straw and spare helmets gave the impression of a large host, while the real Oda army hurried round in a rapid march to get behind Yoshimoto's camp. Fortune, and the weather, favoured Nobunaga, for about mid-day the stifling heat gave way to a terrific thunderstorm. As the Imagawa samurai sheltered from the rain Nobunaga deployed his troops, and when the storm ceased they charged down upon the enemy in the gorge. So sudden was the attack that Yoshimoto thought a brawl had broken out among his men. He realized it was an attack by Nobunaga only when two samurai charged up. One aimed a spear at him, which Yoshimoto deflected with his sword, but the second swung his blade and cut off Imagawa's head.

The Battle of Okehazama only lasted several minutes, but it is one of the most decisive battles in Japanese history. It put Oda Nobunaga into the front rank of military power, and also gained for him his most valuable ally, for the death of Imagawa Yoshimoto freed Tokugawa Ieyasu from his obligation, and in 1561 he joined Nobunaga. The three potential leaders of Japan were now all fighting side by side.

Nobunaga was now faced with a difficult decision. Dare he try to succeed where Imagawa had failed? He was, after all, one province nearer to Kyōto than Imagawa had been, and was separated from the capital only by Mino and Ōmi. To make his position more secure at the rear he married his daughter to Takeda Shingen's son, and in 1564 he married his younger sister to Asai Nagamasa, who controlled northern Ōmi. As Tokugawa Ieyasu was the leading light in Mikawa only

I 'The Samurai'. A warrior leaves the battlefield bearing an enemy's severed head as a trophy. From a nineteenth-century woodblock print. (E. G. Heath collection)

II (left) This dark-blue silk-laced 'Ō-yoroi' armour has been carefully restored, and is one of the finest examples of the armour worn by the samurai of the eleventh and twelfth centuries. (Oyamazumi Shrine Museum, Ōmishima, photograph by Haku-san)

III Samurai of the Minamoto clan present the head of Shinzei to Fujiwara Nobuyori after the 'Heiji Incident', 1160. Details of samurai dress and equipment can be clearly seen in this section of the *Heiji Monogatari Emaki* ('The Scroll of the Heiji War'), taken from a copy of the original. (Collection of L. W. Allen)

V The site of the Battle of Yashima, 1185, looking south from the plateau of Yashima to the mainland of Shikoku across the narrow straits where the Taira fleet was moored. At that time there was no land bridge. (Photograph by the Author)

VI A samurai commander marshals his troops ready for the Mongol invasion. From the scroll *Mōko Shūrai Ekotoba* ('The Mongol Invasion Scroll'). (Imperial Household Collection)

IV A battle between 'sōhei' (warrior-monks) of the Kōfuku-ji and samurai of the Taira clan. The use of the naginata and kumade may be seen. From the scroll *Kasuga Congen Reikenki* ('The Miracles of Kasuga Gongen'), painted 1309. (Imperial House-hold Collection)

VII (above) Three boatloads of
samurai row out to attack the
Mongol fleet. From the *Mōko
Shūrai Ekotoba*. (Imperial Household
Collection)

VIII (below) Japanese samurai attacking a Mongol ship. Takezaki Suenaga decapitates
one Mongol while his comrades attempt to force their way below deck. From the
Mōko Shūrai Ekotoba. (Imperial Household Collection)

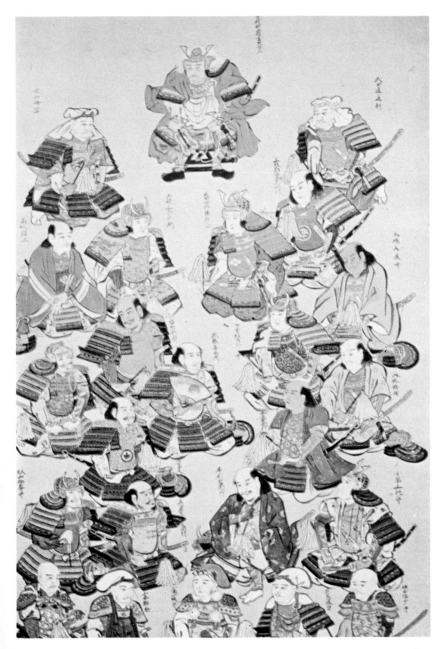

IX Takeda Shingen and his generals. One of the greatest resources possessed by this
renowned warrior was his band of loyal and skilled generals. From a hanging scroll
in the Koya-san Treasure House. (Photograph by the Author)

XIV and XV The Battle of Shizugatake, 1583. From a painted screen depicting the Battle of Shizugatake. (Ōsaka Castle Museum)

X and XI (above) Mounted samurai of the Takeda lead the charge against the palisade at the Battle of Nagashino in 1575. From a painted screen depicting the Battle of Nagashino. (Tokugawa Art Museum, Nagoya)

XII (right) Takeda Katsuyori leads the Takeda reserve in a final charge against the palisade at Nagashino, while the defenders of the castle sally out. From a painted screen depicting the Battle of Nagashino. (Tokugawa Art Museum, Nagoya)

Mino remained in his way. The reader may recall that this province was occupied by the ex-oil merchant, ex-priest Saitō Toshimasa, who was named in the last chapter as an outstanding example of villainy. Nobunaga had been expecting trouble from Saitō for several years, and had taken the precaution of marrying Saitō's daughter. Toshimasa was an unattractive father-in-law, being fond of torture and boiling people, so it was with some relief that Nobunaga had heard of Toshimasa's death at the hands of his son, Nobunaga's brother-in-law, in 1556. Any excuse being better than none Nobunaga declared war on the son to avenge the father. Before the campaign had really begun, however, the son, Yoshitatsu, died of leprosy, leaving his son Tatsuoki to continue the struggle. The task of subduing the last of the Saitō was entrusted to Toyotomi Hideyoshi, who reduced their castle of Inaba-yama (now called Gifu) with little difficulty in 1564.

The road to the Capital was now open, and all Nobunaga needed was an excuse to act. In 1567 it fell on his doorstep, in the person of a young man called Ashikaga Yoshiaki. As his surname implies he was a rich prize indeed, for he was the heir to the Ashikaga Shōgunate, which was still limping along in spite of many vicissitudes. The twelfth Ashikaga Shōgun, Yoshiharu, had abdicated in 1545 in favour of his son Yoshiteru, and then, seeing the approach of his family's ruin, he died of sheer despair. For Ashikaga Yoshiteru, who became the thirteenth Ashikaga Shōgun at the age of eleven, life was a long succession of miseries. He was firmly in the grasp of an elegant but malignant pair of schemers called Miyoshi Chōkei and Matsunaga Hisahide, who eventually had him put to death and raised his cousin to the Shōgunate as their puppet. In the coup that produced Yoshiteru's death his younger brother, Yoshiaki, escaped, and eventually sought refuge with Oda Nobunaga.

On 9 November 1568 Oda Nobunaga entered Kyōto in triumph, bringing with him the heir to a title that had long ceased to have any meaning. It is hardly necessary to say that Yoshiaki became Nobunaga's puppet, the latter reducing the functions of a Shōgun to the performance of ceremonial. It was an excellent opportunity for Nobunaga to indulge his taste for the magnificent, so he raised up a new palace for the Shōgun, and also one for the Emperor who, naturally, was grateful.

While Nobunaga pursued the course of politics his allies and subordinate generals proceeded to eliminate his enemies. The growing power of Nobunaga is shown clearly in these campaigns where he delegated full responsibility to an individual leader such as Ieyasu or Hideyoshi. He rewarded them generously, it is true, but the fact that such alliances could and did work indicates that a little loyalty was beginning to emerge from the confusion of samurai politics. At the centre of the campaign that Ieyasu conducted in 1563 against the Ikkō monks stands the figure of a young warrior, reckless and brave. The Ikkō-ikki, as we saw in the last chapter, were second to none in fanatical power and righteous indignation. They advanced to meet Ieyasu at Azukizaka with tablets in their helmets bearing the legend, 'He who advances is sure of Heaven, but he who retreats of eternal damnation.'

To help the damnation of their enemies they carried a quantity of arquebuses, for the Ikkō leaders had been among the first customers at the arsenal recently established at Sakai.

Seeing Ieyasu in action at this battle reminds one that the age of individual valour was not quite over. Icyasu challenged a monk to single combat. He replied with a deprecating remark, whereupon Ieyasu charged his horse full tilt at him. Several more samurai joined in, and in the fight which followed one of the Ikkō leaguers, perhaps the one who had made the comment, was forced to retire with two long slashes down the back of his armour made by Ieyasu's spear blade. As Ieyasu began a pursuit of his retreating enemy he felt the impact of an arquebus ball against his armour, but it caused him no pain, so concluding that it must have ricocheted he continued the fight. When he finally returned to camp and unfastened his armour two bullets fell out of his shirt. Had the marksman's gunpowder been a little stronger Ieyasu would have gone down to posterity as a typical samurai fanatic who fell victim to his own enthusiasm, and the subsequent history of Japan might have proved very different. The skirmish with the Ikkō–ikki turned out to be as indecisive as Ieyasu's wound. Of all Nobunaga's opponents, those of the various religious factions were to prove the most turbulent, especially the Ikkō-ikki in their impregnable fortress-cathedral of Ishiyama Hongan-ji, and the monks of Enryaku-ji on Mount Hiei. One possible reason for the monks' belligerence was the appearance on the scene of the first rival to Buddhism in eight hundred years.

When the Portuguese arrived in 1543 they brought more than firearms with them. In the wake of the merchants came the missionaries. Outstanding among these was the Jesuit, Saint Francis Xavier.

The impact of Christianity on the samurai is a subject too vast for this book to cover adequately, but certain aspects should be noted. It may be hypothesized that one reason why Christianity made such dramatic inroads was the fact that its evangelists gave the samurai something to respect. The Buddhist Church, after all, had become worldly indeed, but the Christian missionaries were of a different cast. It is significant that they were Jesuits. In 1549 the Society of Jesus was scarcely nine years old since its founding by Saint Ignatius Loyola in 1540. Loyola had been a soldier, and a very successful one, and carried his military organization with him when he founded the Society to 'fight for the Church with the sword of the spirit'.

Rigid discipline and strict obedience were the cardinal virtues, together with a willingness to go anywhere and do anything at a moment's notice, which made Loyola refer to his foundation as the 'cavalry of the Church'. Once the Jesuits got under way the novitiate period was long and hard, and it was only after years of spartan training that a Jesuit was 'fully qualified'. There is a certain analogy here with the training and the values of the samurai, which may give a clue to the initial successes of the Jesuits. While the comparison must not be carried too far, it is tempting to see the Jesuits as the Pope's samurai. To some extent the demands the Jesuits made on themselves in a spiritual sense would be recognized by samurai brought up under the rigours of Zen. A call to put aside all wordly things, and detach one's mind from the here and now of this world of impermanence, could apply as easily to the quest for enlightenment as to a preparation for the work of God.

As Christianity made further converts among the samurai it seems appropriate to ask how a religion that teaches the love of one's neighbour could ever be embraced by men whose neighbour was an enemy simply because he was a neighbour? What, for example, would a samurai make of the Commandment, 'Thou shalt not kill'. The answer is, simply, as little as his contemporaries in Christian Europe made of it, which was pitifully small. Christian strictures against taking life were no great revelation for the samurai, for one of the teachings of Buddha was to see oneself in all that lived, and therefore do not kill. As in all countries the Sixth Commandment was rationalized and fitted into the existing framework. The murderers of the Shōgun Yoshiteru were among the first converts in Kyōto, and the murder actually took place after they had become Christians. Some, of course, cherished their new faith and followed its doctrine. An outstanding example was Takayama Ukon, a daimyō of Settsu, who was converted after losing a debate with Father Gaspard Vilela. He was baptized with all his house, and proved a tower of strength to the Christian Faith.

Early reports of Japan and its people coming to the ears of Saint Francis Xavier, he saw there a glorious vista of missionary activity. On 15 August 1549, Xavier landed at Kagoshima in southern Kyūshū. He received a friendly welcome from the local lord, Shimazu Takahisa. The friendship was reciprocated, and Xavier wrote enthusiastically about the Japanese that they were:

'. . . The best who have as yet been discovered, and it seems to me that we shall never find among heathens another race to equal the Japanese.'

While their mission remained confined to Kyūshū, the missionaries met with great success. The rulers of the island were all keen on extending their trade with Portugal, and had been the first to adopt firearms, while the common people proved receptive to a gospel that promised them bliss. To some extent the faith of which the Jesuit Fathers spoke must have reminded them of the teachings of the Ikkō and Jōdo sects, who also promised salvation by faith. So Christianity flourished, and included among its converts many samurai. The greatest achievement in Kyūshū was the conversion of Ōtomo Sōrin, Lord of Bungo, who proved a loyal supporter of the new religion, for motives probably as political as they were religious.

So the Faith prospered while the slaughter went on. The most bizarre example of the rationalization of the Christian life with the Way of the Warrior occurred in 1567. Shibata Katsuie, one of Nobunaga's leading generals, led a campaign against Miyoshi and Matsunaga, the murderers of the Shōgun Yoshiteru. The forces met in battle near the city of Sakai, where the leading Catholic light was the energetic Father Luis Frois. As the two armies faced each other in battle array Frois invited the faithful from both sides to celebrate High Mass, for it was Christmas Eve. The Christian samurai came to the Mass together, prepared for and partook of the Blessed Sacrament, and before they returned to their camps, 'to show they had all one heart', they brought dishes of fruit and ate at the Fathers' table. As they left they proclaimed, 'We are brothers in Christ'. Next morning, Christmas Day, the Battle of Sakai began. The commanders Matsunaga and Miyoshi fled, and all who did not surrender were put to the sword.

From now on we shall notice increasing reference to Christian daimyō and indeed whole Christian armies. Martyrdom and persecution were many years hence, and the samurai who went into battle shouting, 'Jesu!', 'Santa Maria!', or 'Sant Iago!', and carrying the cross on their banners, were undoubtedly inspired by a faith that was deep and genuine. As for Oda Nobunaga, he never became a Christian, but his support for the Jesuits was substantial. This was largely because they were a useful lever against the Buddhist sectarians.

Nobunaga's next opponents were entirely secular. In Echizen, the second province of the Hokurikudō, lived Asakura Yoshikage, heir to a small well-organized kingdom built up by his grandfather Toshikage. Toshikage had left his grandson a set of rules of conduct, like those of Hōjō Sōun, which included the perceptive observation, 'Swords or daggers of famous warriors ought not to be coveted. A sword worth ten thousand pieces can be overcome by one hundred spears worth only one hundred pieces.'

In March 1570 the heir to this good advice had to face Oda Nobunaga, who chose to command the Hokurikudō expedition in person. He was accompanied by Ieyasu and Hideyoshi, and was about to attack Asakura's headquarters of Ichijō-ga-tani when he received the alarming intelligence that his brother-in-law, Asai Nagamasa, had allied himself with Asakura. As Asai held the passes of Northern Ōmi there was grave danger of Nobunaga's entire army being cut off from Kyōto and surrounded. A retreat was decided upon, so Nobunaga left with the main body of the army, while Hideyoshi and Ieyasu organized a fighting rearguard. It was a masterly operation, considering that Nobunaga's army consisted of 110,000 men, and the two forces succeeded in keeping Asakura back while the rest of the army returned safely. The operation of the rearguard formed a strong bond between Ieyasu and Hideyoshi, both of whom faced considerable danger. Ieyasu is recorded as having made good practice with an arquebus, indicating that he was in the thick of things.

Later in the year Nobunaga returned to Ōmi to attack Asai, which resulted in the furious Battle of the Anegawa. (See map, Fig. 61.)

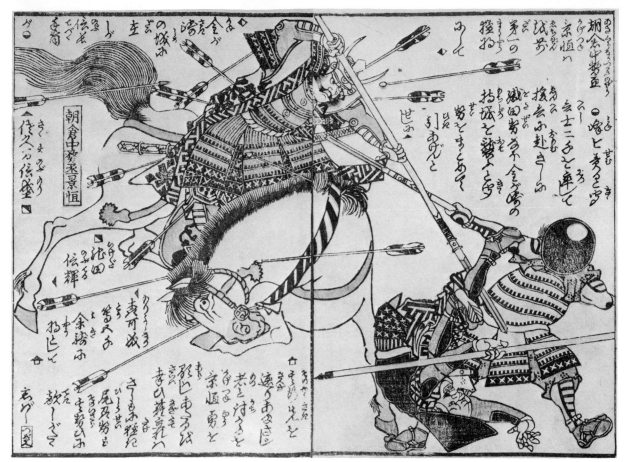

朝倉中務丞景恒

60 Asakura Yoshikage, defeated by Nobunaga at the Battle of the Anegawa, 1570. (E. G. Heath collection.)

Nobunaga proceeded from his headquarters of Gifu, in Mino, along the Nakasendō Road and up the eastern side of Lake Biwa towards Nagahama. On 21 July he neared Ōtani, Asai's headquarters, which he threatened by attacking Yokoyama Castle about five miles to the south-east. Here Ieyasu joined him with 5,000 men of the Tokugawa force from his home province of Mikawa. At this battle we meet for the first time Ieyasu's 'Shi-tennō', his four chief retainers. Their names were Sakai Tadatsugu, Ishikawa Kazumasa, Sakakibara Yasumasa and Honda Tadakatsu. The last named was a particularly flamboyant character, who wore a helmet ornamented with wooden antlers (Figs 50 and 101). He proved himself as a long established and staunch supporter of the Tokugawa house.

The main forces of Asai, augmented by those of Asakura, took up positions straddling the road to Ōtani, with the river Anegawa in between them and Nobunaga's troops. Their plan was to attack at dawn the following day with Asai's 8,000 and Asakura's 10,000. Nobunaga's army outnumbered them by about two to one, and Nobunaga hoped to capitalize upon this numerical superiority by attacking first. In fact his troops were not all reliable, but the questionable contingents had been placed under the watchful eye of Hideyoshi, so Nobunaga had little to fear. He originally intended to let Ieyasu confront Asai, but changed his mind in view of his own relationship, and

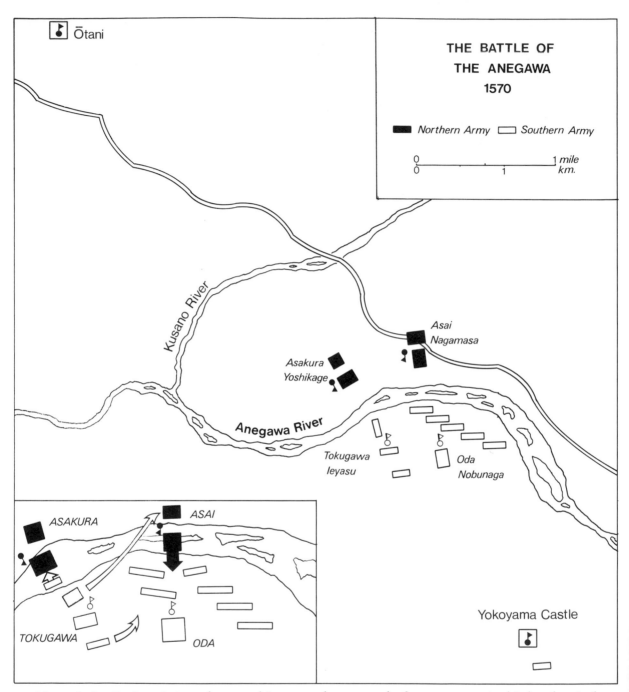

The Battle of
the Anegawa
1570

Northern Army   Southern Army

0   1 mile
0   1   km.

Ōtani

Kusano River

Asai
Nagamasa

Asakura
Yoshikage

Anegawa River

Tokugawa
Ieyasu

Oda
Nobunaga

Yokoyama Castle

ASAKURA   ASAI

TOKUGAWA   ODA

61 Map of the Battle of the
Anegawa, 1570.

drew up his personal command of 23,000 opposite his brother-in-law.
They were arranged thirteen ranks deep to withstand the shock of a
charge.

At 4 am both armies waded into the wide, shallow waters of the
Anegawa. Ieyasu's troops, with Sakai and Ishikawa in front, and
Honda and Sakakibara in the second rank, met and held Asakura's force

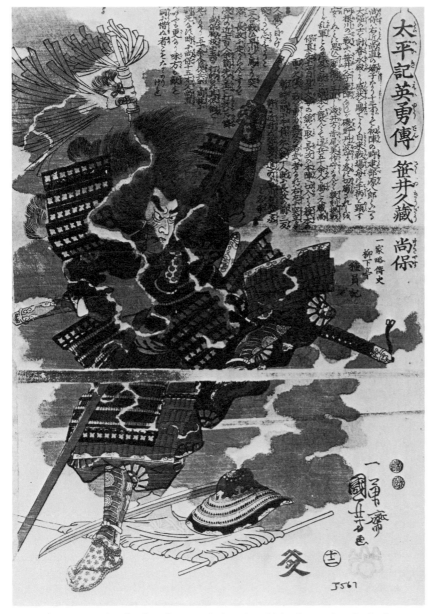

太平記英勇傳 笹井久藏 尚保

62 Spearman against musketry. One of the best known Kuniyoshi prints, depicting the bravery of Sasai Masayasu at the Battle of the Anegawa, 1570. (Victoria and Albert Museum.)

in mid-stream. As the battle raged clouds of black smoke drifted across the river from the arquebuses, and the combatants became soaked with sweat, as well as wetted by the waters of the red-tinted river. Nobunaga's force was not doing so well. Asai had broken through his ranks and was menacing Nobunaga himself. So Sakakibara and Honda detached their divisions from the struggle on the left wing, crossed the river and descended on to Asai's right flank, while Inaba Ittetsu, whom Ieyasu had held in reserve until that moment, supported Nobunaga's left. The battle was joined by the besiegers of Yokoyama Castle, who left their posts and hastily came to the fight. The result was a victory for Nobunaga.

The Northern commanders retired, and half their army lay dead. As a token of appreciation Nobunaga presented Ieyasu with a fine sword, and an arrowhead that once belonged to the 'giant' Minamoto Tametomo. An incident that occurred during the Anegawa campaign is also worth relating. A samurai called Sasai Masayasu entered Asai Nagamasa's headquarters, spear in hand. He was met by a furious barrage of arquebus fire which flung him backwards. In all fifty bullets hit him, and his bravery has been immortalized in one of Kuniyoshi's best known prints, 'Spearman against musketry' (Fig. 62).

The Battle of the Anegawa may have been a victory, but it was far from decisive. Within a few months Asai and Asakura were active again. Their opportunity came when Nobunaga's attentions were directed towards Miyoshi Chōkei. Nobunaga was busily engaging Miyoshi near Ōsaka when the latter was reinforced by Ikkō sectarians from the Ishiyama Hongan-ji, including 3,000 armed with arquebuses. Seeing Nobunaga involved, Asai and Asakura brought an army down through Ōmi. Nobunaga hastily abandoned the unequal struggle with the Ikkō and swung round on the two Northern allies, driving them back up the mountain passes. The deep snows of winter 1570/1 hindered their retreat, and Nobunaga's forces were about to deliver the final blow when they were suddenly attacked in flank by the monks of the Enryaku-ji. The fighting power of this well-established hornets' nest may have paled in comparison with the Ishiyama Hongan-ji but they were still as formidable as ever, and Nobunaga was forced to give ground and fell back to Kyōto. His position, by spring 1571, looked more perilous than ever. Ieyasu was unable to help him, because Takeda Shingen had made an alliance with Hōjō, and it was all that Ieyasu could do to keep this pair of lions at bay. So Nobunaga was encompassed about by enemies on all sides, most of whom seemed to be monks. His defence line stretched from Kyōto to Gifu, and was proving difficult to hold.

To break out of the net Nobunaga decided to launch a full-scale attack on the Enryaku-ji, an operation that reveals the ruthless nature of Nobunaga as does no other incident in his long, eventful career. It will be remembered that the Enryaku-ji had always been held in special respect because of its position next to the capital, and in spite of the appearance of new sects such as Zen and Nichiren the Tendai monastery of Enryaku-ji still exerted an authority that no other foundation could equal. After a preliminary feint in another direction Nobunaga swung round on Mont Hiei with 30,000 men. In vain his own subordinates begged him to reconsider, but he was adamant. 'I am not the destroyer of this monastery' he said. 'The destroyer of the monastery is the monastery itself!' Under cover of darkness his samurai encircled Mount Hiei, and at dawn, when the blowing of conch-shell trumpets gave the signal, Nobunaga's army began slowly to move up the mountain, and simply shot or cut down any person they met – man, woman or child. The Jesuit Father Frois noted that the attack began on 29 September 1571, the Feast of the Archangel Michael:

'. . . he burnt Sakamoto with two other villages at the foot of the mountain, and by favour of the smoke his men climbed up the rocks, entered the fortress [sic] and put all to fire and sword. They made a horrible slaughter of all these false priests. Some, indeed precipitated themselves from the rocks, others took sanctuary in their temples, and others hid themselves in grottos and caves; but Nobunaga had concerted his business so well that not one of them escaped. He set fire to the temple of the God Kwannon, which had cost immensely, and burnt all the other temples and monasteries; in a word, he put his men into every hole or cave, as if he had been in a chase of some wild beasts, and there butchered these miserable wretches. Thus God punished these enemies of his glory on Saint Michael's Day in the year 1571.'

The last sentence sums up the Jesuits' opinion of the Buddhist priesthood. It is hardly surprising that they got on well with Nobunaga.

So one enemy had been crushed, and very great had been the crushing. There was however no likelihood of the process being repeated against the Ikkō. Ishiyama Hongan-ji was a real fortress where, as noted by the active Jesuit Father Vilela, the inmates each made seven arrows daily, and held weekly archery and musketry contests. Their swords, too, could cut through a man 'as easily as a sharp knife cleaves a tender rump'. Ishiyama Hongan-ji would have to wait.

Having settled affairs close at hand satisfactorily Nobunaga could now face up to the threat from the east. Ieyasu had rendered sterling service by holding back Takeda Shingen and Hōjō Ujiyasu. The process had been helped by an alliance between Oda and Takeda against Uesugi and Hōjō. But in 1571 Ujiyasu died, and his son upset the balance of power by coming to an understanding with Shingen. Shingen's rear was now secure, and the only danger would be a possible attack by Uesugi Kenshin, which could be forestalled by moving during the winter when the passes from Echigo were blocked by snow drifts. So in October 1572 Takeda Shingen left Kai to march on Kyōto. He had with him 20,000 samurai and ashigaru, the cream of the Takeda forces, of unquestioning loyalty and fierce fighting spirit. The might of Shingen, joined by 2,000 samurai of Hōjō's, passed south out of Shinano into Tōtōmi, to join the Tōkaidō road at Hamamatsu. The irresistible force was about to meet the immovable object.

The commander of Hamamatsu Castle was Tokugawa Ieyasu. He was now twenty-nine years old, less impetuous perhaps, than when he had fought the Ikkō-ikki, but no less brave and resourceful. Shingen was fifty-one, experienced, proud and corpulent. Supporting him were some of the finest generals in Japan: Yamagata Masakage, Baba Nobuharu, Naitō Kiyonaga and Oyamada Nobutomo.

Ieyasu sent out scouts under Ōkubo Tadayo and Honda Tadakatsu, who were mauled by Shingen's advance guard, and returned rather shaken. Their spirits rose somewhat when 3,000 samurai arrived as reinforcements from Nobunaga, who could scarcely spare them, but who obviously realized that the advance of Shingen was the greatest threat to his position that he had yet faced. Ieyasu was torn between two courses of action. To risk a pitched battle with such odds against him was courting suicide, but to stay within the walls of Hamamatsu would be playing straight into Shingen's hands, who would probably detach a small force to contain the Tokugawa army, and press on to Kyōto unmolested. Takeda Shingen was no Imagawa Yoshimoto!

So Ieyasu boldly led his army out along the road to the north. Three quarters of a mile from Hamamatsu was a stretch of elevated moorland called Mikata-ga-hara. On Ieyasu's right flank ran the Magome River, while on his left the moor stretched for two miles. He drew up his troops in line abreast, or 'stork's wing' as the Japanese poetically call it. He placed the reinforcements from Nobunaga on his right, with Sakai Tadatsugu on the extreme flank where the ground began to slope. His other 'Shi-tennō' were on the left, and Ieyasu himself retained the main body a little to the rear of centre. Opposing them was the Takeda host, whose advance guard alone nearly exceeded the total Tokugawa number. Behind them stood Shingen himself, with the main body of 15,000 men. (See map, Fig. 63.)

As the two armies assembled it began to snow, and snow was falling steadily at 4 pm when the Takeda advance guard moved up to attack the wings of the Tokugawa. The left held firm, but the right, Nobunaga's reinforcements, soon collapsed, leaving Sakai Tadatsugu isolated. As Sakai endeavoured to fight his way back Takeda Katsuyori, Shingen's son, worked round to assail the rear. As it began to grow dark the Takeda centre charged forward forcing the Tokugawa to retreat rapidly. To rally his troops Ieyasu planted his standard, a large golden fan, on high ground to the rear. To avoid alarming the garrison at Hamamatsu, Ieyasu called over a samurai who had taken the head of a cowled warrior, and ordered him to carry it down to Hamamatsu and proclaim it as the head of Shingen.

By now the Takeda samurai were getting perilously close to Ieyasu, and arrows and bullets were whistling past his head. The thought crossed his mind of dying like a true samurai, but the demands of posterity prevailed and Ieyasu galloped away in the direction of Hamamatsu. It was a narrow escape. One of his companions actually kicked a bow out of the hands of an enemy samurai as they rode by, and Ieyasu put an arrow through a samurai who ran at him with a spear. On arrival at the castle Ieyasu gave orders for the gates to be left open and torches lit to guide the retreating troops home. 'It will also confuse the enemy,' he added. 'To shut the gates would make them think we are afraid of them!' Eventually the Takeda samurai did arrive, and noted on their way that all the Tokugawa who had fallen in the retreat had died facing the enemy. No attempt was made to assault the castle that night. If one had been made it may well have succeeded. As it was Ieyasu slept peacefully, and a corps of volunteer samurai descended on Shingen's camp, which he had pitched near Sai-ga-dani. As they

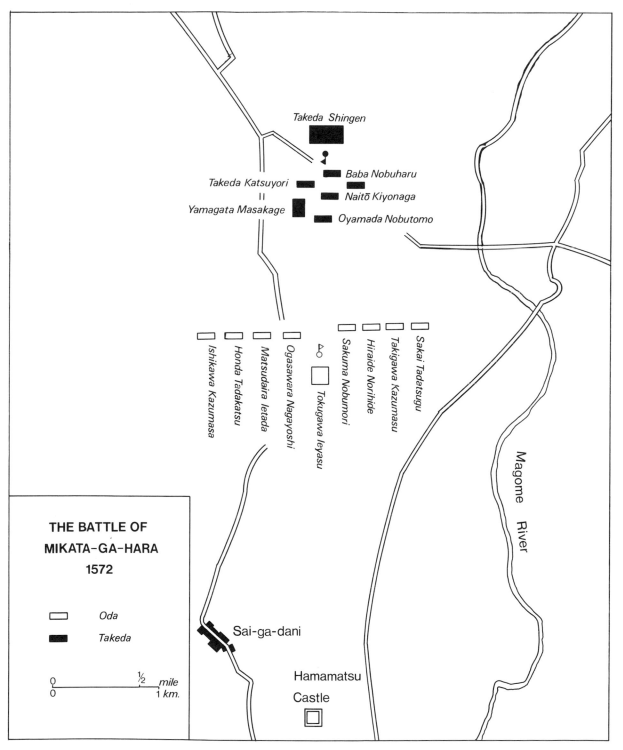

Takeda Shingen

Baba Nobuharu

Takeda Katsuyori

Naitō Kiyonaga

Yamagata Masakage

Oyamada Nobutomo

Ishikawa Kazumasa

Honda Tadakatsu

Matsudaira Ietada

Ogasawara Nagayoshi

Tokugawa Ieyasu

Sakuma Nobumori

Hiraide Norihide

Takigawa Kazumasu

Sakai Tadatsugu

Magome River

THE BATTLE OF
MIKATA–GA–HARA
1572

☐ Oda

■ Takeda

0 ½ mile
0 1 km.

Sai-ga-dani

Hamamatsu
Castle

63 Map showing the Battle of
Mikata-ga-hara, 1572.

64 Tokugawa Ieyasu after the Battle of Mikata-ga-hara, 1572. (Tokugawa Art Museum, Nagoya.)

were on their home ground they managed to get in quite close before opening fire, so the Takeda samurai spent a very disturbed night.

Next morning Shingen called a council of war. The longer they waited for Hamamatsu to fall the sooner would come the spring thaw, and Uesugi Kenshin would be sweeping down from Echigo. So Shingen decided to withdraw, and arrange a concerted attack upon Nobunaga using an unholy alliance of Takeda, Asai, Asakura and the Ikkō-ikki. In early 1573 Shingen returned to the fray, and marched into Mikawa to prepare for the final showdown. His first objective was a castle held by one of Ieyasu's generals. The siege proceeded well, so well in fact that the defenders soon had no food at all, the only provisions in the castle being a rather large quantity of sake. Not wishing to let this precious brew fall into the hands of the enemy the garrison agreed to dispose of the liquor in the most appropriate manner. The sound of carousing carried far on the night air, and Shingen himself approached the ramparts that he might hear more clearly the pleasant sound of a flute being played by a sentry. As he reached the wall a samurai, who was obviously less inebriated than the others, took aim with his arquebus, and shot him in the head. Although the wound was not instantly fatal, Takeda Shingen died in April 1573, unquestionably one of the greatest samurai commanders who ever lived. On hearing of his death Uesugi Kenshin is said to have wept for the loss of the 'best of enemies'.

To the Takeda family Shingen's death was a tremendous blow. His heir, Katsuyori, was brave enough, but quite lacked his father's enormous talents. The old retainers of the family had no confidence in his ability, and the ruin of the house looked imminent. To Nobunaga the news was the best he had received for a long time. As if inspired by Shingen's demise he kicked the Shōgun Yoshiaki out of Kyōto, thereby abolishing the Ashikaga Shōgunate once and for all, and attacked Asai and Asakura so fiercely that they both committed suicide. In summer 1574 he attacked an Ikkō stronghold on the Kiso River, and began a blockade of Ishiyama Hongan-ji. Nobunaga's star was once more on the ascent, and the following year he reached the pinnacle of his success in the Battle of Nagashino, a battle that marked a new era in Japanese warfare.

If Nagashino had been the only victory Nobunaga had ever won his reputation would still have been assured. Nagashino was a castle in Mikawa, built on a naturally strong position where the Takigawa and Ōnogawa rivers joined to form the Toyokawa. At their confluence the rivers were up to a hundred yards wide with steep, high banks, so it was a commanding site. In spite of its obvious strength Nagashino had changed hands more than once, and in May 1575 it was held for Oda Nobunaga by Okudaira Sadamasa, an energetic samurai of twenty-four, a Mikawa man under Tokugawa Ieyasu. On 16 June Nagashino Castle was attacked by Takeda Katsuyori. The garrison put up a spirited defence against all the wiles that a son of Shingen might possess. He had brought with him a company of miners from the Takeda gold

156

mines, who began tunnelling under the walls. The defenders counter-mined. Katsuyori then constructed rafts and floated samurai across the rivers, but the platforms were as vulnerable as sitting ducks. Siege-towers were erected, and dragged up to the walls, but the defenders gleefully blasted away at them with heavy calibre muskets. By 22 June Katsuyori had decided to convert the siege into a blockade, so palisades were built and cables stretched across the river, and the Takeda samurai settled down to starve the defenders out.

As the defenders had only a few days' food left they were becoming alarmed. Requests for help had been sent to Ieyasu, who had forwarded a plea for reinforcements to Nobunaga, but the garrison knew of none of these developments. There then occurred one of those brave incidents that brighten the monotonous chronicle of sixteenth-century campaigns, as the individual samurai spirit asserts itself. A samurai called Torii Suneemon volunteered to take a message out of the beleagured castle to Ieyasu. At midnight on 22 June Torii slipped quietly into the river and swam down past the Takeda sentries, cutting the cable with his dagger. He soon arrived at Okazaki, whereupon Ieyasu and Nobunaga promised immediate aid, so Torii hurried back with the good news. Unfortunately the gallant samurai was too eager to let the garrison know that all was well, for he lit a beacon on a near-by hill, which the Takeda saw and suspected. When Torii swam upstream he found that the cables now had bells attached to them. The ringing of the bells gave Torii away to the Takeda. He was apprehended and brought before Katsuyori, who promised him his life as well as a large reward if he would proceed to the castle walls and warn the garrison that succour could not arrive and that there was nothing left but surrender. He consented, but Katsuyori, not a little suspicious, had Torii bound to a tall wooden cross, which he set up before the castle. The garrison were summoned to the ramparts to receive Torii's message. As an added precaution against trickery a number of footsoldiers encircled the cross and held their spear points against his body, whereupon Torii raised his voice and shouted, 'Before three days are out you will be relieved. Stand Fast!' As he uttered these words the spears were driven into his body. Torii's courageous act is the best example of that most perfect form of samurai courage – a deed that earns respect from friend and foe alike. A certain samurai on the Takeda side was so struck with Torii's example that he had a picture of him on the cross painted on his banner.

The fact remained that reinforcements *were* on their way, and in considerable number. Nobunaga saw in the relief of Nagashino an opportunity to crush finally the Takeda clan, so he was bringing 30,000 men, while Ieyasu had 8,000. The besieging force of the Takeda was scarcely 15,000, so the wise old retainers of Shingen advised their young lord to withdraw. Alas, Katsuyori was for fighting, so Baba and Naitō tried to save the clan's honour, if not its head, by suggesting an all out assault on the castle so that they could occupy it. Katsuyori turned this suggestion down also, and the old generals could do little but prepare to die bravely on the morrow.

Seeing that Katsuyori was resolved on a fight, Nobunaga made his plans accordingly. He knew that Katsuyori had capitalized as best he could on the legacy left by his father of a highly trained, very loyal army, whose great strength was its mobility. Constant practice at Kawanakajima had made the Takeda cavalry a force to be reckoned with, and although Nobunaga had the larger army, his troops were by no means as reliable and could not be trusted to stand up to a charge. The preparations Nobunaga made to withstand this threat have earned him his place in military history. His men were equipped with stakes and rope for making a stockade, which was erected behind a stream on the high ground below Mount Gambo, about a mile from the Takeda lines. It was really a loose palisade, just high enough to prevent a horse leaping over, and with gaps every fifty yards or so for the convenience of counter-attack. Nobunaga's master-stroke was that he did not merely line up his army behind the palisade, but detached from his total force of 10,000 arquebusiers the 3,000 best shots, and lined them up in three ranks of a thousand each under Sasa Narimasa, Maeda Toshiie and Honda Tadakatsu. The orders he gave them indicate how completely he appreciated the potential of the arquebus. He had realized that the chief drawbacks were its short range and slow loading, so the 3,000 men were ordered to fire each rank alternately in volleys, and for all to hold their fire until the enemy were within close range.

On the left wing of his army he placed Sakuma Nobumori in front of the stockade as 'bait' for the Takeda cavalry, and on the right of the stockade Ōkubo Tadayo straddled the road with five hundred arquebusiers ready for a flank attack. The extreme left was held by Toyotomi Hideyoshi and Shibata Katsuie, the victor of Sakai, 1567, while Nobunaga, two of his sons, and Ieyasu, remained behind the stockade with the main body. (See map, Fig. 65.) During the night of 28 June Sakai Tadatsugu of the Tokugawa force took a small band of samurai and disturbed the sleep in the Takeda camp. Dawn broke at 5 am on 29 June 1575, and the Battle of Nagashino began.

Takeda Katsuyori had arranged his army in five groups of 3,000 for the attack, under Baba on the right, Naitō the centre, and Yamagata the left. Katsuyori was to follow the three veterans with 3,000, while the final group maintained the siege. The first group into the attack was Yamagata's, who attacked Ōkubo Tadayo outside the palisade. The assault developed into a fierce hand-to-hand fight, as did the attack by Baba on the Oda left wing. But meanwhile the Takeda centre had launched a charge against the palisade. The ground was uneven, and muddy from the previous night's rain. As soon as the slow progress of the Takeda horsemen brought them to the edge of the stream a devastating volley from a thousand arquebuses tore into them. Volley after volley followed, until men and horses were scattered around the slopes. The right wing under Baba also caught the blast of fire as Sakuma feigned a retreat, and Hideyoshi and Shibata Katsuie swept round to fall on his flanks. Katsuyori then ordered up his reserves,

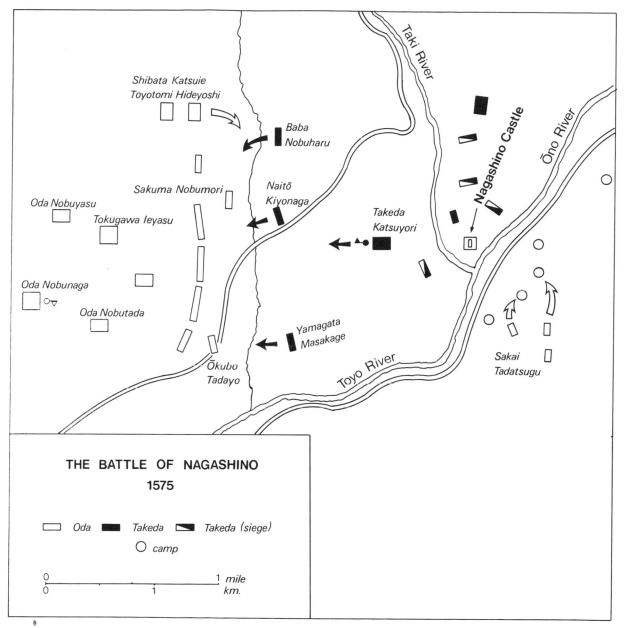

Shibata Katsuie
Toyotomi Hideyoshi

Baba
Nobuharu

Sakuma Nobumori

Naitō
Kiyonaga

Oda Nobuyasu

Tokugawa Ieyasu

Takeda
Katsuyori

Oda Nobunaga

Oda Nobutada

Yamagata
Masakage

Ōkubo
Tadayo

Taki River

Nagashino Castle

Ōno River

Toyo River

Sakai
Tadatsugu

THE BATTLE OF NAGASHINO
1575

☐ Oda   ■ Takeda   ◣ Takeda (siege)
○ camp

0   1 mile
0   1   km.

and personally led an assault on the stockade. But the alternate volleying was still calm, controlled and efficient. Every twenty seconds a hail of bullets tore into the ranks and blasted the Takeda samurai to eternity. Baba Nobuharu, Yamagata Masakage and Naitō Kiyonaga lay among the dead, along with many others of Shingen's old retainers. When the garrison of Nagashino Castle saw that the battle was going their way they sallied out and attacked the Takeda in the rear. At the same time the Oda main body left the palisade and joined in hand-to-hand fighting.

65 Map showing the Siege and Battle of Nagashino, 1575.

The events of that memorable day are preserved in a six-fold painted screen, painted at the end of the sixteenth century. Although obviously stylized it depicts with great vigour the excitement of a samurai battle, and several characters may be recognized. Takeda Katsuyori, with his white banner, is seen leading the reserve; Ieyasu is recognizable by the golden fan standard; Oda Nobunaga is in the top left hand corner, and Hideyoshi is preceded by his 'golden gourd standard'. As Hideyoshi's military career developed he is said to have added a golden gourd for every victory. At the palisade Honda Tadakatsu's antlers make him instantly recognizable.

The Battle of Nagashino was a triumph for Nobunaga's modern methods, but some blame must be attached to Takeda Katsuyori for making the slaughter possible by his impetuosity. Takeda Shingen would never have made such a mistake, as his veterans realized, but loyalty to their young lord overcame their good sense and the tragic charge took place. As for Katsuyori, he escaped from the battlefield and continued his campaigns against Nobunaga on a much reduced scale. It was 1582 before Nobunaga had the satisfaction of seeing his head.

Nobunaga now felt sufficiently secure in the east to concentrate upon the west, where the strongest power had been the Mōri family since the Battle of Miyajima in 1555. Mōri Motonari had died in 1571, and his rich domains, comprising no less than ten provinces, passed to his grandson Mōri Terumoto. The 'Two Rivers', Kobayakawa Takakage and Kikkawa Motoharu, were still active, and led the forces of both collateral families in support of their nephew. Up to about 1575 the Mōri had not ventured to challenge Nobunaga's supremacy, but at the prompting of the deposed Shōgun Yoshiaki they made an alliance with the Ishiyama Hongan-ji, and sent out feelers towards Uesugi Kenshin. Takeda Katsuyori was also approached, but not unsurprisingly declined to join any alliance against Nobunaga.

For some time Nobunaga's 'Admiral', Kuki Yoshitaka, had been blockading Ishiyama Hongan-ji from the Ōsaka seaboard. As the Mōri controlled most of the shipping through the Inland Sea, Terumoto decided to begin hostilities against Nobunaga by running the blockade. This he did quite easily in August 1575, an insult which forced Nobunaga to turn west on Mōri. Ieyasu was still busy chasing Takeda Katsuyori, so the task was given to Nobunaga's two ablest subordinate generals, Toyotomi Hideyoshi and Akechi Mitsuhide. (Ieyasu, of course, was regarded as an ally, and not as a subordinate.) Ever since the time that Hideyoshi had first entered his service as an ashigaru Nobunaga had recognized his great talent, so entrusted him with the most difficult part of the campaign. The attack on Mōri was to be the first real movement by Nobunaga's troops out of their own immediate vicinity, and would involve fighting a way along the Inland Sea. To aid Hideyoshi's advance along the Sanyōdō, Akechi Mitsuhide was to proceed along the San'indō, the Japan Sea coast road. Thus the two generals set off on a campaign that was to keep them occupied for some time to come.

During 1576 Nobunaga began work on his new castle at Azuchi, on the edge of Lake Biwa. If Nagashino can be said to have revolutionized military tactics, then this supreme edifice revolutionized military architecture. From Kusunoki's defence of Chihaya to Okudaira's defence of Nagashino we have seen the concept of a defensive building develop from stockade to castle, but until Azuchi was built the castle was viewed as a purely military structure. Azuchi transcended military needs, and was a great mansion as well as a fortress, which would impress rivals as much by its interior decoration as by its military strength. Azuchi, designed by Niwa Nagahide, one of Nobunaga's generals, expressed in a striking way the character of its owner and the spirit of the age. Its proportions were colossal. It was built on a promontory rising six hundred feet out of the lake. The stone wall enclosing the castle was several thousand feet long and seventy feet high, within which were four concentric baileys. The keep was seven storeys high, and contained, in addition to the castle arsenal and storehouses, the most gorgeously decorated private apartments and audience chambers. Father Frois visited it, and commented:

'. . . his palace and castle, which as regards architecture, strength, wealth and grandeur may well be compared with the greatest buildings of Europe.'

The site of Azuchi had been carefully selected. It was built outside Kyōto, away from the periodic conflagrations that affected the city, where it commanded the main lines of communication to the east. The use of stone, and the loopholes in the battlements showed Nobunaga's regard for firearms, but above all Azuchi Castle was important as a symbol. It displayed Nobunaga's power in a way no army could. Compare Azuchi to Yoshimasa's 'Silver Pavilion', and it will be realized how dramatically the balance of power had shifted in a century. Azuchi's architecture was the brash, splendid style of the military dictator. It is customary to date a new period in art history, the 'Azuchi-Momoyama' from 1576.

While Azuchi was being built Nobunaga continued his campaigns. In June 1576 he led an attack on the Ishiyama Hongan-ji, but was wounded in the leg by a bullet. This made him change his plans somewhat, and in 1577 he led a series of campaigns against the outposts and supporters of the Ikkō leaguers, with the aim of isolating them by land as well as by sea. In 1578 he began construction of six 'iron ships', certain parts of the superstructure of these ships being reinforced with iron plates. They were 72 feet long and 42 feet wide, and equipped with 'cannon'. For 'cannon' we may possibly have to read the large calibre versions of the matchlock musket. Two pieces of Portuguese cannon had been presented to Ōtomo Sōrin in 1551, but they had proved difficult to copy. The large muskets, called 'wall guns' were up to nine feet long, but they saw little action afloat, as the 'iron ships'

66 Suit of armour. The breastplate is patterned with Dutch leather, evidence of the spread of European taste. (I. D. Bottomley collection.)

had serious technical deficiencies. They succeeded in peppering a pirate fleet, but when attacked by Mōri one was boarded and capsized.

In the same year, 1578, Nobunaga received further welcome news. Uesugi Kenshin had died at the age of forty-eight. He had apparently suffered a haemorrhage after an apopleptic fit in his lavatory and died nine days later. His death was so timely for Nobunaga that assassination was definitely suspected, and grisly tales grew up about the activities of *ninja*, but nothing was ever proved.

Meanwhile the Ishiyama Hongan-ji was being pressed from all sides, now that the life-line from Mōri had been finally cut. At last, in 1580, the defiant Ikkō sectarians gave in. With the fall of Ishiyama Hongan-ji the long history of the warrior-monks comes to an end. Two years later Ieyasu brought Nobunaga the head of Takeda Katsuyori, which the latter examined with the greatest of pleasure.

Nobunaga was now free to concentrate upon the defeat of the Mōri. For five years Hideyoshi had been making slow but steady progress, in contrast to Akechi Mitsuhide, whose campaign had been less than successful. Hideyoshi's campaign had been a long succession of sieges, which took time, but he had been helped by the defection to his side of Ukita Naoie, one of Mōri's allies. By April 1582 Hideyoshi had advanced as far as Bitchū, and laid siege to a certain castle called Takamatsu. He first attempted to bribe the commander, but this failed, so Hideyoshi resorted to an ingenious feat of engineering. Takamatsu stood on marshy ground only a few feet above sea level, so Hideyoshi built a dyke over a mile long and diverted the waters of the Ashimori River so that they began to form a lake in the valley where the castle stood. As the waters rose the castle became a refuge for rats and snakes, and Hideyoshi's gunners kept up a steady fire. With hot lead above and water below the commander sent an urgent plea for help to Mōri Terumoto, who soon came on the scene accompanied by the 'Two Rivers'. (See map, Fig. 67.) Faced with the entire Mōri family, Hideyoshi urgently summoned reinforcements from Nobunaga who sent nearly every man he could spare under Ikeda, Hori, Takayama and others, meaning to follow personally soon afterwards. As Ieyasu was in Sakai, enjoying a short rest after his long campaign against the Takeda, Oda Nobunaga was left alone in Kyōto with scarcely one hundred men, in place of his customary bodyguard of 2,000.

Akechi Mitsuhide, the general who had failed against the Mōri, was in Kyōto at the time, and under orders from Nobunaga to march west to reinforce Hideyoshi. As he reached the Katsura River he wheeled his troops round and exclaimed, 'The enemy is in the Honnō-ji!' The Honnō-ji was Nobunaga's Kyōto residence, and Akechi's followers immediately realized the implication of his remark. With their matches already burning in their serpentines they re-entered Kyōto as dawn was breaking on 21 June 1582, and surrounded the Honnō-ji on all sides. The guards were quickly dealt with, and the insurgents entered the courtyard. Nobunaga had just got up and was washing when he heard the sounds of commotion outside. Suddenly an arrow struck

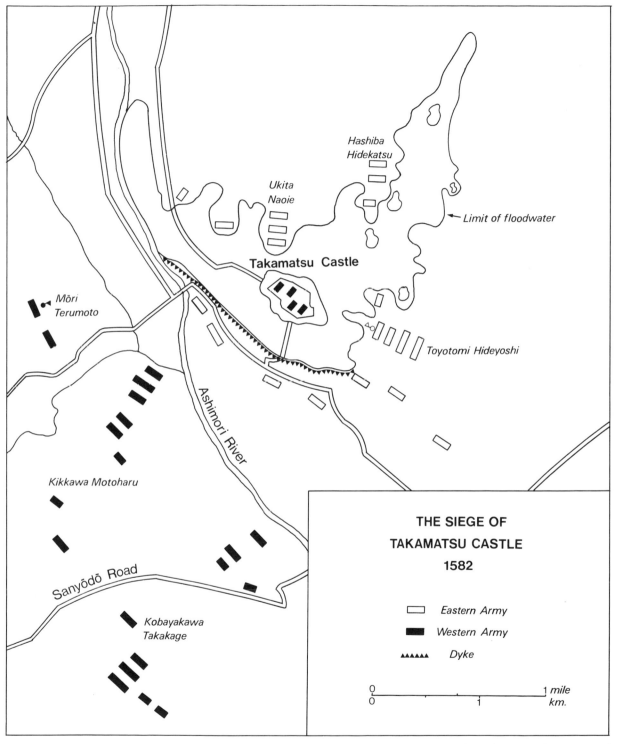

Hashiba
Hidekatsu

Ukita
Naoie

← Limit of floodwater

Takamatsu Castle

Mōri
Terumoto

Toyotomi Hideyoshi

Ashimori River

Kikkawa Motoharu

Sanyōdō Road

Kobayakawa
Takakage

**THE SIEGE OF
TAKAMATSU CASTLE
1582**

☐ *Eastern Army*

■ *Western Army*

▲▲▲▲▲▲ *Dyke*

0   1 *mile*
0   1   *km.*

67 Map showing the Siege of
Takamatsu Castle, 1582.

68 The death of Oda Nobunaga at the Honnō-ji, 1582.

him in the ribs. He drew it out and seized the nearest available weapon, a spear, and laid about him with it until a bullet shattered his left arm. As Father Frois wrote:

'Then he retreated into the rooms and shut the door with great difficulty. Some say that he cut his belly, and killed himself, according to the usage of the Japanese lords, others will have it that he was burned alive in the blazing palace, which the assailants speedily fired. But be that as it may, it suffices that he who before made everyone tremble not merely with a word, but with his very name, is now turned into dust and ashes.'

So perished Oda Nobunaga, aged forty-eight, at the hands of a second-rate general who seized a favourable opportunity. Akechi Mitsuhide's motives can only be guessed at. He was apparently conceited about his skills as a poet, which was much disliked by Nobunaga. Nobunaga drew attention to Mitsuhide's premature baldness by nicknaming him 'the Shaveling'. On one occasion Nobunaga, when drunk, had held Mitsuhide's bald head under his arm and beaten a tattoo on it with his iron war-fan. This series of insults and jealousies may have driven him to murder Nobunaga, but it is tempting to regard Hideyoshi's and Ieyasu's absence from the scene as not merely fortuitous. However, no evidence of a plot was ever furnished, or sought.

Nobunaga's military achievements cannot be overestimated, but it must be recognized how much he owed to men like Hideyoshi and Ieyasu. Yet Nagashino was all his own, and by it he established a reputation that is entirely justified. The destruction of Enryaku-ji is his also. His fighting was efficient, but ruthless and often exceptionally savage. He showed no mercy at any time to anyone. His sole idea of victory was the extermination of his enemy. It was a violent age, it is true, but Nobunaga surpassed it in ruthlessness.

Nobunaga's legacy was seen in Azuchi. The building of a castle that was not merely to be a temporary fortress but a permanent barracks led eventually to the separation of the samurai as a social class. When danger threatened, the warriors would leave the fields to go to the castle, but as the peasant had little to fear from war the castle was needed to protect only the lord and his fighting men. Therefore a distinction grew up between those inside the walls and those outside. A man, in other words, was either a warrior or a farmer, not both. To some extent Nobunaga also helped this trend by disciplining his ashigaru and dressing them in uniforms, so that even the lowest classes became warriors. Over the years the separation of the samurai from the land, and the farmer from the sword, was to be formalized, and Azuchi Castle set the trend in motion.

Fortune, as they say, favours the bold. Oda Nobunaga had been born in exactly the right place at exactly the right time. It is ironic indeed that the master of musketry should be struck down by a musket ball in the last seconds of his life.

9. Tea and muskets

The ten months between June 1582 and April 1583 witnessed the most extraordinary display of samurai energy ever seen in as few months in Japanese history. In June 1582 Toyotomi Hideyoshi was a subordinate general fighting his master's wars. Ten months later he had avenged Nobunaga's death and controlled thirty provinces, a domain which it had taken Nobunaga twenty years to subdue. All this was achieved in a manner which reflected the next twenty years in microcosm, as Hideyoshi showed the world how he intended to win an Empire.

When the news of Nobunaga's death reached Hideyoshi he kept it strictly to himself and proposed peace terms to Mōri. The terms were generous, and soon Hideyoshi was tearing back to Kyōto. Akechi Mitsuhide, meanwhile, was furiously seeking out Nobunaga's relations to put to the sword. Nobutada, the eldest son of Nobunaga, was killed by Akechi's samurai in the Nijō Palace. Akechi then moved on to Nobunaga's fortress palace at Azuchi which he looted, distributing the gold and silver among his troops. He did no damage to the place, but a few days later it was in flames, probably due to looters, and the symbol of Nobunaga's reign was reduced to the level of its stone walls. It has never been re-built. Akechi then began to feel uneasy. He knew that Hideyoshi would soon be on his way, and his henchmen had failed to find Ieyasu. Concerning the latter there is a story told that is so in character that it may well be true. Akechi's men tried to intercept Ieyasu on his way back from Sakai to Okazaki. During his perilous journey he was at one point forced to hide under a pile of rice bales on a cargo boat. Akechi's samurai were searching the boat, and thrusting spears down through the rice bales. The blade of one spear cut his leg, but Ieyasu calmly removed the towel from his head and wiped the blade clean of blood before it was withdrawn.

On 30 June events caught up with Akechi Mitsuhide. No sooner had Hideyoshi's army arrived back in Kyōto than Akechi was attacked at Yamazaki, south west of the capital. Akechi's force was completely overwhelmed. As he escaped through the rice fields he was recognized by peasants out for plunder, who seized him and beat him to death. Only thirteen days had elapsed since he first began mustering troops against Nobunaga; hence his nickname, 'The Thirteen Day Shōgun'.

Hideyoshi thus became the avenger of Nobunaga, and this put him in a very favourable position indeed. As he had risen from the ranks and was the son of a peasant he was very popular with his men,

166

to whom fighting prowess meant everything. In spite of his small, bent stature and a face that several contemporaries compare with a monkey's, he was a veritable war-god on the field of battle. From being an ashigaru whose wedding garments had been made out of Nobunaga's old battle flags, Hideyoshi now had the whole of his former master's domain there for the taking. As an old Chinese proverb says, it would be like shifting a heavy pack from one pair of broad shoulders to another.

The main objectors to a Hideyoshi takeover were, naturally enough, the surviving members of Nobunaga's family. There were also Hideyoshi's comrades to consider, in particular Shibata Katsuie, who had fought next to him at Nagashino and who ranked as highly; Niwa Nagahide, who had so recently seen his creation of Azuchi Castle go up in smoke, Takigawa Kazumasu and Ikeda Nobuteru. Tokugawa Ieyasu was still unavailable for comment. All were men who had served Nobunaga loyally and well, and they were not willing to treat Hideyoshi's succession as apostolic. However, they were dealing with a man of vastly different character from their late lord. Hideyoshi was a cunning and shrewd politician. His suggestion that Nobunaga's grandson should be declared heir would have been an eminently reasonable one had the grandson not been one year old. The Japanese tradition of a puppet ruler was being revived with style!

It was a situation that in the climate of medieval Japan only force could resolve. Thus began four months of furious marching, besieging and battling. Hideyoshi faced a considerable strategic problem. (See map, Fig. 54.) Nobutaka, Nobunaga's third son, threatened the capital from the old Oda fortress of Gifu. Takigawa Kazumasu had conceived an intense hatred of Hideyoshi that may have been motivated by jealousy, and he was installed in the castle of Kameyama in Ise. By far the greatest threat came from Shibata Katsuie, who had distinguished himself during Nobunaga's campaigns against the Asai and the Asakura, and as a reward had been granted the provinces of Echizen and Kaga, which he administered from his castle at Kita-no-shō (now called Fukui). Shibata had marched to attack Akechi after the coup, and was much chagrined when he found that Hideyoshi had beaten him to it. The one factor in Hideyoshi's favour with regard to Shibata was that during the winter months his army was virtually snowbound in Echizen. Apart from that meteorological consideration Hideyoshi would have to rely entirely on his military skill, and the more than likely chance that his three opponents would be unable to coordinate their efforts. Hideyoshi could not count on help from any other daimyō. All, including Ieyasu, were watching Hideyoshi closely to see how he fared. It was success, not sentiment, that would bring support.

If the three allies, Oda Junior, Takigawa and Shibata had succeeded in acting together they may well have triumphed. Instead, the impetuous young Oda Nobutaka declared open war on Hideyoshi in December 1582, while the Echizen passes were still blocked with snow. It was imprudent, to say the least, and Hideyoshi reacted instantly. He led an

69 Portrait of Toyotomi Hideyoshi (1536–98).

167

army into Mino province and surrounded Gifu Castle. This show of force was too much for Nobutaka, who humbled himself and begged for mercy, placing himself entirely in the hands of Hideyoshi, who pardoned him and merely took hostages as a guarantee of good behaviour. How different from Nobutaka's late father! Nobunaga would probably have slaughtered the entire garrison.

Hideyoshi had scarcely returned to Kyōto when he received reports of fresh movements. Takigawa Kazumasu was about to move on Kyōto from Ise, supported by a detachment of Shibata's troops who were installed in Nagahama Castle in Ōmi. Nagahama was commanded by Shibata Katsutoyo, Katsuie's son, and being farther south was not affected by the snows. Forced into precipitate action by the young Oda, Shibata was obviously trying to hold Hideyoshi until the thaw. Hideyoshi, however, fought with gold as well as with steel, and a handsome bribe brought the castle of Nagahama into his hands, together with its entire garrison including the commander. With his rear protected Hideyoshi wheeled round into Ise, and besieged Takigawa Kazumasu in Kameyama Castle. Takigawa surrendered when the castle began to fall about his ears, the first successful use of mines in Japanese history.

By now Shibata Katsuie was desperate for the spring. To ward off any attack from Echizen, Hideyoshi sent a garrison to Nagahama, and threw up a chain of thirteen forts in northern Ōmi. The map in Fig. 71 shows the location of eight of these. They must have been fairly rudimentary affairs, probably the usual stockade with watch-towers, for it was winter and northern Ōmi is very mountainous. The heart of the defences lay just north of Lake Biwa, among the steep wooded hills surrounding Lake Yogo. Two forts overlooked the road that led north from Nagahama: Tagami, held by Hideyoshi's half-brother Hashiba Hidenaga, and Iwasaki-yama, under the command of the Christian Takayama Ukon; while on a mountain over 1,300 feet high stood Shizugatake, under Nakagawa Kiyohide.

All was quiet on the northern front when Hideyoshi heard that Oda Nobutaka had again revolted. No doubt cursing his generosity Hideyoshi set off once more for Gifu, but had no sooner prepared his battle lines than news came from the Ōmi/Echizen frontier. Shibata had sent Sakuma Morimasa on through the melting snow to harass the frontier forts. Sakuma had taken Iwasaki, and the Christian Takayama had been forced to retreat to Tagami. Sakuma had followed up his victory by moving on to besiege Shizugatake. The fortress had not fallen but its commander, Nakagawa, had been killed, and it was now tightly beleaguered.

Hideyoshi asked the courier whether Sakuma had withdrawn. When he replied that he had made no signs of so doing Hideyoshi's expression, sorrowful until that moment, became suddenly one of elation. Here was the one big mistake that would throw Japan into his hands like a ripe peach. And the reason for his confidence? In a word – Nagashino. The experience of that awesome battle was a memory

70 Helmet owned by Toyotomi Hideyoshi, with 'sun-burst' crest. A copy of the original, which is now lost. (Ōsaka Castle Museum.)

168

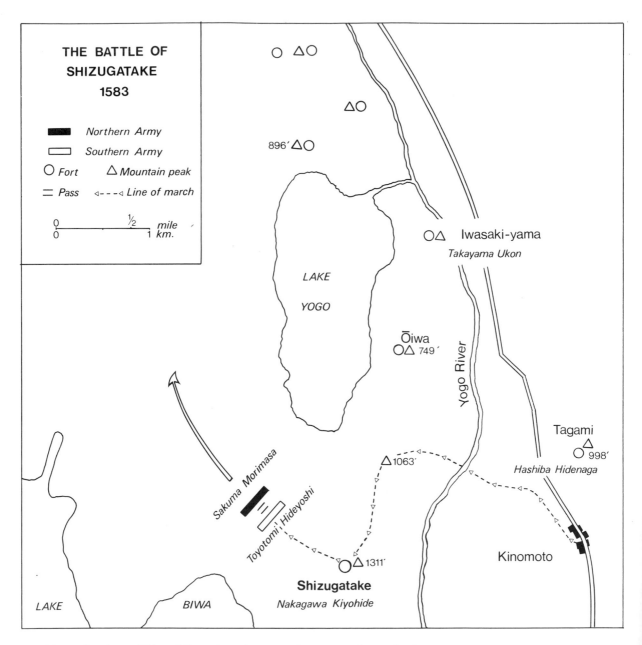

THE BATTLE OF
SHIZUGATAKE
1583

■ Northern Army
▭ Southern Army
○ Fort   △ Mountain peak
═ Pass   ◁----◁ Line of march

0   ½
|_____|_____ mile
0   1 km.

896′ △○

△○

○ △

○△ Iwasaki-yama
Takayama Ukon

LAKE

YOGO

Ōiwa
○△ 749′

Yogo River

Tagami
△
○ 998′
Hashiba Hidenaga

△ 1063′

Sakuma Morimasa
■
▭
Toyotomi Hideyoshi

Kinomoto

○△ 1311′

Shizugatake
Nakagawa Kiyohide

LAKE   *BIWA*

71 Map showing Hideyoshi's 'frontier fortresses' and the Battle of Shizugatake, 1583.

shared by both Hideyoshi and Shibata. Sakuma Morimasa had not been present, and an impetuous frontal attack such as the one he had launched against Shizugatake was suicide against a force that had taken the defensive. What was needed was a vast reinforcement, before Sakuma could be joined by Shibata, who was still fighting his way out of the Echizen passes. In one of those rapid strokes of which he was master, Hideyoshi galloped with a handful of samurai from near Gifu to Tagami, covering a distance òf fifty miles in six hours by night. There he joined his half-brother, and together with the discomfited Takayama led their armies up the mountain paths to Shizugatake. All this was achieved before dawn broke.

Sakuma, meanwhile, had disobeyed repeated commands from Shibata Katsuie ordering him to withdraw to a position. On hearing of Hideyoshi's approach before Sakuma fancied he could even have heard of the attack on Shizugatake, he withdrew to a near-by hill, where at first light his 7,000 or 8,000 troops were assailed by Hideyoshi's 6,000. The colourful screen (Plates XIII–XV), although stylized, gives an excellent impression of the battle fought among the hills and woods. The fight raged until noon, when the Echizen force broke and ran, casting away spears, muskets, swords and even clothes as they scrambled through the dense undergrowth.

There followed a bloody pursuit over the mountains to the very gates of Shibata's castle of Kita-no-shō. Shibata, who had not participated in the battle, recognized defeat when he saw it, and intended to go gloriously to his death. All the windows in the castle were locked shut, and the keep was piled high with straw which Shibata fired. As the flames rose he plunged his dagger into his abdomen. Thus finished the short but decisive Battle of Shizugatake. It gave Hideyoshi control over all that Nobunaga had left behind, and, perhaps more important, it gained him allies and loyal followers. Among the 'Seven Spears of Shizugatake', as he called his seven most valiant samurai that day, we notice the name of Katō Kiyomasa, the son of a blacksmith from Hideyoshi's village, and shortly to become one of his greatest generals.

When Oda Nobutaka heard of the death of Shibata he obligingly followed his ally's example. There was then but one son of Nobunaga still alive, Oda Nobuo, who proceeded to ally himself with the only likely rival to Hideyoshi in the whole of central Japan, Tokugawa Ieyasu. It was a fateful decision, for it brought on to opposite sides two warriors who had been close friends and comrades in arms. Any armed struggle between Hideyoshi and Ieyasu would be a clash of Titans.

Ieyasu was now a lord of five provinces, for the death of Takeda Katsuyori had given him Kai and Shinano, Shingen's old kingdom, to add to Mikawa, Tōtōmi and Suruga. Ieyasu had therefore inherited Shingen's gold mines, his well-run administration, and his trustworthy and fierce retainers. He was a foe to be feared, and this Hideyoshi appreciated.

As soon as the two realized they were irrevocably opposed they began to court allies from far and near. The strategic line-up for their contest, one of the most interesting and yet least well known in Japanese history, was briefly as follows:

Hideyoshi held the home provinces and was allied with Mōri in the west, Niwa Nagahide and Maeda Toshiie in the Hokurikudō, whom Hideyoshi had 'settled' in Shibata's vacated provinces, and Uesugi Kagekatsu, son of Kenshin, in the northern Tōsandō. Among his other land-owning generals Hideyoshi could count on Inaba Ittetsu, Gamō Ujisato and Hori Hidemasa, while nearer home were Ikeda Nobuteru and Mori Nagayoshi (no relation to Mōri). Altogether Hideyoshi's allies outnumbered Ieyasu by three to one.

Ieyasu held a wide band of the Tōkaidō, and had wisely married his daughter to Hōjō Ujinao, of the fourth generation Hōjō from Sōun. In the Hokurikudō he relied on the doubtful potency of Sasa Narimasa, whose military bearing one historian has likened to 'a dried sardine gnashing its teeth'. Shikoku was for Ieyasu, in the person of Chōsokabe Motochika. There were also a number of minor allies, including a samurai named Homo, in the Tōkaidō.

So the two giants assembled their forces. Ieyasu was forty-three, and Hideyoshi forty-nine. The collection of allies has a ring of the Gempei War about it, but on a vaster and more terrible scale. With Hideyoshi and Ieyasu there is the feeling that the 'Middle Ages' are being left behind, and that we are witnessing the clash of two 'Renaissance' armies. The reader is referred to the map in Fig. 73 to follow the campaign of 1584. Comparison with Fig. 54 will show that once again the issue was to be settled in the area surrounding the Nobi Plain, near the present city of Nagoya. It is important to bear in mind, throughout, the influence that Nagashino had had on Ieyasu and Hideyoshi. Both realized the importance of a defensive strategy, in spite of its conflict with traditional samurai ideals.

The campaign began when Hideyoshi's ally Ikeda Nobuteru took the castle of Inuyama, on the Kiso River. This brought him within twelve miles as the crow flies of Ieyasu, who had established his forward base at Kiyosu. To some extent Owari was 'no-man's land' between Mino and Ieyasu's Mikawa. The capture of Inuyama was thus an indirect move against Ieyasu, and when Ikeda's son-in-law Mori Nagayoshi was seen to be moving along the road from Inuyama towards Kiyosu, Ieyasu decided to stop the advance while the force was still isolated. Sakai Tadatsugu and others took a detachment of the Tokugawa force, 5,000 strong, and met the Mori army at Komaki, halfway along the road. Here a fierce battle ensued. Mori managed to hold the Tokugawa force in the village in spite of heavy arquebus fire, until Sakai circled round and attacked him from the rear. Mori hastily retreated, with the loss of 300 men.

Sakakibara Yasumasa then suggested that Ieyasu should move up to Komaki, for near the village was a rounded hill 280 feet high that dominated the flat rice lands. So the Tokugawa soldiery took up the spade, dug trenches and erected palisades around Komaki-yama. The building of fortifications took a week, and, as no immediate danger threatened, Ieyasu ordered the repair of two old forts at Hira and Kobata. Shortly after Ieyasu's chain of earthworks had been established Hideyoshi arrived on the scene. On 7 May 1584, he entered Inuyama Castle, where he was told of the position by Ikeda Nobuteru. Hideyoshi left Inuyama to make a reconnaisance of Ieyasu's positions, and paid his rival the compliment of the sincerest form of flattery by commencing the erection of a series of forts opposite those of Ieyasu. He established his headquarters at Gakuden, behind his front-line which stretched

72 War fan used by Toyotomi Hideyoshi. It is decorated with gold and pearls, on a scarlet silk gauze. (Tokugawa Art Museum, Nagoya.)

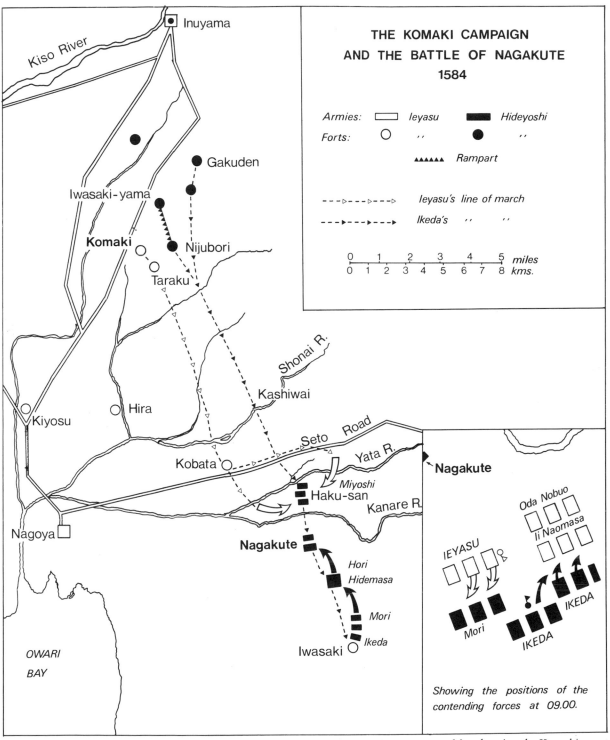

THE KOMAKI CAMPAIGN
AND THE BATTLE OF NAGAKUTE
1584

Armies: ☐ Ieyasu   ■ Hideyoshi
Forts: ○ ,,   ● ,,

▲▲▲▲▲▲ Rampart

— ▷ — ▷ — ▷   Ieyasu's line of march
— ▶ — ▶ — ▶   Ikeda's ,,   ,,

0	1		2	3	4		5	miles
0	1	2	3	4	5	6	7	8 kms.

Inuyama

Kiso River

Gakuden

Iwasaki-yama

Komaki

Nijubori

Taraku

Shonai R.

Kashiwai

Hira

Kiyosu

Seto Road

Kobata

Yata R.

Miyoshi
Haku-san

Kanare R.

Nagoya

Nagakute

Hori
Hidemasa

Mori

Iwasaki Ikeda

OWARI
BAY

Nagakute

Oda Nobuo

Ii Naomasa

IEYASU

Mori   IKEDA   IKEDA

Showing the positions of the
contending forces at 09.00.

73 Map showing the Komaki campaign and the Battle of Nagakute,
1584.

from Iwasaki-yama to Nijubori. Between these two forts, which were about a mile and a half apart, he built a rampart fifteen feet high and three feet thick. Ieyasu responded by erecting another fort at Taraku, but he did not copy the rampart. Nevertheless two armies of samurai were now 'dug in' as securely as in a trench system of the First World War. From behind the lines both commanders waited, fearing to launch a frontal attack and meet the fate of Takeda Katsuyori. Hideyoshi had no less than 80,000 men under his command, and was rather bored by the situation, as he wrote to Mōri Terumoto:

> 'Our encampments extend for a distance of ten or fifteen chō [about a mile] along the front of Komaki Castle. Although we have tried to force the enemy to fight it out in the open, Ieyasu absolutely will not come out of his castle at Komaki. So there is no use in being here. . . .'

It was obvious that such a stalemate could not last long in sixteenth century Japan. After less than a week of waiting Ikeda Nobuteru went to Hideyoshi and suggested a raid on Mikawa province. As half the samurai in Mikawa were now sitting behind palisades on Komaki-yama this sounded a reasonable suggestion if surprise could be guaranteed. Hideyoshi agreed, and prepared to launch a frontal attack on Ieyasu's positions as a diversion.

Ikeda set off at midnight, 15/16 May. His force numbered 20,000 in all, and as an aid to secrecy with such a large host, Ikeda himself left first with 6,000, followed by Mori Nagayoshi with 3,000, Hori Hidemasa with 3,000 and Miyoshi Hidetsugu with 8,000. Dawn of 16 May found them camping at Kashiwai. An army of 20,000 is not easy to conceal, and that afternoon some farmers informed Ieyasu of the presence in the Kashiwai region of a large number of enemy samurai. At first he was disinclined to believe them, but that evening a scout confirmed the report, and Ieyasu prepared to move.

By this time, of course, Ikeda's army had moved on, more slowly now, marching through the day after a short rest. On the night of 16/17 May they crossed the Yata River, and the vanguard of Ikeda was rapidly approaching the outpost of Iwasaki, held for Ieyasu by Niwa Ujishige. The army was now spread over about five miles, and at dawn on 17 May Ikeda's samurai assaulted Iwasaki, which they took with little trouble. The rest of the army breakfasted happily along the road, oblivious of the approaching Tokugawa army.

Ieyasu had left Sakai, Honda and Ishikawa in charge of Komaki, and had set off at eight o'clock on the evening of 16 May. His advance guard under Mizuno Tadashige had reached Kobata about 10 pm, where they were joined by Ieyasu at midnight. Ieyasu had correctly guessed Ikeda's strategy, and despatched Mizuno, after a two-hour sleep, to catch the rear of Ikeda's columns.

The surprise was complete. The Ikeda rearguard under Miyoshi

Hidetsugu were caught as they breakfasted on 'Haku-san' or White hill. They were suddenly attacked by Mizuno from the right and Sakakibara from the left. As they were unprepared the attack was completely successful, and Miyoshi only just managed to escape with his head. Their third division, the nearest source of help, lay about three miles farther along the road, but the sound of arquebus fire carried to them and Hori Hidemasa hurriedly wheeled his army round and marched back towards the sound of firing. They soon reached the hamlet of Nagakute, and took up positions in two companies on a hill, with the Kanare River between them and the advancing Tokugawa troops. Hori Hidemasa was a wise general, and saw the stretch of water in front of him as a defence potentially as decisive as the palisades of Nagashino. It was seven o'clock in the morning of 17 May. Hori ordered his men to light their matches, and load ready to fire when the enemy were about twenty yards away. As an added inducement he offered 100 *koku* of rice to anyone who brought down a horseman.

On came the Tokugawa troops at a run, straight into the range of the arquebuses. A hail of bullets swept their ranks, and seeing them reel Hori led his men in a vigorous charge which flung the Tokugawa samurai aside. It would have been Nagashino all over again, but as Hori's 3,000 hit the Tokugawa 4,500 and split them wide open, Hori saw on the horizon the golden fan standard of Ieyasu leading the Tokugawa main body. So Hori prudently withdrew, and again took up his position together with the first and second divisions under Mori and Ikeda, who had hurried back from Iwasaki. Ieyasu had made a wide sweep as he arrived, collecting up the remnants of his embarrassed vanguard. There was a pause while both armies dressed their ranks, and then at 9 am the 'real' Battle of Nagakute began.

The positions of the contending forces are shown in Fig. 73. The Tokugawa numbered 9,000 in all, split almost equally between the three commanders shown. Ii Naomasa was one of the pillars of the Tokugawa house. He had served with Ieyasu since 1578, and, on a suggestion from Ieyasu, dressed all his samurai and ashigaru in red lacquered armour. This was an idea Ieyasu had adopted from Shingen's old retainers, who had remarked on the habit of Yamagata Masakage of putting all his front rank men in red armour at Kawanakajima. Against Ii's 'Red Devils', as they were called, were Ikeda's two sons Terumasa and Yukisuke with 4,000 men. Mori Nagayoshi was on the left with 3,000, while Ikeda Nobuteru stayed in reserve with 2,000. This made the sides almost equal. There was no advantageous position, no palisade, and no surprise.

The battle began with the Tokugawa arquebusiers blazing away at their opponents, which goaded the two Ikeda sons into attacking Ii Naomasa, who held them off with fierce arquebus fire. Ikeda senior moved over to aid his sons, but neither Mori nor Ieyasu had yet fired a shot. Mori was waiting for Ieyasu to support his left wing, whereupon Mori could take him in flank, but Ieyasu was not fooled. He suddenly charged his whole contingent forward in two sections, and the impact alone made Mori's samurai stagger. Mori rode up and down in front of his lines and waved his war fan frantically. He stood out conspicuously in his white surcoat, and one of the Red Devils took careful aim and shot him through the head. It was a very public death, and acted as a signal to Oda Nobuo to swoop round and fall on Mori's flank. In vain did Ikeda Nobuteru send his men forward in support. The whole Mori force gave way, and Ikeda collapsed on his camp stool knowing that all was lost. A young samurai called Nagai Naokatsu ran up and speared him through, acquiring a prize head. By 1 pm the battle was over. Ieyasu sat down and was shown 2,500 heads of the defeated. He was pleased to hear that their own losses had been less than 600.

The Battle of Nagakute is illustrated in Figs 74 and 75 and Plate XVI. The centre panel of the screen (Plate XVI) shows several interesting features, including the large red standard of the Ii family bearing the first character of their name, and the death of Ikeda Nobuteru.

Meanwhile, back at the two bases, speculation was growing about the outcome of the expedition. When Hideyoshi heard of the 'breakfast battle' at Haku-san he immediately set off with reinforcements, while Honda Tadakatsu made ready to take him in flank. In fact, it never

74 The Battle of Nagakute, 1584. The troops of Hideyoshi, under Gamō Ujisato, retreat from the Tokugawa force. From a painted screen. (Tokugawa Art Museum, Nagoya.)

came to a battle, for Hideyoshi's force was so vast as to make him extremely sympathetic to Honda's bravery, and although they could have annihilated this most talented Tokugawa captain they did not even threaten him. Honda therefore carried on to Kobata, where he met Ieyasu. Soon both armies were safe behind the lines, and the previous stalemate began again.

The stalemate lasted for several months, while allies of the two rivals fought in other parts of the country, notably in the Hokurikudō, where Maeda Toshiie chastised Sasa Narimasa. From the end of 1584 the relations between Ieyasu and Hideyoshi changed from military campaigning to politics. Eventually each saw that the other was worth more with a head than without one, so Ieyasu submitted. Hideyoshi, he reasoned, could not last forever, and between them they could conquer the rest of Japan. Ieyasu had judged his time right, and well deserves his reputation as the man who won the Empire by yielding.

Between 1582 and 1586 Hideyoshi built Ōsaka Castle. It was to remain his centre of power until his death, and like Azuchi, symbolized the power of its owner. It was built on the site of Ishiyama Hongan-ji, the Ikkō's fortified cathedral, which had itself been built with an eye for strategy. Ōsaka could watch the Inland Sea with one eye and

75 The Battle of Nagakute, 1584. The heads of the slain are carried off in triumph. From a painted screen. (Tokugawa Art Museum, Nagoya.)

76 The keep of Ōsaka Castle, a modern reconstruction. (J.T.B. Kyodo News Service.)

Kyōto with another. One unusual feature in its construction was the use of cyclopean blocks of granite. The largest stone of all is forty feet long and twenty feet thick. Ōsaka Castle has suffered many vicissitudes, and its present re-building is but a shadow of its former self.

With Ieyasu on his side, and Ōsaka as a base, Hideyoshi now felt sufficiently confident to pursue the conquest of Japan. The only major clans in Japan who did not now acknowledge Hideyoshi's supremacy were, in Honshū, Hōjō and Date, both of whom were cut off by Hideyoshi's allies, and the inhabitants of Shikoku and Kyūshū. Shikoku was the first to fall, in a campaign so brief that it requires only a short mention. Hideyoshi's invading force numbered 80,000, including the Mōri family. Chōsokabe Motochika soon surrendered. He was allowed to keep Tosa province, while the rest of the island was carved up among Hideyoshi's generals.

By 1587 Hideyoshi's strength had developed so much that he was able to contemplate the ultimate campaign – the invasion and conquest of Kyūshū. The great Southern Island had always remained out of the mainstream of Japanese politics. During the Gempei War local rivalries had affected it, and Kyūshū only played a real part when Noriyori led his expedition which got no farther than thirty miles into the island. The major events of the War between the Courts served the Kyūshū samurai with little more than excuses for developing their own territorial gains. The Mongol invasions had been defeated by Kyūshū samurai acting almost alone. In short, Kyūshū was another world and, before describing Hideyoshi's invasion, it is worthwhile to examine what had been happening in Kyūshū during the Sengoku Period.

From Chapter Six it will be recalled that the growing power in southern Kyūshū was the Shimazu family of Satsuma. The Shibuya, who had opposed the Shimazu so doggedly eventually capitulated, leaving the Shimazu to enjoy undisputed power over Satsuma from their capital of Kagoshima (map, Fig. 77). It was on Shimazu territory that the firearm-carrying Portuguese had landed in 1543, and it was noted that the earliest recorded use of firearms in battle was by Shimazu Takahisa (1514–71) in 1549. In that same year he had received St Francis Xavier in audience at Kagoshima. So although Kagoshima was remote from Kyōto it was by no means a cultural backwater. Indeed the reverse was more likely true, for all trade and commerce tended to arrive first in Kyūshū, and Kyōto had to keep itself abreast of fashion.

In 1556 the Shimazu began a planned programme of conquest aimed at giving them the mastery of the whole island. It is a familiar pattern, with parallels in the rise of the Hōjō and the Tokugawa. In 1556 Ōsumi was annexed, and a seven-year campaign began against the Itō clan in Hyūga. Itō Yoshisuke capitulated in 1578, and fled north to seek support from the Christian lord of Bungo, Ōtomo Sōrin. The Ōtomo moved against the Shimazu with as many as 100,000 soldiers, and after a fierce battle on 10 December 1578 half that number lay drowned in the River Mimi-gawa or strewn dead for miles around. Ōtomo Sōrin withdrew to Bungo, vowing a most un-Christian vengeance. Hyūga was occupied by the Shimazu.

Their attention now turned towards Higo, and a vast Shimazu army besieged Mina-mata, just inside the Higo boundary. The garrison surrendered overnight on 17 September 1581, and soon nearly all of Higo was in Shimazu hands. Half of Kyūshū was now theirs. Bungo was still held by the Ōtomo, and the Ryūzōji clan controlled most of the north west. The outlying forces of Shimazu and Ryūzōji occasionally came to grips, but it was not until spring 1584, the same time that Hideyoshi and Ieyasu were preparing for the Komaki campaign, that the two clans collided. Ryūzōji Takanobu was 'mopping up' a number of samurai clans which had been left intact by the fighting. He assaulted the one independent clan in his sphere of influence – Arima, a Christian daimyō of Hizen. Arima appealed to the unbelieving Shimazu for aid, which was given in the shape of Shimazu Iehisa, the third son of the late Takahisa.

On 24 April 1584 the Shimazu entrenched themselves on high ground in front of Shimabara where they met a fierce attack from the

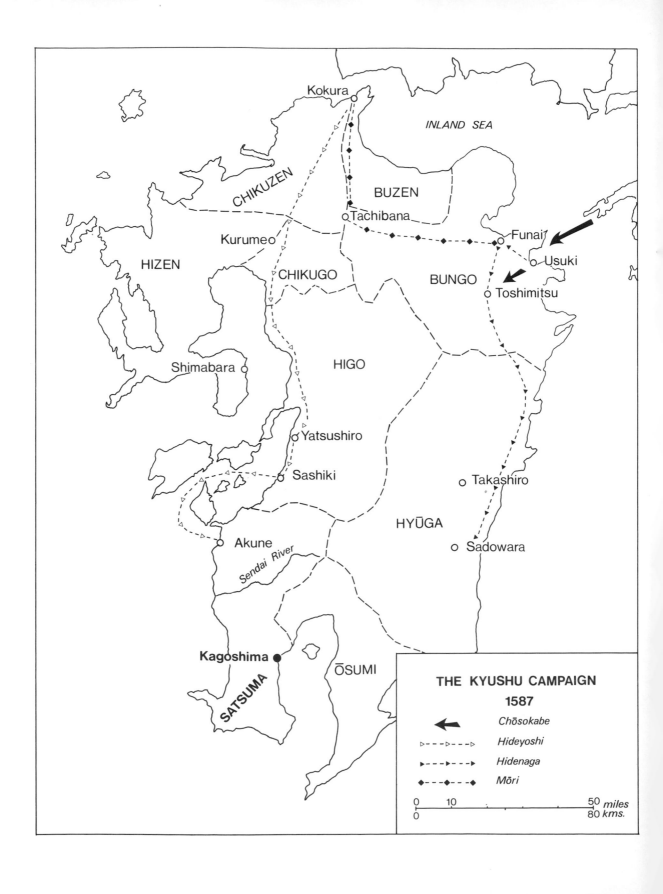

Kokura

INLAND SEA

CHIKUZEN

BUZEN

Tachibana

Kurume

Funai

Usuki

HIZEN

CHIKUGO

BUNGO

Toshimitsu

Shimabara

HIGO

Yatsushiro

Sashiki

Takashiro

HYŪGA

Akune

Sendai River

Sadowara

Kagoshima

ŌSUMI

SATSUMA

THE KYUSHU CAMPAIGN
1587

→ *Chōsokabe*

▷–▷–▷ *Hideyoshi*

►–►–► *Hidenaga*

♦–♦–♦ *Mōri*

0	10		50 *miles*
0			80 *kms.*

Ryūzōji, who were well supplied with firearms including large calibre muskets. They attacked the Shimazu and Arima in three columns, one advancing by the road, one over the hills, and the other along the beach. The latter column soon received a taste of their own medicine when the Christian Arima supported their allies by firing on the Ryūzōji from boats kept close in shore. The boats contained arquebuses, muskets and two pieces of cannon, which one assumes were probably Portuguese. As the attacking column was so thick, and advancing in front of them, they could hardly miss, and the religious significance of Christian samurai blasting Buddhist samurai did not escape them. Nor did it escape the pen of Father Frois:

'. . . the pattern to which they kept was really something to see: that, first of all, piously kneeling down with their hands turned towards Heaven, they began reciting, "Our Father, which art in Heaven, hallowed be thy name. . . ." The first phase of the strategy having thus been accomplished, turning impatiently to load the cannon with balls, they fired with such force against the enemy that with one sole shot the whole sky could be seen to be filled with limbs. Then once more on their knees they fell. The petitions of their Sunday Oration followed, and in this way they inflicted heavy losses on the "gentiles", who had not the courage to go on any farther. One part retreated and the other joined the middle column.'

In other words, 'Forgive us our trespasses . . .' and those who trespass against the Arima are sent flying in a hail of bullets! The victory of Shimabara was clinched when a flying column of Shimazu samurai burst through the Ryūzōji lines and took Takanobu's head.

The Battle of Shimabara placed all of north-western Kyūshū under Shimazu control, and made a renewed conflict inevitable between the greedy Shimazu and the revengeful Ōtomo, much to the annoyance of the Christian Arima, no doubt, whose devout behaviour had helped the Shimazu on their way. From 1585 the Shimazu made plans for the conquest of Bungo, the last major step in the conquest of Kyūshū, not dreaming what fate lay in store for them. Ōtomo Yoshimune had sent for help from Toyotomi Hideyoshi!

A request for aid was the very excuse Hideyoshi had needed. It would make his subjugation of Kyūshū infinitely easier if he could be seen to be acting on behalf of one of the indigenous clans. Taking Ōtomo's part with Gladstonian opportunism Hideyoshi wrote in the name of the Emperor to Shimazu Yoshihisa, commanding him to cease hostilities with the Ōtomo and withdraw to Satsuma whence he had come. Yoshihisa, who hardly realized that with Hideyoshi they were dealing with a military genius and a master of politics, treated the letter with contempt. He did, however, reply, and contrasted Hideyoshi's rise in power from peasant boy to dictator with the centuries of Shimazu rule in Satsuma – an observation that must have struck

77 Map showing the provinces of Kyūshū and Hideyoshi's campaign against the Shimazu of Satsuma, 1587.

181

Hideyoshi where he was most sensitive.

The Shimazu attack on Bungo began in November 1586. The Shimazu brothers, Yoshihisa, Yoshihiro and Iehisa led three great armies by way of Higo and Hyūga into Bungo. An army led by allies laid siege to Tachibana, on the Bungo-Chikuzen border, while the brothers aimed separately at Funai (now called Ōita) the capital of Bungo. Yoshihisa first advanced upon Usuki, where lived Sōrin, the older Ōtomo. Events indicated that it was a little more than the usual clan strife. A Jesuit Father complained that: 'A troop of bonzes (Buddhist monks) had joined the Satsuma army. Nothing they met with in their passage was spared by these madmen; everywhere nothing was seen but the wreck of churches and missionaries in flight.'

Meanwhile another Satsuma army was besieging Toshimitsu. As it was holding out against them, a detachment was left to cover it while the three brothers united in an attack on Funai. By now the vanguard of Hideyoshi's army had arrived in Kyūshū. The Mōri clan, under Kobayakawa and Kikkawa crossed the straits from Honshū and raised the siege of Tachibana. This was the first reverse that the Shimazu had suffered in thirty years of fighting, but this setback was offset by the speed of their advance into Bungo. The castle of Funai had, however, been reinforced by another contingent sent by Hideyoshi under Sengoku Hidehisa and Chōsokabe Motochika, who had crossed the Bungo Strait from Shikoku and landed at Usuki. Hideyoshi's orders had been to relieve Funai, but Sengoku and the younger Ōtomo disregarded their orders, in spite of pleas by Chōsokabe, and the Shikoku force marched to relieve Toshimitsu. When the Shimazu heard of the approach of the allies they made a supreme effort and took Toshimitsu by storm on 20 January 1587. When the Shikoku samurai arrived in front of the castle, they found the black-cross-in-a-ring of the Shimazu flying from the battlements. In the battle that followed the Shikoku army were utterly vanquished, and Chōsokabe's son was killed. Chōsokabe fled to the coast to re-embark for Shikoku, but the tide was out and the boats could not be reached across the quicksands. He was about to commit suicide when a samurai arrived with a message from the pursuing Shimazu Iehisa:

'We regret exceedingly to have killed your son in yesterday's engagement. Meanwhile we perceive how difficult it is to get to your boats over that quicksand. Wait tranquilly till the tide comes in. I wish you a safe return.'

The age of chivalry was not dead.

On 24 January 1587 the Shimazu entered Funai in triumph. It was a victory from which they never recovered.

Four days before the fall of Funai Hashiba Hidenaga, Hideyoshi's half-brother, had landed in Kyūshū with 60,000 men. He was joined by the 'Two Rivers', who had relieved Tachibana, and their united

command of 90,000 samurai advanced upon Funai. Faced with this fresh allied threat the Shimazu thought it no shame to fall back, and almost before the allies knew they had begun retreating they were over the border into Hyūga. Hidenaga followed in pursuit, and met with no opposition until he reached the fortress of Takashiro. This stronghold was about ten miles to the right of his line of march, and where the great Hideyoshi would have detached a division to mask it, and continue the pursuit, Hidenaga revealed his lack of talent by sitting

78 A so-called 'Three plate helmet', typical of the robust and practical designs of armour used in the Momoyama Period. (L. J. Anderson collection.)

down in front of Takashiro with all his 90,000 men.

As the siege began a message arrived from the gallant and chivalrous Shimazu Iehisa giving notice that he intended to raise the siege in due course. Thus warned, Hidenaga detached 60,000 men from the besieging force to face the Shimazu army, and fortified a position against them. The Shimazu had acquired for themselves a reputation for courage and dash, and although their province had been the first to receive the blessing of firearms, their remoteness from the centre of Honshū had left them unacquainted with the lesson of Nagashino. Hidenaga prepared accordingly. Long rows of entrenchments were dug, trees were felled by the score, and their fallen trunks arranged as barricades. Behind the lines he erected towers from which marksmen could fire on the Satsuma ranks.

The Shimazu unwisely relied upon old ideas of warfare, a trait which makes the gallant Satsuma warriors most like the cherished ideal of the typical samurai. As Gubbins relates:

'First came a picked force of 3,000 swordsmen, who were directed to abolish the entrenchments. Behind these was stationed a body of cavalry in readiness to charge over the barricades the moment that practicable breaches had been made. In the rear of the cavalry the main body of the army was drawn up, while a force of 1,000 men was sent to assail the Imperialists in the rear.'

On came the Shimazu with their customary élan, straight into the gunfire. However, the defenders were almost hoisted with their own petard, for the hottest fire was directed against the occupant of a camp stool, dressed in a magnificent suit of armour, who appeared to be directing the attacking party.

'Five times was the object of this concentrated fire shot off its seat, and each time its place was promptly filled. The marksmen were congratulating one another upon the accuracy of their aim when one, keener sighted than the rest, discovered that the supposed general was nothing more than a straw figure placed in a conspicuous position to draw the fire of the defenders. Meanwhile the assailants had effected a breach in the entrenchments, and feigning a retreat they made way for the cavalry, who dashed in and made themselves masters of this portion of the line of entrenchments.'

In spite of such an auspicious beginning the Shimazu were in their turn worsted by a simple trick, which appears all the more ironic after the incident described above. Scouts came and reported to Iehisa that a large army had arrived between them and their base of Sadowara. The large army was composed of paper streamers and old spears tied to trees, but it succeeded in making the Shimazu withdraw. The

'Imperialists' followed, and a handful of Satsuma samurai fought a desperate rearguard action, forming a half-circle round their fallen comrades. Their sacrifice was not in vain. The Satsuma army regained Sadowara, while the stolid old Hidenaga returned to sit down once more in front of Takashiro. His patience was at last rewarded when the castle gave in to starvation. Iehisa was then cooped up in Sadowara by Hidenaga's troops, which should have happened weeks before. The elder brother, Shimazu Yoshihisa, assumed control of Satsuma affairs from Kagoshima.

The castle of Takashiro must have fallen about the end of May, by which time Hideyoshi had been making steady progress. He had arrived in Kyūshū on 22 February 1587, a month after leaving Ōsaka with no less than 30,000 men. This put his total command, including Hidenaga's and Mōri's contingents, to over a quarter of a million men, drawn from as many as thirty-seven provinces. Twenty thousand pack horses carried provisions for 300,000. Only a commander with Hideyoshi's resources could conceive of such a host, organize it and transport it hundreds of miles. Incidentally, only one possessed of Hideyoshi's cunning could persuade the rich merchants of Sakai to finance it.

It was also a sign of Hideyoshi's political insight that he realized that not every Satsuma ally in Kyūshū had to be quelled. Many, he reasoned, were allies only under duress, and would willingly change sides if given the chance. The first opportunity to test this theory came when Hideyoshi drew up outside the castle of Ogura, which was held by Akizuki Tanezane. That same night Akizuki evacuated the castle and retreated to another. His eventual submission to Hideyoshi is a rather fanciful story. When Hideyoshi entered Ogura he found that the castle was unfinished, the work having been done in such haste that the walls had not been given the finishing coat of white plaster. He at once gave orders to cover the outer defences with white paper. Next morning a scout reported to Akizuki that such was the power of Hideyoshi that the castle had been entirely plastered overnight! So Hideyoshi gained one ally, confirming his view that a stealthy approach, gaining support from the clans the Satsuma had coerced, was the right one. He addressed his generals, saying:

'Let us proceed with caution, and concentrating our strength, add to it daily by winning over to our side those barons who are vassals of Shimazu. Then, when Satsuma stands alone, like a tree shorn of its leaves and branches, we will attack and destroy the root. . . .'

By the end of May Hideyoshi had reached Yatsushiro in Higo, and was almost parallel with his half-brother in Takashiro. Here he received the allies he so desired. The 'Lords of the Isles', Matsuura of Hirado, the Christian Arima Harunobu, Gotō from the islands of that name, all came to submit, and their ships crowded the narrow channel.

It was a vote of confidence in Hideyoshi, so he gave the order for a general advance against the Shimazu, all of whom had now been funnelled into their home province of Satsuma. As Hideyoshi was about to set off he was joined by Ryūzōji Masaie, who proceeded with him to Satsuma by sea, landing near Akune. Hideyoshi, along with thousands of Kyūshū samurai seething with thirty-one years' lust for revenge, was now established in Shimazu territory. Sixty thousand men were left at Akune to advance on Kagoshima by sea, while Hideyoshi pressed on with 170,000 by land.

Meanwhile a council of war was being held in Kagoshima, attended by every person of note in the Shimazu clan. The question at issue was whether some attempt should be made to dispute the passage of the enemy, or to allow him to march down Satsuma and decide the campaign from the capital. To some extent their minds had been made up for them by Niiro Tadamoto, a leading vassal of the Shimazu, who had refused to withdraw from the Sendai River, and was guarding this natural barrier with 20,000 men. So 30,000 men were immediately despatched to assist him, and Shimazu Yoshihiro set up a further line about eight miles north of Kagoshima.

On 6 June Hideyoshi's army came in sight of the Shimazu for the first time since the campaign had begun. Sixty thousand samurai were drawn up to dispute his passage across the Sendaigawa, and Hideyoshi noted to his surprise that they had chosen to fight with the river at their backs. On came the huge army. When they were about a mile from the river they stopped, and the officers began dressing the ranks. Seeing them halt, Niiro Tadamoto led his personal force of 5,000 men in a wild charge against the 170,000 of Hideyoshi! As the army was just reforming its ranks the force of the charge carried Niiro Tadamoto clean through the first rank, and the second, and they were heading for Hideyoshi's golden gourd standard when they came up against the samurai of Fukushima Masanori and Katō Kiyomasa. At this point the remainder of the Satsuma samurai piled into the Imperialists. But though the much-vaunted superiority of the Satsuma swordsmen told in the hand-to-hand struggle, the sheer weight of numbers gradually forced them back to the river. A charge by mounted samurai diverted the Imperialists' attention sufficiently for the Satsumese to withdraw, but not until a personal combat had been fought between Niiro Tadamoto and Katō Kiyomasa. Niiro was unhorsed, and at the mercy of his antagonist, who generously refused to take advantage of the brave samurai, and spared his life. As darkness fell the Satsuma army, or what was left of it, melted away into the night.

The second line of defence, as noted above, lay eight miles from Kagoshima. Here the Shimazu conceived a daring plan of ambush. All the roads to Kagoshima lay over high passes or through deep ravines, which the volcano of Sakurajima had sculpted in centuries of volcanic ash. As knowledge of the topography of the district was most carefully guarded it was hoped that a whole army could be held up, whereupon it was planned to fire the undergrowth and cut the Imperialists down under cover of a smoke screen. Unfortunately this part of the trap was set off prematurely when the vanguard of Hideyoshi's army got detached and lost itself in the maze of gullies.

There was but one thing the Shimazu had not allowed for, and that was treachery. For some time Hideyoshi had had spies acting in the Kagoshima area in the unlikely persons of Ikkō monks. These monks were to act as guides for Hideyoshi's army through the volcanic wilderness. Hideyoshi now made his final dispositions. The 60,000 that had been left at Akune embarked and set off to sail round the south of the peninsula and up the gulf. At the same time Hidenaga would advance by the main road, while columns under Katō Kiyomasa, Fukushima Masanori and Kuroda Yoshitaka made their way through the defiles and gullies, led by the monks.

The first intimation Shimazu Yoshihiro had of the advance was the appearance of Hidenaga on the main road. The Satsuma samurai held him off with ease, when alarming news came of the amphibious force landing on the coast. Suddenly Katō and Kuroda appeared from the secret pathways, and Hidenaga charged forward. Yoshihiro fled and the Satsuma army pulled back.

Nothing remained now but the earthworks and palisades round Kagoshima itself; the final assault, slaughter, and perhaps the biggest mass suicide in the history of the samurai. But there was no more fighting. Through the mediation of Iehisa, who had been taken prisoner at Sadowara, Shimazu Yoshihisa, head of the Satsuma clan who had fought their way from one end of Kyūshū to another, was brought face to face with Hideyoshi for the first time. He saw a man of small stature with a wizened, monkey-like face, but there was innate nobility in the demeanor of the great General, and Yoshihisa was filled with awe. Hideyoshi's terms were simple. Yoshihisa was to proceed to Kyōto as a hostage, while his brother Yoshihiro took over in Satsuma. The Shimazu would retain control of Satsuma, Ōsumi and half of Hyūga. The terms were generous, and in line with Hideyoshi's far-sighted policy. He had been generous with Mōri and Chōsokabe, who had gone on to fight for him in Kyūshū. He did not wish to exterminate his enemies, but to reduce them and use them. So the great Kyūshū campaign, the largest military undertaking seen in Japan, came to an end. The best of Hideyoshi's generals, including Katō Kiyomasa and Kuroda Yoshitaka, were granted lands in Kyūshū where they could keep an eye on Satsuma. At the beginning of July the army started for home.

There is a curious epilogue to the story which has a modern ring to it. On the day of the final disaster to the Satsuma army the brave Niiro Tadamoto, a samurai if ever there was one, took to the hills rather than see the shame of his clan's defeat. Here he planned to continue the struggle, unaware that terms had been arranged and that the war had ceased. As the vanguard of Hideyoshi's 150,000 troops defiled through one of the narrow passes on the Satsuma border they found their way barred by Niiro and his ragged samurai. In vain did the

Northern samurai assure Niiro that peace had been declared. He brandished his sword more fiercely and would have charged into the vanguard had it not been for the arrival on the scene of Hideyoshi's entire army. Niiro then saw the absurdity of his intentions, and became the last Satsuma samurai to lay down his sword. The Japanese soldiers who are still being found on Pacific islands have an honourable ancestor.

Hideyoshi's return was triumphant. He had succeeded where generals from Minamoto Noriyori to Imagawa Ryō-sun had failed. Well does Hideyoshi deserve to be called 'The Napoleon of Japan'.

Hideyoshi's unification of Japan was not exclusively military. He had more weapons in his armoury than swords and guns. One was tea, and it may be said that Hideyoshi won the Empire by combining tea and muskets. The Japanese tea ceremony is difficult to describe in a few sentences. It is a cult of elegant simplicity, politeness and aesthetic appreciation, centred round having a cup of tea in the best way possible. Hideyoshi, above all others, appreciated that the tea ceremony was a way to win friends and influence people. To him we owe the raising of the tea ceremony from a fashionable pastime to a veritable cult, as a means of taming the spirit of those who would question his authority.

The cultivation of tea was introduced to Japan during the ninth century A.D., but its culture really begins in the twelfth. At first the drinking of tea was regarded with some suspicion, but when a Shōgun discovered that it cured his hangovers, tea began to be held in the highest esteem. During the Kamakura Period the fine leaf was highly prized and very expensive. A jar of tea was sometimes presented to warriors performing some uncommon exploit, who would gather their friends and relatives to share in the precious gift. Here, perhaps, we have the tea ceremony in embryo.

From its inception the tea ceremony was closely associated with Zen. The quiet contemplation of simple things was common to both, and the Zen priests had earlier found that tea helped their meditations by acting as a mild stimulant. The Japanese love of ceremonial and formality led to the 'rules' of the ceremony. Ashikaga Yoshimasa, the Shōgun of the Ōnin War, was instrumental in formulating the tea ceremony as it later came to be understood. The Zen aspect of tea commended itself to the samurai. From the middle of the sixteenth century tea anecdotes abound, as the newly powerful daimyō joined in with the fashion. Oda Nobunaga gave many tea ceremonies, and there are few daimyō from then onwards about whom there is no tale of something that happened during a tea ceremony. Hideyoshi was an expert on tea. Any occasion to indulge his passion for the cult was eagerly seized upon. On returning from Nagakute he stopped to have tea by the roadside, while after the Kyūshū campaign he held a tea ceremony on the beach at Hakata. Ishida Mitsunari, who will play a large part in our story, first attracted Hideyoshi's attentions when he served him with tea. When Ōtomo came up to Ōsaka to beg help from Hideyoshi, the meeting that led to the Kyūshū invasion, the tea ceremony formed part of his entertainment.

Utensils for the tea ceremony were highly prized, and pieces by the most renowned potters were very valuable. A gift of a tea jar by a famous potter was a reward more valued than a fine sword. When Ieyasu submitted to Hideyoshi after the Komaki campaign the latter presented him with a tea jar. But not all tea ceremony utensils were the prerogative of the very rich. A certain Ueda Shigeyasu was riding along under fire when he noticed a particularly fine bamboo beside the road. He calmly dismounted, ignoring the bullets whizzing past him, and cut a section of bamboo for a vase in his tea house.

Some warriors, of course, remained suspicious of the tea ceremony. Kuroda Yoshitaka once remarked to Hideyoshi that the pleasures of tea were no business of a samurai. It was risky, he argued, for host and guests to be seated so close together unarmed. At the next tea party he attended Hideyoshi sat next to him and discussed military affairs in a quiet voice. Kuroda then saw one advantage of the peace of the tea room. Of course Hideyoshi was abusing the very essence of the tea ceremony, which emphasises things not of this world, but that was his way. Kuroda was fortunate that Hideyoshi's abuse of his passion stopped at wordly conversation. Both Oda Nobunaga and Katō Kiyomasa are known to have planned assassinations during tea ceremonies. Oda Nobunaga's intended victim was Inaba Ittetsu, who composed such a charming poem during the tea ceremony that Nobunaga admitted the plot and begged forgiveness. Katō's plot was more bizarre. His quarry was the tea master in charge of the ceremony, whom he hoped to catch off guard while engrossed in the serving of the tea. However the master proved so alert and controlled that he gave Katō no opportunity, who grudgingly praised his host's deportment after the ceremony was concluded. One great tea master is said to have warded off a sword thrust with his tea ladle.

Many tea stories recall Zen proverbs. A personal favourite of the Author's concerns the great daimyō of Northern Honshū, Date Masamune, who was noted for his self control. Once, when examining a very valuable tea bowl he nearly dropped it, and gave an involuntary exclamation. It so ashamed him that he could face a battle unflinchingly, and yet start at the fear of smashing a tea bowl, that he took the bowl and flung it on to the stones, where it broke into a thousand pieces.

It is impossible to understand the mind of the samurai without appreciation of the hold that tea and the rituals surrounding it had on them. Hideyoshi was obsessed by it, from the simple ceremony with one guest to the lavish and extravagant party he gave at Kitano after returning from Kyūshū, attended by hundreds of guests and with scores of tea vessels bubbling away as the greatest in the land wallowed in aestheticism.

Hideyoshi's other work of social control was less graceful. For two centuries peasants, priests and pirates had fought alongside samurai, and through such an exacting test of merit men like Hideyoshi himself had risen to great power. It was now vital to Hideyoshi's aim of uniting the country under him that this disordered state of affairs should not continue, thus denying to others the opportunities that had been afforded to him. In other words, one Hideyoshi was enough. A means to this end was the great land survey, and another was Hideyoshi's celebrated 'Sword Hunt', whereby Hideyoshi planned to disarm the peasantry by turning the swords, if not actually into ploughshares, then into something equally pacific. This was Hideyoshi's pious engineering project, the construction of another Great Buddha. The confiscated swords were to be melted down and used to make nails and bolts for the statue, which was to be of wood, because bronze-casting took too long. The Buddha began to take shape in 1586. It was built to the east of Kyōto, and involved the labour of 50,000 men over six years. As if a warning to those who erect graven images, an earthquake disposed of the idol in 1596, but it had served its secular purpose.

The actual order for the Sword Hunt was issued on 29 August 1588. Part of it is worth quoting:

'1. The people of the various provinces are strictly forbidden to have in their possession any swords, short swords, bows, spears, firearms or other types of arms. The possession of unnecessary implements [of war] makes difficult the collection of taxes and dues and tends to foment uprisings. . . . Therefore the heads of provinces, official agents, and deputies are ordered to collect all the weapons mentioned above and turn them over to the government.

'2. Swords and short swords thus collected will not be wasted. They shall be used as nails and bolts in the construction of the Great Image of Buddha. This will benefit the people not only in this life but also in the life hereafter. . . .'

Hideyoshi's resources were such that the edict was carried out to the letter. The growing social mobility of the peasants was thus flung suddenly into reverse. The ikki, the warrior-monks, became figures of the past, as all their weapons had been taken from them.

The importance of the Sword Hunt in the development of the samurai as a class cannot be over-estimated. As the Sword Hunt proceeded the growing mania for castle building, which had begun under Nobunaga, reached its peak of activity. Consequently the social trend whereby a man was almost literally forced to choose between the station of a soldier or a farmer, being within the walls or without, was now dramatically accelerated. An ashigaru may have been a low rank of warrior, but he was a warrior, a swordbearer, not a peasant. This was the real beginning of the social stratification of Tokugawa Japan, the samurai becoming the 'two-sword man', the badge of distinction which gave him power of life and death over the subject classes. From the time of the Sword Hunt the word 'samurai' loses its loose connotation and becomes ever more clearly defined.

One other innovation of Hideyoshi's was significant. We have seen repeatedly how throughout the years the samurai almost always expected a reward for his services. Up to the time of Nobunaga it had been customary to make this in terms of grants of land, that were slowly but thoroughly distributed on receipt of proof of service. Hideyoshi began to give gold and silver to his samurai, and gave it more essentially the character of a 'prize'. During the Kyūshū campaign he found a certain castle, called Ganjaku, a tough nut to crack, because it was desperately defended. Hideyoshi watched the progress of the battle from the summit of a near-by hill, surrounded by boxes of coins. When samurai returned bearing heads they were rewarded on the spot from the chests. Compare this to Hori Hidemasa's promise at Nagakute of 100 *koku* of rice to anyone who shot a horseman, and it will be seen how things were changing.

In 1600 when Kuroda Yoshitaka was recruiting for the struggle recounted in Chapter Eleven, he put up a notice inviting rōnin (masterless samurai) into his service, offering prizes of gold and silver. On 'pay day' Kuroda noticed that the rōnin were getting impatient while their coins were being weighed out. He told his commissioners not to worry if the coins were a little overweight. In addition Kuroda instructed his officers to wink at those, if any, who slipped into their pockets a few stolen pieces of gold. 'It is all very well,' said he, 'when dealing with merchants, to be scrupulous about weighing, but here the best policy is liberality, which will make me famous and attract many rōnin.'

79 The keep of Odawara Castle, seat of the Hōjō and the object of Hideyoshi's 'picnic campaign' of 1590. A modern reconstruction. (Kyodo News Service.)

We will close this chapter with an account of the final step in the reunification of the Empire. Subsequent events in Hideyoshi's life fill a chapter of their own.

The provinces of Northern Honshū had always been as remote politically as they were geographically. The Kantō in particular had little to do with Hideyoshi's triumphant campaigns. The Kantō was of course the seat of the Hōjō, whose founder, Hōjō Sōun, provided such a vivid illustration of the process of *gekokujō*. His son and grandson faithfully followed Hōjō Sōun's testament of twenty-one articles, but in the succeeding generation, Hōjō Ujimasa, became lax. He was perhaps tired of instructions from his late great-grandfather, but probably the fact that his father had handed him the Kantō as a *fait accompli* made him careless. Since the death of his father in 1570 the Hōjō had become increasingly inward-looking, seeing the natural barrier of the Hakone mountains as a defence not only against samurai but also against cultural innovation. For example, they were well aware of the existence of the arquebus, but Ujimasa was satisfied to set more importance upon bows and arrows than guns, and 'drilled' his soldiers by making them chase dogs. Odawara was also rather old fashioned in its customs, which it would take a Japanese to appreciate.

In 1589 Hideyoshi obtained an excuse for a campaign against the Hōjō, and planned an attack of Kyūshū-style proportions. The daimyō were required to muster between 40 and 70 per cent of their soldiery, the actual number depending on their distance from the Kantō. Thus the heaviest burden fell on Tokugawa Ieyasu, whose lands were next to Hōjō's, and who had neatly avoided the Kyūshū campaign by using the same argument in reverse. He was to advance on Odawara from along the Tōkaidō Road with Gamō Ujisato and Oda Nobuo, while Uesugi Kagekatsu and Maeda Toshiie approached from the north. As Ieyasu's provinces stretched along the Tōkaidō he hurriedly made arrangements for the great road to be tidied up. Rest-houses were built along it and old castles renovated. To help the flow of troops a pontoon bridge was built across the Fuji River, site of the 'water-birds' incident four centuries before. Hideyoshi's preparations regarding ammunition and provisions were placed in the hands of Nagatsuka Masaie, who arranged for 200,000 *koku* of rice to be taken from Ōsaka and transported by sea along the Tōkaidō. On top of that, 10,000 large gold coins were spent on buying rice in the Tōkaidō provinces.

The Hōjō were hopelessly outnumbered. They could muster up to 50,000 men, and had first intended to fight in open country, but faced with possibly 200,000 enemies they withdrew to their castle of Odawara where they placed three muskets and one cannon at each loophole.

Hideyoshi left Kyōto on 5 April 1590, in a parade that for size and magnificence defied all description. His progress along the Tōkaidō was stately and flamboyant. Ieyasu had already moved off to begin the siege. His field orders have been preserved and they give a good indication of the nature of warfare in the Momoyama Period:

'If anyone advances on reconnaissance, unless orders have been given, he shall be punished.

Anyone who presses on too far forward, even to make a name for himself . . . he and all his family shall be punished.

Anyone who is found in another company [while on the march] without due reasons shall be deprived of his horse and his weapons.

All troops on the march shall keep to the main roads.

When troops are on the march all flags, guns, bows and spears are to be carried according to regulations.

Long spears are not to be carried except when in the ranks.'

Regulations follow against letting horses stray, looting and burning, and the proper place for the baggage train. The orders end:

'May all the Gods of Japan, both great and small take heed!

'May they blast without pity any who transgress the above orders!

'So be it.

IEYASU.'

Gamō Ujisato played his part in helping the gods to blast transgressors. On his tour of inspection of the samurai under his command he noticed one who was not keeping his place. The samurai was sharply reprimanded, and ordered back into the ranks. Some time later Gamō found him out of place once again, so without a word he drew his sword and struck off the man's head. There were no more discipline problems after that.

It turned out that there was little fighting to be done. Ieyasu's men took a few outlying forts, but when the rest of the army arrived at Odawara they merely sat down and waited for the Hōjō to be starved into submission. So peaceful was it that a temporary town grew up round the walls, where samurai entertained their wives, played Go, performed the tea ceremony and grew their own vegetables. The Hōjō, too, contrived to be as merry as possible within their well-stocked castle, which contained as much sake as gunpowder. The only real attack on the castle during the four-month long siege was made by the Tokugawa force. Ieyasu brought some miners from Kai who dug under one part of the wall, so that a sudden storm brought the masonry down. The Ii Red Devils charged into the breach and a fierce fight took place. However, such actions did more service by relieving boredom than gaining ground. An observer noted that:

'. . . the leaguers now attempted no assault, but passed the time in giving feasts. Dancing-girls, musicians and actors were brought into the various camps, and merrymaking was the order of the day. It was indeed more like a gigantic picnic party than a host intent upon slaughter.'

Eventually the Hōjō submitted, and Ujimasa committed suicide. The rest of the family were treated as generously as the Shimazu had been, but did not in fact keep their provinces. In a prophetic gesture Hideyoshi presented the Kantō to Ieyasu, and suggested that an appropriate location for his capital would be – not Odawara – but the little fishing village near Kamakura called Edo. Ieyasu agreed, and set up the Tokugawa homelands around this small town. How successful this settlement was may be gathered from the fact that Edo is nowadays called Tōkyō.

The only daimyō who had not submitted was Date Masamune, from the far north of Honshū. Although remote, the Date clan were up to date with all military developments, as shown by their armour (Figs 81 and 82). Date Masamune was a striking character, nicknamed 'The One-Eyed Dragon', because he was disfigured by one eye, having been wounded, hanging out on his cheek. He later cut it off, in case an enemy should seize hold of it in battle.

Date came to submit to Hideyoshi after, or perhaps during, the Odawara campaign. His allegiance made Hideyoshi's supremacy complete. For the first time since before the Ōnin War Japan was one nation, and one under the sword of the son of a woodcutter. To Hideyoshi's everlasting regret he never became Shōgun, because he was not a Minamoto, but was known as 'Kwampaku' or 'Regent'. His lack of a distinguished pedigree always embarrassed him, and it is interesting to speculate that the elaborate decoration of 'mon' on his armour (Fig. 83) might reveal an obsessive quest for identity.

80 Suit of armour of cowhide, owned by Tokugawa Ieyasu. He is traditionally supposed to have had this unusual armour made as a reply to a taunt from Hideyoshi referring to him as 'The cow of the Kantō', an allusion to the country provinces which Ieyasu received after the fall of the Hōjō. (Tokugawa Art Museum, Nagoya.)

81 'Yukinoshita-dō'. This style of armour, with its bullet-proof reflecting surfaces and solid plate construction, is a fine example of Momoyama armour. (L. J. Anderson collection.)

82 Rear view of the Yukinoshita-dō shown in Fig. 81. Note the attachment for a sashimono holder. Date Masamune (1566–1636) equipped all his retainers in armour of this type. (L. J. Anderson collection.)

83 Suit of armour owned by Toyotomi Hideyoshi, with a design of a red rising sun on blue. The extensive use of 'mon' is an unusual feature. (Tokugawa Art Museum, Nagoya.)

10. Hideyoshi's Korean war

Now that Toyotomi Hideyoshi had made himself master of Japan the way was open for him to realize his greatest ambition, the conquest of China. This grandiose scheme was no sudden obsession, but an idea that had been growing in his mind for many years. As early as 1578 he had confided his thoughts to Oda Nobunaga before setting off to chastise the Mōri clan on Nobunaga's behalf. In an extraordinary speech, considering that he was then but one, albeit the ablest, among Nobunaga's generals, he looked beyond his present commission to the reduction of Kyūshū and further conquests overseas, until, with the aid of a pacified and friendly Korea he could finally humble China herself. 'I shall do it,' he told Nobunaga, 'as easily as a man rolls up a piece of matting and carries it under his arm.'

By 1586 his plans were taking a definite shape, and he felt sufficiently confident of their eventual execution to approach the Jesuit Fathers with a view to obtaining two Portuguese ships, armed and crewed, for use in the invasion.

His growing interest in this project had its amusing side, for, five years later, while the siege of Odawara was under way, Hideyoshi took a break from the business of starving out the Hōjō, and paid a visit to the Tsurugaoka Hachiman shrine near Kamakura. This was the shrine of the tutelary deity of the Minamoto, and the last resting place of Minamoto Yoritomo who died in 1199. Hideyoshi approached the bronze statue of the great Shōgun, and patting it on the back addressed the image of his illustrious predecessor:

'You took all the power under Heaven, and you and I are the only ones who have been able to do this. But you were born of high descent, while I am sprung from the peasants. But as for me, after conquering all the Empire, I intend to conquer China. What do you think of that?'

Hideyoshi may well have had a further motive for wishing to conquer China, for the now united Japan contained upwards of half a million unemployed samurai. How was Hideyoshi to maintain his rapidly acquired supremacy? Without the opportunity for the exercise of their force his hardy subjects would never remain quiet, and this Hideyoshi had foreseen. To expend their energies in an overseas war was the most promising solution, and this consideration was probably in Hideyoshi's mind as well as any grand design to place the Emperor of Japan upon the Dragon Throne of Peking.

Between Japan and China lies Korea, a proud, independent country since being united in 1392. It was still under the protection of China, but nevertheless able to regard itself as the equal of Japan. Relations between Japan and Korea had been cool for some years, largely owing to the activities of the Japanese pirates. In 1587 Hideyoshi attempted to re-open diplomatic exchanges, realizing that, for his plans to succeed, Korea would either have to ally with Japan or be conquered. The first Japanese ambassador sent to Korea by Hideyoshi returned without having seen the Korean King, so Hideyoshi had him decapitated *pour encourager les autres*. This suitably spurred on his successors, and at last word was received that the King would be willing to entertain representatives if they would bring him some Japanese pirates for execution. Three were collected and despatched, and the Japanese ambassador was finally called to the Palace in August 1589, and presented the King with a peacock and some matchlock muskets. Significantly, these were the first ever seen in Korea, and this simple illustration of the superiority of Japanese military technology made the threat of conflict with Japan a daunting proposition.

In April 1590 the Japanese returned with three Korean envoys and a letter from the King. Hideyoshi received them, and at length replied in grandiloquent terms, which made his intentions abundantly clear.

'. . . taking wings like a dragon, I have subdued the East, chastised the West, punished the South, and smitten the North. Speedy and great success has attended my career, which has been like the rising sun illuminating the whole earth.

'. . . I will assemble a mighty host, and invading the country of the Great Ming, I will fill with the hoar frost from my sword the whole sky over the four hundred provinces. Should I carry out this purpose, I hope that Korea will be my vanguard. Let her not fail to do so, for my friendship with your honourable country depends solely on your conduct when I lead my army against China.'

From the tone of this letter and observations made during their stay in Japan, the Korean ambassadors were convinced that war between the two countries was inevitable, for the Koreans had no intention of standing idly by while the Japanese marched through their country to China. There would be no road for them unless they cut one for themselves with the sword. The Korean ambassadors, as scornful of Hideyoshi as he had been of them, added that his idea of conquering China would be as absurd as a bee trying to sting a tortoise through its armour.

Such a reply filled Hideyoshi with rage, and rumours of his intentions soon reached Peking, whence messengers were sent to Korea to assertain the truth. Korea could only confirm its own worst suspicions, and warn the Chinese of their impending danger.

If attacking China was like a bee worrying a tortoise, conquering Korea was likely to prove like a dog fighting a rabbit, the rabbit being lame, blind and stupid. For in spite of their brave diplomacy no country can have been less fitted to face the might of Japan than was Korea in 1592. It was a society that consisted of but two classes, the aristocracy and the slaves. The former lived lives very similar to the languid Heian nobles, but with no samurai to protect them against aggressors, for indeed there were none to trouble them. Jealousies plagued their court, and political rivalry was so savage and ruthless as to make the Fujiwara despots look like Athenian democrats. The horde of peasants who constituted the Korean army were no more than a mob, whose notions of patriotism could be conveniently set aside by the payment of a sum of money which relieved them of the duty of military service. All who could afford it bought themselves out, so that the defence of their country fell to the poorest of the poor and the lowest of the low.

In its equipment too the Korean Army showed a marked inferiority to the Japanese, notably in their swords which were short, double-edged stabbing weapons. The bow and several varieties of straight and curved spears were used, as well as the curious Korean 'flail'. This was a form of mace with a long handle and a spiked head connected by three links of chain, a weapon wielded by the Korean cavalry and one in which they placed great faith. The lack of matchlocks has already been noted, although the Koreans did have cannon, but no attempt seems to have been made to copy the specimens brought by the Japanese ambassadors. For defensive armour the officers and cavalry wore a large coat, reinforced with leather and metal rivets, over a suit of chain mail, and a simple helmet of leather or iron. The mass of poor foot-soldiers bore weapons of even more primitive design, and wore no armour whatsoever. And this nation, already reeling under the corruption of its rulers and the wretchedness of its people, had to face the military strength of a country whose well-trained army could have proved a match for any in contemporary Europe!

There were two factors in Korea's favour. First there was their homeland itself. Korea is mountainous throughout, with many a hidden gorge and valley. The winters can be very severe, and taking these things into account it became clear that Korea was an ideal setting for guerrilla warfare. Now this was something that the Japanese had never had to face, for they had never fought in a foreign country. The Japanese civil wars had developed into clashes between rival barons, and affected the ordinary farmer very little as, for him, they merely resulted in replacing old oppressors with new. No resistance movement could thrive in such conditions. But in Korea, where the hurt would be so keenly felt and the aggressor so readily identified, there would be hostility at each corner, and danger behind every wall.

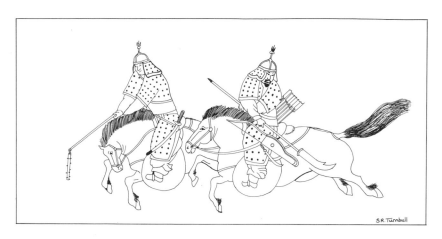

The second advantage that Korea possessed was the simple logistical fact that should a resistance movement get under way, and the Japanese find burnt fields and hostile faces, then every bullet, every ounce of gunpowder and every grain of rice would have to be brought across fifty miles of open sea. And although the ill-armed and ill-led Korean army may have been dying on its feet the Korean Navy was potentially a decisive threat to Japan, with a well-manned fleet that could sever the lifeline as easily as a samurai's sword cleft a Korean lance.

With a high disregard for such dangers, preparations began for the army of invasion. In autumn 1591 a base was set up on the north-west coast of Kyūshū at Nagoya, now called Karatsu, and here were gathered samurai, footsoldiers, horses, ships and all the paraphernalia of warfare. Hideyoshi's plans were meticulous. He organized everything and provided the finance for practically nothing, for the cost in money and human lives was to be borne by the daimyō. The greatest burden was to be shouldered by the daimyōs of Kyūshū, who were to provide 600 fighting men for every 10,000 *koku* of assessed revenue. Other daimyō on Shikoku and Honshū supplied lesser numbers in proportion to the distance of their lands from Kyūshū. Daimyō whose fiefs bordered on the sea had also to make available two junks per 100,000 *koku* to be crewed by fishing villages in their domain at the ratio of ten sailors for every hundred houses.

Hideyoshi's strategy showed a comparable 'grand design'. The army of invasion was in two parts. The initial assault was to be made by seven divisions of troops, assembled ready on the island of Tsushima, who were to pacify Korea and occupy it. Then three reserve divisions would land and join their comrades for the advance on China, hopefully with the now-friendly Korean army in tow. The table below shows how each division was organized, consisting of the troops of several daimyō, with one daimyō in overall command.

The Initial Assault

First Division (*Kyūshū*)

Konishi Yukinaga	7,000
Sō Yoshitomo	5,000
Matsuura Shigenobu	3,000
Arima Harunobu	2,000
Ōmura Yoshiaki	1,000
Gotō Mototsugu	700
	18,700

Second Division (*Kyūshū*)

Katō Kiyomasa	8,000
Nabeshima Naoshige	12,000
Sagara?	800
	20,800

Third Division (*Kyūshū*)

Kuroda Nagamasa	6,000
Ōtomo Yoshimune	6,000
	12,000

Fourth Division (*Kyūshū*)

Shimazu Yoshihiro	10,000
Mōri Yoshinari	2,000
Takahashi Mototane	2,000
Akizuki Tanenaga	1,000
Itō Suketaka	1,000
Shimazu Tadatoyo	1,000
	17,000

Fifth Division (*Shikoku*)

Fukushima Masanori	5,000
Toda Yasunaga ?	4,000
Hachisuka Iemasa	7,200
Chōsokabe Motochika	3,000
Ikoma Chikamasa	5,500
	24,700

Sixth Division (*Kyūshū*)

Kobayakawa Takakage	10,000
Mōri Hidekane	1,500
Tachibana Muneshige	2,500
Takahashi Mototsugu	800
Tsukushi Hirokado	900
	15,700

Seventh Division (*Honshū*)

Mōri Terumoto
Kikkawa Hiroie } 30,000
Mōri Motoyasu

Thus the initial army of invasion was to consist of 138,900 men.

Reserve

Eighth Division (*Honshū*)

Ukita Hideie	10,000
Masuda Nagamori	3,000
Ishida Mitsunari	2,000
Ōtani Yoshitaka	1,200
Maeno ?	2,000
Katō Mitsuyasu	1,000
	19,200

Ninth Division (*Honshū*)

Asano Nagamasa	3,000
Miyabe Tsugimasu	1,000
Nanjō ?	1,500
Kinoshita Katsutoshi	850
Nakagawa Hidemasa	3,000
Inaba Masanari	1,400
	10,750 (plus minor Daimyō)

Tenth Division (*Honshū*)

Hashiba Hidekatsu	8,000
Hashiba Tadaoki	3,500
Hasegawa ?	5,000
Kimura Shigekore	3,500
Onogi ?	1,000
Kamei Korenori	1,000
	22,000 (plus minor Daimyō)

Total of the three reserve divisions: 51,950+

85 Portrait scroll of Katō Kiyomasa (1562–1611), one of Hideyoshi's ablest generals and the leader of the Second Division during the Korean War. (Author's collection.)

These figures show the immense scale of the operation which Hideyoshi had planned. Yet, in spite of the impressive figures, human nature was to provide complications. As Hideyoshi did not intend to accompany the army during the first wave there was effectively no commander-in-chief, and the old samurai tradition of individual achievement was not dead. Consequently relations between the divisions were far from cordial, especially in the case of the first two divisions, who were to be the vanguard of the invasion. Each division was led by a fine soldier, but it is hard to see how Hideyoshi, with his meticulous attention to detail, could have chosen such an ill-assorted duo for a task that needed cooperation above all. In command of the first division was Konishi Yukinaga, a Christian who hated Buddhists, while leading the second division was Katō Kiyomasa, a Buddhist who hated Christians. As their antagonism was to prove a major factor in the campaign it is well to consider certain details about them.

Both were men who, like Hideyoshi, had risen from the ranks. Konishi was the son of a medicine dealer in Sakai, and had first attracted Hideyoshi's attention by his skill at serving tea, an accomplishment which immediately endeared him to the latter. He was as gifted in the profession of arms, and had risen rapidly to the post of Commander of the first division at the age of only twenty-three. After the Kyūshū expedition he had been granted half the province of Higo as his fief. He had been baptized in 1583 by the Jesuit missionaries and given the name of Don Augustin, and was to remain faithful unto death. Consequently the Jesuit accounts paint a rosy picture of him as a 'verray parfit gentil' samurai, and by and large he lived up to it. Hideyoshi presented him with a fine war horse as a parting gift, saying 'Gallop over the bearded savages with it!'

Katō Kiyomasa, in command of the second division, was very different. In place of Konishi's Catholicism Kiyomasa was a disciple of Nichiren, the ardent Buddhist evangelist who had inspired the Japanese against the Mongols, and gone on to found the only really bigoted Buddhist sect, complete with bible and musical accompaniment. Kiyomasa carried his faith high, to the extent of emblazoning his standard in big red characters with the text: 'Namu myōhō renge kyō' (Glory to the Holy Lotus), which was the prayer and legend of his sect. Kiyomasa was born in 1562, the son of a blacksmith, and although only seven years senior to Konishi Yukinaga he had many more years of service to Hideyoshi to look back on. In return for his service in Kyūshū Hideyoshi had given him the other half of Higo province, thus making Konishi his nextdoor neighbour. He was fond of wearing elaborate helmets with particularly high crowns built up on a wooden framework. He also sported a growth of whiskers, which he claimed made tight helmet cords more comfortable. For all his eccentricities he was utterly ruthless, and became a savage persecutor of the Christians.

Strangely enough, Konishi Yukinaga's division was almost entirely Christian, the only exception being the Matsuura clan of Hirado island. So was the third division, the two commanders having been baptized as Damian and Constantine. The former, Kuroda Nagamasa, was another young leader at the age of twenty four, and the son of another great general. He had lived a samurai life from the day he had been entrusted to Hideyoshi's care. His troops were instantly recognizable by the black disc on their banners, an example of a Japanese heraldic pun, for Kuro-da means 'black field' (Fig. 88).

The composition of the fourth division indicates the hold Hideyoshi now had on Southern Kyūshū, for it was commanded by his former enemy Shimazu Yoshihiro, who had responded as well as his straitened circumstances allowed him. The following is a record of the Shimazu's contingent, which not only indicates the reliance placed upon the firearm, but the timeless nature of military bureaucracy:

'The military service of Shimazu-dono in the Korean expedition:

15,000 men	Mata-ichirō-dono.
300 banners; 5 hand-spears (te-yari)	Yoshihisa
300 spears, of which 200 are long spears (naga-yari) and 200, hand-spears	Yoshihiro

'Besides these, the men should provide hand-spears according to their capacity. . . . In a retinue or in front of camp, it is not sightly to have nothing but long spears.

| 1,500 guns | 1,500 men with bows. |

600 men with small banners (sashimono); these should be armoured.

'Only distinguished men should be mounted; however, all those who cannot go on foot should be mounted. Therefore, the number of mounted is indefinite. The mounted men might well bear helmet and armour.

'These regulations shall be observed with zeal.'

Mata-ichirō-dono was Yoshihiro's eldest son Hisayasu, killed in Korea in 1593. Yoshihisa was the same who fought against Hideyoshi in Kyūshū.

From the other divisions one or two names stand out. Kobayakawa Takakage (VI Division) is the victor of Miyajima (1555), now sixty years old and still of a warlike disposition. Kikkawa Hiroie and Mōri Terumoto (VII Division) are his nephews, the latter the builder of Hiroshima Castle in 1591.

It will be noticed that the composition of the first seven divisions does not bear out the view sometimes expressed that Hideyoshi shipped off to Korea his most dangerous rivals merely to get them killed. The attack was to be led by his ablest and loyalest commanders, all men who owed their position and prosperity to Hideyoshi. If he had wished to sap the strength of likely opponents he would have made sure that men such as Date Masamune and Tokugawa Ieyasu were the first to step on enemy soil. As it was, it was these who, owing to the distance of their domains from Kyūshū, found it easiest to refuse. They contented themselves with supplying the garrison at Nagoya, which numbered 100,000 men.

So in the year 1592 Toyotomi Hideyoshi was able to put in the field an army of 300,000 men, fully armed, and amply provisioned. It is in sad contrast that we see the naval force that was to accompany them. We have noted Hideyoshi's methods of requisitioning ships. It resulted in an overnight fleet totally unprepared when it was sent to the continent. His earlier attempt to buy two Portuguese warships had failed, and the ships which were sent in response to his demands were an odd collection. Most had a single square sail, with additional oar propulsion because they could not tack. Hideyoshi was no sailor, and he fondly believed that he would have a superior fleet as soon as he had collected many war vessels and filled them with soldiers. In fact he had already crippled his naval potential in 1587 by curbing the pirates, an act which led to the rapid decay of the only organized naval force in Japan.

So the huge, clumsy fleet gathered, laden with the finest and noblest samurai in the land. Behind them straggled junks laden with sake, salt meat, dried fish, soy beans, arrows, musket balls, war fans and all the vast un-named necessities of war. Nothing was forgotten:

'... Provision for these men (12,433) for five months, 10,522·9 *koku*, inclusive of supplies for boatmen and their chiefs.

'272 horses. Their provisions 816 *koku* of beans, being for five months, at the rate of one fiftieth of a *koku* per day (for each horse).

'Rice and beans together 11,438·9 *koku*.'

It had taken about seven or eight months to assemble the armada. Now they awaited the order that would speed them on their way against a despised but as yet unmeasured foe.

Meanwhile the rivalry between Konishi Yukinaga and Katō Kiyomasa grew increasingly bitter. As we have seen in previous chapters, great honour was obtained by being the first into battle, so both commanders were determined that their division should be the first to set foot on Korean soil. The early morning of 24 May 1592 was misty, and Konishi took the opportunity to elude both the Korean Navy and Katō Kiyomasa. Soon, sentries on the southern coast of Korea spotted the troopships that carried the first division. By nightfall the division had landed, while Katō Kiyomasa was still invoking the aid of his Buddhist deities to fill his sails with wind, or rather cursing his Catholic rival for having appropriated most of the transport ships. This sudden beginning to the invasion might well have spelled disaster against any other foe, for in his presumptuous start Konishi had left Tsushima while the Japanese armada was still gathering at Nagoya. A small Korean

86 Helmet owned by Katō Kiyomasa. The 'court-cap' design is built on a wooden framework over a simple helmet bowl. It is lacquered silver, with a red sun's disc on either side. (Tokugawa Art Museum, Nagoya.)

flotilla could have caused havoc, but as it was no ships appeared to worry Konishi, or Katō Kiyomasa, who arrived four days later, much chagrined at having been outstripped by his younger rival.

Before following the land campaign it is worth considering the nature of the task with which the Japanese were faced. Korea is a peninsula running roughly north to south, with the Sea of Japan to the east, and the Yellow Sea to the west. From the port of Pusan, which is practically the nearest point to Japan, it is about 550 miles to the Chinese border. Seoul, the capital in 1592 of all Korea, lies just over half way up. So the Japanese had to traverse the entire length of Korea before coming within sight of their ultimate objective, and this Konishi's division began to do with amazing rapidity. Pusan was the first to fall, after a short but brave resistance by the young governor, and then Tong-nai, a fortress a few miles to the north. Konishi Yukinaga took a prominent part in the fighting and at Tong-nai was the first to mount the bamboo scaling-ladders set up against the walls. He then set his army on as direct a route north as he could determine (Fig. 88).

Meanwhile the other divisions had not been idle. Katō Kiyomasa's Buddhist brigade had landed near Pusan on 28 May, and, loath to follow the line of victory of his rival, headed northwards on a road to the east of the route chosen by Konishi. The other Christian division, the third, under Kuroda Nagamasa, with no wish for shared glory, chose a third road to the north-west of the others' lines of advance. Thus three Japanese divisions were independently battering their way up Korea, and the race for the capital was on.

87 Portrait of Kuroda Nagamasa (1568–1623), commander of the Third Division during the invasion of Korea, 1592.

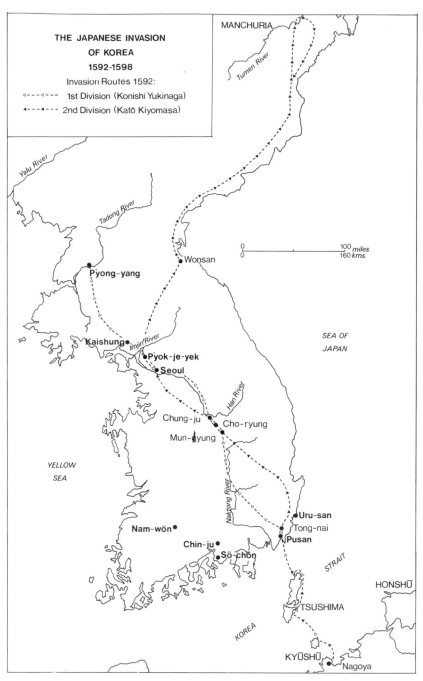

THE JAPANESE INVASION
OF KOREA
1592-1598
Invasion Routes 1592:
◁---◁--- 1st Division (Konishi Yukinaga)
◀---◀--- 2nd Division (Katō Kiyomasa)

MANCHURIA

Tumen River

Yalu River

Tadong River

100 miles
160 kms.

Wonsan

Pyong-yang

Kaishung ● Imjin River

Pyok-je-yek

Seoul

SEA OF
JAPAN

Han River

Chung-ju ● Cho-ryung
Mun-gyung

YELLOW
SEA

Naktong River

Uru-san
Tong-nai
Pusan

Nam-wön ●

Chin-ju ●
Sö-chön

KOREA
STRAIT

HONSHŪ

TSUSHIMA

KYŪSHŪ
Nagoya

88 Map of the Korean War, 1592–8.

Konishi and Katō briefly joined forces on 5 June at Mun-gyung,
and their united commands headed for the Pass of Cho-ryung, a potential
death trap for an invading army. However, owing to the appalling lack
of military talent among the Korean generals the pass was left undefended, and the Japanese marched through in high spirits. The
Korean generals had in fact decided to meet the Japanese in the flat

XIII The frontier fortress of Shizugatake, attacked by Sakuma Morimasa, holds out until the arrival of Toyotome Hideyoshi. From a painted screen depicting the Battle of Shizugatake. (Ōsaka Castle Museum)

XVI The Battle of Nagakute, 1584. In the lower centre of the picture, Ikeda Nobuteru is killed by Nagai Naokatsu. From a painted screen depicting the Battle of Nagakute. (Tokugawa Art Museum, Nagoya)

XVII Katō Kiyomasa fighting a tiger in Korea. Katō Kiyomasa's division were the only Japanese troops to cross into China during the Korean War, 1592-8. Tiger hunting was a popular relaxation. (Author's collection)

XIX and XX The Battle of Sekigahara, 1600. Tokugawa Ieyasu commands (bottom right) and the Ii samurai charge forward. At left are the Shimazu, with their mon of a black cross in a ring. From a painted screen. (Ii Art Museum, Hikone Castle)

XVIII Kumamoto Castle, Kyūshū, first built in 1600 by Katō Kiyomasa. The present keep is a modern reconstruction. (Photograph by the Author)

XXII The 'Summer Campaign' of
Ōsaka, 1615. Ii samurai charge on
the troops of Kimura Shigenari.
From a painted screen. (Ii Art
Museum, Hikone Castle)

XXI Tokugawa Ieyasu commands the Tokugawa besieging force during the siege of
Ōsaka Castle, 1614-15. From a painted screen. (Ōsaka Castle Museum)

XXIII The fall of Ōsaka Castle, 1615. Defenders flee as the Tokugawa army crosses the inner moat. From a painted screen. (Ōsaka Castle Museum)

XXIV The keep of Hikone Castle. Hikone was started by Ii Naokatsu in 1603, and became the residence of his brother Ii Naotaka in 1623. (Photograph by the Author)

不嫉武備
詩實為盞友
疆國家

XXV Matsuura Seizan Kiyoshi, daimyō of Hirado from 1775 until 1806. Seizan Kiyoshi, aged 81, is dressed in black. From a hanging scroll. (Matsuura Historical Museum, Hirado)

XXVI An eighteenth-century samurai's town house. An excellently preserved example in Sendai.

XXVII A beautifully made suit of Japanese armour, bearing the mon of the Niwa clan. A good example of the elaborate Edo style of armour, that was never intended for fighting. (Courtesy of Christie's)

land beyond the pass, where they fondly hoped their cavalry would sweep down upon the invaders with their flails. Thus the Japanese were given full opportunity to manoeuvre around the battlefield the Koreans had selected, which was bordered on one side by the River Tamguemda, and on the other three sides by the mountains, giving the area the appearance of a vast amphitheatre from which the only exits were narrow passes at each end. Gradually the Japanese clambered around the foothills of the mountains, and at a given signal began a hot fire from their matchlock muskets. This they followed up with a devastating charge, which forced the Koreans to the banks of the river. Soon the army, which consisted in the main of the only garrison between Pusan and Seoul that had not already fled or been defeated, lay dying at the water's edge, or crammed into the northern pass in its headlong flight.

Beyond the battlefield the road forked, so the two divisions again parted. Katō swung off to the west, hoping thereby to sweep round on Seoul ahead of Konishi, who continued on his original course. On 12 June it seemed as if Katō had succeeded, for after some speedy marching the second division arrived at the southern bank of the Han River, which forms a natural moat to Seoul. The city appeared deserted, and having crossed the river Katō discovered the reason for its placidity; Konishi had arrived in Seoul four hours previously! Both, however, must have been disappointed to learn that had they cooperated and arrived four days earlier, they would have captured the Korean King and all his treasure.

On 16 June they were joined by Kuroda Nagamasa and Ukita Hideie, commander of the eighth division whom Hideyoshi had sent on with his troops to act as Commander-in-Chief once Seoul had fallen. One by one the other divisions arrived, and Ukita began to implement Hideyoshi's orders for the subjugation of the country. These orders delineated certain spheres of influence for each Japanese division. Konishi and Katō were to press on separately to the north, the former on the direct route to the nearest point of the Chinese border where it is marked by the Yalu River, and the latter to the north-east, where Korea borders Manchuria. The other divisions were to spread out from Seoul, Ukita's remaining in the capital as a garrison. Incidentally, Ukita's progress so far had not been without incident, for on their way from Pusan his army had been defeated by a Korean general, who in turn had fallen foul of a jealous rival. The rival accused his colleague of treason and reported the matter to the King. Such were the machinations of Korean politics that the general, responsible for Korea's one success since the war had begun, was confronted by an executioner sent from the King, who performed his 'particularly vital function' before the hero could protest his innocence.

When Hideyoshi received the news of the fall of Seoul his delight knew no bounds, and indeed it was a remarkable achievement in so short a time. Within nineteen days Konishi's division had fought three battles and several skirmishes, and travelled 250 miles with

18,700 men. Katō had seen less action, and had made the journey to Seoul in fifteen days, at a respectable average speed of sixteen miles a day. The speed of the advance so far convinced Hideyoshi that the rest of the campaign would have similar results, and in July he wrote to his nephew Hidetsugu telling him of the collapse of the Korean capital, and giving much fascinating detail of the business of Empire-building:

'Your highness must get ready to start for the front. You must set out in the first or second month of next year. The Korean capital has fallen in two days. You must therefore cross the sea without delay. I now intend to command the country of the Great Ming. [You can] cross by ship from Hyōgo. . . . Though you are not likely to meet any opposition in the Three Countries, yet you must for your reputation's sake see most carefully to the condition of your weapons and accoutrements. And this you must strictly impress on all ranks.

'The rice in the castle at Kyōto is not to be touched. I have already set aside thirty thousand *koku* of rice for army use, and if this is not enough you are to draw on the Taikō's own store.

'A thousand swords with metal mounts and short swords are to be provided. If they are too big they will be troublesome for such a long journey, so let the swords be of about seven *ryō* in weight [about 500 grammes], and the short swords about three.

'You had better take thirty halberds with metal mounts and twenty spears of the same kind. More are superfluous. The shafts of the long spears are to be mounted with metal, and you do not need any scabbards with fur on them. Since there are seasoned oak spear shafts in store at Ōsaka, you can take what you need from them. You need only take five or six suits of armour. More will be unnecessary.

'When his Majesty the Mikado deigns to proceed to China, the Imperial progress will be made with all due ceremony.

'The conquest of Korea and China will not take long.'

On 27 June, after a well-earned rest, the first division under Konishi Yukinaga left Seoul for the north. The natural moat of the Han River having been breached when the Japanese entered Seoul, the Koreans had now fallen back to the northern bank of the Imjin River, which empties into the Yellow Sea near the present border between North and South Korea. Here they resolved to stand, and in fact the point that they had selected made stubborn defence a practical proposition. The road north led to the Imjin via a narrow pass between high cliffs, while the northern bank was a wide expanse of sand, and here the Korean army drew up, covering the only ferry point on the fast flowing river with their archers. It was an impossible situation for the two Japanese commanders, Katō having arrived a few days later, and for ten days the Japanese sat down and waited.

89 Katō Kiyomasa leads the Japanese samurai in a charge against Korean soldiers. (Studio M.)

Had the Koreans managed to keep the invaders pinned down at the Imjin the subsequent course of events might have proved very different. As it turned out it was the lack of control they possessed over themselves, rather than over their adversaries, that proved their undoing. Konishi and Katō put into operation the oldest trick in the book, and as the Koreans gazed across the river they observed what appeared to be the Japanese firing their camp and heading off south. Inevitably one or two hotheads among the Korean staff were eager to pursue the retreating army, and, as was their way, replied to wiser counsels with orders of decapitation. Needless to say the Korean force that crossed were ambushed and annihilated within full view of the watchers on the northern bank. All was not lost, however, for the Japanese had no command of the ferry, but here the Korean commanders came most gallantly to the aid of the invaders by ordering a general retreat, and set an example to their countrymen by fleeing with all the speed their steeds could muster.

After crossing the Imjin the two Japanese divisions separated once again. As noted above Katō Kiyomasa had been given the less glamorous task of subduing the North East, thus preventing flank attacks against Konishi's lines of communication from Seoul to the Yalu River. Katō thus set in motion a fierce campaign that was to occupy him throughout the winter of 1592–3 among the frozen snowdrifts of North Korea. No great pitched battles were fought, but many sieges and skirmishes were undertaken, during one of which Katō captured some important hostages including two Korean princes and a girl reputed to be the most beautiful in the kingdom. In pursuit of the enemy the Japanese were led into wild and lonely regions and into the depths of trackless mountains where they met not only human foes, but faced the tiger disturbed from his lair. They were often obliged to camp in places where these dangerous beasts attacked the sentries or the sleeping soldiers. Tiger-hunting became a popular break from chasing Koreans, and Katō Kiyomasa himself slew a tiger with his lance after a desperate struggle, a scene often represented in Japanese art (Plate XVII).

Let us follow Konishi Yukinaga on the road to Peking. Only one fortress now lay between him and the Chinese border. This was the town of P'yong-yang, strongly defended and guarded by another river, the Tadong. Konishi arrived there on 15 July, and was once again faced with the problem of a swiftly flowing river with unknown fords. As the Koreans seemed unwilling to repeat their previous manoeuvre at the Imjin, Konishi tried the last refuge of every frustrated general – he sent a message across the river proposing a peace conference. The resulting interview was held in boats anchored in midstream, and as the Japanese demands were for an open road to China the meeting proved abortive, so Konishi was rowed back to shore to await developments. Delay made the Japanese less vigilant. The Koreans noticed this and planned to surprise them with a night attack. But the summer nights were short, and the Korean army was so badly organized that dawn was already breaking by the time the various detachments charged down upon Konishi's camp. Kuroda's division, who had joined their comrades but recently, counter-attacked smartly, trapping the Koreans by the river and driving them back across the fords, thus revealing their location to the excited Japanese. After breakfast the entire army followed in pursuit, and by afternoon P'yong-yang was theirs – magazines, weapons, provisions and all. The final Korean fortress had fallen, and the undefended Chinese border lay less than eighty miles away. Yet not one of the samurai that stood that day on the walls of P'yong-yang was destined to cross it, and P'yong-yang was to become the last outpost of a premature Empire.

However, the jewel of conquest was not to be snatched dramatically from Japanese hands. The 'blitzkrieg' of the past two months had gone according to plan, and now the second phase of the operation was to begin. As will be recalled from Hideyoshi's original plans, it had been realized right from the start that the seven divisions, having fought their way through Korea in six or seven weeks, would be insufficient to subdue China unaided. This was to be the task of the 52,000 reserves, who were now to be ferried up the west coast of Korea to join Konishi at P'yong-yang. That this second force never arrived, and that consequently the invasion of China never took place, was due to the bravery of one Korean, Admiral Yi Sun Sin.

Reference was made earlier to the potential of the Korean Navy. It has also been noted that seven Japanese divisions managed to land at Pusan without even the sighting of a Korean ship. This was partly due to the fact that the Koreans were taken by surprise, but more to the character of the admiral in charge of K'yung-san province, where lies Pusan, a certain Won-kiun. Won-kiun was an alcoholic, and an example of Korean aristocracy at its worst. On catching sight of the Japanese armada he was torn between two courses of action, both typical of him, and both equally fatal. One alternative was to scuttle his entire fleet, and the other was flight. Fortunately for the future history of Korea he chose the latter, and hurried to beg aid from the admiral of neighbouring Chulla province, Yi Sun Sin. Admiral Yi was made of sterner stuff than Won-kiun. He had been born in 1545, the same year as his contemporary whom his career so closely resembles, Sir Francis Drake. The meeting with the hapless Won-kiun took place on 7 June, as the Japanese were racing towards Seoul. Admiral Yi rose to the needs of his country, and set off to inflict upon the Japanese their first real taste of defeat.

When Hideyoshi had made up his mind to invade Korea the preparations he had set in motion were detailed, extensive and as far as his previous experience of warfare could teach him, entirely adequate. Yet throughout his years of campaigning he had never had to move his armies across any hostile seas, or indeed across any seas at all save the narrow straits that divide one Japanese island from another. His total naval enterprise depended upon a handful of enthusiastic daimyō with some family history of piracy, especially the brothers Kurushima Michifusa and Michiyuki, and Kuki Yoshitaka, who had served Nobunaga in naval actions against the Mōri, and had held joint command of Hideyoshi's 'fleet' during the Kyūshū and Odawara campaigns. His fellow commanders during this time had also come to Korea. They were Wakizaka Yasuharu and Katō Yoshiaki (no relation to Kiyomasa). But their experience was not of the high seas, nor indeed were their ships, for the history of Japanese piracy was one of seaborne raids on coastal or river towns. Besides, most of the Japanese fleet presently engaged were essentially transport vessels, both in function and design, and the Japanese idea of a warship was no more than a floating platform for samurai.

So much for the Japanese. In contrast, the Korean vessels were warships – big, fast and, if certain obstinate Korean traditions are to be believed, at least three hundred years ahead of their time. For it is stubbornly maintained by certain authorities that Admiral Yi commanded one, and perhaps several, iron clad battleships! These were the turtle boats, pride of the Korean Navy. That the turtle boat, or boats, existed is beyond doubt, but it is not entirely clear whether this remarkable vessel was one flagship, or a type. The latter seems most likely, for one ship alone, even of such an unusual design, would not be very effective. So we may assume that there were a number of these turtle boats which as the name implies, were shaped like a turtle

90 Admiral Yi Sun Sin, whose fleet broke the Japanese lines of communication during the Korean War. From the only known likeness of Yi (1545–98).

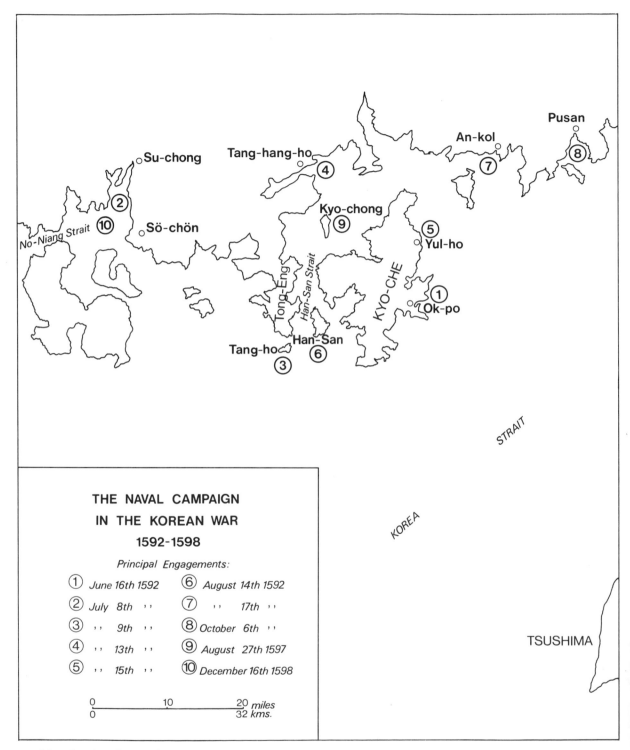

Su-chong

Tang-hang-ho
④

An-kol
⑦

Pusan
⑧

②

⑩ Sö-chön

No-Niang Strait

Kyo-chong
⑨

⑤
Yul-ho

Tong-Eng

Han-San Strait

KYO-CHE

① Ok-po

Tang-ho
③

Han-San
⑥

STRAIT

KOREA

THE NAVAL CAMPAIGN
IN THE KOREAN WAR
1592-1598

Principal Engagements:

① *June 16th 1592*   ⑥ *August 14th 1592*
② *July 8th ,,*   ⑦ *   ,,   17th ,,*
③ *,,   9th   ,,*   ⑧ *October 6th   ,,*
④ *,,   13th ,,*   ⑨ *August 27th 1597*
⑤ *,,   15th ,,*   ⑩ *December 16th 1598*

```
0            10            20  miles
0                          32 kms.
```

TSUSHIMA

91 Map showing the naval campaign of the Korean War, 1592–8.

shell. From descriptions which survive it is possible to build a vivid picture of these craft. They were about 100 feet long and 30 feet wide, powered by means of a sail and oars. In the bows was a large carved dragon's head, while the shell of the turtle was a curved roof of planks that completely covered the deck, thus discouraging boarders as well as affording protection for the gunners, whose cannon projected through portholes on either side. Now it has been said earlier that the Koreans had no firearms in the form that the Japanese knew, i.e. arquebuses. But they were well acquainted with gunpowder, and it was in the form of cannon that Korean firepower had developed. The guns fitted to the turtle boats were about three feet long and fired either shot or steel-headed darts. Fire arrows could also be projected at enemy vessels, and bombs similar to those used during the Mongol invasions were thrown, probably by catapult. With a total of forty or more guns per ship their armament was truly formidable, but it is in its means of defence that the turtle boat is so tantalizing. When going into action the mast was folded down into the deck, and after bombarding the enemy the fleets would probably close and boarding would be attempted. To hinder boarders still further the 'shell' was studded with iron spikes, which were concealed under bundles of straw. Some descriptions go further than this, and claim that the 'shell' was covered in iron sheets. This is difficult to prove either way, but the use of armour plate notwithstanding, the turtle boat was far superior to anything the Japanese possessed at the time, as were Admiral Yi's battle tactics. These included the use of the smoke screen – a sulphurous smoke that rolled 'like a fog' out of the jaws of the dragon head, and the line-ahead formation. As the Korean fleet drew near the enemy the left wing luffed before the wind, thus permitting the right wing to pull ahead until what had been a broad arrow in reverse became a line-ahead formation. Drake had used similar tactics against another armada four years previously. Yi also made use of his knowledge of Korean waters, with which the Japanese had not endeavoured to acquaint themselves, and most important of all, Yi was in sole command, in sad contrast to the fortunes of his countrymen on land.

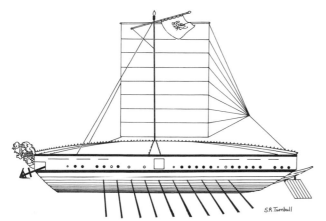

92 Artist's impression of one of Admiral Yi's 'turtle ships'. (By the Author.)

On 16 June 1592, as Kuroda Nagamasa's third division was entering Seoul, Yi's battle fleet, for he had now absorbed the unfortunate Won-kiun within it, bore down upon the Japanese at Okpo on the coast of Kyo-che island opposite Pusan. The Japanese fleet consisted of about fifty ships in all, while the Koreans had twenty-four turtle boats, fifteen smaller vessels, and forty-six 'sea-ear' boats, which are presumably open boats. In his ship's log Admiral Yi described his first impression of the Japanese samurai in their hideous face masks and elaborate helmets. 'They were,' he wrote, 'like beasts or devils and enough to frighten anyone.' Anyone, that is, except Admiral Yi, who sailed in with his turtle boats and sunk forty of the Japanese.

Surprised though the Japanese were by this sudden display of vigour on the part of an enemy who was being driven back on land with relentless speed, they were not dismayed and began moving the fleet round the coast to support the army. While the Japanese forces were crossing the Imjin, Yi found the Japanese Navy drawn up by the shore at Su-chong. As things were, the Koreans could do little, for if they went in closer they would ground, and the distance was too great for their fire to be effective otherwise. So Yi pretended to retreat. The Japanese followed, thirsting for action and the chance to get to grips with a turtle boat. Wakizaka Yasuharu sprang on to the gunwales of his ship with a pronged rake, and ordered it to be directed full tilt at the nearest turtle. Shielding himself with his armoured sleeves and the neck piece of his helmet Wakizaka flung the rake down into the planking of a turtle boat and leapt on board, followed by the boldest of his samurai. Wrenching off several of the planks they penetrated its defences before the Koreans had a chance to fend them off, so one prize at least fell to the Japanese.

However, the loss of but a single ship was enough of a challenge for Yi to let loose a volley of fire-arrows on to the Japanese fleet. As the ships blazed the turtle boats opened out to left and right to let Won-kiun's squadron through to attack the stricken Japanese. They replied with arquebus fire, putting Admiral Yi himself on the casualty list with a bullet through his left shoulder, but he paid no attention to it and went on directing the battle. When it was over he cut the bullet out with his dagger. The wound was several inches deep, which greatly alarmed his colleagues but daunted Yi not a bit. Had the shot struck a little lower it might have altered the whole history of Asia.

After a short rest Admiral Yi again attacked some Japanese ships, this time at Tang-ho, on the end of the Tong-eng peninsula. If any news of the war on land reached his ears, it did nothing to deter him from his duty. By the middle of July the King had fled to China and Konishi was before P'yong-yang. But at sea the positions, and indeed the characters of the opposing commanders, were completely reversed. Life on board the Japanese flagships bore a strange resemblance to the Korean Court. Yi's log recorded that:

'He [Kurushima Michiyuki] used to sit on the quarter deck attired in yellow brocade with a gilt head-dress and everything about him was luxuriously appointed. Every evening the captains of the other ships used to come aboard and salute him and receive his orders, sitting awhile in a humble attitude with their heads to the mats. Anyone who disobeyed him was immediately decapitated.'

The above account was related to Yi by a young Korean girl who had been captured by the Japanese. She was rescued by the Admiral's squadron during their next offensive at Tang-hang-ho on 13 July. Kurushima's flagship was Yi's primary target. It was a large ornate vessel, with a triple tower in the bow painted red and green like a Buddhist temple. Yi sailed in close and blazed away at the superstructure. In the mêlée that followed the Korean archers came within range of Kurushima, and sank ten arrows into him. Being mortally wounded he retired and committed hara-kiri, the only Japanese admiral to meet his end in the whole campaign.

These actions so far were by no means decisive battles, but were the thin end of the wedge that Admiral Yi was driving between Japan and Korea. The transport of supplies had already been cut drastically, and the ships still in Korean waters felt safe only in Pusan harbour. But a decisive battle was to come. Yi had the measure of his rival and from the end of July began regular patrols along the southern coast of Korea. He had divined what Hideyoshi's grand strategy must have been, and in mid-August his patience was rewarded when one of his scouting vessels appeared with the intelligence that a large Japanese fleet was shortly to appear over the horizon. The second wave of the invasion, that was to march triumphantly into Peking, was finally on its way.

Yi's fleet was a large one, having been reinforced by other admirals besides the ineffectual Won-kiun. They were resting at Tang-ho when the news arrived that the Japanese were at anchor at Kyon Nae Riang, about half way up the straits. Setting off in pursuit the Koreans soon came across two Japanese scouting vessels, which immediately bolted back into harbour. Admiral Yi saw that he could do them little damage in port, for the harbour was narrow and there would be ample opportunity for the Japanese samurai to escape on to land. So he determined to draw them out to the vicinity of Han-San Island, which lay well out to sea between the two promontories at the mouth of the strait. Here there would be no escape except to the uninhabited island itself.

The resulting Battle of Han-San took place on 14 August 1592. The Japanese fleet was under the command of Kuki, Katō and Wakizaka, and consisted of thirty-six big vessels and fourteen medium sized, with an indeterminate number of junks. To lure them out Yi sent forward six ships only, and once again caution was thrown to the winds as Wakizaka came careering out, leaving the rest behind. Eventually the others followed, and having taunted them for sufficiently long Yi ordered his fleet into 'stork's wing formation', that is line-abreast with the two wings somewhat in advance of centre. This gave the Japanese the impression of sailing into a semicircle of hostile craft. Immediately a hot fire was directed on to the Japanese ships, and of Wakizaka's squadron only fourteen ships escaped unscathed, and four hundred men were forced to swim to the comparative safety of Han-San Island. Wakizaka came near to losing his life as fire-arrows rained down upon his ship, and might well have captured a prize had it not been for the samurai insistence upon individual glory at all costs. Wakizaka and Kuki Yoshitaka had both flung grappling irons on to the same ship. Wakizaka ordered one of his men to cut the other's rope. Kuki, irritated, wanted to fight his colleague, and while a heated squabble raged the Korean ship slipped out of reach.

With Wakizaka coming close to a watery grave the other admirals decided to make with all speed for An-kol harbour. The Korean fleet hung on to their flanks and bombarded them so that they sustained considerable damage, the mast of Kuki's ship being shot away, and it was only owing to the approach of nightfall that they were able to evade the pursuers. The four hundred survivors of Wakizaka's squadron who had swum to Han-San Island appeared to be trapped, and had to look forward to an indefinite period of eating seaweed and pine cones. That they eventually escaped was due to Won-kiun, whom Yi had left in charge of guarding the island while the main body of the Korean fleet pursued the Japanese. Rumours reached Won-kiun of the approach of another Japanese fleet, so he hastily retired, leaving the marooned Japanese free to improvise rafts from wreckage and reach the mainland safely.

Meanwhile Yi had chased the Japanese fleet to An-kol, and on 17 August bore down upon them. They had twenty-two large ships and fifteen medium, with six transport junks. The large ships were drawn up at the harbour mouth, protecting the transports behind. Yi sent his fleet in as ones and twos, delivering a broadside and then retiring, their place being occupied by a following pair. Eventually this goaded the Japanese into making a full scale attack, which had the expected result, and then Yi dealt decisively with the transports. Fifty-nine ships were sunk during the Battles of Han-San and An-kol, although many of the crews escaped during this last engagement. As Yi recorded in his log, 'The rascals fled in all directions and if they saw so much as the sail of a fishing boat they were terrified and knew not what to do.'

All that remained was for Yi to deliver the *coup de grâce* by destroying the Japanese base at Pusan. But Pusan proved too tough a nut to crack, and when Yi sent a large fleet against it in October he was faced with four hundred and seventy Japanese ships, as well as some land fortifications. He withdrew after a short struggle, for the Japanese were not to be lured out again, and contented himself with a bloackade of the port, secure in the knowledge that if he could not save his own country, he had certainly saved China. By the action of Han-San the invasion of China was postponed indefinitely, and the entire course of the

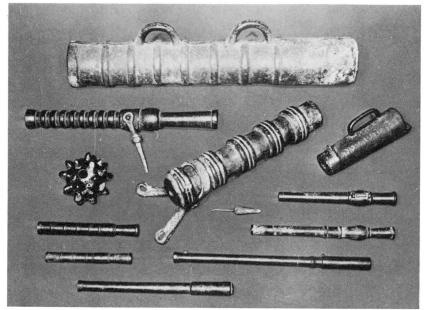

93 Types of Chinese and Korean cannon: (*top and centre right*) Cartridges for breech-loading heavy cannon; (*left centre*) Ōji type, length 61 cm., firing darts, used by the Korean Navy, and a porcelain hand-grenade; (*centre*) Koson type bronze cannon, length 52 cm., used by the Korean Navy; (*bottom*) Spoon for gunpowder, and Chinese handguns of the Ming Dynasty.

Korean War was changed dramatically.

Let us return to Konishi Yukinaga in P'yong-yang. He had entered it about 20 July, and spent the next month strengthening the line of communications that Yi was now breaking at its southcrn-most point. He established a chain of forts from P'yong-yang to Seoul, each a day's march from the other, and continually scanned the horizon for signs of the reinforcements that were destined never to arrive. He was burning with a desire for action, but advance was out of the question until fresh troops arrived, and every day the news from the South got worse. A vigorous guerrilla campaign had opened, led by younger, more able leaders than the cowardly old generals who had now fled to China. They attacked Japanese outposts and ambushed scouting parties. They led bands of samurai into dead-end valleys and massacred them. They pelted wandering foragers with rocks, and slit the throats of sentries in the dark. Besides the actual damage they did in cutting off stragglers, they wore down the enemy, both men and horses, by keeping them perpetually on the alert and in motion, and by subjecting them to the strain of a haunting sense of insecurity. Those regular Korean troops that were left shut themselves up in walled towns and castles, and held off the most furious onslaughts of the Japanese, who, with the ever present fear of the unseen knife in the dark, felt more like besieged than besiegers. Kuroda Nagamasa failed to capture the fortress of Yu-nan, and the Seventh Division sustained a positive disaster when they attempted to take the castle of Chin-ju in the South. A new spirit seemed to have animated the Koreans. They had been swept aside by the whirlwind advance of the Japanese, but 'he that is down need fear no fall'. The Koreans had nothing further to lose, and everything to gain.

It was at this point, when the fortunes of Korea were beginning to look brighter on land and sea, that the course of the war took a further dramatic turn. As summer became autumn, Konishi's ever-vigilant pickets observed the approach of a force of five thousand men. It was not the longed-for reinforcements, for they were coming from the North, and as they drew near to P'yong-yang the Japanese noticed their yellow silk banners, inscribed with the characters 'Tai Ming' (Great Brightness) – the distinctive blazon of the Ming Dynasty of China.

China's decision to aid Korea by a direct invasion had not been undertaken lightly. The Chinese had been so surprised by Korea's rapid capitulation that they suspected collusion with the Japanese, and it was only after urgent appeals from Korea that they agreed to act. Konishi, however, was nothing daunted by the sight of this comparatively small Chinese force, and made plans accordingly. When the Chinese arrived at P'yong-yang they found the city gates open, and marched into one of the simplest and deadliest of traps possible. The Japanese were concealed in every house and first decimated the Chinese by arquebus fire and then sprang on them with their swords. The new invaders were completely routed, and the few survivors fled with all haste to beyond the Yalu River.

This gesture from the North turned Konishi's mind from plans of immediate further conquest and, as autumn gave way to a bitter winter, consolidation became his theme. The government at Peking, too, were deep in thought, and were now beginning to understand the power of the Japanese. In order to gain time an emissary named Chin Ikei was sent, independently of the Koreans, to treat with the Japanese. His manly bearing and conduct impressed Konishi greatly, so a truce was agreed, probably as much to the relief of Konishi as to the Chinese. It was to last fifty days, and gave the Japanese a welcome breathing space, during which they further strengthened the chain of forts stretching to Seoul, and redoubled their efforts against the persistent guerrillas. Meanwhile the Chinese were busy raising a huge army to push the Japanese out of the peninsula. The numbers of this host are variously given as forty or two hundred thousand. Whatever its actual size it was well equipped, still with no matchlock muskets, but included a large artillery train of small field pieces, and formidable numbers of cavalry. As 1592 drew to its close, the fresh Chinese army set out. The march over the mountain passes of Liao Tung was such severe going that the horses are said to have sweated blood. They crossed the Yalu in the dead of winter, on 27 January 1593, and in early February stood before the walls of P'yong-yang.

Konishi's alternatives lay between the risk of battle and a retreat. He decided on the former, and fortified the city as best he could. To the north of P'yong-yang lay a hill, on which the Japanese reared earthworks out of the frozen ground and built palisades from the wood of ice-bound trees. Here it was planned to hold off the Chinese with arquebus fire, with the city walls to fall back on. Encirclement was unlikely because of the presence of a mountain to the west, and to the south and east the Tadong River, which the Japanese had crossed with such exhilaration scarcely seven months previously.

As dawn broke on 10 February the Chinese launched a furious assault along the whole line. At first the Japanese muskets took their toll, but soon the Chinese pressed them back by sheer weight of numbers and by nightfall on the second day of the siege the defenders were forced within the walls of the city, leaving two thousand Japanese dead in the breastworks. At this point the Chinese commander, Li jo sho, sent a messenger with a summons of surrender. The answer he received was the headless body of the messenger flung from the city walls. Seeing that the Japanese were prepared to defend the city to the last, and that his own troops were exhausted after forty-eight hours of non-stop fighting, Li jo sho gave the order to return to camp, expecting to renew the offensive in the morning. As the Chinese withdrew Konishi took advantage of the lull in the fighting to evacuate the city. Under the cover of night the Japanese slipped out of the southern gate, and across the ice of the frozen Tadong River. In this masterly retreat little was left behind but corpses. Weary, footsore, and suffering from cold and hunger, the once proud samurai began the long march southwards. Their task was made more difficult by the cowardly Ōtomo Yoshimune, who had been placed in charge of the communications fort next to P'yong-yang. At the approach of the Chinese he had fled, as had the commander of the second fort. So the Japanese were faced with a two-day march before provisions could be obtained. This they accomplished unmolested, for the Chinese made no attempt to pursue them, and no Korean force nearby felt strong enough to attack. The Koreans did have the satisfaction of beheading some sixty unfortunate stragglers who, from sickness or fatigue, were unable to keep up with the rest of the army.

The fall of P'yong-yang was the first serious reverse suffered by the Japanese on land, and as Konishi's troops fell back on Seoul they left Katō Kiyomasa isolated in the north-east. As mentioned previously, his efforts had not been entirely unrewarded as the presence in his camp of two royal captives showed. Flushed by success, the Chinese commander who had taken P'yong-yang sent an envoy with a haughty summons of surrender to Katō. To this Katō replied with a note of defiance and guarded his royal prisoners more vigilantly. In an act of sheer cruelty designed solely to intimidate the Chinese envoy he put to death the beautiful Korean girl captive, by transfixing her with his spear from waist to shoulder while bound to a tree, as the envoy looked on. But as news reached him of Konishi's withdrawal he decided to fight his way back through the snows of North Korea, and join up with his rival. It mortified Katō to have to take such action, for during his winter campaign he had actually crossed the Tumen River and briefly entered Manchuria. The Koreans had been active in Katō's area, including the capture of a fortress, which had caused the Japanese much alarm, as the following account shows:

'A man called Ri Cho Son invented a cannon which he called Shin-ten-rai or Heaven-shaking-thunder, which by his art he secretly brought to the foot of the castle. It was put in operation and shot into the castle, where it fell in the courtyard. The Japanese troops were ignorant of its construction, and rushed forward to see what curious missile had been shot at them by the enemy, when all of a sudden the gunpowder poison burst forth, with a noise which made heaven and earth tremble, and it broke up into splinters of iron, which caused instant death to any one whom they struck. More than thirty men were killed in this way, and even those who were not killed were flung to the ground.'

It appears that we have here the inventor of the mortar and the bomb. The delayed action was due to the slow burning of Korean gunpowder, which contained an excess of sulphur, but like the turtle

94   Bronze cannon owned by Katō Kiyomasa, with a design of a celestial nymph. (Tokugawa Art Museum, Nagoya.)

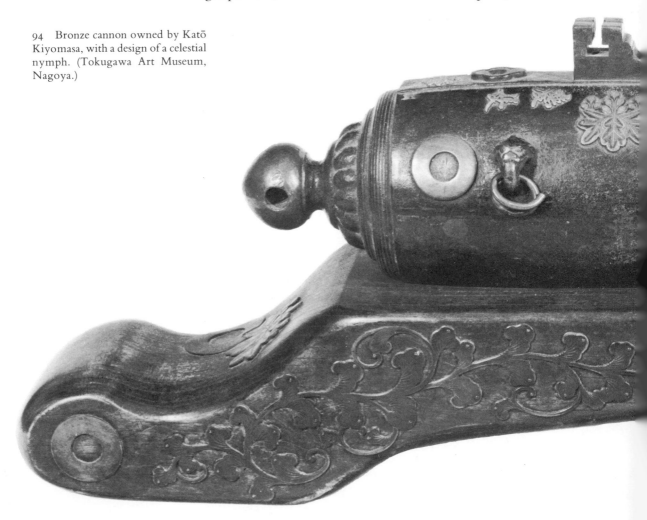

boat the 'Flying Thunderbolt', as it is sometimes called, was regarded as not being of human manufacture.

Konishi and Katō joined forces at Kaishung, just north of the Imjin River, and decided to withdraw to Seoul all Japanese divisions north of the Han River. This order was promptly obeyed by all commanders except Kobayakawa Takakage, the grizzled sixty-one-year-old warrior, commander of the Sixth Division. When the order for withdrawal reached him he stoutly refused to budge. It was pointed out gently that he was needed to fight a general action against the Chinese, who had now begun to advance. He then agreed to retire if he were assigned the place of danger in the forthcoming battle. As he began a dignified withdrawal the advance guard of the Chinese caught up with him, but he brushed them off and continued on towards Seoul. On arrival he refused to enter the city, saying that he had gone back far enough, and that it was time for an old hand like himself to show the young ones how to turn defeat into victory. This was no mere samurai bravado, but a calculated attempt at a rearguard action while the Japanese regrouped. So Kobayakawa Takakage, possibly the oldest samurai in

the Japanese army, prepared to meet the entire Chinese army. The younger commanders were somewhat shamefaced at this riposte, so two bands of 3,000 were sent out to join him, including Katō Kiyomasa who was always ready for a fight. Kobayakawa had 10,000 from the Sixth Division, mainly his personal retainers, and chose to meet the Chinese at P'yok-je-yek, a few miles north of Seoul.

The battle, on 25 February 1593, was destined to prove the largest and bloodiest of the whole campaign. P'yok-je-yek was a rounded hill, and Kobayakawa stationed his division behind it, while the other Japanese armies occupied its northern slopes in two groups of 3,000 men each. The snow was beginning to melt with the distant approach of spring, and the battlefield was a sea of slush and mud, which Kobayakawa hoped would slow down the Chinese cavalry and lay them open to the sharp blades of the Japanese. Until P'yok-je-yek no real pitched battle had been fought, and apart from Konishi's division the samurai had had no opportunity to test their mettle against the Chinese. The Chinese opened the attack at dawn, and launched themselves against the forward positions of the Japanese. Once again the arquebuses blazed away, but the Japanese were slowly but surely pushed back up the hill by the colossal Chinese army, swollen by Korean troops who had flocked to the victorious standard of Li jo sho. As they reached the crest of the hill the Chinese thought victory certain, and began a headlong pursuit with both foot soldiers and cavalry down the reverse slope towards Kobayakawa's 10,000. Kobayakawa waited until the enemy were too far distant from their camp to receive reinforcements, and watched the Chinese become more exhausted and disordered as their horses bogged down in the mud. Then the order to charge was given, and 10,000 samurai and footsoldiers bore down upon the enemy, their curved blades glinting in the weak winter sun. The battle then became a gigantic hand-to-hand fight, on a scale never before witnessed in Korea. For the first time the Japanese sword was measured against the shorter Korean and Chinese version, with devastating results for the latter. The lower-class Japanese also did terrible execution, piling on to the Chinese horsemen mired in the churned-up slush. The samurai wielded their long cross-bladed spears, tearing the Chinese from their saddles with the cross-pieces, and then finishing them off with a slash or a thrust. Particularly active in this was Katō Kiyomasa, whose silver helmet stood out in the midst of the fray. This close fighting continued from

ten till noon, by which time it was all over, and the Chinese had lost 10,000 men. Their commander, Li jo sho, is said to have been so disheartened that he cried all through the night. As for old Kobayakawa, here a cross between Marshal Ney and John Wayne, he was very modest about having saved the Japanese army from annihilation. 'When Empress Jingō of yore invaded Korea,' he said, 'she was helped by the Gods. In the present case who knows but the Gods helped us again?'

95 The decisive weapon of the Japanese samurai, the standard fighting sword, or 'katana'.

The victory of P'yok-je-yek proved to be only a temporary respite for the Japanese. The long winter rains made the samurai despondent and gloomy enough to commit hara-kiri, while the state of the roads and the dashing courage of the guerrillas, who were now bold enough to push their raids to the very gates of Seoul, made foraging an unpopular duty among the men. In such discomfort winter wore away, and tardy spring approached. In this state of affairs the Chinese and Koreans were willing to offer, and the Japanese to consider, terms of peace. A meeting was arranged, which proved to be short and businesslike. The Korean terms were blunt. The Japanese had to release the two Korean princes captured by Katō, and withdraw their armies to the extreme south-west of the country. These demands inevitably reopened the enmity between Konishi and Katō, for the former was in favour of them, while Katō saw his chief prize of the campaign being given away. But at length he was forced to agree, and in the name of Hideyoshi, Konishi and Katō agreed to evacuate Seoul on 9 May 1593, almost a year after they had triumphantly entered it. On 20 May the Chinese entered the city, and witnessed the horrors the Japanese had left behind. Starving people fought one another, even turning to cannibalism in their desperation. Typhus was rife, and the dead bodies of its victims lay all along the road, the head of one pillowed on the breast of another.

The Japanese proceeded southwards, no longer disturbed by the Koreans or their Chinese allies. Indeed the only engagement fought was the reduction of the fortress of Chin-ju, and this was merely to satisfy Hideyoshi's desire for revenge, for Chin-ju was the fortress before which Mōri Terumoto's Seventh Division had failed. With such a large concentration of troops in the South the Japanese were able to launch a massive attack under an enthusiastic Katō Kiyomasa, eager to make a speedy capture and so irritate the Koreans as to prevent the peace he feared. He surrounded the castle which the Koreans had failed to reinforce, but the stout resistance of the garrison, who threw down rocks on to the heads of the assault parties, forced him to try an enterprising innovation in siege-warfare. Collecting several hundred green hides, and dry hardening them in the fire, he covered four heavily built slant-roofed wagons with them. These vehicles, called 'kame-no-kosha' or tortoise-shell wagons, were pushed forward to the foot of the walls. While the matchlock men in the ranks engaged those fighting on the ramparts the soldiers under the protecting shell of the tortoise wagons began to dig under the foundations. Thus undermined the stones were prised out, and soon fell in sufficient numbers to cause a breach, through which fresh soldiers rushed and quickly stormed the castle.

After this affair Konishi's division garrisoned a series of fortified camps along the south coast, and most of the other troops who had served throughout the campaign were withdrawn, while prolonged peace negotiations began. The business of negotiation eventually dragged on for four years, while the Japanese stayed within their camps in Korea. Conditions were demanded, readily accepted, and then as easily broken, while Konishi strutted back and forth between Japan and Korea as Hideyoshi's chief negotiator. Even the forces of nature played their part to frustrate the successful conclusion of peace, as a mighty earthquake laid low most of the important buildings in Kyōto, and the Chinese Embassy, who arrived on 21 October 1596, had to be accommodated in a wing of Ōsaka Castle. The much delayed meeting was held in great pomp and splendour. The Chinese brought with them a letter which, Konishi had assured Hideyoshi, contained an agreement to all his demands. However, Hideyoshi did not receive them kindly, and when he came to the part of their letter demanding the demolition of the Japanese fortresses and the withdrawal of the remaining troops he became so angry, 'that vapour exhaled from his head'. Insult was added to injury by the pantomime which followed, for Hideyoshi was presented with a crown and a robe of state that he fondly believed made him Emperor of China. The reality became apparent when the document of investiture was read: 'We do therefore specially invest you,' it ran, 'with the dignity of King – of Japan!' Hideyoshi was roused to the most intense fury, and sent for Konishi that he might cut off his head on the spot. Konishi protested his innocence, and in view of his martial prowess was reprieved. The ambassadors were immediately shown the door.

On 19 March 1597 orders were issued for a second invasion of Korea. That a further attempt at conquest would have little chance of succeeding where the first had failed seemed obvious to everyone except Hideyoshi, who was quickly losing control of his reason. It was an utterly pointless exercise, and Hideyoshi's revenge was its only excuse. Nevertheless there was no shortage of volunteers to lead the new attack, and the honour fell to the ever-willing Katō Kiyomasa, while the fleet was to be placed under the control of Konishi Yukinaga. The Japanese had learnt a severe lesson at the hands of Admiral Yi, and now made sure that all their vessels were equipped with cannon.

Overall command of the army was given to an up-and-coming samurai called Kobayakawa Hideaki, the adopted son of Kobayakawa Takakage and Hideyoshi's nephew. Such august patronage had assured him this high post at the tender age of twenty. Kuroda Yoshitaka, Nagamasa's father, was sent along to keep an eye on the young lad. Needless to say this appointment provoked great jealousy among the others, particularly a certain Ishida Mitsunari, formerly a staff officer of Ukita Hideie in the first invasion. He lost no time in accusing the young commander of incompetence, and was quick to pounce on any fault once the invasion got under way.

Together with the garrison already in Korea there were 149,000 troops returned to Korean soil, five divisions from Kyūshū, two from Shikoku, and two, Mōri and Ukita, from Honshū. It is perhaps surprising that the second invasion managed to land at all, but the Korean Navy was not what it had been in 1592. Even the gallant Admiral Yi Sun Sin was not proof against the machinations of colleagues, and had been relieved of his post by the wily Won-kiun, who now had supreme command. The Japanese had little trouble in trouncing Won-kiun when they came across his fleet near Kyo Chong in August 1597. The Korean governor of the district summoned Won-kiun and had him flogged. But this only made him seek solace in drink and the other commanders could not rouse him to any action at all. Eventually he went on shore where he sat drunk under a pine tree and watched through half-glazed eyes the destruction of his country's Navy. Noticing the absence of Admiral Yi the Japanese attacked with alacrity, boarding every Korean vessel they closed with. Nabeshima Katsushige, a young samurai of seventeen and the son of Katō Kiyomasa's comrade in arms, described the sight of the destruction of so many Korean ships as being greater 'even than that of viewing the cherry blossoms of Yoshino'. One hundred and sixty Korean ships were sunk, and the second army of invasion landed in Korea with as little trouble as the first had done in 1592.

For Katō Kiyomasa the landing was a vindication of his view that peace ought never to have been considered, but once in Korea there was to be no rapid advance northwards, for the Chinese had already sent an army into Southern Korea, and it was against a detachment of this that Katō Kiyomasa first directed his forces. The Chinese had entrenched themselves within a powerful fortress town called Nam-wön, encircled by stone walls twelve feet or more in height. While one of his generals prevented a relief column from coming to the aid of Nam-wön Katō led his army in a siege against it. Konishi, in charge of the fleet, sailed along the coast and landed reinforcements at the mouth of the River Sem on which Nam-wön stood.

The preparations for defence were all that Chinese science could suggest. The walls contained high towers, and a dry moat, three hundred feet wide, bristled with an abattis of tree trunks with their branches outwards. After some desperate fighting the Japanese took the moat, and then put into operation one of the warlike stratagems at which

Katō Kiyomasa excelled. Large numbers of men were sent into the rice fields which the farmers, in hope of peace, had sown. Reaping the green, juicy stalks they gathered an enormous quantity of sheaves and waited with these and their stacks of bamboo scaling-ladders until night. In the darkness, and in perfect silence, they moved to a part of the wall that was twenty feet high and thus lightly guarded, and began to build a platform of the sheaves. By the time the ruse was discovered the pile was quite high, and when the alarm was raised the matchlock men swept the walls with bullets, and the piling became fast and furious, so that the mass of green rice stalks, both firm and fireproof, reached the level of the walls. Hundreds of samurai leapt into the castle and the whole garrison was put to the sword. For the first time the Japanese had the opportunity of complying with Hideyoshi's orders issued before they left for Korea, that the commanders were to furnish him with visible proof that they were doing their duty. Consequently they began to sever the heads of the garrison, which came to 3,726 in all. The heads of the officers, and the noses of the private soldiers were pickled in salt and lime and sent in barrels to Hideyoshi, surely the strangest evidence yet of Hideyoshi's declining mental powers.

So the Japanese pressed on for Seoul, but as they proceeded on their way they heard news that struck terror in their hearts – Admiral Yi had returned! Soon communications were again broken, with the Japanese a mere seventeen miles from Seoul. Their advance had been slow. It was now mid-October, and as the bitter Korean winter would soon be upon them the generals resolved to fall back upon the chain of fortified camps in the south, and renew the offensive in the spring. When the fortresses were reached orders were immediately given to strengthen their defences, for one of the Chinese generals had determined to close the war as quickly as possible by a massive attack on the Japanese positions that would drive them into the sea. The General, Yang Ho, erected an altar in the presence of his troops and offered sacrifices to propitiate the spirits of Heaven and Earth, praying for victory against the invader. Then seeing to his supplies he gave orders for a general march against Yol-san, known to the Japanese as Uru-san, which was the most easterly of all the Japanese forts. This position was held by Katō Kiyomasa's division, and was strongly built with inner and outer defences, the southern side of the fort lying on the sea. The operations of the war, which had hitherto covered large spaces of the country, now found their pivot at this place situated thirty-five miles north of Pusan. The allied army, reinforced by a fresh Chinese army of 40,000 advanced to lay siege and arrived just too late to prevent Asano Yukinaga from entering with his men.

At the beginning of January 1598, the Chinese army suddenly assaulted the castle. A small detachment, evidently a decoy, attempted to scale the wall, but were driven back by arquebus fire and forced to retreat. Seeing this the Japanese recklessly opened the gate and began pursuit of the enemy thinking they were only Koreans. Lured on to a distance they found themselves surrounded by 80,000 Chinese. Only after hard fighting did the remnants of the sortie manage to drag themselves back to the walls. They had lost heavily in casualties, reducing the garrison to but five thousand men.

The following day the war conch sounded again in the Chinese camp, and the ears of the besieged were deafened by the yells of the besiegers as their full force was flung against the walls. Though seven attacks were repulsed the wall was breached and the garrison was driven into the inner defences. Next morning the Japanese were awakened by showers of arrows, and the fighting recommenced. In spite of the intense cold the samurai perspired so much that the sweat froze on their armour. Over their own heap of corpses the Chinese attempted to force one of the gates, while from the walls above the Japanese continued to fire musket balls down upon them. In February the Chinese were again beaten off, and at night the sentries gathered hoar frost on their helmets. Some of the Japanese samurai noticed that their shinguards kept slipping down, though adjusted repeatedly. The fact was that their flesh had shrunk until their bones were nearly visible, and their legs were as lean as bamboo sticks. Another warrior, taking off his helmet and face mask, was seen to have a face as thin and wizened as one of those hungry demons of the nether world, which they had seen so often depicted in temple pictures at home.

By the end of February the Chinese general, who had looked upon Uru-san as a small affair to be settled by the way, tried negotiation. The Japanese turned down all offers, and profited from the brief break to make fires of broken arrows and enjoy a dinner of hot horse meat, stripped from the carcasses of their steeds. The next day was quiet, but intensely cold, and many of the worn-out samurai, sitting under the sunny side of the towers for warmth, were found later frozen to death. To hunger was added the torture of thirst, for as there was no well in the castle the Japanese had sallied out at night and brought water from the mountain brooks, and now this was stopped by the besiegers. The soldiers who fought by day stole out at night and licked the wounds of the slain, and even secretly ate the raw flesh sliced from the corpses of the Chinese. They chewed paper, trapped mice and ate them, and braved the arrows of the Chinese sentries to search the clothes of their dead enemies for stray grains of parched rice. One night the Chinese succeeded in capturing one hundred of the garrison, prowling like ghouls among the corpses of the slain. The siege was now a complete blockade, and famine and cold daily took their toll.

Eventually tidings reached the other Japanese commanders, who hurriedly assembled a relief column to raise the siege of Uru-san. Kuroda, Hachisuka and Nabeshima marched with 50,000 men, and arrived as a fresh assault was taking place. Without hesitation they flung themselves against the rear of the Chinese host, and at the same time Konishi's fleet braved Yi's blockade to bring in supplies by sea. The suffering was now over for the valiant defenders, who had fought on without food and water, save melted snow. With a feeling of being raised from the dead they took off their armour. For the commanders

Of Uru-san, Katō Kiyomasa and Asano Yukinaga, it was a personal triumph. A few days later Asano wrote an excited letter to his father Asano Nagamasa, a veteran of the 1592 invasion. In it he stressed the power of the Japanese weapons, for although the Koreans and Chinese had by now armed some of their troops with matchlocks the advantage was still with the Japanese:

'When troops come [to Korea] from the province of Kai, have them bring as many guns as possible, for no other equipment is needed. Give strict orders that all men, even the samurai, carry guns.'

With the coming of spring the Chinese received further reinforcements, and Konishi advised the evacuation of the fortresses and a concentration in Pusan. But Hideyoshi would not hear of it. He recalled the greater part of the army, however, leaving only the Kyūshū divisions and a few others to hold the camps, against which the Chinese kept up fruitless attacks throughout the summer. One of these camps was held by the Shimazu clan under Shimazu Yoshihiro. This family's service so far had been undramatic, although Yoshihiro had lost his eldest son Hisayasu in 1593, but now they were to have the distinction of taking part in the last land battle of the Korean War. This was the Battle of Sö-chön, fought on 30 October 1598, and was a pitched battle like P'yok-je-yek. The Chinese casualties were heavy, and to comply with Hideyoshi's demands for proof the Satsuma warriors sliced the ears off 38,700 heads and sent them, pickled in salt, to Kyoto, where they were buried in a mound known as the 'Mimi-zuka' or ear tomb, a ghastly memorial to a ghastly war. The battle was not long over when the news reached Korea of the death on 18 September of Toyotomi Hideyoshi. With his death faded the dream of Empire that had become a nightmare, and the order to embark for home was everywhere gladly cheered in the Japanese camps.

But the war was not quite over, for there was one round left to play, as the Japanese still had to evacuate the remainder of their armies. To ensure a safe withdrawal the knowledge of Hideyoshi's death was kept a close secret from the neighbouring Koreans, lest they should attack during the embarkation. But Korean spies in Japan soon learnt the Japanese intentions, and as Konishi was on his way out through the straits of No Niang on 16 December 1598, he was surprised to hear the sound of cannon. He soon came upon Shimazu's Division, which had left its base at Su Chong, and had been met by Admiral Yi, eager to strike a last blow at his departing foes. The attack had begun at midnight, and the fight was now fast and furious. The Shimazu warriors were a stubborn bunch and managed to board the ship of Yi's second-in-command and slew him. Admiral Yi sailed to assist, and just then a bullet struck him in the armpit and he fell. 'Don't let anyone see or it may hinder the battle,' he said to a sailor beside him, so they covered him with a shield and no one spread the news. At length the Japanese drew off. Shimazu escaped with fifty ships and Konishi took advantage of the fighting to slip away into the open sea. 'But when the death of their Great Admiral was known the lamentations of both Koreans and Chinese sounded far over the oceans.' So died Admiral Yi, as the last Japanese samurai left Korea.

Thus ended the Korean War, unique in Japanese military history in being the only time when the energies of the samurai were directed in an act of aggression against a foreign country. It had begun as the first stage of a grandiose project for conquering China, and had ended without territorial, financial or political gain. In Japan it is picturesquely called the 'dragon head and snake tail campaign'. That is, the Japanese started furiously, but gradually tailed off. Nevertheless the war had an important influence on later generations when ideas of another Asian Empire were being considered, and the success of the samurai on land was regarded as a 'flower to adorn Japanese history'. Before the cynical reader condemns this view of a campaign that laid Korea waste let him compare the popular English attitude towards Henry V's French expedition, and remember that the Korean War was the sole case of overseas aggression in six hundred years. Moreover, the intervention of the Chinese late in 1592 was almost as great a disaster for Korea as the Japanese landings. When the Chinese crossed the Yalu the Koreans had already begun to turn the tables, and it is quite conceivable that had no Chinese arrived to share the already dwindling supplies of the Korean Army then Korea could have turned itself into one vast besieging camp. The evacuation of North Korea would then only have been a matter of time. As it was, Korea was subjected to the ravages of both nations, and watched helplessly while two great powers fought on her soil, not for the last time in Korea's history. Also, when the Japanese evacuated the peninsula in 1598, the Chinese left a garrison of 34,000 men, which did nothing to help the re-generation of Korea.

The effect on Korea was tragic. The whole country had been a battlefield, and there was no way of seeking redress. Cities and villages lay waste, and the country presented a picture of frightful confusion, where starving people and refugees were preyed on by thieves, and corrupt officials took advantage of the unhappy conditions to line their own pockets.

The war also dealt a blow to Ming China. The government had already been facing internal difficulties when the war began, and the cost of the campaigns ran up a vast bill. For the second invasion alone the Chinese army got through 118,000 fire-arrows and 41 tons of gun-powder, as well as swords, fodder and rice. This not only weakened the nation's resources, but, as most of the troops were drawn from Northern China her defences there were weakened, and this led to the eventual conquest by the Manchus.

As for Japan, the war had been a failure. It had failed because Hideyoshi did not realize that command of the sea was necessary for success on land. It was not a question of better ships, or army and navy cooperation, even though these were improved before the second invasion set sail, but of the need to bottle up or utterly destroy the enemy's fleet before one samurai was landed. Had this been done when Won–kiun was still in command the future course of the campaign might have been very different. But this whole idea was completely contrary to the Japanese view of a ship as a platform for soldiers, and there was nothing in the experience of Hideyoshi or anyone else to make them think differently. It is left to the reader to speculate what might have happened had the second wave landed and marched on to China.

So what did Japan get out of it? In military or political terms nothing at all. There was plenty of loot brought home, including such bizarre items as stones for castles and garden trees. The oddest result of the Korean War, and its most enduring memorial, was the arrival in Japan of scores of Korean potters who, as a result of the Japanese passion for the tea ceremony, were brought to Japan to carry on their craft. They were without exception well treated, some intermarrying and others maintaining their Korean blood and the pure pottery style. Thus there was one peaceful result from the cruel Korean War.

11. The final reckoning

When the weary samurai returned home from Korea they found Japan a different country from the one they had remembered. The great dictator had left behind him the foundations of modern Japan, but had died in a manner all dictators dread. He had died leaving an infant son to inherit. Toyotomi Hideyori was five years old when his father died, and although the evidence suggests that Hideyoshi was gradually losing his reason as his end approached, he was sufficiently lucid to safeguard Hideyori's future as best he could. To this end he appointed a board of five regents to administer during Hideyori's minority. His choice is interesting, and each name will be familiar to the reader. They were Ukita Hideie, Maeda Toshiie, Mōri Terumoto, Uesugi Kagakatsu, and Tokugawa Ieyasu.

The parallel between 1598 and 1582 is particularly striking. In 1582 Hideyoshi had declared Nobunaga's one-year-old grandson as heir. He then asserted his strength politically, and waited for his rivals to give an excuse for war. Hence the Shizugatake campaign, which gave Hideyoshi control of Nobunaga's domain within ten months. In 1598 the part of Hideyoshi was being played by Tokugawa Ieyasu, who was by far the most powerful daimyō in Japan, with a revenue of 2,557,000 *koku*. When one remembers that a *koku* is the amount of rice necessary to feed one man for one year, it is a truly colossal sum. In second equal place were Mōri Terumoto and Uesugi Kagekatsu, whose revenues were each about half of Ieyasu's. Of the two, Mōri was the more influential, 'ruling' the Inland Sea from his castle at Hiroshima, while Uesugi's daimyate lay in the north of Honshū. However, Mōri had fought in Korea, while Uesugi had not. Neither, for that matter, had the Tokugawa troops.

Ieyasu was now fifty-six years old. His lithe figure had given way to bulldog-like corpulence. No longer was he the dashing young samurai, swinging his spear at the Ikkō monks, but a cool, intelligent general. He had retained sufficient respect for the realities of war to appreciate that battles could not be won by merely sitting on a camp stool giving orders. He once remarked that victories were not won by gazing at the backs of one's samurai. Nevertheless he no longer jeopardized the future of the Tokugawa house by charging into the fray. He had many captains who would do that for him, including a clutch of fine sons, one of whom, his heir Hidetada, was being trained in the arts of war.

96 Portrait scroll of Tokugawa
Ieyasu (1542–1616). (Tokugawa Art
Museum, Nagoya.)

Ieyasu's ambitions were soon made plain. The main opposition to them came not from his fellow regents, but from a civil servant called Ishida Mitsunari. We have heard his name mentioned twice before in this narrative. He entered Hideyoshi's service after proving his ability at serving tea, leading to his appointment as one of Hideyoshi's commissioners. During the first invasion of Korea he served on the staff of Ukita Hideie as Inspector General of the Forces, an appointment which he took very seriously. As a result he made several enemies, including Kuroda Nagamasa, who, according to Ishida, was more interested in playing 'Go' than in fighting the war. Ishida had also objected to the appointment of Kobayakawa Hideaki as commander-in-chief of the second invasion. Their resulting antagonism was to prove a more fateful quarrel than either realized at the time.

Ieyasu looked to Ishida to play the part of Shibata Katsuie, and divide the council of regents down the middle, thereby precipitating a quarrel, out of which Ieyasu would emerge on top. Ieyasu had to move very carefully. In particular he had to be seen not to be opposed to Hideyori directly. That would look too much like disloyalty to his late comrade-in-arms. Ishida would provide the sounding board, and Ishida most obligingly did.

Ieyasu had made his temporary headquarters in the late Hideyoshi's Ōsaka Castle, where, in 1600 he received in audience the first Englishman ever to set foot in Japan, Will Adams. Adams was a pilot on a Dutch vessel that had docked in Kyūshū. By all accounts he was a real Elizabethan sea-dog, and had commanded one of the English ships that had defeated the Spanish Armada. Ieyasu is said to have found Adams an interesting and informative fellow, but his ship's cargo was perhaps a more welcome arrival. The cargo was impounded by Ieyasu, increasing the Tokugawa arsenal by several fine pieces of European cannon, not to mention 500 arquebuses, 5,000 iron cannon balls, 300 chain-shot, two tons of gunpowder, the European variety being much prized, and 350 fire-arrows.

While Ieyasu was increasing his stock of weaponry the daimyō of Japan were dividing themselves into two factions, for Ishida Mitsunari or for Tokugawa Ieyasu. It was a division far more complete than had been the taking of sides in 1582. The well known names throwing in their lot with Ishida, who maintained respectability by declaring that he represented the interests of Hideyori, were Mōri Terumoto, accompanied of course by Kobayakawa Hideaki and Kikkawa Hiroie, all Korean War veterans; Ukita Hideie, formerly commander-in-chief, Korea; Shimazu Yoshihiro, whose Satsuma samurai always seemed ready for a fight; Chōsokabe Morichika of Shikoku, Konishi Yukinaga and Uesugi Kagekatsu.

Fortunately for Ieyasu, many of Hideyoshi's 'Old Guard' supported him because he was a soldier first and foremost, unlike Ishida, whom Katō Kiyomasa described as a 'civilian poking his nose into military matters'. So Katō declared for Ieyasu, thus putting himself in the opposite camp to his old rival Konishi Yukinaga. He was joined by

Asano, Hosokawa Tadaoki, Kuroda Nagamasa and his father Yoshitaka, as well as the usual Tokugawa collaterals.

The first move was made by the Ishida side, who are usually referred to as the Western Army. Ishida's ally Uesugi Kagekatsu was observed to be building castles at a furious rate up in his Northern provinces. In May 1600, Ieyasu invited him to come to Ōsaka to explain his conduct. The reply he received from Uesugi's chief counsellor, Naoe Kanetsugu, who told Ieyasu to mind his own business, pointed out that while Ieyasu and his city samurai collected tea bowls, out in the country they tended to collect weapons instead. From his subsequent manoeuvrings it is clear that Ieyasu understood fully what was going on, and that Ishida wished him to move east to face the threat from Uesugi while Ishida and his allies seized Ōsaka and cut off Ieyasu from behind. As Ieyasu's plans were as well laid as Ishida's he thought it advisable to make his rival think he had him fooled, so he began to move east in a leisurely fashion. He left Ōsaka on 26 July and reached Edo on 10 August. He then moved farther north, ostensibly to combat Uesugi, but all the while keeping in close touch with affairs in the capital. The campaign against Uesugi was of minor importance, because Ieyasu had valuable allies in Date Masamune, the 'One-Eyed Dragon', and Mogami Yoshiakira, who were already keeping Uesugi well in hand. At midnight on 1 September Ieyasu was aroused from sleep to receive a messenger, who had brought definite intelligence of a revolt in the West, led by Ishida, acting no doubt on the bold but erroneous assumption that Ieyasu would be pinned down by Uesugi.

Ishida's first move was made against the strategic fortress of Fushimi Castle, which Hideyoshi had built a few miles south of Kyōto to complete, with Ōsaka, the defences of the Kinai. Because of its position Fushimi commanded the approaches to the capital, and Ieyasu had entrusted its defence to Torii Mototada, an old friend then aged sixty-two. Before leaving for the east Ieyasu paid a visit to Torii, and their meeting ended with an emotional parting, as both knew that once hostilities began, Fushimi would be the Westerners' first target.

The assault on Fushimi began on 27 August, and was repulsed for ten days with unparalleled fanaticism. Torii knew that he must play for time, time for Ieyasu to seize the strategic fortresses along the Tōkaidō and Nakasendō while a large proportion of Ishida's samurai were banging their heads against the wall of Fushimi Castle. The garrison fought bravely, and only began to yield when a traitor, whose wife and children had been threatened with crucifixion by Ishida, set fire to one of the towers. Even then Torii would not give in, and rejected a suggestion that he should commit suicide. What was of the essence, he pointed out, was not his own honour but the need to delay Ishida as long as it was humanly possible. So he led his two hundred samurai, the remnants of the brave garrison, in a charge out of the gate. After five such sallies the number of men left was reduced to ten, and Torii finally retired into the castle and collapsed. A certain samurai called Saiga Shigetomo ran at him with a spear, intending to take his head.

The old man called out his name, so the young samurai waited respectfully while Torii committed suicide, then cut off his head. His delaying tactics had worked, and in addition had given the Ishida party the dubious satisfaction of a Pyrrhic victory, for they had lost 3,000 men in the attack.

The fall of Fushimi meant that Ishida's Western allies could safely come and join their leader, who was at that time at Ōgaki, near to Gifu Castle. The only contingents so far with him were Shimazu and Konishi. Consequently both he and Ieyasu were playing for time for a similar reason.

The reader is referred back to the map in Fig. 54 to appreciate Ieyasu's immediate strategic problem. He was in Edo, which was connected with the Kinai area by two main roads, the Tōkaidō and the Nakasendō. The two roads are at their nearest point near to Gifu, where the gap between them is about twenty miles, before they finally join near the southern tip of Lake Biwa. The 'neck' between the two roads was dominated by the fortresses of Gifu and Kiyosu, both formerly important bases for Nobunaga. If the Western forces could hold the two castles they could control all traffic from Eastern Japan, and perhaps hold Ieyasu until Uesugi could break free in the Tōsandō. In September 1600 each fortress was held by supporters of one army. Gifu was controlled for Ishida by Oda Hidenobu, who was a grandson of Oda Nobunaga, and the very baby that Hideyoshi had proclaimed as heir in 1582, a remarkable link with the past! Kiyosu was held by Ōsaki Gemba on behalf of Fukushima Masanori, who was with Ieyasu.

While Ishida was assaulting Fushimi Castle Ieyasu began to move. He sent a mobile force along the Tōkaidō to secure Kiyosu and capture Gifu. The first division he sent, included Kuroda Nagamasa, Fukushima Masanori, Hosokawa Tadaoki, Honda Tadakatsu and Ii Naomasa, at the head of 16,000 men. The second division, 18,000 strong, marched under Ikeda Terumasa, Asano Yoshinaga, and Yamanouchi Kazutoyo. On 21 September they entered Kiyosu Castle, and five days later launched themselves at Gifu. The attack nearly met with disaster before it had begun, for once again the samurai nemesis appeared. Ikeda and Fukushima quarrelled over whose army should be the first to attack. Fukushima actually challenged Ikeda to a duel, but fortunately for the Eastern cause someone suggested a compromise whereby Fukushima attacked the front gate and Ikeda attacked the back. So when Ieyasu arrived at Kiyosu on 17 October he found both armies reconciled and in possession of both castles.

The rivals were now very close. Ishida, at Ōgaki, was about sixteen miles from Gifu. Ōgaki was in an awkward position. Unlike Gifu it did not sit on the Nakasendō but some miles off it. As Ieyasu controlled both roads there was a great danger that he could detach a force to bottle up Ishida in Ōgaki while the main body of the Eastern army proceeded unmolested along the Tōkaidō and Nakasendō. The threat was so obvious that Ishida had to take steps to prevent it, and that was just what Ieyasu hoped. Ieyasu desired above all to force Ishida into fighting a pitched battle, so spies and traitors fed Ishida the false information that Ieyasu was indeed going to mask Ōgaki and continue Westward. Consequently on 20 October Ishida gave a general order to withdraw to a convenient place where the Eastern army might be stopped in its tracks. His allies had been arriving in dribs and drabs over the past few weeks. Those who had not proceeded to join him at Ōgaki had camped their armies along the Nakasendō from Lake Biwa. The last to arrive had been Kobayakawa Hideaki, who had stationed himself at what seemed to Ishida an ideal place for a stand, the little village of Sekigahara.

Sekigahara lay about twelve miles to the rear of Ōgaki, at the foot of Mount Ibuki on an important crossroads in the Nakasendō. At Sekigahara a spur from the Tōkaidō joins the Nakasendō, while another road branches off north, round Mount Ibuki, to the Hokurikudō. Early in the evening of 20 October 1600, the Western Army made ready for their twelve-mile march back to Sekigahara. The weather was foul. A fine drizzle began as they began to withdraw with Ishida at their head. Before they had gone far the rain developed into a downpour, while a gale blew up from the direction of Lake Biwa and flung the rain into the faces of the samurai. The road was narrow, and the wind was funnelled between the mountain slopes as the rainwater poured off the sides of the hills. The feet of 50,000 marching troops churned up the road into a mud-bath as they squelched along in the pitch darkness. Ishida's division reached Sekigahara at one o'clock on the morning of 21 October. The higher-ranking officers took shelter in houses along the Hokurikudō road while the other ranks were posted on the hills around. At 4 am the Satsuma contingent arrived, followed later by Konishi Yukinaga and finally Ukita Hideie, whose sodden and muddy samurai entered Sekigahara shortly before dawn. Dawn, in fact, proved as ineffectual as night, for the whole area was enveloped in a dense, damp, fog which brought the visibility down to about six feet. The weary samurai took what sleep they could and at about 7 am began wringing the water out of their clothes, while those who were not so fortunate as to possess waterproof covers for their arquebuses tried to dry out their weapons, and the commanders arranged their ranks as best they could in the impenetrable fog.

The road to the north was covered, on the left wing, by Ishida Mitsunari, who established his headquarters in a clump of trees on top of a low hill. In front of him was his chief military adviser, Shima Sakon, and Gamō Hideyuki, known as 'Bitchū', son of the late Gamō Ujisato, together with troops from the Ōsaka Castle garrison. On the right of the road were the Shimazu of Satsuma under Shimazu Yoshihiro with Shimazu Toyohisa in front. He was the son of the late gallant Iehisa, and surprisingly carried a bow, which was regarded as being very old-fashioned. The centre of the Western armies comprised the two large divisions of Konishi Yukinaga and Ukita Hideie. Towards the Nakasendō stood the samurai of the minor daimyō Kinoshita, Toda, Hiratsuka and Ōtani Yoshikatsu. Across the Nakasendō, at the

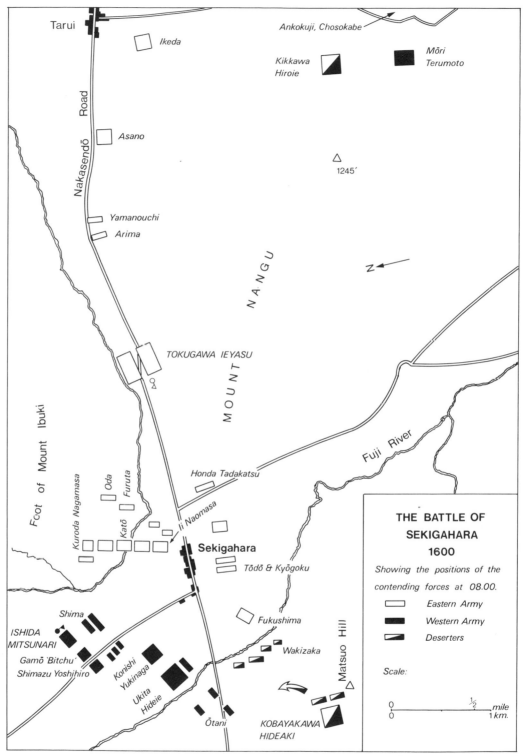

Tarui

Ankokuji, Chosokabe

Ikeda

Kikkawa
Hiroie

Mōri
Terumoto

Nakasendō Road

Asano

△
1245′

N

Yamanouchi

Arima

N A N G U

TOKUGAWA IEYASU

Foot of Mount Ibuki

M O U N T

Fuji River

Honda Tadakatsu

Oda

Furuta

Kuroda Nagamasa

Katō

Ii Naomasa

Sekigahara

Tōdō & Kyōgoku

THE BATTLE OF
SEKIGAHARA
1600

*Showing the positions of the
contending forces at 08.00.*

☐   *Eastern Army*

■   *Western Army*

◨   *Deserters*

Scale:

Shima

Fukushima

Matsuo Hill

ISHIDA
MITSUNARI

Gamō Bitchu

Wakizaka

Shimazu Yoshihiro

Konishi
Yukinaga

0   ½   mile
0   1 km.

Ukita
Hideie

△

Ōtani

KOBAYAKAWA
HIDEAKI

97 Map showing the Battle of
Sekigahara, 1600.

foot of Matsuo Hill, stood Wakizaka Yasuharu, the ex-admiral from the Korean War, and Ōtani Yoshitsugu who was a leper and had to be carried in a palanquin. On top of Matsuo Hill was Kobayakawa Hideaki, whose troops thereby formed the right wing of Ishida's army. His kinsmen, incidentally, were posted way up on the rear slopes of Mount Nangu, where they threatened the left flank of the Eastern Army. (See map, Fig. 97.)

The Western Army consisted in all of 80,000 troops. Another 13,000 had been left behind at Ōgaki, or were covering other fortresses. This compares favourably with Ieyasu's 74,000, but certain elements in the Western Army were of doubtful allegiance, particularly Kobayakawa Hideaki. Relations between him and Ishida had never been good since the appointment of Kobayakawa as commander in Korea, and now this unreliable and vituperative ally held the most commanding position in the Western dispositions! In fact Ieyasu had been reliably informed that he was willing to change sides once the battle had begun.

The Eastern Army had begun to march towards Sekigahara at 3 am. By this time the worst of the storm that had so battered the Westerners had abated, but it was still raining steadily making the Easterners as wet as their enemies. However they encountered the worst of the fog. Fukushima Masanori's vanguard actually collided with the rear ranks of Ukita Hideie's Westerners, who were only just reaching the end of their march. It is questionable which side was the most surprised, but both armies managed to part without shots being fired. At about 7 am the Easterners drew up their battle lines, encountering the same problems that had beset the Westerners. Only the rattle of armour and the shouting of commands indicated to the waiting samurai that the most celebrated battle in Japanese history was about to begin.

The foothills of Mount Ibuki extended to within a few hundred yards of the Nakasendō. The main body of the Eastern Army settled itself in this gap. Kuroda Nagamasa, his helmet ornamented with huge wooden buffalo horns, held the right wing. Hosokawa Tadaoki, wearing his helmet decorated with a rather wet and bedraggled pheasant's tail, stood next to him. Farther along were Katō Yoshiaki and Tanaka Yoshimasa, while with his left flank on the road was Ii Naomasa and the Red Devils. Across the Nakasendō, and a good way ahead, was Fukushima Masanori, who had previously met his enemy. Behind him were Kyōgoku Takatomo and Tōdō Takatora, while behind them, straddling the Southern Road, was 'old faithful' Honda Tadakatsu, now aged 52.

Thus Ieyasu planned to fight the most decisive battle of his career. His last moments before setting out were characteristically undramatic. He had a meal of boiled rice, and put on his armour. He did not put on his helmet, but just wore a hood of brown crêpe silk. A few brief words with his retainers assured them that he would scatter the Western confederates as he had formerly scattered his enemies at Nagakute. His short speech finished with a typical statement. There were but two alternatives, he said, either to come back with a bloody head in your hands, or to be brought back without your own. With this chilling remark Tokugawa Ieyasu, aged 58, rode out into the darkness.

For an hour the front lines of both armies peered into the impenetrable fog that still covered the battlefield. The only clue that either army had of the presence of its foes, who were scarcely two bow-shots away at the nearest point, was the hum of voices, the chink of horses' bits, and the occasional testing shot from an arquebus. In the all embracing grey fog, what thoughts must have been passing through their minds? For Ieyasu, his thoughts must have kept flying to one question, 'Where is Hidetada?'. His son and heir was somewhere on the Nakasendō between Edo and Sekigahara with 38,000 men. He had waited to lay siege to Ueda Castle and was now hurrying for all he was worth to join his father. It was now 8 am, and he had still not arrived.

At eight o'clock in the morning of 21 October 1600, the fog suddenly lifted, then rolled away up the bulky foothills of Mount Ibuki. For a split second the armies stood gazing at each other, their wet banners indicating their loyalties. The tension was broken by a yell from the Eastern side, as Ii Naomasa led thirty samurai forward against a band of Western skirmishers. The spear-swinging Red Devils crashed into the Western samurai and knocked them headlong, while the rest of the Ii retainers followed on towards Ukita's division. Simultaneously Fukushima launched his men across the Nakasendō on to Ukita, and the men who had been ghostly shapes at six o'clock now came to grips. Arquebuses were fired, then discarded as the samurai slithered, sword in hand, over the muddy ground. As this initial attack developed into a vast hand-to-hand combat the remainder of the Eastern front line made straight for Ishida, while the second rank moved up to attack Konishi. Shima Sakon, Ishida's adviser, received a bullet wound and retired to the rear. The Satsuma samurai had not yet moved, for Shimazu Yoshihiro did not consider the time was right, in spite of orders, demands and then pleas from Ishida. Konishi's division had practically caved in under the attack of the Easterners, but the balance was redressed a little by the Ōtani, who were well-trained shock troops, and pushed back Tōdō and Kyōgoku as they advanced.

Their success indicated to Ishida that it was time to deliver a full attack, so he signalled to Kobayakawa to descend from Matsuo Hill on to the flank of the Eastern Army. But Kobayakawa did not move. Ishida's signals became all the more frantic. Konishi and Ōtani sent messengers up the hill urging him to attack, but still not a man moved. Suspicious thoughts began to cross Ōtani's mind, for he had been half suspecting some treachery when he had seen the Eastern Army ignore Matsuo Hill in their attack. So his right wing under Yoshitsugu was turned through ninety degrees in case of an assault by Kobayakawa upon them.

The Western army were not the only ones watching Kobayakawa closely. Ieyasu sat tensely on his horse, biting his fingers. To remind

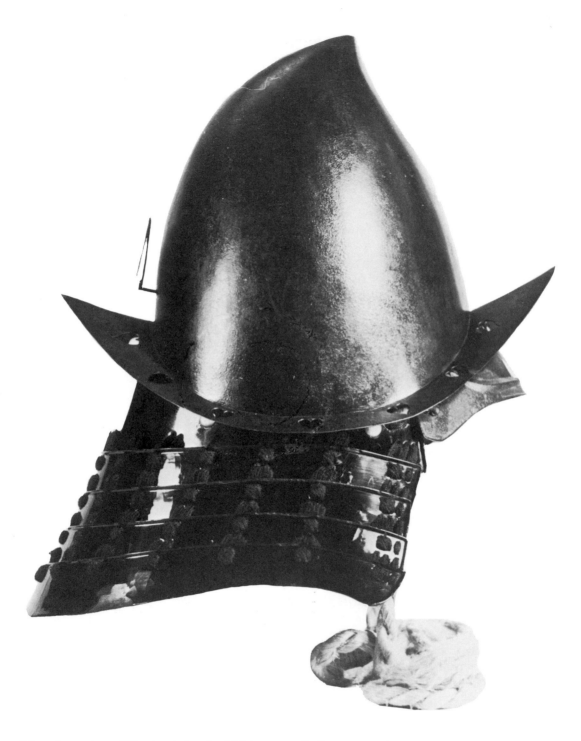

98,99 Side and rear view of 'Namban kabuto', which is a copy of a European morion by Saotome Ietada, *c.* 1600. Tokugawa Ieyasu is supposed to have worn an armour of Spanish style at Sekigahara. (L. J. Anderson collection.)

Kobayakawa of the seriousness of the situation he sent a few arquebusiers forward to fire on him and see what he would do. This seemed to wake him up, and the Kobayakawa samurai charged down the hill on to Ōtani. Ōtani's men were quite ready for the treacherous attack and blasted away at them with their firearms so that they tumbled down Matsuo in heaps. The mere proof of Kobayakawa's intentions was enough for Ieyasu, who ordered a general attack along the line.

Ōtani was still holding his own against the deserters and the new wave of Easterners when there came a totally unexpected development. 'Admiral' Wakizaka joined Kobayakawa's defection and fell on Ōtani. This was the decisive moment. The Ōtani samurai were scattered, and Yoshitsugu asked a retainer to put an end to him.

In the meantime Konishi's division had been gradually driven back. Kobayakawa's men swept through the wreck of Ōtani's troops, round the rear of Ukita, and fell on Konishi from behind. Cries of 'Treachery!' went up from all sides as the awful news spread along the ranks. Ukita's division was the next to be attacked. Ukita plunged through the mass of muddy, bloody samurai to personally decapitate the traitor Kobayakawa, and might well have done so, had not some of his brother officers seized him and forced him to join them in retreat. The Western centre was now utterly broken, and Ishida felt the full force of the Eastern Army as they attacked his hillock. Soon he too fled, leaving only the Shimazu clan. Toyohisa fell, and Shimazu Yoshihiro found himself alone at the head of about eighty samurai in the middle of a raging sea of ghastly enemies. Ii Naomasa detached himself from the rout of Ukita's division to engage Yoshihiro in personal combat, but he was a conspicuous target in his brilliant red armour surmounted by gold horns, and a Satsuma arquebusier put a bullet into his left arm. Shimazu Yoshihiro spurred his horse, and the remnants of the Shimazu charged headlong through the mob of yelling samurai and galloped away down the road to the south-west. As they rounded Mount Nangu they came in contact with scouts of the Mōri and Kikkawa contingents, who had spent the morning listening to the sounds of battle from the valley below. The Shimazu apprised them of the intelligence that the battle was indeed lost, a fact that Kikkawa had gone some way towards realizing by joining Kobayakawa's defection, and thus preventing Mōri Terumoto from causing any sort of diversion on Ieyasu's left.

By two o'clock Ieyasu knew that the day was his. He sat on his camp stool and at last put on his helmet, twisting the cords securely round his face-mask, saying, 'After a victory tighten your helmet cords,' a remark which is now a Japanese proverb. Then, baton in hand, he began the ceremony of viewing the heads. One by one his commanders came to report to him. He greeted them warmly; first, Kuroda Nagamasa, then Honda Tadakatsu and Fukushima Masanori, his own son Tadayoshi and the wounded Ii Naomasa, whose arm Ieyasu bandaged. Then all turned at the approach of Kobayakawa Hideaki, who knelt before Ieyasu without saying a word. His disloyalty had wrecked a coalition, but saved an Empire.

That afternoon a shamefaced Tokugawa Hidetada arrived, and his father tore him off a strip for missing Japan's most famous battle.

Because of its dramatic nature, and the large numbers who took part, Sekigahara's importance has tended to be overestimated. By his victory Ieyasu had destroyed an alliance of daimyō and assured the Tokugawa ascendancy, but he had not defeated the greatest opposition to his ambitions, Toyotomi Hideyori, who was still the heir of his father and still alive. Sekigahara was Ieyasu's Shizugatake, but it was not his Waterloo. Nevertheless he had triumphed over Ishida, but even if Sekigahara had been lost it is doubtful whether Ieyasu could have been stopped in his tracks. Uesugi was firmly held in check, and Hidetada was approaching with a fresh army. As it was Ishida lost, largely because of Kobayakawa's defection, but also because the Western Army was not under one supreme commander.

It is interesting to note that while the Sekigahara campaign was under way the allies of both sides were taking the field in other parts of the country. Hosokawa Yūsai, the aged parent of Tadaoki, who was with Ieyasu, was besieged by the Western faction in his castle. So respected was the old man, who was a noted poet and scholar, that the besieging army had bombarded his castle with cannon into which they had deliberately omitted to put any projectiles. Yet another senior samurai was playing his part in Kyushū. Kuroda Yoshitaka, whose son Nagamasa was at Sekigahara, conducted a vigorous recruiting campaign. As all the able-bodied samurai were with Nagamasa he assembled an odd collection of old men, youths, rōnin, farmers and tradespeople, armed with rusty weapons and armour whose plates hung by a thread. His open-handed way of rewarding his recruits has already been referred to in Chapter Nine. The most active of the Easterners in Kyūshū was Katō Kiyomasa, whom Ieyasu had requested to stay in the island. For the veteran warrior it was a golden opportunity to pay off some old scores. Konishi Yukinaga, who owned Southern Higo, was of course at Sekigahara, so Katō took advantage of his rival's absence to ravage his domains. Katō's troops surrounded Konishi's castle, which surrendered unconditionally on hearing the result of Sekigahara.

As for Konishi Yukinaga himself, his end was noble and as tragic as any samurai's could be. He had fled to the hills after the battle, but was soon captured and ordered to commit suicide. He refused, saying that God had given him his life, and that it was not up to him to dispose of it. He therefore resolved to die like the true Christian knight that he was. He requested to be allowed to see a priest, but his captor would not permit it. It is strange to relate that he was in fact held by Kuroda Nagamasa, who must have completely abandoned his faith since the Korean War.

Two other captives accompanied Konishi to the execution ground. One was Ankokuji Ekei, and the other was Ishida Mitsunari, who had managed to elude the Eastern search parties for three days. Determined as ever, he had attempted to escape to the sea, but he contracted dysentery and was soon handed over in a very sorry state. The three were put on donkeys and paraded blindfold through the streets of Ōsaka, then taken through Kyōto in a cart. When they reached the Rokujō execution ground, where Minamoto Tameyoshi had knelt four-and-a-half centuries before, Konishi called on Christ to receive him, and held a picture of the Saviour heavenward as the sword fell. With Konishi out of the way, Katō Kiyomasa was able to show his true colours and began

100 Iron cannon in the shape of a dragon, owned by Tokugawa Ieyasu. The Japanese never really developed cannon, preferring to use those of European manufacture. (Tokugawa Art Museum, Nagoya.)

a savage persecution of the Christians in Higo. One day he boasted of his success to Hosokawa Tadaoki, who retorted, 'I do not know if there is anyone among my retainers who is a Christian. But I do know this much, my retainers are all honest and loyal subjects.'

After Sekigahara Ieyasu began to concentrate upon building up a stable central government for Japan. This is dealt with in more detail in the following chapter. The continued existence of Hideyori was

awkward, but not embarrassing. He would be dealt with in time, and time, between the years 1600 and 1614, wrought many changes, not the least being the deaths of many who had inscribed for themselves a name across the pages of samurai history. Within those fourteen years the White Jade Pavilion received as guests Kuroda Yoshitaka, Katō Kiyomasa, Asano Nagamasa, Asano Yukinaga, Ikeda Terumasa, Maeda Toshinaga (his father Toshiie had died in 1599), Ii Naomasa and Honda Tadakatsu. In 1603 Tokugawa Ieyasu was proclaimed Shōgun, the office that had been held in abeyance since Nobunaga deposed Ashikaga Yoshiaki thirty years before. Whereas Nobunaga and Hideyoshi were not of Minamoto descent, Ieyasu could point to a pedigree stretching back to Minamoto 'Hachiman-taro' Yoshiie. With the appointment of the first Tokugawa Shōgun the military government founded by Yoritomo became military once again. Ieyasu ruled from Edo, not Kyōto, so it is as the Edo Period that the time of Tokugawa rule is known. It was a triumph for Ieyasu's work, and for the foundations laid by Nobunaga and Hideyoshi, that the government of the samurai, by the samurai and for the samurai did not pass from the Earth, but existed under Tokugawa Shōguns from 1603 until 1868.

For the daimyō who did not die the years between 1600 and 1614 were times of great upheaval. First, their lands were either reduced or increased according to the side they had been on at Sekigahara. Second, they commenced the construction of a number of large castles, many of which still stand today. Himeji dates from this period, as does Hikone (Plate XXIV) and Katō Kiyomasa's Kumamoto (Plate XVIII). Edo Castle, which is now the Imperial Palace in Tōkyō, was of course the most splendid of all. One result of all this architectural endeavour was the near bankruptcy of several minor daimyō. Unfortunately for Ieyasu the same trick did not quite work on Hideyori.

It will be recalled that the swords confiscated during the 'Sword Hunt' of 1588 were melted down and converted into nails and bolts for the construction of a great image of Buddha, 'for the good of the nation'. The Great Buddha had been completely destroyed by the earthquake of 1596, during Hideyoshi's lifetime, and the rebuilding of the idol had been one of his great ambitions. Ieyasu therefore suggested that Hideyori and his mother should take the work in hand for the repose of Hideyoshi's spirit. By 1602 the rebuilding had proceeded as far as the idol's neck, at which point the scaffolding somehow caught fire, and all their work was brought to nothing. In 1608 the reconstruction began again, involving 100,000 men in its execution, and much gold from the store room in Ōsaka Castle. However, Hideyori's finances appeared bottomless, but the Great Buddha was capable of embarrassing Hideyori in another way.

The precedent for a split with Hideyori came not from the idol itself, but from the great bell that was cast to accompany it. When finished in 1614 this bronze giant was fourteen feet high and weighed 72 tons. It was the inscription on its side that caused the downfall of the Toyotomi family. It began, 'May the State be peaceful and pros-

101 Portrait of Honda Tadakatsu (1548–1610), the companion of Ieyasu in all his campaigns.

248

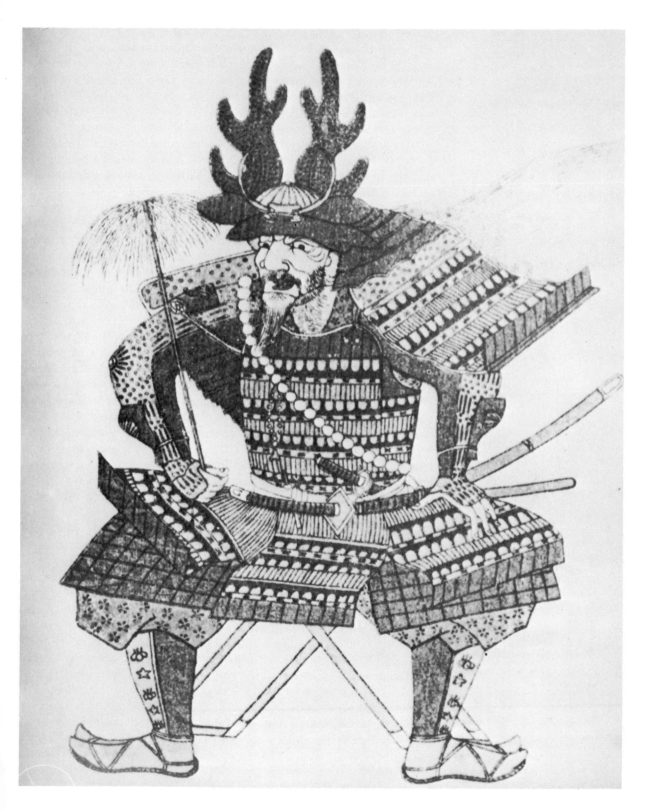

perous', or, in Chinese 'Kokka ankō'. Now the characters with which this sentence was written contained the ideographs 'Ie' and 'yasu' (ka and kō in Chinese). As his name had been split in two on the bell Ieyasu affected to be much offended by it. Also the sentence, 'In the East it greets the pale moon, and in the West bids farewell to the setting sun', was taken as alluding to the Lord of the East, i.e. Ieyasu at Edo, being inferior to Hideyori in the West.

It was a weak complaint, but a strong enough pretext for Ieyasu. Rumours began circulating that Hideyori was recruiting rōnin for the defence of Ōsaka. Maeda Toshitsune allegedly received a letter from Hideyori telling of the large stocks of rice now held in the castle, and asking him to come to Ōsaka. Toshitsune forwarded the letter to Ieyasu. In the midst of all the rumours was the pathetic figure of Hideyori, who had so little thought of war that in June 1614 he had actually sent back a large quantity of gunpowder to the English factory at Hirado because he was unable to sell it! However, Ieyasu was so determined that by October Hideyori was forced to convert rumour into reality, and took steps to arm himself against the gathering storm.

The powder which Hideyori had sent back to Hirado had been bought with alacrity by Ieyasu, who at the same time purchased five cannons. Four were of the 'culverin' type, firing a shot of 18 pounds. The other was a 'saker', which fired a shot of 5 pounds. The English guns were greatly preferred to any of Japanese manufacture. It was noted that Ieyasu had obtained some Dutch guns before Sekigahara, but it is unlikely that they were used in the battle, as the weather and land conditions were entirely inappropriate. Once preparations for war got under way the English 'arms dealers' did good trade with Hideyori as well. Between June and October there was a sixty per cent price rise for English gunpowder, and by December the price of the inferior Japanese gunpowder was nearly four times what the better English product had been in March.

Hideyori issued an appeal for help to all the great daimyō, but so effective had been Ieyasu's fourteen years of power that not one responded. In contrast, those to whom the victory of Sekigahara had meant the confiscation of property and the virtual extinction of their family's name responded with a will. Consequently we find few familiar names among the list of defenders of Ōsaka Castle. Those already with Hideyori included Ōno Harunaga and his brother Harufusa; Kimura Shigenari, who is believed to have been a Christian; and Oda Yuraku, brother of Oda Nobunaga, once again the family supplying a strange link with the past. Among those who came to join them was Chōsokabe Morishige, who had fought at Sekigahara and surrendered to Kuroda Nagamasa, and Gotō Mototsugu, another Christian whose family had supported Hideyoshi when he invaded Kyūshū. Finally we may note Sanada Yukimura. Sanada, together with his father Masayuki, had been responsible for holding up Hidetada and his 38,000 troops at their castle of Ueda on the eve of Sekigahara. He was a master of siegecraft, and a useful addition to Hideyori's forces.

The rest of the 90,000 samurai who packed Ōsaka Castle were rōnin, samurai whose masters had been dispossessed or executed. To defend Ōsaka was an opening for revenge as well as employment. They had nothing to lose by defeat, and everything to gain by victory. Among the rōnin there were not a few Christians, and a certain Jesuit called Father Girao recorded that:

'. . . there were so many crosses, Jesu's and Sant'Iago's on their flags, tents and other martial insignia which the Japanese use in their encampments, that this must needs have made Ieyasu sick to his stomach.'

As for the besiegers, they included the scions of some very noble houses, as well as many familiar faces. Date Masamune, the 'One-eyed dragon' was there, so was Uesugi Kagekatsu, his submission to Ieyasu complete. Among the sons of famous samurai we may note Asano Nagaakira, son of Nagamasa; Honda Tadamasa and Tadatomo, sons of Tadakatsu; Ii Naotaka, who now led the Red Devils; Maeda Toshitsune, son of Toshiie; Wakizaka Yasumoto, son of Yasuharu; and Shimazu Iehisa, son of Yoshihiro and named after his gallant uncle. A number of the sons of Ieyasu took part. Their father was now seventy-three years old, 'the terrible old man' to his enemies, and still as cunning as ever.

The defences of Ōsaka Castle are illustrated in the map of Fig. 102. The castle, built on the site of Ishiyama Hongan-ji, which had held out for so long against Nobunaga, was unquestionably the strongest fortress in the whole of Japan. The topography of Ōsaka, which has changed considerably since 1614, was exploited to the full. At that time the sea was several miles nearer to the castle than it is now, and formed its western moat. To the north flowed the Temma, Yodo and Yamato rivers, which divided the flat rice-fields into a bewildering array of muddy islands. The castle itself was built with two moats surrounded by massive walls 120 feet high. These walls still exist (Fig. 103), but the keep contained within them is a rebuilding dating from the Second World War. In 1614 the keep was a purely military building, with the castle living-quarters situated within the inner bailey. In preparation for the siege Hideyori greatly increased the castle defences. To the west of the castle was a canal, and on the east a stream, so his rōnin set to work and joined them by digging a moat 240 feet wide and 36 feet deep, which filled with water to a depth of between 12 and 24 feet. Inside this new moat a 10-foot-high stone wall was built. When the work was finished a tour of inspection of the outer defences of Ōsaka Castle would have entailed a walk of nearly nine miles. Sanada Yukimura increased it still further by building a barbican called the Sanada barbican, in front of the Hachome gate, with a wall and an empty moat, and palisades on either side of the moat and inside it. Besides this the defenders manned a number of outposts on the outskirts of Ōsaka,

251

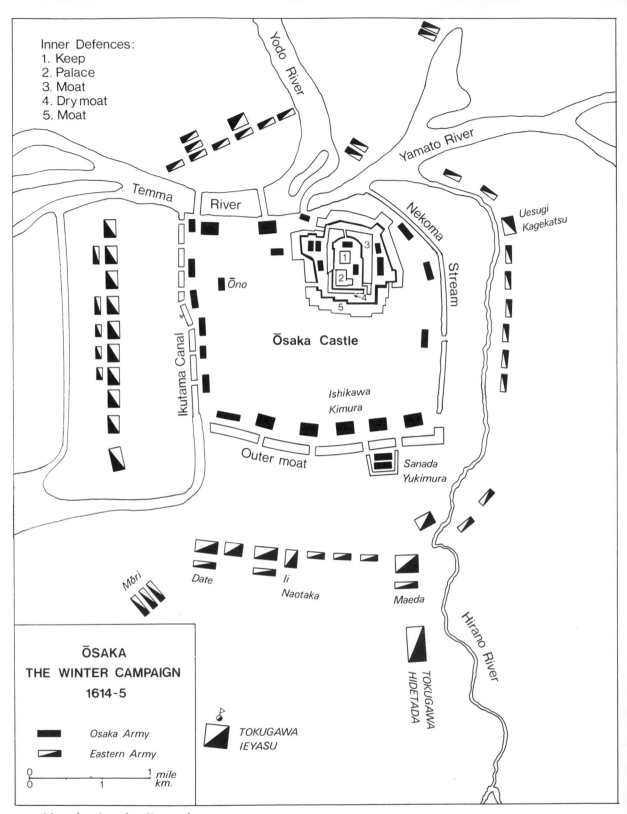

Inner Defences:
1. Keep
2. Palace
3. Moat
4. Dry moat
5. Moat

Yodo River

Yamato River

Temma

River

Nekoma Stream

Uesugi
Kagekatsu

Ōno

Ōsaka Castle

Ikutama Canal

Ishikawa

Kimura

Outer moat

Sanada
Yukimura

Mōri

Date

Ii
Naotaka

Maeda

Hirano River

TOKUGAWA
HIDETADA

ŌSAKA
THE WINTER CAMPAIGN
1614-5

Osaka Army

Eastern Army

TOKUGAWA
IEYASU

0   1 mile
0   1   km.

102 Map showing the Siege of
Ōsaka Castle during the winter of
1614–15, known as the 'Winter
Campaign'.

103 The inner moat and walls of Ōsaka Castle. (Kyodo News Service.)

and were well supplied with artillery, including large wall guns up to nine feet long, and cannon. Two cannon in particular were placed on either side of the main gate. Everywhere the walls bristled with guns, and every few hundred yards was placed a fire-projecting mangonel. From within these walls Hideyori's 90,000 outcasts prepared to face the 'terrible old man'.

On 2 November 1614, Ieyasu gave orders to Hidetada to mobilize all available forces in Edo. On 5 November the daimyō in residence departed for their territories to collect troops, while Ieyasu set off for Ōsaka, arriving in Kyōto on the 24th, where his fifth son Yoshinao was waiting for him with 15,000 troops from his new castle of Nagoya. That same day the main body began to leave Edo, Tokugawa Hidetada leading 50,000, Date Masamune 10,000, Uesugi 5,000 and Satake 1,500. By 10 December the whole Eastern Army, 180,000 in all, exactly twice the Ōsaka garrison, had come down 'like a wolf on the fold'.

Ieyasu's characteristic self-confidence had not deserted him over the years. His troops could be counted on for loyalty, if only because their families were virtual hostages in Edo. There was certainly no danger of a rear attack, but his opponents were an unknown quantity. For the vast majority of Hideyori's rōnin the prospect of Ieyasu's head impaled on the castle gate was something to fire the very blood of fanaticism. The one weak link in the Ōsaka defence, and one that Ieyasu hoped to manipulate, was the presence within the fortress of Yodo-gimi, Hideyori's mother and therefore the widow of the great Hideyoshi. But psychological warfare would not be needed if military strength prevailed, so the full force of the Tokugawa military machine advanced on the castle walls.

The first fighting involved the capture of the outposts, which was accomplished by the end of 1614, though not without heavy losses to the Easterners. On 3 January 1615, Ieyasu ordered an attack upon the castle's southern defences. Maeda Toshitsune's troops advanced before dawn towards Sanada's barbican. Sanada sent some samurai up on to the wall to taunt their enemies. A few insults soon had the calculated result, and the Maeda samurai tried to scale the wall, whereupon Sanada's men laid them low with heavy and accurate arquebus and musket fire. A further contingent came up, and they too were assailed by a barrage of Nagashino proportions. Further along the wall the Ii Red Devils managed to scale the ramparts, but on descending into the outer bailey they were confronted with Kimura Shigenari and 8,000 samurai, most of whom were armed with some form of firearm. So another division was cut to pieces. An attack the next day was beaten off by Chōsokabe.

The mettle of the defenders having been tested Ieyasu ordered the erection of a stockade and rampart around the outer walls. Hidetada was in favour of a full-scale assault, and could not understand his father's hesitation. Ieyasu, however, had realized that the castle was too strong to be taken by direct assault, so he ordered a bombardment, which was to continue for three consecutive days at dawn and at ten o'clock at night, while miners endeavoured to dig under the outer towers. Ieyasu kept up a personal reconnaissance, exposing himself to considerable danger in so doing. One day the defenders noticed the Tokugawa banner flying from one of the siege-towers and opened up on it with cannon and musket, but Ieyasu was unharmed.

Ōsaka was no picnic campaign like Odawara. The gentlemanly defeat of the Hōjō had been accomplished during the height of summer, and it was now the depths of winter. In spite of the intense cold, more worrying to besiegers than besieged, the samurai contrived to stay cheerful. Furuta Shigenari, a noted tea master as well as samurai, was one day patrolling the palisades erected by Satake's troops to the east of the defences. As he walked along he noticed an aesthetically pleasing piece of bamboo in the palisade, so he reached over and cut it for a tea spoon. As he did so a vigilant sharpshooter behind the castle wall aimed at his head and put a bullet into the bowl of his helmet. Furuta was unperturbed, and to the astonishment of his retainers drew a purple napkin out of his armour and carefully wiped the blood off his cheek.

So the siege went on. There was a little skirmishing, particularly on the northern side, where the defenders had actually reinforced their defences by using sandbags, but little advantage was gained either way. The truth was that as long as the garrison stood united the castle was impregnable. A guard ship floated in the Yodo River, but a blockade was an irrelevance, for 200,000 *koku* of rice had been unloaded into the castle granaries shortly before the siege began, and this was but a fraction of the total amount. The castle had its own well, was amply stocked with powder and ball, and could theoretically hold out on full rations for several years. Also, according to some authorities, 35,000 out of Ieyasu's 180,000 men had been put *hors de combat* before the end of 1614. It was Ieyasu's turn to worry, for time was on the side of Hideyori. For six weeks he had made fools of the mightiest powers in the land, and cracks were beginning to appear in the façade of Tokugawa invincibility. If Hideyori could hold out it would soon be apparent which of the Tokugawa allies were there merely by coercion, making a mass desertion by certain troops a possibility. In short, the fortunes of the house of Tokugawa stood in greater peril than they had done on the eve of Sekigahara.

It was fortunate for the 'terrible old man' that he was fully conversant with the situation. In fact, the failure of his earlier attacks had made him completely rule out a military solution. Bribery was so common in siege-work as to be almost respectable. A willing traitor was found, but the unfortunate man was shortened by the length of his head before he could get anywhere near to opening the gates. Ieyasu then tried to bribe the brave Sanada, of all people, by offering him the whole of Shinano province, but Sanada was not to be bought, and proudly broadcast the offer in the castle as an example of the desperation of the Tokugawa.

Bribery having failed, Ieyasu turned the full force of his guile on to the weak link previously alluded to – Hideyori's mother. A lady called Acha Tsubone was sent by Ieyasu to negotiate a set of entirely spurious peace terms. To get Yodo-gimi in the right frame of mind for peace negotiations the besieging army opened up a furious bombardment from a hundred large calibre guns, which prevented the ladies from enjoying any sleep. The best gunners in the Tokugawa artillery trained a few pieces of cannon on to the ladies' quarters, and succeeded in dropping a thirteen-pound shot through the wall, which hit Yodo-gimi's tea cabinet and killed two servants. A few days later the same gunners landed a cannon ball in the shrine built to the memory of Hideyoshi, narrowly missing Hideyori's head.

While the pressure continued Acha Tsubone conducted negotiations. Ieyasu seems to have understood Yodo-gimi's mood perfectly, for she began to plead with her son for a settlement. Such a pacifistic attitude was scorned by the garrison commanders. Gotō emphasized the need for unity at all costs, and Hideyori stated that he was prepared to make

255

the castle his tomb if need be. Both were adamant about one thing, that Ieyasu could not be trusted. He had in fact been guilty of similar sharp practice many years before, when campaigning against the Ikkō monks. Peace negotiations had begun, and one of the terms successfully concluded was that the monks' temples should be restored to their original state. Immediately after the conclusion Ieyasu's men set fire to the temples and burned them to the ground. When the monks protested at this breach of faith Ieyasu pointed out that the 'original state' had been green fields with no temples thereon!

Meanwhile the bombardment continued, and the Eastern Army added to the discomfort of those within by adopting the tactics of Joshua before Jericho and raising a periodic shout in front of the ramparts. The walls did not come tumbling down, but 100,000 or so samurai yelling in unison added considerably to Yodo-gimi's fears.

Incredibly, it may seem, Hideyori was swayed, with the help of Ōno and Oda, who saw in a Tokugawa victory the means of regaining what they had lost. The peace terms were drafted, agreed and sealed in grand style with the blood from the tip of Ieyasu's finger. It was the most treacherous and fraudulent document in the history of the samurai. Peace was the last thing that Ieyasu wanted. His sole aim in producing the terms was to weaken the castle in readiness for a further siege. The terms were quite simple, a free pardon for all the rōnin, complete freedom of choice for Hideyori as to where to live, in return for a solemn undertaking not to raise a rebellion against Ieyasu. What was important was what the document did not say. During the protracted negotiations Ieyasu had casually mentioned to the mediator from the Ōsaka side that as the war was now ending the outer moat of the castle ought to be filled in. This extra condition was mentioned by Ieyasu and his representatives on at least three separate occasions, yet the levelling of the moat was never properly discussed or demanded, nor included in the final terms.

On 22 January 1615, the day after the terms had been sealed, Ieyasu made a great show about disbanding his army. All that it amounted to was Shimazu marching off to the nearest harbour. On the same day practically the entire Tokugawa force began to fill in the outer moat. The demolition contract was entrusted to the supervision of the Honda clan, who spurred on the samurai to such strenuous exertions that within a week the outer wall of the defences had been transferred whole-sale into the outer moat, which now no longer existed. Naturally enough the Ōsaka commanders protested, and their protests became all the more frantic when the Honda 'navvies' turned their attentions to the second moat. Honda apologized, and explained that his officers must have misunderstood his orders. In the presence of the Ōsaka representative he personally ordered the filling-in to stop. As soon as the representative left, the work continued with renewed vigour. Yodo-gimi then complained, and went to Kyōto to protest to the senior Honda, Masanobu. He assured her that he would certainly see to it that no more destruction was done. Unfortunately, he explained, he was suffering from a bad cold, but would communicate with his nephew when he was feeling better.

True to his word Honda Masanobu went to Ōsaka, where he reprimanded Masazumi for his 'foolishness', but, as he added to Yodogimi, to dig up the second moat would take ten times the labour that had been so erroneously expended in filling it. Surely, now that peace had been established, there was really no need to have a moat at all!

Within twenty-six days of the start, the second moat had been completely levelled, and the defences of Ōsaka had been cut down to one moat and wall. It is small wonder that to the Japanese the 'Winter Campaign of Ōsaka' has become a by-word for the folly of pacifism.

Three months later Ieyasu attacked Ōsaka Castle once again. In the 'Summer Campaign', as it is called, he was determined to crush Ōsaka 'finally, drastically, effectively'. All he required was an excuse for so doing, and reports that Hideyori was feverishly re-excavating the second moat was all the pretext necessary to accuse him of breaking the agreement. A few rumours spread judiciously round Kyōto that the rōnin of Ōsaka were back, and were planning to pillage the capital, were sufficient to make Ieyasu appear almost a saviour.

Hideyori had in fact succeeded in digging out large areas of the second moat, and had erected palisades around it by the time the Summer Campaign began. He had also succeeded in attracting to his standard, or rather his late father's 'golden gourd' standard which put heart into all who saw it, many more rōnin than before. The total number of troops mustered by Hideyori was about 120,000 – 60,000 more than in the Winter Campaign, again including a large Christian contingent. Six great banners bore the Cross as their device, and several foreign priests were inside the fortress. It is not known for certain how big was the Tokugawa force, but it may have been a quarter of a million.

It was the Ōsaka troops who first took the offensive. On 28 May Ōno Harufusa led 2,000 troops into Yamato province, burning as they went, and reaching as far as Nara. On 30 May he set off again for the South, to block the advance of Asano's contingent, and burned the town of Sakai. A new spirit had animated the Ōsaka garrison. They had been humiliated during the Winter Campaign, but they had not been defeated. If they could smash the various divisions of the Tokugawa army before they reached Ōsaka then a second siege of their treacherously weakened castle might not take place. They very nearly succeeded. On 1 June an army set off to block the passes leading from Nara. Unfortunately the main body got lost in a fog, leaving 2,400 under Gotō Mototsugu, whose small force was soon overwhelmed by sheer weight of numbers. Meanwhile Chōsokabe and Kimura had attempted to hold Tōdō and Ii, but they too were driven back, and the garrison withdrew into what was left of Ōsaka Castle.

At a council of war held on 2 June 1615, it was resolved to meet the Tokugawa force in battle on the open ground to the south of the

257

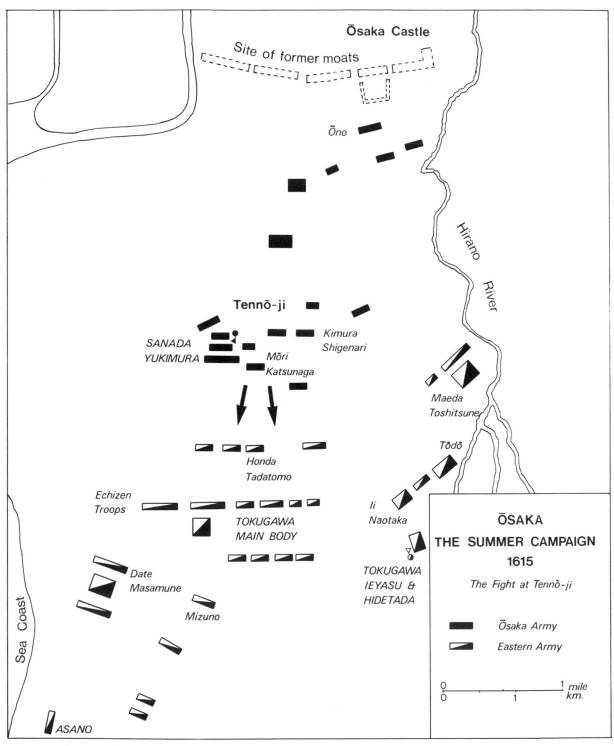

Ōsaka Castle

Site of former moats

Ōno

Hirano River

Tennō-ji

SANADA YUKIMURA

Kimura Shigenari

Mōri Katsunaga

Maeda Toshitsune

Tōdō

Honda Tadatomo

Echizen Troops

TOKUGAWA MAIN BODY

Ii Naotaka

Date Masamune

Mizuno

TOKUGAWA IEYASU & HIDETADA

Sea Coast

ASANO

ŌSAKA
THE SUMMER CAMPAIGN
1615

The Fight at Tennō-ji

▰ *Ōsaka Army*

◪ *Eastern Army*

0   1 mile
0   1   km.

104 Map showing the 'Summer Campaign' of Ōsaka, 1615.

former outer moat. This battle, the Battle of Tennō-ji, was destined to be what Sekigahara is always supposed to be, the last samurai battle in Japanese history. Apart from minor revolts and skirmishes, 3 June 1615 witnessed what the world would never see again, a clash between two huge armies of Japanese samurai.

The plan was as follows: Sanada, Ōno and their fellow commanders would launch a holding attack against the Tokugawa front, while Akashi Morishige made a wide sweep round to assault the Tokugawa rear. When Akashi attacked, the garrison were to sally out with Hideyori at their head, bearing aloft the golden gourd standard of Hideyoshi. It was a plan so grand that it deserved to succeed.

At noon on the fateful day the opposing forces occupied the positions shown in Fig. 104. The Tokugawa troops stretched from the Hirano River to the sea. On the right was Maeda Toshitsune, with Tōdō on his left, then Ii Naotaka and the Red Devils. Naotaka wore a suit of armour similar to that worn by his father at Sekigahara. It weighed 120 pounds, and Ieyasu had blamed the weight of Naomasa's armour for the wound he had received at Sekigahara. The Tokugawa main body had as vanguard the younger Honda son, Tadatomo. On the left, and slightly to the rear, was Date Masamune, while well at the rear, his forces reaching to the sea-shore, was Asano Nagaakira. According to their father, the battle was to be 'useful practical experience' for Ieyasu's young sons Yorinobu and Yoshinao. Ieyasu had placed Hidetada in overall command.

The Ōsaka forward troops, numbering some 54,000, drew up their main body beyond Tennō-ji opposite the Tokugawa centre, under Sanada Yukimura and Mōri Katsunaga, who was no relation to the other Mōri. Behind them divisions of reserves reached back as far as the castle, where Ōno Harunaga took up a position in front of the former Sanada barbican.

It was a clear summer's day. With no fog to mask their movements there was no confusion, merely the meticulous marshalling of troops, the lighting of matches and the swaying of the tall banners in the gentle breeze. Ieyasu had recommended his samurai to leave their horses a furlong behind, and go in on foot with their long spears. For a while both armies stared at each other, perhaps conscious of the finality of the bloody work in which they would shortly be engaged. Win or lose, it would be the last battle in which any would take part. Four centuries previously there would have been a duel of arrows at this stage, and challenges to individual combat. Instead the impetuous rōnin under Mōri Katsunaga opened up on the Tokugawa troops opposite with their arquebuses. Sanada, anxious to avoid a precipitate engagement lest Akashi should be delayed in his encircling movement, ordered them to cease fire, but they only doubled their efforts and brought down a number of the enemy. After a hurried consultation with Sanada, Mōri decided to take advantage of his men's adrenalin and led them forward in a charge, which crashed clean through the Tokugawa front ranks and carried them to the main body behind.

105 Suit of armour worn by Ii Naotaka (1590–1659), who led the Ii samurai during the 'Summer Campaign' of Ōsaka, 1615. The armour is lacquered red. (Ii Art Museum, Hikone Castle.)

Sanada now realized that as the battle had begun, so must it continue, and he despatched his son at full gallop towards the castle to tell Hideyori to charge out immediately, while he led his troops against the Echizen levies on the Tokugawa left wing. They fell upon the 15,000, and were helped in their shock attack by a most unexpected manoeuvre, for approaching along the sea coast, and heading towards the Tokugawa left wing, were the samurai of Asano Nagaakira. This surprise movement was too reminiscent of Sekigahara to be ignored, and again cries of 'Treachery!' went up from all sides. The Echizen rear rank ran pell-mell back into the Tokugawa main body, who were fully stretched holding off Mōri's rōnin, who fought like wildcats. The hand-to-hand fight swayed this way and that, and Ieyasu was so alarmed that he rode up into the fray to steady his troops. There is a persistent tradition which says that Ieyasu was wounded during the rally by a spear that cut him near the kidneys. It is certain however, that the apparent treason by Asano caused so much panic among the men that Ieyasu was fully prepared to commit hara-kiri.

106 Honda Tadatomo (1582–1615) leads an attack against the samurai of Sanada Yukimura (1570–1615) during the 'Summer Campaign' of Ōsaka, 1615. Sanada is on the left. From a painted screen. (Ōsaka Castle Museum.)

It was the younger Honda who saved the day. He led his troops against Sanada, and together with the rallied Echizen men managed to push him back towards Tennō-ji (Fig. 106). Sanada was exhausted, and sat down on a camp stool to recover his wits. A samurai called Nishio Nizaemon spotted him, but Sanada was too tired to accept a challenge. He merely introduced himself and took off his helmet. Soon the samurai was riding off with the head of the bravest man in the field.

107 Portrait scroll of Date Masa-mune (1566–1636). His sashimono bears a red sun's disc on white. (Sendai Municipal Museum.)

The quickly proclaimed news of the death of Sanada put new heart into the Eastern Army, who had now realized that Asano's suspicious move was a rather thoughtless attempt at reinforcement. Hidetada detached Ii and Tōdō from the right wing and sent them across to support the main body, who were now beginning to push the Ōsaka troops back towards the castle. A fine painted screen in Hikone Castle illustrates what happened next. The Red Devils charged across into the left flank of the Ōsaka troops under Kimura Shigenari (Plate XXII). Kimura was seized by a group of Ii retainers and done to death. The anonymity of war was felt also by the Tōdō troops when a landmine exploded under them.

As soon as Hidetada had released the Ii and Tōdō troops he began frantically signalling for them to return, for Ōno had taken advantage of the fighting in the centre to launch his samurai against Hidetada. Maeda, on the right, was also summoned to help but did not move. Again treachery was suspected, but the Maeda inaction turned out to

108 The explosion of a land mine. Print by Utagawa Kuniyoshi (1798–1861). (Victoria and Albert Museum.)

262

be due solely to the fact that they had not yet finished eating lunch. Seeing the Ōsaka troops making headway against the 'household' troops, Ii Naotaka wheeled round and hurried back in support. The Ōsaka troops were well supplied with arquebuses, and shot the two Ii standard bearers carrying their red banner and the 'fly-trap' device seen in Plates XIX–XX. Ii's men were driven back on to Hidetada's division, where all was confusion. Hidetada himself plunged into the fight, but two officers grabbed hold of his bridle and pulled him back while Katō Yoshiaki and Honda Masanobu managed to get some order into the ranks. The Maeda troops, suitably refreshed after their meal, were now engaging Ōno, who had pressed his attack rather far from the castle walls. Date Masamune, meanwhile, had dealt with fresh suspicions of treachery on his flank by shooting samurai who, it turned out, were too exhausted to move. Had the Ōsaka surprise attack materialized then it may well have succeeded, but Akashi had been intercepted in his progress, and Hideyori had not yet appeared. By the time he emerged from the gate it was too late. The sheer mass of Eastern troops had pushed the Ōsaka garrison right back under their walls.

The next moves in the drama are confused. The Eastern Army penetrated the wall, and began fierce hand-to-hand fighting with the inner garrison. Mizuno Katsushige, of the Eastern force, managed to plant his standard in front of the Sakura gate, the southern gate of the innermost citadel. Soon this too fell, and the Eastern Army swarmed inside, while civilians and servants fled in terror. Hideyori retired to the keep, where Ieyasu asked Ii Naotaka to keep guard. Ii interpreted the order as an excuse to blast away at the keep with cannon. By now flames were rising from various parts of the castle, the first fire allegedly having been started by Hideyori's cook. By 5 pm the whole of the castle was in Ieyasu's hands, with Hideyori a prisoner in the keep. Ii Naotaka continued to fire on it during the night, and by next morning Hideyori concluded that he could receive no quarter, and soon flames were to be seen rising from the keep itself. In the midst of the conflagration Hideyori and Yodo-gimi committed suicide, and the keep of Hideyoshi's great fortress became the funeral pyre of the Toyotomi family.

As the ashes cooled the retribution began. No rebellion must in future be allowed to disturb the reign of Tokugawa Ieyasu. Accordingly the eight-year-old son of Hideyori was decapitated. He was the last of the Toyotomi. Chōsokabe was also beheaded, along with such a large number of rōnin that their displayed heads stretched from Kyōto to Fushimi.

The reader cannot help but notice the decline in the fighting quality of the Tokugawa samurai. It was forty years since Mikata-ga-hara, and the samurai at Ōsaka were a different generation from those who had fought against Shingen. No longer were they a brave little clan fighting for survival. They were now the army of the Tokugawa Shōgunate, the establishment. In contrast the rōnin within Ōsaka fought with the desperation of survival, and most of the heroics appear to be on their side. Sanada Yukimura is fit to rank with the noblest of samurai.

One alone on the Tokugawa side remained unchanged. Tokugawa Ieyasu had fought his first battle at the age of seventeen, and had covered Nobunaga's retreat from Echizen at the age of twenty-seven. He was now seventy-four, and still the consistent yet sinister hero. The fall of Ōsaka completed the military side of the Tokugawa grand design, but Ieyasu was not to enjoy his triumph for long. The following spring he was taken ill from what is believed to have been cancer of the stomach. His active life had kept him remarkably healthy for his age. He brandished a sword on his deathbed, and departed for the White Jade Pavilion a few days later. There was no rebellion, no upheaval. The package of government was safely transferred to Hidetada's broad shoulders, and Ieyasu was buried in the most magnificent tomb in the world, the temple of Nikkō, one of the wonders of Japan. Here he was deified, and worshipped as Tō-shō-gū, the Sun God of the East. He could have asked for nothing more.

12. Decline and triumph

Having mastered the arts of war the Tokugawa Shōgunate could turn to the problems of peace. Chief among its problems was the maintenance of what was clearly, after Ōsaka, a peacetime army. The army of the Tokugawa daimyate was now the army of the Japanese state. It had grown considerably since the young Ieyasu had led his samurai into battle, and had undergone at least one major change in organization. We have seen how, after the defeat of the Takeda, Ieyasu absorbed into his ranks the former retainers of the great Takeda Shingen. It is not generally known that Ieyasu owed Shingen more than merely a supply of some of the best samurai in Japan. In fact he was forced to completely reorganize his army sometime around 1584, when one of his 'Shi-tennō', Ishikawa Kazumasa, defected to Hideyoshi (this was the time of the Komaki campaign) and informed him of the layout, organization, supply and dispositions of Ieyasu's army. The model Ieyasu chose on which to base his re-formed army was that of Takeda Shingen. So successful did it prove that the overall scheme was retained throughout the entire life of the Tokugawa Shōgunate.

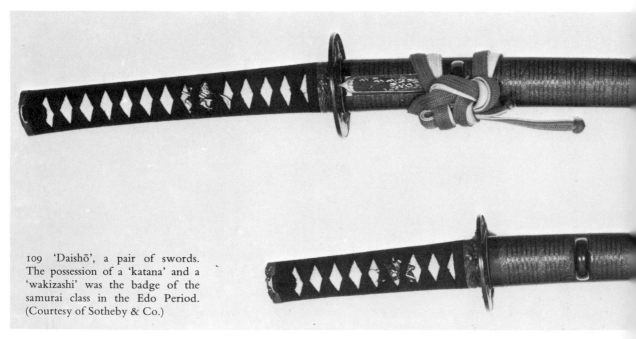

109 'Daishō', a pair of swords. The possession of a 'katana' and a 'wakizashi' was the badge of the samurai class in the Edo Period. (Courtesy of Sotheby & Co.)

Apart from the Tokugawa, who owned 20 per cent of the land, were a number of other names, some former allies, others former enemies, who ruled their domains in a similar way to their lords at Edo, but on a much smaller scale. Largest of these 'daimyō' was Maeda of Kaga, whose income was about a quarter of that of the Tokugawa. Once the Tokugawa Shōgunate became established the title 'daimyō', hitherto a loose title for a large landholder, became formally defined as a landowner who received an annual income of 10,000 *koku* or over. The daimyō, therefore, were the highest division of the samurai class under the Shōgun. The rapid growth of castle towns, and the settlement of daimyō into provinces specified by the Tokugawa, accelerated the trend begun under Nobunaga that the samurai should be an entirely separate class. Hideyoshi had deprived the peasants of their weapons. Ieyasu and his successors now began to deprive them of their self respect. If a peasant offended a samurai he might be cut down on the spot by the samurai's sword. The story is told of an old oil seller who abused Ieyasu, whereupon one of the latter's retainers struck the man at the base of the neck with a blow from his sharp sword. The blade cut clean through the offender so quickly that the oil seller walked on several paces and then fell clean in two. Such swift retribution was mercifully rare, but the two swords thrust through the samurai's belt remained the symbol of his authority which the lower orders of society had no choice but to recognize.

From a military point of view the organization and personnel of the Tokugawa military machine became more effete and bureaucratic as the years of peace went by. Below the daimyō were two further subdivisions of the samurai class, the 'hatamoto', or 'bannerman', and

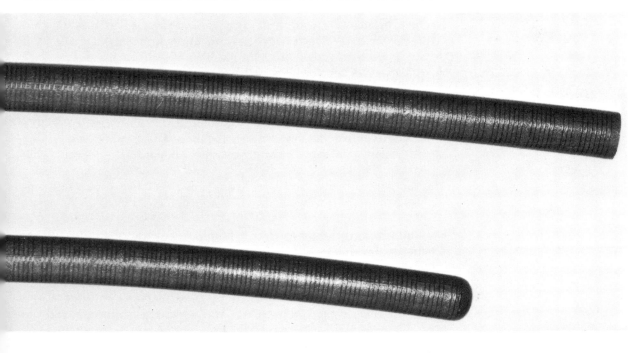

the 'go-kenin' or 'houseman'. The hatamoto, a name that literally means 'under the standard', were samurai with incomes between 100 and 10,000 *koku*. The housemen had stipends of less than 100 *koku*. Strictly speaking the words refer only to the samurai of the Tokugawa Shōgunate, but there were corresponding subdivisions for the retainers of the daimyō.

The essential military function of the bannermen and housemen was to form the standing army of the Shōgunate. In times of an emergency the bannermen were required to muster housemen according to fixed ratios regarding number and weaponry, based on the bannerman's income. Very roughly, at the time of the beginning of the Shōgunate, we can work on a figure of three men per hundred *koku*, from which calculations have been made of the contribution made by various daimyō at the time of Sekigahara. It may be noted that at the time of the Korean War Hideyoshi required six men per hundred *koku* from the daimyō of Kyūshū, and lesser proportions from others, depending on the distance of their fiefs from Kyūshū. The schedules for the breakdown of weaponry were revised in 1616, 1632 and 1649, that of the last year serving for the rest of the Shōgunate's existence. Using the 1649 schedule a bannerman with a stipend of, say, 200 *koku* would be required to furnish one swordsman of samurai (houseman) rank, one spearman (ditto) and three non-samurai servants; a total, including himself, of six persons. A bannerman of 1,000 *koku* would have to supply one arquebusier, one archer, two spearmen, five swordsmen and five non-samurai servants. This fits with a contemporary description by a European observer of a daimyō being required to provide 20 foot and two mounted men per 1,000 *koku*.

The élite of the Tokugawa army was the 'Ō-ban' or 'Great Guard', which originally consisted of three companies. When Ieyasu's contingent went to Nagoya for garrison duty during the Korean War there were five, and in 1623 the number was raised to twelve. Each company had one captain (ō-ban kashira), four lieutenants (ō-ban kumigashira) and fifty guardsmen (ō-ban). Each captain had thirty housemen at his command, and the subordinate ranks above mentioned furnished housemen and others according to the schedules. As well as the Great Guard there were also the Bodyguard (Shoin-ban), who guarded the Shōgun's person; the Inner Guard (Koshō-ban) who guarded Edo Castle; and the New Guard (Shin-ban), who guarded nothing in particular, and were formed in 1643, allegedly to find employment for the relatives of the many concubines of the third Tokugawa Shōgun, Iemitsu.

In addition to the *ban* were a number of specialized units, largely concerned with different weapons, such as the 25 squadrons of 100 men on horseback, armed with guns, known as the 'teppō hyaku-nin-gumi'. Though militarily more efficient than the élite mounted swordsmen of the Great Guard they were vastly inferior in status. Enrolment in a *ban*, particularly the Great Guard, was a symbol of prestige and the beginning of a military career. It did not, however, indicate any prowess

in military skill. With no enemy to fight it soon became difficult to maintain an effective fighting force. In 1650 a law was brought in forbidding duelling and feuding between idle ban members, followed by laws enjoining them to keep their military equipment in good order. In 1694 there even had to be a law forcing the samurai in the Shōgunal army to practise the martial arts, a strange contrast to the popular view of the samurai. Many of the Great Guard, it was discovered, were unable to swim, let alone use a sword. The energetic Shōgun Yoshimune tried in 1701 to revive the spartan virtues, but his pleas fell on deaf ears.

It was not only the lack of opportunity to put the martial arts to the test that caused a samurai decline. By the end of the seventeenth century the samurai was more occupied with the need to keep financially solvent than with the finer points of swordplay. The annual rice stipend ensured for the samurai a fixed income in a world of inflating prices. As early as 1630 the increased expenditure entailed by living in Edo for periodic guard and other duties, was leading to financial difficulties. The luxuries demanded by life in the (unofficial) capital were expensive to obtain, and pressed heavily on a bannerman's ability to maintain the armed retainers the schedules demanded. In 1633 stipends were

110 Samurai firing matchlock pistols. It is unlikely that firearms were much used from the saddle. From *Budo Geijutsu hiden zue*, painted by Ichiyusai Kuniyoshi, 1855. (National Diet Library, Tōkyō.)

111 (*overleaf*) Samurai firing a short arquebus. This picture is unusual in that it depicts the use of a shield. From *Budo Geijutsu hiden zue*, painted by Ichiyusai Kuniyoshi, 1855. (National Diet Library, Tōkyō.)

短筒打之圖

短筒手櫃持之図

raised, but not sufficiently to keep many samurai out of the pawn-brokers' and moneylenders'. One samurai in 1673, whose stipend was 300 *koku*, found himself faced with a fearful budgetary problem. His stipend was equivalent to a cash value of 75 *ryō* in silver coinage (equivalent to about $1\frac{1}{2}$ kilogrammes of gold), but during that year he spent 38 *ryō* on wages to housemen and servants, 10 on the purchase of a horse and its fodder, 12 for firewood, 18 for oil, vegetables, salt and other daily needs, and 30 for clothes, paper and sundries, a total of 108 *ryō*! The deficit was made up at the moneylenders. One samurai at the end of the eighteenth century sold his rice stipend to pay the rent. The samurai may have had the privilege of carrying two swords, but the despised merchant class had the cash.

The most striking example of the samurai's increasing poverty comes in 1856, towards the end of the Tokugawa Period, when a certain samurai was forced to borrow money from the farmers who worked his lands. The farmers, over whom the samurai theoretically had powers of life and death, threatened to resign as village leaders if he did not cut expenditure, beginning, they suggested, by getting rid of his idle and wasteful brother.

Incidentally, not all the samurai in Tokugawa Japan were employed in exclusively military occupations. A large number of the samurai who strutted around Edo were off to settle nothing more dramatic than the repair of a castle wall or an inspection of flood damage. Though the idea of a civil service armed to the teeth may strike us as amusing, these men were samurai too, and classified in the same way as the members of the standing army, with the same theoretical responsibility to furnish armed retainers according to the schedule. It was as if the desks of one's Town Hall were filled by the members of the local branch of the Territorial Army. Yet like their colleagues in the *ban*, they faced the same economic problems.

One way to ease the financial burden was to obtain promotion. This was by no means as easy as it sounds, for the Tokugawa stratification mentality tended to leave a man on the level where he had been born. In the early years of the regime service on the battlefield was an aid to promotion, as it was to most other things. Thus in the years of the Shōgunate's foundations a samurai may have seen his position and his income rise as a result of service during, for example, the Ōsaka campaigns. An outstanding example is a certain Uemura Iemasa. Iemasa's father was a rōnin whom Ieyasu employed as a mercenary. He died in 1599 when Iemasa was only eleven, and the lad was made a page by Hidetada, becoming in 1608 a captain of footsoldiers. He served in this capacity during the siege of Ōsaka where he distinguished himself by leading a patrol through the Ōsaka lines. This earned him an additional 1,000 *koku*, and in 1623 a Captaincy in the Great Guard. He later benefited from the Tokugawa policy of giving former enemy castles to trusted retainers, being given, in 1640, the castle of Takatori with an income of 25,000 *koku*. He therefore became a daimyō. Of course such dramatic advancements were not possible in peacetime, and indeed after about 1600 the forces that Hideyoshi and Ieyasu had set in motion were almost certain to prevent such a rise happening again.

When money is a problem it is always those in the lowest income groups who suffer most, and the same applied to the samurai. The lowest samurai were the housemen, whose income was supposedly up to 100 *koku*. In the majority of cases it was much less. The Housemen did not have the same responsibilities as the bannermen which included maintaining servants, but he had to keep himself as a true samurai, and on his low income this often proved a problem. The poverty of some housemen-samurai was so great that they are known to have sold the blades of their swords and replaced them with bamboo. In some cases they sold their swords altogether and borrowed a pair from a colleague when on duty. Fortunately for the houseman-samurai he was allowed to supplement his income by taking a part-time job. If his wife was working too then the family's problems were much reduced. Among the occupations listed for samurai are: making paper lanterns, making umbrellas, raising crickets and selling bamboo-shoots. In extreme cases a samurai could literally sell his birthright, although to do so was strictly illegal. A wealthy merchant who desired samurai status for his son could arrange for him to be adopted by a houseman, at the right price.

The foregoing remarks apply to the samurai in the service of the Shōgunate. For the samurai who were retainers of daimyō the position was similar but worse, some samurai having a lower income than commoners. Although prices were as a rule lower in the provinces, a samurai would have a taste of life in Edo when he accompanied his master on his biennial peregrination to pay respects to the Shōgun. This device, designed to make the daimyō waste their money on as lavish a scale as possible, required all daimyō to reside in Edo and in their home provinces for alternate years, except those in the Kantō, who changed their residence every six months. The 'Alternate Attendance' system was the brainchild of the Shōgun Iemitsu, and its most practical result was that the daimyō, accompanied of course by a large retinue, spent most of their time either marching towards Edo or marching away from it. As their wives and families had to stay in Edo as permanent residents it had the advantage of being a huge hostage system. Hostages had of course been exacted since time immemorial, and soaking the daimyō was hardly new, but like a lot of things under the Tokugawa the Alternate Attendance System was formalized and codified.

Certain daimyō in outlying areas with special defence responsibilities had a reduced obligation. In particular the Sō daimyō, on the strategic islands of Tsushima, reported to Edo for only four months in every three years. Apart from such concessions the daimyō had to follow the rules, and the great roads of Japan, particularly the Tōkaidō, must have been a splendid and colourful sight, as witnessed by the famous prints of Hiroshige (Fig. 116). In spite of the financial burden it imposed, the daimyō vied with one another in the splendour of their retinues.

112 A footsoldier putting on his armour. Note the 'jingasa' or 'war hat', and the bags of rice, which fastened in front of the arms and behind the neck.

As the processions were a decadent survival of warlike columns of men marching to battle, arms were carried by all, but primarily as objects of display. As tastes grew more luxurious so did the lavishness of the processions. Maeda Tsunayoshi (1642–1724) could command a host of 4,000 men on his processions, but as the financial burden grew even this daimyate was forced to reduce the number to about 1,500 by 1747. For the rest of the Tokugawa Period the average size of a daimyō's procession ranged from 150 to 300 samurai. Unexpected expenses on the journey could boost the cost tremendously. In 1852 the Inaba daimyō was overtaken by darkness on his way over the Hakone mountains, which necessitated the hiring of 200 extra porters and 45 lantern bearers, plus the purchase of 8,863 candles and 350 pine torches.

One way a daimyō could cut his overall cost of living was to cut the stipends of his samurai. As a result part-time jobs were not merely tolerated but positively encouraged. The Odawara samurai produced, among other things, fish-hooks and toothpicks. Other samurai ran pawnshops and sold vegetables. In Saga province they actually became farmers, an interesting reversion of role! From the military point of view the most interesting diversification is the making of suits of armour. In Kaga province (the Maeda daimyate), so much armour was produced that today 'Kaga' work is well known.

As samurai employment grew it was noted by contemporaries that the samurai character was changing for the worse. Murata Seifu (1746–1811) wrote about 1780:

'For years now, the samurai have suffered poverty, and their thoughts are preoccupied with the need to make ends meet. "Buy this, sell that", "pawn this to pay for that" have become all of their existence. It is inevitable that even those dedicated to their duties debase themselves and engage in unsavoury conduct. Only their swords in their belts remind them of their status. . . .'

No doubt if the worthy writer had ventured to examine certain swords more closely he would have received a nasty shock!

Some samurai, of course, refused to let monetary and other matters interfere with their duties as warriors. One such was Kumazawa Banzan (1619–91), who was not a bloodthirsty wandering samurai cherished by the motion-picture industry, but an accomplished man of letters. He had begun his military career as a rōnin, entering the service of Ikeda Mitsumasa of Okayama at the age of fifteen. As a young samurai he took his profession seriously, and practised the martial arts with an assiduity that would have done credit to any of Nobunaga's front rank samurai. To keep his weight down he gave up eating rice, and also abstained from sexual intercourse for ten years, presumably for the mortification of the flesh. While on guard duty at Edo he practised fencing with a wooden sword during the night, and kept fit by running along the roofs of Edo Castle, much to the amusement of his colleagues, who thought he was possessed by a hobgoblin.

Banzan eventually attained a high administrative position, and set his mind to the philosophical and economic questions of the samurai life. His writings must be viewed against the background of peace and indolence that he saw were having such a debilitating effect on the class. Banzan believed that the Manchus, who had conquered China in the wake of the Korean War, might well attempt to copy Kublai Khan and invade Japan. With this constantly in mind he inveighed against the wastage of rice and the wastage of talent that afflicted the country. Instead of giving a rice stipend to the samurai, he argued, the rice

113 A wood-block print of an
actor in the role of a samurai. Once
wars had ceased, the ideal samurai
rapidly acquired the romantic image
that he possesses today. (Courtesy of
Christie's.)

114 Firecloak and helmet. One of the samurai's most frequent duties during the Edo Period was to organize the fighting of the large fires that tended to sweep the city. (Richards collection, Manchester Museum.)

produced by the farmers should be stored in case of foreign invasion, and the samurai should return to their former status as 'samurai-farmers'. 'Ever since the samurai and farmers have become separate classes,' he wrote, 'the samurai have become sickly and their hands and feet have grown weak.' In particular Banzan directed a fierce torrent of criticism against the Alternate Attendance System.

The invasion which Banzan so feared never in fact materialized, but while Banzan was still a young man the samurai had been greatly embarrassed by an incident that had occurred far nearer home. This was the Shimabara revolt, an outbreak which, because of its religious connotations, has attracted a good deal of attention from Western historians. The actual revolt began as a peasant uprising, led by a handful of determined rōnin who rebelled against the monstrous excesses of the local daimyō, Matsukura Shigeharu. This repulsive character was given to torturing his peasants in sundry painful ways, including binding their hands, dressing them in straw rain cloaks, and then setting fire to the straw. Very few of the insurgents had any weapons when the outbreak began, a deficiency they speedily corrected by ambushing a samurai punitive column. They then shut themselves in Hara Castle on the Shimabara peninsula, which they quickly restored from its ruined state. Soon Christian banners and large wooden crosses began appearing on the walls, as Hara Castle became a focus for resistance against all forms of persecution. There are believed to have been 37,000, including women and children, inside the castle, which was attacked by Itakura Shigemasa at the head of 50,000 men. To the samurai's great surprise and indignation they were repulsed with heavy loss. On Japan's New Year's Day, 1638 a further assault was launched during which Itakura was killed, so his successor Matsudaira Nobutsuna began a blockade. Once more in Japanese history the European 'arms dealers' came in useful. Dutch cannon were used to bombard the castle from land, and a Dutch ship fired on it from the sea. The Dutch contribution soon ended, however, when the garrison shot arrows into the besiegers' camp bearing messages ridiculing them for relying on foreigners. By 4 April 1638, provisions were getting low, and a sally by defenders to capture supplies failed miserably. On 12 April an assault on the debilitated garrison succeeded in breaking through the outer wall. After two more days of fighting the castle fell, the last defenders falling as they wielded cooking pots and cauldrons as weapons.

The Shimabara Revolt came as a shock to the Shōgunate. A band of Christian farmers and rōnin had managed to hold off supposedly well-trained samurai. It was a portent of the samurai decline.

The most immediate result of the Shimabara Revolt was the cancellation of an ambitious project, which, had it gone ahead, might have added some remarkable chapters to the history of the samurai. In 1624 some ships belonging to Matsukura Shigemasa, daimyō of Shimabara and father of the tyrant Shigeharu mentioned above, were carried by the wind to Luzon in the Philippines. The sailors entered into communication with the natives, and reported back to Matsukura on their return. The description given of the Philippines led Matsukura to consider an invasion, so he asked the Shōgun for permission. Such a ludicrous scheme would never have been entertained had it not been for the current rivalry in Japan between the Dutch Protestants and the Spanish Catholics. The Dutch saw the plan as an ideal way of reducing Spanish influence in the area, and supplied the Shōgun with maps, charts, cannon and endless recommendations. They even offered to ferry the entire Japanese invasion force, which was to consist of about 10,000 men, and to protect the fleet against the Spanish galleons. The project received a setback when Matsukura died in 1630, but in 1637 the Shōgun gave permission for the invasion to go ahead. Of course, in 1637 the son of Matsukura Shigemasa was pre-occupied with the Shimabara Revolt, and when the Revolt ceased the futility of the invasion was seen clearly, so that it was directly abandoned.

115 An enterprising Japanese improvement to the arquebus—waterproof covers for the serpentine and touch hole. From *Budo Geijutsu hiden zue*, painted by Ichiyusai Kuniyoshi, 1855. (National Diet Library, Tōkyō.)

279

One military result of the Shimabara Revolt was that the Shōgunate took a fresh look at European military technology. The failure of the bombardment of Shimabara made the Japanese aware of the need for some form of mortar, in case such a revolt should occur again. The Dutch had in fact suggested mortars, perhaps as an excuse for their own ineffective bombardment, but anyway in 1639 the Dutch were demonstrating the new weapon to the Japanese. The samurai had met bombs before, but the Dutch mortars greatly impressed them. The bombs were twelve inches in diameter, indicating a tremendous destructive potential. A piece of land with five houses on it was selected as the target area for the tests. The unfortunate inhabitants were moved out, and the demonstration began. The first shot fell short, and landed in a deep marshy rice field. The Japanese observers concluded that it must have been lost, when suddenly it burst with such violence that vast quantities of mud were flung high into the air.

The second shot exploded in the barrel, causing great damage. The Japanese were, however, not dismayed, so that after wounds had been dressed the demonstration continued. The third shot also fell short of the houses, but this time on to hard ground, where its explosion produced a crater nine feet in diameter and six feet deep. The fifth shot burst in mid-air, which the Japanese greatly wondered at, so the Dutch gunner explained that he had done it just to make them laugh! Eleven bombs in all were fired, convincing the Japanese that if landed in a castle they would do great harm, but they were a little disappointed that none had hit the houses. The Dutch were consequently asked to place a bomb in one of the houses and light the fuse. This was done. The bomb exploded with a tremendous roar, igniting the timbers of the roof. So excited were the watchers that they broke into a spontaneous round of applause.

The supply of mortars and other guns ensured for the Dutch a certain immunity against the expulsion of foreigners in 1640. Throughout the next two centuries the small Dutch trading post provided a nucleus for the spread of European military lore. Apart from this concession, no foreigner was allowed to land, and no Japanese was permitted to leave. Although the closing of Japan was by no means as total as is popularly believed, it had far-reaching effects on Japanese history.

A further example of the samurai decline is furnished by Japanese armour. The long wars of the sixteenth century had raised armour to its point of perfection, producing a design that was proof against arquebus shots, yet allowed the wearer the maximum possible freedom of movement. New forms of body armour had been developed where the weight was taken off the shoulders and transferred to the hips, and simple armour had been mass-produced for ashigaru, including a 'jingasa', or 'war-hat', which Ieyasu recommended should be of iron so that the soldiers could cook their rice in it.

As the warlike Momoyama Period gave way to the peaceful days of Edo those features of armour that had made it such a good 'battle dress' were either reduced or obscured. An increase in decoration meant

more places where a spear point might be retained. In particular the use of embossing reduced the strength of an armour plate to such an extent that it could never withstand an arquebus shot. The Myōchin family, who had earned a reputation as practical armour makers, turned their attentions towards producing works of art. The elaborate and eye-catching suit of armour shown in Plate XXVII would have been little use in battle. In fact such armours, which are rare and expensive nowadays, were rare and expensive when they were made. The samurai below daimyō rank purchased armour as his pocket dictated, and to the vast majority of samurai the notion of a 'suit of armour' did not exist. He would choose a body armour, sleeves, helmet etc., from the armourer's selection at a price he could afford. Thus the lower ranks were likely to choose armours that were simpler and therefore more effective in warfare.

One aspect of the decadence in armour making was a revival of old styles of armour, a trend which was given considerable impetus by the publication in 1725 of the book *Honcho Gunkiko* by the historian Arai Hakuseki. Hakuseki cherished the old 'yoroi' styles, and contemporary smiths tried to imitate them, producing on occasions some weird and wonderful 'mongrels'. The combination of a sixteenth-century sashimono and a fourteenth-century flat neckguard was likely to produce a severe pain in the neck to anyone unfortunate enough to wear it, but such were made. Nevertheless some superb armour was made

116 'Yellow Dusk at Numazu', from Hiroshige's 'Fifty-three Stations of the Tōkaidō'. During the Edo Period this great road echoed to the tramp of marching feet in the daimyō processions. (Courtesy of Sotheby & Co.)

(Fig. 117), and for the first time armour was introduced for the samurai's horse.

While armourers strove to dress the samurai in fitting panoply, writers like Kumazawa Banzan attempted to deck his mind with thoughts of similar richness. One of Banzan's contemporaries added a major contribution to the samurai philosophy. This was Yamaga Sokō (1622–85). His life bears many similarities to Banzan's, but his writings concentrate far more on the military aspects of the samurai. Yamaga saw intelligence as one of the martial virtues, and drew attention to the need to study Western weapons and tactics. Above all he, like Kumazawa Banzan, was concerned with the prolonged inactivity of the samurai class. This is not to say that he was advocating an invasion of Korea or the Philippines, far from it. He believed that the samurai had to justify his special status over and above being skilled in the martial arts. It was not enough, argued Sokō, for the samurai to receive his stipend, to eat the food that others grew and wear the clothes that others wove, unless he cultivated those ideals which would enable him to serve as an example to the rest of the population. The other classes performed their functions, so a samurai should perform his, in the way of serving his lord with exemplary devotion, denying personal gain. Sokō therefore was stressing the spartan values of austerity, self-discipline and readiness to face death, to a society that was becoming increasingly divorced from such demands as a natural part of life. To exhort the samurai before Ōsaka's walls to be samurai was prosaic. To do so in 1690 when they were in debt to the moneylender and bored by office work was an anachronism.

Yet Sokō was wise enough to realize that the martial virtues would have to be converted into the ways of peace if the samurai class was going to survive. His creed was not all martial discipline, for he desperately believed that there had to be a re-awakening and a re-deployment of the samurai spirit if the ruling class were to give the intellectual and moral leadership that the country needed. 'Within his heart,' wrote Sokō, 'the samurai keeps to the ways of peace, but without he keeps his weapons ready for use.' Those samurai who have no concept of their calling should join one of the lower classes and take up a trade. For Sokō, the first rule for the samurai was 'Know thyself'.

In Sokō's writings we discern one of the earliest expositions of what has come to be known as 'bushi-dō', the 'Way of the Warrior', a term as familiar to Western ears as 'samurai' itself. The following passage has a familiar ring to it:

'Korea was subjugated, and its royal castle made to surrender. Japanese military headquarters was established on foreign soil and Japanese military prestige was supreme over the four seas from the earliest times to the present day. Our valour in war inspired fear in foreigners. As for invasion from abroad, foreigners never conquered us or even occupied or forced cession of our land. In fact, in the making of armour for man and horse, in the making and use of

117 A suit of armour by the Myōchin family. It is signed 'Myōchin Kiyasukiyo', 1847. It was made for Nakagawa Mochinori, a retainer of the Nagato daimyō. (I. D. Bottomley collection.)

283

118 An armour of the
Unkei school. (I. D. Bottomley collection.)

sword and spear, and again in military science, strategy and tactics, no other country can equal us. Within the four seas, then, are we not supreme in valour?'

This is Sokō at his best. The reader can judge for himself whether, in the light of the Shimabara Revolt, embossed armour and grasping moneylenders, this passage is an accurate assessment of the Japanese military capacity about the year 1670. Nevertheless it is an excellent example of how the samurai spirit could flourish when unhampered by the need actually to win battles. The simple truth of the matter is that between 1615 and 1860 the samurai were essentially an unproductive bunch of under-employed parasites.

119 An unusual three-piece face mask. (L. J. Anderson collection.)

285

As to the 'Warrior's Code' or the 'Way of the Warrior' it may be argued that a warrior's code must have existed in the sixteenth century for the sheer sake of survival. However, fighting cannot be learned from textbooks, and the writing of a warrior's code was left to the peaceful days of Edo. The best indication of a warrior's code in the sixteenth century comes from Tsukuhara Bokuden, a great teacher of swordsmanship. He merely states that 'the warrior who does not know his business is like a cat that does not know the way of ratting'. In other words the way of the warrior is being a warrior. That is all there is to it. The reader will recall that Hōjō Sōun's testament to his son ended with the words: 'The literary and martial arts are . . . to be practised always. Letters are the left hand and militarism the right. Neither must be neglected.'

In the comfort of the Edo Period armchair samurai (or rather 'straw-mat samurai', to keep the analogy correct), could sit back and enumerate the virtues of the ideal warrior. This is the 'bushi-dō' we know today. The main virtues emphasized are the samurai's bravery, integrity, loyalty, frugality, stoicism and filial piety. How far are these justified in the light of the history of the samurai?

Bravery goes without saying. Throughout history their death-defying courage never fails to impress. As was noted with Torii Suneemon at Nagashino, the highest respect is earned for bravery that is so outstanding that it can be admired by friend and foe alike. Examples of actual cowardice are very rare. In fact the samurai tradition of suicide to save one's honour may have lost Japan many fine generals who would otherwise have lived to fight another day. It is instructive to look at Admiral Yi Sun Sin, who was utterly disgraced, tortured and imprisoned after the victories of the first invasion had raised the ire of Won-kiun. Had Yi been a Japanese admiral he would certainly have committed suicide, whereas Yi withstood all his degradation and returned to attack the Japanese again in 1598.

Suicide was never an easy way out of a difficulty, for only the Japanese have ever insisted that suicide must be painful. It was however both honourable and dramatic. We have seen many striking examples, but the Author cannot resist mentioning what is surely the most spectacular example of suicide in Japanese history. It was performed by the admittedly semi-legendary samurai known as Tōgō Shigechika, who had vainly attacked an enemy fortress. In despair he allowed himself to be buried alive, fully armoured and mounted on his horse, swearing ghostly vengeance on his enemies!

Loyalty and integrity are more elusive virtues to find, the former being certainly an early casualty of war. Mōri Motonari's recommendation to trust no one, particularly relatives, sums up the Sengoku Period, the age which produced such paragons of samurai virtue as Hōjō Sōun. In fact, the period which saw the military spirit at its highest also saw the virtues of loyalty at their lowest. Akechi Mitsuhide, surely our best authority on disloyalty, said that the warrior's lies were called strategy, while the only honest people were the farmers and townsmen.

It is easy to poke fun at a nation when it idealizes its early history. Every nation does so. What is certain is that the opinions and ideas of writers such as Yamaga Sokō and Kumazawa Banzan did find a place in the hearts of the samurai. Appeals to put aside self and take up an obviously idealized model of samurai behaviour were not wasted. The most striking example of Yamaga Sokō's success is the story of the famous '47 Rōnin', without whom no history of the samurai would be complete. The leader of the 47 Rōnin, Ōishi Kuranosuke, was a pupil of Yamaga Sokō. What is remarkable in this classic tale of revenge is the length to which the plotters went to put their intended victim off his guard. They made it appear to him that they were no longer concerned with the fate of their late master's house, turning to drunkenness and debauchery as a screen behind which they could hatch their plot. On 14 December 1702, the 47 Rōnin attacked their enemy's mansion and killed him, placing his head on their late master's grave. This act of revenge startled the authorities. Were they to punish the Rōnin for the crime of murder, or reward them for behaving more like the idealized samurai than anyone had done for a century? In the end the law prevailed, and the 46 remaining Rōnin (one having died during the attack) committed hara-kiri 'en masse'.

It is questionable whether the 47 Rōnin did anything for contemporary Japan except provide her with endless plots for plays and stories, and to demonstrate how primitive Japan was when compared with the outside world. The positive contribution that bushi-dō made is best exemplified in the person of Mito Mitsukuni (1628–1700), from the Mito branch of the Tokugawa, who cultivated the study of Japanese history. Of particular interest is his extolling of the virtues of Kusunoki Masashige and Masatsura, which caused them to be the popular heroes they are today.

The true worth of bushi-dō came much later when, as Yamaga Sokō had hoped, the samurai class, or at any rate members of it, rose above their idleness, their poverty and their demoralization to become the brains of the Restoration movement, and the makers of modern Japan. They were then truly an aristocracy, giving an example to the people, and inspiring them by their leadership. There is no space here to describe adequately the great events of the Meiji Restoration and the emergence of Japan from its cloistered cell, but certain features relevant to our story may be noted.

The families who played a major part in the Restoration have names familiar to us. Tokugawa (Mito) Nariaki was a descendant of Mitsukuni and a great advocate of samurai training in the days when European and American ships began to be seen off Japan. In 1853 he was entrusted with the defence of his country, but the obvious superiority of the foreign powers made such preparations irrelevant. He faced fierce opposition on the question of foreign intervention in the person of Ii Naosuke, a direct descendant of Naomasa and Naokatsu, the Red Devils of Hikone. In 1858 Naosuke signed a treaty with the United States and, soon after, with England and France. These treaties roused

120 Arquebuses against bows, the collision of two primitive technologies. A year before this was painted Commodore Perry of the United States Navy had landed in Japan. From *Budo Geijutsu hiden zue*. Painted by Ichiyusai Kuniyoshi, 1855. (National Diet Library, Tōkyō.)

雨中連砲之圖

strong resentment among the conservative, anti-foreign group and in 1860 Naosuke was assassinated by rōnin of the Mito daimyate.

The Restoration brought about all the changes that its opponents had feared. The samurai were abolished as a class, and compensation was given for their stipends which it was hoped would help them to set up in business. In 1876 the wearing of swords was forbidden to all except members of the armed forces, who were now organized on a national conscript basis.

One samurai in particular found this too much to stand, and Saigo Takamori returned to his native Satsuma where he began training the young samurai in the arts of war. The government, foreseeing danger, did all in its power to bring Takamori back, but all in vain. The insurrectional movement was brewing and finally broke out as the 'Satsuma Rebellion' in 1877. On 15 February, Takamori, at the head of 15,000 men, took possession of Kagoshima, then, marching on the Kumamoto army, defeated it and laid siege to Kumamoto Castle. On hearing the news the government despatched a conscript army under Arisugawa Taruhito. The rebels withdrew under the pressure of superior numbers and entered Hyūga where, in spite of great valour, they were defeated in several encounters. Eventually Saigo's army was driven back to Kagoshima. Resistance became impossible. Surrounded on all sides, by sea and by land, the last of the samurai prepared to sell his life dearly. The final battle took place at Shiroyama on 24 September 1877. Saigo fell, wounded in the leg by a bullet from a European-trained conscript, and one of his faithful retainers, at his request, put an end to his life.

It is a long journey from Prince Yamato, via Yoshitsune, Kusunoki Masashige and Oda Nobunaga, to Saigo Takamori, yet the pattern remains the same. The hero is a lonely, solitary figure who dies tragically while fighting overwhelming odds. Here was the spirit of the samurai. In the words of the greatest chronicle of samurai heroics, the *Heike Monogatari*:

'The sound of the bell of Gionshōja echoes the impermanence of all things. The hue of the flowers of the teak tree declares that they who flourish must be brought low. Yea, the proud ones are but for a moment, like an evening dream in springtime. The mighty are destroyed at the last, they are but as the dust before the wind.'

Appendix 1. Selected genealogies

1. Taira

Only the most prominent of this extensive and active clan are shown.

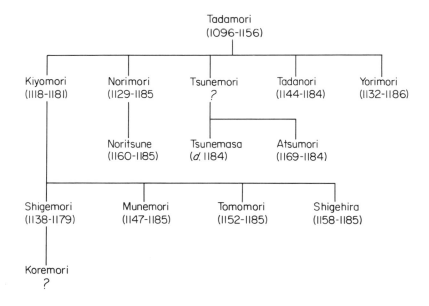

2. Minamoto (*Seiwa–Genji*)

Only names mentioned in the text are included in this family tree.

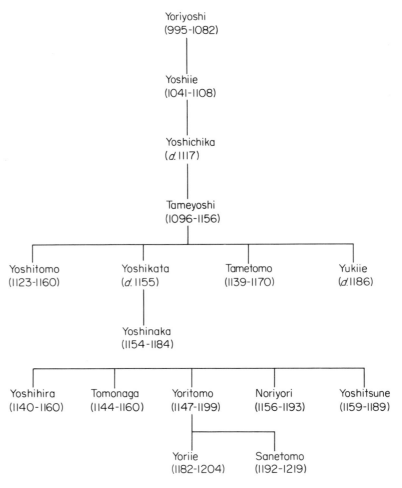

3. Shimazu

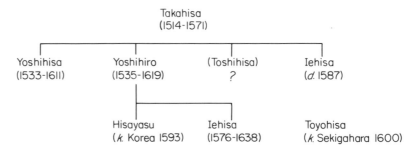

4. Shibuya (*Iriki*)

Few dates of birth or death are known for this family during the period described in Chapter 6 of text.

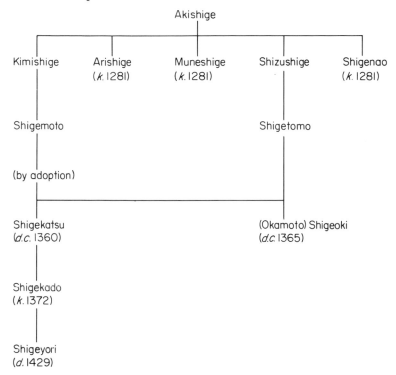

Akishige

Kimishige — Arishige (*k.*1281) — Muneshige (*k.*1281) — Shizushige — Shigenao (*k.*1281)

Shigemoto — Shigetomo

(by adoption)

Shigekatsu (*d.c.*1360) — (Okamoto) Shigeoki (*d.c.*1365)

Shigekado (*k.*1372)

Shigeyori (*d.*1429)

The three brothers noted as having been killed in 1281 died from arrow wounds received during the Second Mongol Invasion.

5. Hōjō (*Odawara*)

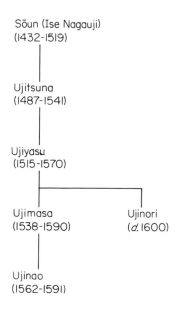

Sōun (Ise Nagauji) (1432-1519)

Ujitsuna (1487-1541)

Ujiyasu (1515-1570)

Ujimasa (1538-1590) — Ujinori (*d.*1600)

Ujinao (1562-1591)

Appendix 2. Chronological list of Shōguns

Minamoto

Yoritomo	1192
Yoriie	1199
Sanetomo	1203

Hōjo Regency (*Shikken*)

Tokimasa	1199
Yoshitoki	1205
Yasutoki	1225
Tsunetoki	1242
Tokiyori	1246
Nagatoki	1256
Tokimune	1270
Sadatoki	1284
Morotoki	1300
Takatoki	1315

Following the fall of Kamakura the Office of Shōgun was held by Prince Morikuni

Ashikaga

Takauji	1338
Yoshiakira	1358
Yoshimitsu	1367
Yoshimochi	1395
Yoshikazu	1423
Yoshinori	1428
Yoshikatsu	1441
Yoshimasa	1443
Yoshihisa	1474
Yoshitane	1490
Yoshizumi	1493
Yoshitane	1508
Yoshiharu	1521
Yoshiteru	1545
Yoshihide	1565
Yoshiaki	1568

'Administrators'

Oda Nobunaga	1573
Toyotomi Hideyoshi	1582
Toyotomi Hideyori	1598

Tokugawa

Ieyasu	1603
Hidetada	1605
Iemitsu	1623
Ietsuna	1651
Tsunayoshi	1681
Ienobu	1709
Ietsugu	1713
Yoshimune	1717
Ieshige	1745
Ieharu	1762
Ienari	1787
Ieyoshi	1837
Iesada	1853
Iemochi	1858
Yoshinobu	1866

Bibliography

N.B. *TASJ*: *Transactions of the Asiatic Society of Japan.*

TJSL: *Transactions and Proceedings of the Japan Society of London.*

Alex, W.: Japanese Architecture. London, 1968.

Anderson, L. J.: Japanese Armour. An
· illustrated guide to the work of the Myōchin and Saotome families from the fifteenth to the twentieth century. London, 1968.

'The Yukinoshita-dō'. (*Journal of the To-ken Society of Great Britain*, I, ii. London, 1966.

Asakawa, K.: The Documents of Iriki. Yale University, 1929.

'Some aspects of Japanese feudal institutions'. *TASJ*, 46, I. 1918.

Aston, W. G.: 'Hideyoshi's invasion of Korea'. *TASJ*, 9– . 1878–83.

Ballard, G. A.: The Influence of the Sea on the Political History of Japan. London, 1921.

Barr, P.: The Coming of the Barbarians. London, 1967.

The Deer Cry Pavilion. London, 1968.

Bertin, L. E.: Les grandes guerres civiles du Japon. Paris, 1894.

Bonar, H. A. C.: 'On maritime enterprise in Japan'. *TASJ*, 15. 1887.

Boots, J. L.: 'Korean Weapons and Armour'. *Transactions of the Korea Branch of the Royal Asiatic Society*, 23. 1934.

Bottomley, I. D. and Hopson, J.: The Armour of Feudal Japan (in preparation).

Boxer, C. R.: The Christian Century in Japan. University of California Press, 1951.

Jan Compagnie in Japan. The Hague, 1950.

'Notes on Early European Military Influence in Japan (1543–1853)'. *TASJ*, 2nd Ser. 8. 1931.

Bramsen, W.: 'Japanese chronological tables'. *TASJ*. 37. 1910.

Brinkley, F.: Japan, its History, Arts and Literature. Boston, 1901.

Brown, D. M.: 'The impact of firearms on Japanese warfare 1543–1598'. *Far Eastern Quarterly*, 8. 1948.

Chamberlain, B. H.: Handbook for Travellers in Japan. London, 1913.

Cole, W.: Kyōto in the Momoyama Period. Oklahoma University, 1967.

Conder, J.: 'The history of Japanese costume, II Armour'. *TASJ*, 9. 1881.

Cooper, M.: The Southern Barbarians. Tōkyō, 1971.

They came to Japan. London, 1968.

Davis, F. H.: Myths and Legends of Japan. London, 1913.

Dautremer, J.: 'The vendetta or legal revenge in Japan'. *TASJ*, 13. 1885.

Dening, W.: The Life of Toyotomi Hideyoshi. London, 1930.

Dilts, M. M.: The Pageant of Japanese History. New York, 1938.

Diosy, A.: 'Yoshitsune, the Boy Hero of Japan'. *TJSL*, 10. 1911.

Dunn, C. J.: Everyday Life in Traditional Japan. London, 1969.

Fisher, G.: 'Kumazawa Banzan'. *TASJ*, 45 (ii). 1918.

Frederic, L.: Daily Life in Japan at the time of the Samurai. London, 1972.

Fujioka, M.: Japanese Castles. Tōkyō, 1968.

Garbutt, M.: 'Japanese armour from the inside'. *TJSL*, 9. 1912.

'Military works in Old Japan'. *TJSL*, 8. 1907.

Gilbertson, E.: 'Japanese archery and archers'. *TJSL*, 4. 1895.

'Japanese blades'. *TJSL*, 4. 1895.

'The decoration of swords and sword

furniture'. *TJSL*, 3. 1893.

Gilbertson, E. and Kowaki, G.: 'The genealogy of the Miochin family'. *TJSL*, 1. 1892.

Goedertier, J.: A Dictionary of Japanese History. New York, 1968.

Griffis, W. E.: Corea the Hermit Kingdom. New York, 1882.
The Mikado's Empire. New York, 1906.

Gubbins, J. H.: 'Hideyoshi and the Satsuma clan in the sixteenth century'. *TASJ*, 8. 1880.

Hall, J. C.: 'Japanese feudal laws'. *TASJ*, 34, 36, 38, 41. –1913.

Hall, J. W.: 'The castle town and Japan's modern urbanization'. *Far Eastern Quarterly*. 1955.

Hall, J. W. and Mass, J. P.: Medieval Japan. *Essays in Institutional History*. Yale University Press. 1974.

Hall, M. P.: Koya-san. Los Angeles, 1970.

Harada, T.: The Faith of Japan. New York, 1926.

Hawley, W. M.: Introduction to Japanese Swords. Los Angeles, 1973.

Hayashi, G.: 'The fall of the Tokugawa government'. *TJSL*, 4. 1895.

Hearn, L.: Kokoro. Hints and echoes of Japanese inner life. London, 1914.

Herrigel, E.: Zen in the Art of Archery. London, 1953.

Hikone, City of: How to see Hikone. 1970.
Guide to Hikone Castle. 1969.

Hirai, K.: Feudal Architecture of Japan. Tōkyō, 1973.

Hulbert, H. B.: The History of Korea. Seoul, 1905.

Jennes, J.: A History of the Catholic Church in Japan. Tōkyō, 1959.

Joly, H. L.: Legend in Japanese Art. London, 1908.

Kasuga Shrine: Catalogue of Objects in the Kasuga Shrine Museum, Nara. 1968.

Kellogg, E. R.: 'Selective Translation of *Hōgen Monogatari*'. *TASJ*, 45 (i). 1917.

Kiralfy, A.: 'Japanese naval strategy', in E. M. Earle (ed.), Makers of Modern Strategy. Princeton, 1943.

Kirby, J. B.: From Castle to Teahouse. Japanese Architecture of the Momoyama Period. Rutland, Vermont. 1962.

Knutsen, R.: Japanese Polearms. London, 1963.

Koop, A. J.: 'The Construction and Blazonry of Mon'. *TJSL*, 9. 1910.

Kurata, H.: Shinran. Tōkyō, 1964.

Kuno, Y. S.: Japanese Expansion on the Asiatic Continent. Berkeley, 1937.

Kunōzan: Catalogue of Armour etc. in the Kunōzan Tōshōgū Shrine Museum. 1965.

Laures, J.: The Catholic Church in Japan, A Short History. Tōkyō, 1954.

Lee, G. A.: 'Some notes on Japanese heraldry'. *TJSL*, 8. 1910.

Lewis, A.: Knights and Samurai. London, 1974.

Ley, C. D.: Portuguese Voyages, 1498–1663. London, 1947.

Longford, J. H.: The Story of Old Japan. London, 1910.

Marder, A. J.: 'From Jimmu Tenno to Perry—Sea power in early Japanese history'. *American Historical Review*, 51. 1945.

Martin, F. C.: Arms and Armor of Ancient Japan. Los Angeles, 1964.

Mass, J. P.: Warrior Government in Early Medieval Japan. Yale University Press, 1974.

McClatchie, T.: 'The feudal mansions of Edo'. *TASJ*, 7. 1879.
'Japanese heraldry'. *TASJ*, 5. 1876.
'The sword of Japan, its history and tradition'. *TASJ*, 3. 1873.

McCullough, H.: The Taiheiki. Columbia University, 1959.
Yoshitsune. Stanford University, 1966.

Miyamoto, M.: A Book of Five Rings, translated by V. Harris. London, 1974.

Morris, I.: The World of the Shining Prince. London, 1964.

Moule, G. H.: The Spirit of Japan. London, 1913.

Murdoch, J.: A History of Japan. London, 1925.

Nishino, S.: Tokugawa Mitsukuni (Giko). Mito, 1961.

Nishioka, I.: Shin nihon-shi zuroku. Tōkyō, 1958.

Nitobe, I.: Bushidō, the Soul of Japan. New York, 1905.

Ogasawara, N.: Japanese Swords. Tōkyō, 1970.

Ogawa, K.: Military Costume in Old Japan. Tōkyō, 1893.

Okada, Y.: Japanese Family Crests. Tōkyō, 1941.

Orui, N. and Toba, M.: Castles in Japan. Tōkyō, 1935.

Papinot, E.: Historical and Geographical Dictionary of Japan. Yokohama, 1909.

Possonby, S. T.: 'Japanese naval strategy'. *U.S. Naval Institute Proceedings*, 70. 1944.

Purnell, C. J.: 'The Logbook of Will Adams'. *TJSL*, 13. 1914.

Purvis, F. P.: 'Ship construction in Japan'. *TASJ*, 47. 1919.

Redesdale, Lord: Tales of Old Japan. London, 1910.

Reischauer, E. O.: Japan, Past and Present. New York (2nd Ed.), 1952.

Robinson, B. W.: Arms and Armour of Old Japan. London, 1951.
The Arts of the Japanese Sword. London, 1961.

Robinson, H. R.: The Armour Book in Honcho Gunkiko. London, 1964.
The Manufacture of Armour and Helmets in Sixteenth-Century Japan. London, 1962.

Rotermund, H. O.: Die Yamabushi. Monographien zur Volerkunde) Hamburg, 1968.

Sadler, A. L.: 'Heike Monogatari'. *TASJ*, 46. 1918; 49, 1921.
Cha-no-yu, the Japanese Tea Ceremony. New York, 1962.
The Maker of Modern Japan, the Life of Tokugawa Ieyasu. London, 1937.
'The Naval campaign in the Korean War of Hideyoshi'. *TASJ* (2nd Ser.), 14. 1937.
A Short History of Japan. London, 1963.

Saito, R.: Japanese Coiffure. Tōkyō, 1939.

Sakakibara, Kōzan: Chuko Kachu Seisakuben. Edo, 1800.

Sanson, G. B.: A History of Japan. (3 volumes.) London, 1959.

Sendai Municipal Museum: Catalogue of an Exhibition of objects belonging to the Maeda family. 1966
Catalogue of objects belonging to the Date family. 1970.

Schegel, G.: 'On the invention and use of firearms and gunpowder in China prior to the arrival of the Europeans'. *T'oung pao*, 2nd Ser. 3. 1902.

Shinoda, M.: The Founding of the Kamakura Shogunate. Columbia University, 1960.

Spohr, C.: Gempei, The Civil Wars of Old Japan. (Privately published.) Chicago, 1967.

Spuler, B.: The Mongols in History. London, 1971.

Smith, B.: Japan, a History in Art. London, 1972.

Summers, J.: 'Notes on Osaka'. *TASJ*, 7. 1879.

Takekoshi, Y.: The Economic Aspects of the History of the Civilisation of Japan. London, 1930.

Totman, C.: Politics in the Tokugawa Bakufu. Harvard University Press, 1967.

Tsunoda, R. *et al.*: Sources of Japanese Tradition. Columbia University, 1958.

Uesugi Museum: Catalogue of objects in the Uesugi Shrine Museum, Yonezawa. 1970.

Underwood, H. H.: 'Korean boats and ships'. *Transactions of the Korea Branch of the Royal Asiatic Society*, 23. 1934.

Vianello, G.: Armi in Oriente. Milano, 1966.

Varley, H. P.: The Ōnin War. Columbia University, 1967.

Waterhouse, D. B.: 'Firearms in Japanese history, with notes on a Japanese wall gun'. *British Museum Quarterly*, 27. 1963.

Yamada, N.: Ghenkō, the Mongol Invasion of Japan. New York, 1916.

Yamagami, H.: Japan's Ancient Armour. Tōkyō, 1940.

Yamamura, K.: A Study of Samurai Income and Entrepreneurship. Harvard, 1974.

Yoshida, K.: Research into Tosei Gusoku of the Edo Era. (Unpublished MS.) 1973.

Yoshioka, S.: Collection of Antique Guns. Tōkyō, 1965.

Index